Cisco Routers Little Black Book Quick Reference

Command Line Interface (CLI)

Cursor Manipulations

You can use the following keystrokes to perform simple manipulations with the cursor:

- To move the cursor to the beginning of the line, press ^A
- To move the cursor to the end of the line, press ^E
- To move the cursor one word back, press Esc+B
- To move the cursor one word forward, press Esc+F

Normally, all these keystrokes are available by default. If they are not, you can enable them using the command **terminal editing**.

CLI Command History Feature

The CLI allows you to edit commands that have been entered previously using the up and down arrow keys or ^P and ^N, respectively. The number of the commands the router can remember depends on the size of the history buffer. By default, it is equal to 10 commands. You can change this setting either on a per session basis or permanently. To change the size of the history buffer on a per session basis, enter the command **terminal history size** followed by the number of commands to remember in the EXEC mode. To change it permanently, enter the command **history size** followed by the number of commands to remember in the line configuration mode. For example:

```
router#config t
Enter configuration commands, one per line.
  End with CNTL/Z.
router(config)#line vty 0 4
router(config-line)#history size 50
```

CLI Help Features

The following help features are available:

- Pressing ? in the middle of a word (without a space between the last character entered and ?) displays all possible complete words beginning with the characters already entered. The already entered part of the command line is preserved and the cursor is placed exactly where it was when ? was entered.

  For example:
  ```
  router#show co?
  compress   configuration   context
    controllers

  router#show co_
  ```

NOTE: Here and below the _ sign indicates where the cursor is placed.

- Pressing ? separated by a space from the last non-space character produces all possible optional arguments that can be used in the place of the cursor. The already-entered part of the command line is preserved and the cursor is placed exactly where it was when ? was entered.

  For example:
  ```
  router#show ip eigrp ?
    interfaces   IP-EIGRP interfaces
    neighbors    IP-EIGRP neighbors
    topology     IP-EIGRP Topology Table
    traffic      IP-EIGRP Traffic Statistics

  router#show ip eigrp _
  ```

- Pressing Tab in the middle of a word completes the word. If the word has multiple completions, it is completed to the point where the possible completions begin to differ.

  For example:
  ```
  router#show ip ac<TAB>
  router#show ip acc_
  ```
  or
  ```
  router#conf<TAB>
  router#configure _
  ```

CLI Terminating Keystrokes And Keywords

The following keystrokes and keywords can be used to terminate certain modes of the router CLI:

- If a router's CLI is in the configuration mode other than the global configuration mode, pressing ^Z or entering **end** terminates the configuration mode and transfers CLI to the privileged EXEC mode.

- If a router's CLI is in the configuration mode other than the global configuration mode, entering **exit** transfers CLI to the previous level of configuration mode. In most cases this previous level is the global configuration mode.

- Pressing ^Z when a command is entered, executes the command and transfers CLI to the EXEC mode. For example if the CLI is in an interface configuration mode and you type in **ip address 10.0.0.1 255.0.0.0** and then press ^Z, this executes the command and transfers CLI to the privileged EXEC mode. If in this situation you need to transfer CLI to the privileged EXEC mode without entering the command press ^C.

W9-BLD-901

- If a source of routing information tries to install a route for a network prefix for which another route already exists in the routing table, the administrative distance of the source and the administrative distance of the existing route is used to resolve the ambiguity. The route with the smallest administrative distance is installed into the routing table, the other route is ignored.

- The router uses the routing algorithm when making forwarding decisions. It only looks for the longest match in the routing table to find the best route for the destination.

- A distance vector routing protocol does not advertise a route that it did not install into the routing table.

Table A Useful **show** commands.

Command	Action
show interfaces	Displays the state of all interfaces
show interfaces <Interface>	Displays the status of the interface <Interface>. The parameter <Interface> includes the name of the interface and its number.
show ip interface	Displays IP-specific information available for all router interfaces.
show ip interface <Interface>	Displays IP-specific information for the interface <Interface>. The parameter <Interface> includes the name of the interface and its number.
show ip interface brief	Displays summary of IP specific information for all interfaces.
show ip route	Displays the whole routing table
show ip route <network prefix>	Displays routing information for a network prefix <network prefix>. The parameter <network prefix> can be either an individual subnet or a classful network address. The latter version either displays the routes for all subnets of the network address, or if none are available the route for the network address itself. If no routing information is available for the specified network prefix, the command's output is **% Network no in table**.
show ip route <source>	Displays routing information installed in the routing table by the source of routing information <source>. The <source> parameter can take the values shown in **Table B**.
show ip route summary	Displays the summary of routing information.
show ip protocols	Displays information on the configured IP routing protocols.
show startup-config configuration	Displays the router configuration stored in the NVRAM, use the or **show** command.
show running-config or write terminal	Displays the router's current operating configuration. Notice that this configuration is different from the one stored in the NVRAM if you entered some commands in the router configuration mode and did not save the configuration into the NVRAM.

Table B The keywords available for the <source> parameter of the command show ip route; the keywords denote the sources of routing information.

Keyword	The Routing Information Source
bgp	Border Gateway Protocol (BGP)
connected	Connected
egp	Exterior Gateway Protocol (EGP)
eigrp	Enhanced Interior Gateway Routing Protocol (EIGRP)
igrp	Interior Gateway Routing Protocol (IGRP)
isis	ISO IS-IS
odr	On Demand stub Routes
ospf	Open Shortest Path First (OSPF)
rip	Routing Information Protocol (RIP)
static	Static routes

Table C The relation between the lengths of subnet masks and the maximum number of hosts the network prefixes using the corresponding subment masks can accommodate.

Number Of Hosts	Subnet Length	Subnet Mask
up to 2	/30	255.255.255.252
up to 6	/29	255.255.255.248
up to 14	/28	255.255.255.240
up to 30	/27	255.255.255.224
up to 62	/26	255.255.255.192
up to 126	/25	255.255.255.128
up to 254	/24	255.255.255.0
up to 510	/23	255.255.254.0
up to 1022	/22	255.255.252.0
up to 2046	/21	255.255.248.0

Table D The default distances of the sources of routing information available on the Cisco routers.

Route Source	Default Distance
Connected interface	0
Static route	1
Enhanced IGRP summary route	5
External BGP	20
Internal Enhanced IGRP	90
IGRP	100
OSPF	110
IS-IS	115
RIP	120
EGP	140
Internal BGP	200
Unknown	255

Table E The default values of the weights used in the formulas to calculate IGRP and EIGRP route metrics.

Weight	Default Value
k1	1
k2	0
k3	1
k4	0
k5	0

CORIOLIS
Technology Press
©1999 The Coriolis Group. All Rights Reserved.

Two other useful options of the command **ping** are **Datagram size** and **Repeat count**. These two can be used to make the router generate intensive traffic for testing purposes.

Traceroute

Entering the command **traceroute** without parameters or followed only by the optional keyword **ip** also produces a set of options similar to those of the command **ping**.

Telnet

The command **telnet** can be sometimes used as a network troubleshooting tool. For example, this command can be followed by the optional parameter **/source-interface** *<interface>*, where the sub-parameter *<interface>* is used to specify the source IP address for the Telnet connection.

IP Addressing

Table C provides the relation between the length of the subnet mask and the number of hosts it produces.

IP Routing

Administrative Distances Of The Routing Information Sources

The administrative distances of dynamic routing protocols can be changed using the command **distance** *<new distance>* in the router configuration mode. This command can be followed by optional parameters allowing setting different administrative distances depending on the source of the routing updates and on the advertised network prefixes.

The administrative distance of static routes can be set using the numeric distance option of the command **ip route**.

Setting administrative distance of any source of routing information to a value of 255 disallows the router to put the corresponding routes to the routing table.

The administrative distances of connected router and EIGRP summary routes cannot be changed.

Table D shows the default administrative distances of all sources of routing information available in the Cisco IOS.

IGRP And EIGRP metrics

IGRP uses the following formula to calculate route metrics:

B_{IGRP} is the IGRP bandwidth of the path, which itself is calculated using the following formula:

$$B_{IGRP} = \frac{10^7}{B_{MIN}}$$

where B_{MIN} is the minimum logical bandwidth of the path expressed in kilobits per second (Kpbs). D_{IGRP} is the IGRP delay of the path, which is equal to the sum of the delays of all segments along the path expressed in 10 microsecond units. L is the IGRP load of the corresponding interface ranging from 1 to 255; 1 is the minimally loaded interface, and 255 is the 100 percent loaded interface. R is the IGRP reliability of the segment to which the corresponding interface is attached. R can range from 1 to 255; 1 is the minimally reliable segment, and 255 is the 100 percent reliable segment. Parameters $k1, k2, k3, k4$, and $k5$ are administratively configurable weights, whose default values are shown **Table E**.

When applied, the default values of the weights reduce the formula for calculating the IGRP metrics to the following:

$$M_{IGRP} = B_{IGRP} + D_{IGRP}$$

EIGRP uses IGRP metrics multiplied 256, as follows:

$$M_{EIGRP} = M_{IGRP} * 256$$

Being redistributed into each other, IGRP and EIGRP do not reset the metrics of the redistributed routers, but scale them by 256 whereby preserving accumulated values.

RIP Metrics

RIP uses hop-counts as route metrics. In other words, RIP advertises the routes it learned from its neighbors with the metrics increased by 1.

OSPF Metrics

OSPF computes the metrics as the sum of costs of all segments constituting the routes. The cost of the segment is calculated in accordance with the formula below:

$$C = \frac{10^8}{B}$$

where B is the logical bandwidth of the corresponding interface measured in bits per second.

Routing Rules

These are the rules the router follows when populating the routing table with routes and making routing decisions:

- The router uses the routing metrics only in the scope of a particular dynamic routing protocol. If a distance vector routing protocol receives multiple routing updates that advertise the same network prefix, the protocol chooses the one with the best metric. This route is submitted for installation into the routing table. The link state routing protocols use the Dijkstra shortest path first algorithm to populate the routing table with the routes.

Terminal Features

Producing Long Output

If you would like a router to produce long output without stopping at the end of each page indicated by the —**More**— marker and waiting for your input, type in the command **terminal length 0**. This command takes effect on per-session basis. You can revert this command by entering **terminal length** followed by the (desired) number of the lines on a page. Alternatively, you can simply terminate the current terminal session and then log in to the router again.

Enabling debug Output Using Network Terminal Connections

If you connected to a router using Telnet (or some other network terminal connection, such as rlogin, PAD, and so on) and would like to see the output of the **debug** commands, be sure to enter **terminal monitor**. By default, only the console displays the output of the **debug** commands.

Displaying And Terminating Network Terminal Connections

If you need to verify who is currently connected to a router, use the command **show users all**. If you notice that someone has connected to the router without permission, you can disconnect that user using the command **clear line** followed by the line name and number taken from the output of the command **show users all**. For example:

```
router#show users all
    Line     User      Host(s)
Idle Location
   0 con 0
00:00:00
   1 aux 0
00:00:00
*  2 vty 0   you       idle
00:00:00 10.0.1.111
   3 vty 1   badguy    idle
00:00:02 10.1.2.120
   4 vty 2
00:00:00
   5 vty 3
00:00:00
   6 vty 4
00:00:00

router#clear line vty 1
[confirm]<ENTER>
 [OK]
router#
```

Disabling DNS Lookup

If you make a typing mistake while entering a command, the router may assume that you're trying to connect to some network device using a network terminal connection, such as Telnet. If the router is not configured to perform DNS lookup, it may take a while before the connection times out, especially if the connection cannot be terminated using the keystroke ^^ (Control+^ or Control+Shift+6). Also, the output of the commands **ping** and **traceroute** on the routers not configured to perform DNS lookup is delayed because the routers still try to resolve the IP addresses to names. You can eliminate this nuisance by configuring the router not to perform DNS lookup at all using the command **no ip domain-lookup** in the global configuration mode.

If you need to configure the router to perform DNS lookup, you will have to enter the command **ip domain-lookup** and also specify the correct domain name using the command **ip domain-name** *<domain>* and one or more domain name servers using the command **ip name-server** *<IP address>*.

Unfortunately, the command **terminal no domain-lookup** (available on a per-session basis) only disables domain lookup in the **show** commands.

Useful show Commands

The **show** commands shown in **Table A** are especially useful when you need to quickly get IP related information from a particular router.

Network Troubleshooting Tools

Ping

If entered without parameters or if followed by the optional keyword **ip**, the command **ping** provides a very useful set of options. One of the most valuable of these options is the ability to specify the source IP address for the ping packets. For example:

```
router#ping ip
Target IP address: 10.1.0.111
Repeat count [5]:
Datagram size [100]:
Timeout in seconds [2]:
Extended commands [n]: y
Source address or interface: 10.23.34.101
...
Sending 5, 100-byte ICMP Echos to
10.1.0.111,
 timeout is 2 seconds:
!!!!!
Success rate is 100 percent (5/5), round-trip
 min/avg/max = 4/8/12 ms
```

NOTE: Some of the optional parameters were skipped and replaced by an ellipse (...).

Cisco Routers
for IP Routing

Little Black Book

Innokenty Rudenko

Tsunami Computing

Publisher
Keith
Weiskamp

Acquisitions Editor
Stephanie Wall

Marketing Specialist
Diane Enger

Project Editor
Michelle Stroup

Technical Reviewer
Jennifer Watson

Production Coordinator
Meg E. Turecek

Layout Design
April Nielsen

Cover Design
Jody Winkler

Cisco Routers for IP Routing Little Black Book

The Coriolis Group, LLC
14455 N. Hayden Road, Suite 220
Scottsdale, Arizona 85260

480/483-0192
FAX 480/483-0193
http://www.coriolis.com

Library of Congress Cataloging-in-Publication Data
Rudenko, Innokenty.
 Cisco routers for IP routing little black book / by Innokenty Rudenko.
  p. cm.
 Includes index.
 ISBN 1-57610-421-4
 1. TCP/IP (Computer network protocol) 2. Internetworking
(Telecommunication) I. Title.
TK5105.585.R83 1999
004.6'2–dc21   99-258444
                                                       CIP

Printed in the United States of America
10 9 8 7 6 5 4 3 2 1

This book was written without oversight or approval by Cisco Systems, Inc.

CORIOLIS

14455 North Hayden Road, Suite 220 • Scottsdale, Arizona 85260

Dear Reader:

Coriolis Technology Press was founded to create a very elite group of books: the ones you keep closest to your machine. Sure, everyone would like to have the Library of Congress at arm's reach, but in the real world, you have to choose the books you rely on every day *very* carefully.

To win a place for our books on that coveted shelf beside your PC, we guarantee several important qualities in every book we publish. These qualities are:

- *Technical accuracy*—It's no good if it doesn't work. Every Coriolis Technology Press book is reviewed by technical experts in the topic field, and is sent through several editing and proofreading passes in order to create the piece of work you now hold in your hands.

- *Innovative editorial design*—We've put years of research and refinement into the ways we present information in our books. Our books' editorial approach is uniquely designed to reflect the way people learn new technologies and search for solutions to technology problems.

- *Practical focus*—We put only pertinent information into our books and avoid any fluff. Every fact included between these two covers must serve the mission of the book as a whole.

- *Accessibility*—The information in a book is worthless unless you can find it quickly when you need it. We put a lot of effort into our indexes, and heavily cross-reference our chapters, to make it easy for you to move right to the information you need.

Here at The Coriolis Group we have been publishing and packaging books, technical journals, and training materials since 1989. We're programmers and authors ourselves, and we take an ongoing active role in defining what we publish and how we publish it. We have put a lot of thought into our books; please write to us at **ctp@coriolis.com** and let us know what you think. We hope that you're happy with the book in your hands, and that in the future, when you reach for software development and networking information, you'll turn to one of our books first.

Keith Weiskamp
President and Publisher

Jeff Duntemann
VP and Editorial Director

Look For This Other Book From The Coriolis Group:

Cisco LAN/WAN Little Black Book

To my dear wife Adelya
for her love and support
—Innokenty Rudenko

About The Author

Innokenty Rudenko, a principal consultant with Tsunami Computing, Inc, is currently working as a consultant at J.P. Morgan in New York. His primary area of specialization is computer networks based on Cisco routers and switches. Innokenty holds an M.S. in computer science and is a CCIE #3805 and MCSE.

Acknowledgments

There are many people whom I would like to thank for contributing to this book.

First, I would like to express my gratitude to my partner Elliot Goykhman, the president of Tsunami Computing—it was his idea that it'd be great if we wrote a book. After I started writing, he continually supported me by providing all necessary resources to successfully complete the book.

I would like to thank the Coriolis team, which made this book possible. Special thanks to Michelle Stroup, my project editor—it was such a great pleasure for me to work with her and Colleen Brosnan—I'm really impressed with the work she did and how much she improved my English. I would also like to thank Stephanie Wall, the acquisitions editor; Jennifer Watson, the technical reviewer; and Meg Turecek, the Production Coordinator.

I want to express my gratitude to my colleagues at Tsunami Computing and J.P. Morgan. I want to thank Howard Poznansky for his advice on the English language. I am very grateful to Frank Kettles, without whom working on this book would have been much less fun.

Special thanks to Gregg Messina and Mike Strumpf for their advice on equipping the lab that I used when writing this book, and to Boris Guzman who did some excellent reviews on some parts of this book.

I would like to thank Cornelius Hull, Anuj Kumar, Pat Coen, Roger Hampar, George Young, Carl Vitale, Mike Andrascik, Redginald Dancy, Ronnie Sun, Albert Mui, Julie Yip, Bill Hammill, Walter Sacharok, Dmitri Tcherevik, Valery Tsyplenkov, Artem Letko, and all those I have missed in this listing for their insight and inspiration.

And last but not least, I want to thank my dear wife Adelya, to whom I dedicate this book, for her love, support, and patience with me during all the time I was writing the book.

Contents At A Glance

Chapter 1 The Layered Communication Model And
Internet Protocol

Chapter 2 Bridging With Cisco Routers

Chapter 3 Static Routing

Chapter 4 Dynamic Routing: Distance Vector
Routing Protocols

Chapter 5 Dynamic Routing: Link State Routing Protocols

Chapter 6 Controlling Data Flow And Routing Updates

Chapter 7 Special Cases Of Routing

Chapter 8 IP Multicast Routing

Appendix A Connecting Two Cisco Routers Back-To-Back
Using Two Serial Cables

Appendix B Configuring Frame Relay Switching On A
Cisco Router

Appendix C Using RSH And RCP With Cisco Routers

Appendix D Ping With Time Stamps

Appendix E Using Windows NT Computers As Hosts

Table Of Contents

Introduction xvii

Chapter 1
The Layered Communication Model
And Internet Protocol 1

In Brief
A Layered Communication Model   2
The OSI/RM   5
The Internet Model   7
Invisible Components   9
The Internet Protocol   12
    TCP/IP Protocol Suite   13
    IP Service Characteristics   14
    Operation Of IP Routing At A Glance   15
    IP Datagrams   17
IP Addresses   23
    Evolution Of IP Address Design   24
    Subnetting   29
Internet Control Message Protocol   33
    ICMP Control Messages   34
IP And Network Access Layer Technologies   38
    Interlayer Addressing And IP Routing   39
    Filtering Packets   42
Useful Tools   43
Immediate Solutions
Using IP Over LAN: ARP And ProxyARP   45
Configuring Serial Interface   52
    Using HDLC Encapsulation   52
    Configuring IP Over Frame Relay: Static Mapping
      And InverseARP   53
Configuring IP Over ISDN   58

Chapter 2
Bridging With Cisco Routers 61

In Brief
MAC Address   62
Transparent Bridging   64
 Spanning Tree Algorithm   64
Source-Route Bridging   68
Immediate Solutions
Configuring Transparent Bridging   72
 Using A Single Bridge Group On A Single Router   73
 Using Multiple Bridge Groups   75
Configuring Mixed-Media Transparent Bridging   77
 Bridging Over HDLC   78
 Bridging Over Frame Relay   79
 Bridging Over ISDN   83
 Configuring Concurrent Routing And Bridging   86
 Configuring Integrated Routing And Bridging   87
 Tuning The Spanning Tree Parameters   89
Configuring Source-Route Bridging   97
 Using Pure Source-Route Bridging   97
 Configuring Remote Source-Route Bridging   98
 Configuring Source-Route Translational Bridging And
  Transparent Bridging   100

Chapter 3
Static Routing 105

In Brief
Routing Algorithm   107
 Load Splitting   109
Immediate Solutions
Using Connected Interfaces To Perform
 Basic Routing   110
Configuring Basic Static Routing   111
Using Metrics With Static Routes   115
Using Output Interface Instead Of Next-Hop Router With
 Static Routing   119
Configuring Classless Routing   123
Configuring A Default Gateway On A Router   125
Configuring Individual Host Routes   125
Configuring Equal Cost Load Balancing Using Static Routing   126
Configuring Unequal Cost Load Balancing Using Static Routing   132

Chapter 4
Dynamic Routing: Distance Vector Routing Protocols............. 137

In Brief
Distance Vector Algorithm   139
Distance Vector Algorithm Refinements: Split-Horizon Rule,
    Holddowns, And Triggered Updates   141
    Split Horizon   143
    Holddowns   144
    Triggered Updates   144
Administrative Distance   144
Classful And Classless Routing Protocols   146
Immediate Solutions
Configuring Classful Routing Protocols   148
    Configuring RIP   148
    Using Individual Host Addresses With RIP   158
    Configuring RIP To Originate The Default Route   160
    Using RIP In The Presence Of Secondary IP Addresses   161
    Preventing RIP From Sending Routing Updates
        On An Interface   165
    Using Unicast Routing Updates With RIP   167
    Discriminating Incoming Routing Updates   169
    Configuring Equal Cost Load Balancing With RIP   173
    Changing RIP Metrics   175
    Configuring RIP Over Non-Fully Meshed Frame
        Relay Networks   177
    Configuring IGRP   182
    Understanding IGRP Metrics   184
    Configuring Equal And Unequal Cost Load Balancing
        With IGRP   187
Configuring Classless Routing Protocols   192
    Dividing IP Address Space For Use With VLSM   192
    Configuring RIP Version 2   202
    Disabling RIP Version 2 Auto-Summarization   208
    Using RIP Version 1 And RIP Version 2 Simultaneously   209
    Configuring EIGRP   210
    Understanding EIGRP Metrics   213
    Disabling EIGRP Auto-Summarization   213
    Configuring Route Summarization With EIGRP   214
    Configuring EIGRP Over Non-Fully Meshed Frame
        Relay Networks   216

Chapter 5
Dynamic Routing: Link State Routing Protocols **219**

In Brief
OSPF   220
Protocol Overview   221
Dijkstra's Shortest Path Algorithm   222
OSPF Network Types   225
Hierarchical Routing Model   227
Link State Advertisements   228

Immediate Solutions
Configuring OSPF With A Single Area   230
Understanding OSPF Costs   234
Configuring OSPF With Multiple Areas   235
Originating Default Information   240
Displaying An OSPF Link State Database   241
Configuring OSPF Stub Areas   242
Using OSPF Virtual Links To Restore A Partitioned Backbone   245
Using OSPF Virtual Links To Connect Remote Areas   255
Configuring OSPF Over NBMA Networks   261
Configuring OSPF Over Fully Meshed NBMA Networks   261
Configuring OSPF Over Non-Fully Meshed NBMA Networks   268

Chapter 6
Controlling Data Flow And Routing Updates **281**

In Brief
Routing Information Redistribution   282
Filtering Routing Information While Redistributing   284
Potential Problems Associated With Redistribution   284
Immediate Solutions
Using Access-Lists To Filter Data Traffic   287
Using Standard Access-Lists   287
Using Extended Access-Lists   291
Using Named Access-Lists   293
Controlling Routing Updates   294
Using Redistribution   297
Configuring Basic Redistribution   298
Assigning A Default Redistribution Metric   308
Using One-Way Redistribution   309
Using Access-Lists To Filter Routing Updates
During Redistribution   312
Using Route-Maps To Filter Routing Updates
During Redistribution   315

Using Redistribution With EIGRP   323
Using The **Null** Interface For Route Summarization   318
Redistributing Between EIGRP And IGRP Configured With The
Same AS Number   324
Redistributing Between EIGRP And IGRP Configured With
Different AS Numbers   329
Using Redistribution With OSPF   332
Understanding And Configuring ASBRs   333
Understanding And Configuring NSSAs   342

Chapter 7
Special Cases Of Routing 351

In Brief
Policy-Based Routing   352
Network Address Translation   352
NAT Terminology   353
Hot Standby Router Protocol   354
Dial-On-Demand Routing   357
Immediate Solutions
Configuring Policy-Based Routing   358
Using Policy-Based Routing For Routing Over
A Dedicated Link   359
Using Application-Sensitive Policy-Based Routing   365
Configuring Network Address Translation (NAT)   369
Configuring Static Translation Of Inside IP Addresses   369
Configuring Dynamic Translation Of Inside IP Addresses   374
Configuring NAT With Overloading Global Inside
IP Addresses   385
Configuring NAT To Translate Between Overlapping
Address Spaces   386
Configuring NAT For TCP Load Balancing   390
Configuring Hot Standby Router Protocol (HSRP)   394
Configuring Basic HSRP   394
Using MHSRP For Load Balancing   401
Configuring Dial-On-Demand Routing (DDR)   405
Configuring Snapshot Routing   405
Configuring Dial Backup   410

Chapter 8
IP Multicast Routing 417

In Brief
Basics Of Multicast Routing   419
Mapping Multicast IP Addresses To MAC Addresses   419

Source-Based Trees   420
Shared Trees   422
Multicast Routing Table   423
Reverse Path Forwarding Algorithm   423
Existing IP Multicast-Related Protocols   423
Internet Group Management Protocol (IGMP)   424
Protocol Independent Multicast-Dense
Mode (PIM-DM)   424
Protocol Independent Multicast-Sparse
Mode (PIM-SM)   425
Other Multicast Routing Protocols   425
Immediate Solutions
Configuring PIM-DM   427
Configuring PIM-SM   433
Configuring PIM-SM And PIM-DM On The Same
Interface Simultaneously   437
Configuring PIM-SM Over NBMA Networks   437

Appendix A
Connecting Two Cisco Routers Back-To-Back
Using Two Serial Cables 445

Appendix B
Configuring Frame Relay Switching On A Cisco Router 447

Appendix C
Using RSH And RCP With Cisco Routers 453

Appendix D
Ping With Time Stamps 459

Appendix E
Using Windows NT Computers As Hosts 461

Index 463

Introduction

You might be wondering: If there are already so many books in the bookstores about configuring Cisco routers, why would anyone bother writing another one? Well, this book is different from the other books in two aspects: its approach, and the problems to which it offers solutions.

This book takes a systematic approach to working with networks, which should tie the principles of modern networking to the operation of the Cisco routers. Reading this book should help you develop a certain way of thinking when working with Cisco routers whereby you will be able to deal with the problems you've never dealt with before or with those that are not covered in the available resources.

Networks, because of their distributed nature, always seem to be more complex than single computers. Likewise, the problems associated with networks seem to be more complex—and thus less approachable—than the problems associated with standalone computers. Plus, networks are built with devices like routers, which, though they are computers themselves, are at the same time so different from the computers that we are used to, like PCs, Macintoshes, and even Unix boxes. For instance, Cisco routers, with their proprietary command line interface and uncountable number of commands, may at first seem to be pretty tough creatures.

But are networks so complex? Not at all; the principles that the networks are based upon are in most cases not overly complex. These principles will be explained in this book. The principles we are going to discuss have been around for quite a few years already, and during this time they have been going through an unceasing process of research and improvement. So now, as they are theoretically proven and perfected, predicting the behavior of a network in most cases should not present a big problem. In other words, the "solvability" is very much achievable—and using a systematic approach should be even more feasible.

Cisco routers themselves are not too complex, either. In fact, they are much simpler than Macintoshes or PCs running Windows 95 or Windows NT—not to mention Unix. The number of the commands that can be entered on a Cisco router at any time is pretty limited and most commands are self-explanatory. For instance, if you compare what can be done with a router and what can be done with a PC running Windows 95, the router would seem like a very primitive device. Still, most IT professionals are not overly challenged by administering Windows 95.

This book covers some rather difficult cases of configuring Cisco routers, cases not found in most other books. For every example in this book, the author provides an explanation of why each action should be taken, and how it is related to the corresponding principles of networking.

Many people think of working with the networks more as an art than a technology. Technology here means applying well-defined methods of working with a certain problem that gradually draws you to a solution, as opposed to art whereby solutions are born sporadically. One may indeed think of working with networks as an art, but only to a certain extent.

Let's take as an example VLSM (Variable Length Subnet Masks). The theory behind the operation of the routing protocols employing VLSM is simple: the routers send the subnet mask along with the network address in the routing updates, which allows several masks to coexist within the same network address. But it's not generally considered easy to create an addressing scheme using VLSM. Problems arise when addresses overlap or the address space is not fully used, and so on. So, designing addressing schemes using VLSM is generally considered an art. In this book, however, the author presents a "technology" that allows you to design addressing schemes using VLSM without wasting address space.

But that's just one of the examples, and although there are more, some things about networking remain an art. Still, this book tries to change the perception of networking as less of an art, and more as an approachable technology.

This book is also for those who are working on attaining the CCIE status. Some configuration examples used in this book can be particularly useful during preparation to the CCIE lab exam.

How This Book Is Organized

The organization of this book is that of a typical *Little Black Book*. Each chapter has an "In Brief" section, followed an "Immediate Solutions" section.

The "In Brief" sections introduce the subject and explain the principles it is based upon. The content of this section does not delve too deeply into details, but instead elaborates only on the most essential points that are important for understanding the "Immediate Solutions." The "Immediate Solutions" section presents several tasks on a subject, which are all based on the material presented in the "In Brief" section. These tasks may vary from very simple to very complex. The wide range of task levels provides as broad a coverage of the subject as possible.

This book contains eight chapters. Some additional information can be found in the Appendices A through E. Let's take a quick look through the chapters.

Chapter 1: The Layered Communication Model And Internet Protocol

After glancing at the title of this chapter, you may guess that it isn't the most exciting one in the book. However, this chapter should be read first because it introduces the basic networking concepts referred to throughout the book.

Chapter 2: Bridging With Cisco Routers

This chapter deals with two types of bridging—Transparent Bridging and Source-Route bridging. This chapter, although a digression from the main subject, clears up the confusion that obscures how a router operates when configured for both routing and bridging. Also, some aspects of bridging are either based on IP or substantially affect IP operation, and to skip them would make for an incomplete presentation of IP.

Chapter 3: Static Routing

This chapter introduces routing and the types of routing that are available. The "In Brief" section contains a description of the routing algorithm that routers follow when making routing decisions. In the "Immediate Solutions" section there are several configuration tasks involving static routing.

Chapter 4: Dynamic Routing: Distance Vector Routing Protocols

This chapter deals with the oldest and most popular versions of dynamic routing protocols—the distance vector routing protocols. It also introduces VLSM. The "Immediate Solutions" section presents scenarios involving RIP version 1 and 2, IGRP, and EIGRP.

Chapter 5: Dynamic Routing: Link State Routing Protocols

This chapter is devoted to OSPF. It presents several different configurations for OSPF, including the infamous (and often loathsome) ones involving fully and non-fully meshed frame relay. Special attention is paid to the topologies involving multiple areas, parted backbone, and virtual-links.

Chapter 6: Controlling Data Flow And Routing Updates

Filtering and redistribution are two most important things about routing. This chapter describes different scenarios and points out some dangers and side effects of filtering and redistribution.

Chapter 7: Special Cases Of Routing

This chapter covers Hot Standby Router Protocol (HSRP), policy-based routing, network address translation (NAT), and Dial-On-Demand Routing (DDR).

Chapter 8: IP Multicast Routing

This chapter introduces multicast IP and provides guidelines on basic configuration of multicast IP, including Protocol Independent Multicast (PIM) Sparse and Dense modes, on the Cisco routers.

How To Use This Book

This book is mostly a practical guide on configuring Cisco routers, and the chapters can be read in any order.

Your feedback on this book is welcome; the author can be reached at irudenko@hugewave.com. Also, all the configuration examples used in this book, as well as some useful utilities, such as multicast IP test application called MCASTER, are available for free at Tsunami Computing's Web site at: **www.hugewave.com/blackbook**.

## Chapter 1

The Layered Communication Model And Internet Protocol

If you need an immediate solution to:	*See page:*
Using IP Over LAN: ARP And Proxy ARP	45
Configuring Serial Interface	52
Using HDLC Encapsulation	52
Configuring IP Over Frame Relay: Static Mapping And InverseARP	53
Configuring IP Over ISDN	58

In Brief

This chapter consists of two logical parts. In the first part, I describe two layered communication models: the Open System Interconnection Reference Model, which is often abbreviated as OSI/RM, and the Internet Model. If you've read about OSI/RM (and almost everybody who works with networks has done so at least once), you'll remember that OSI/RM consists of seven layers, each one with a well-defined purpose not found in the other layers. The Internet Model is similar to the OSI/RM, with few exceptions. For that reason, I'll skip detailed explanations of each layer in both models and concentrate only on the most important elements, which I will refer to in later chapters.

The second part of this chapter describes the Internet Protocol, or IP. This book is called "Cisco Routers for IP Routing," and therefore in addition to the Cisco routers, I believe it's necessary to provide a rather comprehensive description of IP. Readers who are very familiar with IP can use the material presented in the second part as a reference. Readers who may not be as familiar with IP will find all of the material that I consider important and necessary for understanding IP, and other important IP-related topics, in the second part of the In Brief section, which starts at the subsection "Internet Protocol."

Most of the IP-related discussion in this book is based on the Internet documents called "Requests for Comments," or RFCs. RFCs represent a really invaluable source of information, which is often underestimated. For example, all Internet standards, such as Internet Protocol, Transmission Control Protocol, and so on, are published as RFCs in full detail. In addition, all RFCs are free of charge and publicly available. When a reference to a particular RFC document is necessary, I will provide it in the format RFC XXXX, where XXXX will be the RFC number. Unless completely necessary, I will not use other sources of information.

For those of you who are interested in where RFCs can be found, www.rfc-editor.org is a good place to start.

A Layered Communication Model

A layered communication model consists of several layers, and each layer carries out certain well-defined functions not found in the other layers. An implementation of a layer on a network node is sometimes referred to as an *entity*. An entity that can communicate with other entities belonging to the same layer is called a *peer*. Peer entities do not communicate with each other directly; instead, they communicate using services offered by the entities that belong to the previous adjacent layer. In other words, a layer N entity communicates with its peers using services provided by a layer N-1 entity. The lowest layer entities communicate directly, using the physical media.

The rules that define the format of the data exchanged between the peer entities and how the exchange is performed are collectively called *protocols*. The data units defined by a protocol are often called *protocol data units*, or PDUs. Any single entity can be associated with only one protocol. The services provided by a layer N-1 entity to a layer N entity are accessed using a *service access point*, or SAP. The model also assumes that only the peers are aware of the protocol they use, and only they can understand it. No other entities on any other layers can understand the protocols that do not belong to them. Figure 1.1 depicts the relation among layers, entities, protocols, SAPs, and PDUs.

Figure 1.1 shows two entities, A_N and B_N, on Layer N, and two entities, X_{N-1} and Y_{N-1}, on Layer N-1. Entities A_N and B_N exchange a PDU, using $Protocol_N$. Although the PDU is addressed by entity A_N to entity B_N, it is sent using a service provided by entities X_{N-1} and Y_{N-1}.

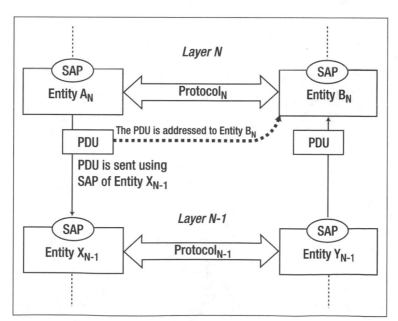

Figure 1.1   Protocols, PDUs, and SAPs.

One of the most important principles of the layered model states that an entity at the destination will receive exactly the same PDU sent by its peer entity at the source. This principle allows layers to be independent of each other and makes protocols possible.

The layered model allows several layer N entities to coexist within the same node and use a single layer N-1 entity service. It is possible through processes called *multiplexing* and *demultiplexing*. Multiplexing occurs when several layer N entities use an SAP of the layer N-1 entity. Demultiplexing occurs when a layer N-1 entity distributes PDUs to the appropriate layer N entities. Figure 1.2 shows how multiplexing is performed.

The purpose of the layered communication models is to make it easier to develop the network software and hardware. Because each protocol on each layer is guaranteed data integrity during transfers, the designer can concentrate on one protocol at a time without worrying about how the protocols on the other layers are performing.

The layered model, with multiplexing and demultiplexing, allows for modular design of the software and hardware. The entity in a layered model is essentially a network module, such as a software driver or even a piece of hardware. The layered model allows you to separately load network modules that belong to different layers and to have several network modules operating on Layer N to use a single network module on Layer N-1.

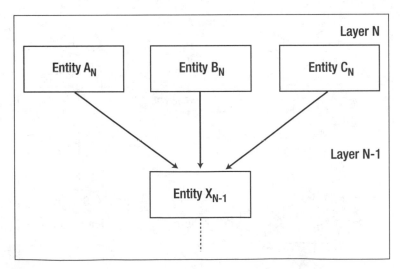

Figure 1.2   Multiplexing.

As I mentioned previously, *entity* and *network module* are essentially the same terms; therefore, they can be used interchangeably. I will use the term *entity* when I refer to the entity in general, and I will use the term *module* when I describe an entity of a particular implementation of the layered model in the situations specific only to this model.

The OSI/RM

In the preceding section, I talked about a generalized layered communication model. By itself, this model makes little sense. In real life, we need a model that helps design communication systems in accordance with our needs. It should not be too simplistic, because if it were, the protocol designers would have to pack too much functionality in each protocol. The model should not be too complex either, because complexity places too many restrictions on what the protocol can and cannot do.

One real-world model, called the *Open Systems Interconnection Reference Model*, or *OSI/RM*, was first introduced in 1984 by the standards body called the *International Standards Organization*, or *ISO*. The model consists of the following seven layers:

- *Application*—Specialized network functions such as virtual terminal, file transfer, and email.
- *Presentation*—Data formatting, character translation, and encryption.
- *Session*—Establishing sessions between a user and a network node, such as a network logon.
- *Transport*—Reliable or unreliable end-to-end delivery of data.
- *Network*—Routing PDUs across multiple networks. Handling intermediate congestion.
- *Data link*—Formatting the data into frames and transmitting them error-free across a physical network.
- *Physical*—Transmission of bits over a physical communication media.

In addition to the functionality found in any layered communication model, OSI/RM introduces *packet encapsulation*. Packet encapsulation is a way to preserve the required integrity of PDUs exchanged between peer entities using the service provided by the lower layer entities.

The PDU on each layer, except for the Physical Layer, consists of two components: a *header* and *data*. The header contains auxiliary information used only by the entity of each particular module. The data is received from the upper adjacent layer for servicing across the network. As you remember, the layered model guarantees that the destination entity will receive exactly the same PDU that was sent by the source entity. OSI/RM conforms with this rule, making the source entity pass the whole PDU, including the header it formed, to the lower adjacent entity as the data. In other words, the upper layer entity's PDU is *encapsulated* in the lower entity's PDU. When the lower entity's counterpart at the destination performs demultiplexing of the data to the upper layer entity, this upper layer entity receives exactly what it was sent. This process works for all layers except for the Application Layer, in which the data is the actual payload received from the network application.

You may notice that the encapsulation on the Data Link Layer also adds a trailer, a piece of information similar to the header, which is only used by the Data Link Layer entities. Because this trailer is not important to our discussion of encapsulation, I'll skip over an explanation of it.

It's still unclear, however, how multiplexing and demultiplexing are supported through the encapsulation process. The primary purpose of encapsulation is to ensure the integrity of the PDUs as they are exchanged between the peers. It does nothing, however, to address the needs of multiplexing and demultiplexing. Thus, to provide multiplexing or demultiplexing, the encapsulation itself is not enough; something else is needed.

If the upper layer entity needs to pass the data to the lower layer entity, it needs to know only the SAP (service access point), which is actually an interface to the service. Even if more than one upper layer entity exists, these entities still can use the service of a single lower layer entity. Thus, you can conclude that SAPs are needed to perform multiplexing. When the lower layer entity's counterpart, operating at the destination, receives a PDU containing the data for the peer of the source upper layer entity, it needs to know how to distinguish that PDU from the other PDUs it receives, which can be destined for the other upper layer entities. The format of the PDUs, passed as the data to the lower layer entity, is part of the protocol that the upper layer entities use and that only they can understand. Therefore, the lower layer cannot look into the data to figure out its receiver. As a result, the only way for the lower layer entity to know the receiver is to label the data using its own header. The labeling is done using an identifier that the lower layer entity stores in the header of its own PDU. This identifier is often referred to as a *demultiplexing key*. The demultiplexing key is used to perform the demultiplexing.

The Internet Model

Although OSI/RM is a rather comprehensive layered communication model, it has certain limitations. OSI/RM was primarily designed to provide a framework for protocols operating over homogeneous local area networks (LANs); therefore, OSI/RM is less suitable for heterogeneous networks, especially those involving wide area networks (WANs). Despite the fact that the routing function is present on OSI/RM's Network Layer, it is not sufficiently developed to provide comprehensive functional specification for routers, the network nodes that are used to connect mixed physical networks whereby providing end-to-end connectivity.

One of the most popular alternatives to the OSI/RM is the Internet Model, also known as the TCP/IP model. Unlike OSI/RM, the Internet Model was designed to provide a framework for protocols operating across incongruous networks, often including WANs and LANs.

The Internet Model has four layers, as follows:

- *Application*—Specialized network functions such as virtual terminal, file transfer, and email.
- *Transport*—Reliable or unreliable end-to-end delivery of data.
- *Internet*—Routing data across heterogeneous networks and performing basic congestion control.
- *Network Access*—Formatting the data into frames and transmitting them error-free across a physical network. Transmission of bits over a physical communication media.

The functionality of these layers is similar to the functionality of the corresponding layers of OSI/RM, with the exception of the Network Access Layer, which simply covers two OSI/RM layers—the Data Link Layer and Physical Layer—and has the combined functionality of the two. Also, the Application Layer of the Internet model can be internally expanded to cover the functionality of the Session Layer and Presentation Layer, if necessary.

What further distinguishes the Internet Model from OSI/RM is that it addresses the communication issues associated with the presence of diverse physical networks by explicitly introducing routers. The Internet Model has two types of layer stacks: one for the end nodes (or *hosts*, according to Internet terminology), and one for the routers (referred to in the early days of the Internet as *gateways*, which may sound a bit confusing today). These two types of layer stacks are shown in Figure 1.3.

The Internet Model provides two distinct names for PDUs of the Transport and Internet Layers: *segment* and *datagram*, respectively. As Figure 1.4 suggests, the datagram created by the IP module of host A may not necessarily be sent to the IP module of host B. Instead, the datagram can be sent to the Internet module of the router along the way to the destination host B, providing that more than one intermediate physical network exists. What is not shown in Figure 1.3 is that the router can and does change some fields in the headers of the datagrams while processing them. It can also break large datagrams

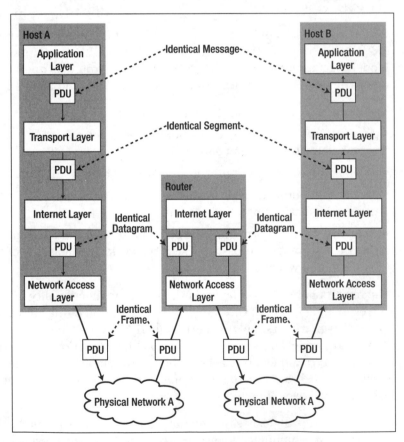

Figure 1.3   Two types of layer stacks in the Internet Model.

into parts if they do not fit into the Maximum Transfer Unit, or MTU, of the network across which it sends them. In other words, the IP module of the destination host B may not receive intact datagrams created by the IP module of host A.

However, this doesn't represent as significant a deviation from the OSI/RM as it may seem. As Figure 1.3 shows, the datagram stays intact while traversing the physical network between the two adjacent nodes, whether these are hosts or routers. If the receiving adjacent node is a router, it changes some fields in the header of the datagram and can also break the datagram into parts, thereby creating one or several new datagrams. These new datagrams traverse the next intermediate network intact. This process does not affect the segment created by the Transport Layer module and carried inside the datagrams; this segment stays intact as it traverses multiple intermediate networks. Because the routers do not have the Transport Layer modules, the segments created by the Transport module of host A are destined for the Transport module of host B. But, the routers do have the Internet modules, and therefore the datagrams can be destined for the Internet modules of the routers. Moreover, the latter always occurs if the datagram needs to traverse multiple intermediate networks. Thus, you can conclude that the PDUs in the Internet Model do remain intact when they arrive at the corresponding destination on each layer.

To accommodate this new encapsulation scheme, the Internet model introduces two layer-dependent types of communication: *end-to-end* (sometimes also called *host-to-host*) and *hop-to-hop*. The end-to-end communication assumes that the PDUs are sent by the source node to the destination node, regardless of the number of intermediate physical networks. Hop-to-hop communication occurs only between the nodes separated by a single physical network. Obviously, the Transport Layer in the Internet Model provides end-to-end communication, whereas the Internet Layer provides hop-to-hop.

Invisible Components

So far, I have discussed the components of both models that are pretty obvious because they were inherited from the concept of the layered communication model. I have not yet touched on some invisible components, and they play a very important role during the whole communication process.

Because this further discussion requires choosing a single layered model to work with as an example, I have chosen the Internet Model.

In general, whenever possible, I will use the Internet Model because it provides for use of routers. In some cases, however, I will use OSI/RM because it gives a thorough description of the two lowest layers: the Data Link Layer and the Physical Layer. Unfortunately, the Internet Model provides a faceless Network Access Layer in place of Data Link and Physical Layers, which often is not sufficient.

Figure 1.4 shows a very simple network consisting of two nodes—say, a PC running Windows and a Unix server, connected via an Ethernet segment. Let's take a closer look at what happens when a user establishes a connection from the PC to the server using Telnet.

To connect to the server, the PC user should enter the following:

```
C:\>telnet 10.1.0.1
```

Here, 10.1.0.1 is the server's IP address. Using this address, the telnet.exe application connects to the telnetd application residing on the Unix server.

The telnet.exe and telnetd applications are peer entities on the Application Layer that communicate using the Telnet protocol. Apparently, both applications should use the communication service of some module that operates on the Transport Layer. The Telnet protocol specification requires using TCP; therefore, the applications should use the TCP module. The TCP module is used by both telnet.exe and telnetd on each side of the connection to service the exchange of Telnet messages across the network. In this process, the Telnet protocol data is encapsulated into TCP segments, which are, in turn, passed to the IP module. The IP module encapsulates the TCP segments into IP datagrams and calls the Ethernet driver to send the datagrams across the physical network inside the Ethernet frames.

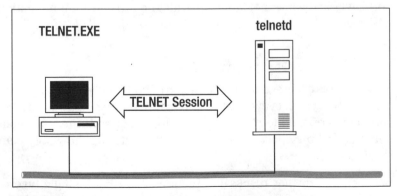

Figure 1.4   Telnet session between a PC and a Unix server.

You know already that Telnet is not the only Application Layer protocol that belongs to the TCP/IP suite of protocols. Others include FTP, HTTP, Finger, and so on. The TCP module should perform multiplexing and demultiplexing across multiple Application Layer protocols. TCP does so using TCP ports, which are stored as two-byte fields in the headers of the TCP segments.

The TCP ports are essentially addresses used to identify the Application Layer protocols during communication, which will be tied to the actual Application Layer modules by the operating system of the host. The two types of ports in TCP are *well-known* and *random*. The well-known ports are used to identify the modules performing server functions—that is, the modules that reply to the requests. The random ports are normally used to identify the modules performing client functions—that is, the modules that issue requests. For instance, in the case of the Telnet session, telnet.exe is the client module, and telnetd is the server module. The random ports, allocated by the operating system, are always unique. On the other hand, the well-known ports are permanently assigned and always stay the same, no matter how many server modules are running. Moreover, the well-known ports must be the same on every host that is claimed to be TCP/IP compliant, which explains why these ports are called "well-known." Because you can launch multiple Telnet sessions going to the same host, you can conclude that the TCP ports are not enough to uniquely identify the application modules, at least not the server ones. In other words, if you have launched several Telnet sessions to the same host, the TCP module cannot figure out which telnetd module to use if it has only the TCP ports for identification purposes.

The only thing that seems to be truly unique in this situation is the combination of both TCP ports and both IP addresses. This combination is used when the TCP module performs demultiplexing of the connections back to the Application modules. When the TCP module calls the IP module, it uses the IP addresses to identify the destination to which the segments need to be sent. But, as you know, TCP is not the only Transport Layer protocol in the TCP/IP protocol suite; UDP (User Datagram protocol) is also available. Theoretically, the Internet model is not limited to only these two Transport Layer protocols; therefore, the model should provide for whatever Transport protocol a user wants. In other words, the IP module must be able to identify the Transport Layer protocol to which the payload of the arriving datagrams belongs. The IP module uses the protocol number, which is stored as a one-byte field in the datagram header. Luckily, having multiple instances of the same Transport Layer module over a single instance of the IP module is impossible. Therefore, the IP module has no problem uniquely identifying the Transport module using only the protocol field.

The problem may seem to disappear on the Network Access Layer because IP is the cornerstone of the Internet model and therefore is the only Internet Layer protocol. Unfortunately, that is not quite the case. Some other suite of protocols may use the Network Access Layer module along with TCP/IP. For instance, it's quite possible—and nowadays, quite usual—to have TCP/IP and IPX/SPX running on the same machine. Therefore, the Network Access Layer module, such as an Ethernet network interface card (NIC) and its driver, also needs to know which Internet Layer module receives the payload of the arriving frames. Again, this process is done in a fashion very similar to IP or TCP: A field in the header of the frame stores the number of the Internet Layer protocols for which the data is destined.

This simple example shows that, although the operation of the Internet model is not really complex, some components of it are not obvious. Luckily, we will be working only with routers in this book, and so it may seem you won't have to worry much about the details of the Transport and Application Layer protocols. Unfortunately, the Cisco routers are not very simple. They have a lot of control over how the Transport, and even the Application Layer modules of the hosts residing on the network, communicate. In this book, you'll come across some situations in which you need to understand what happens on other layers besides the Network Access and Internet Layers.

The Internet Protocol

According to the Internet Model, the Internet protocol (IP) performs two functions: routing datagrams and basic congestion control. The first function—routing—is unique to IP. No other protocol on any other layer of the Internet Model can perform routing packets across multiple heterogeneous intermediate networks. Although a somewhat similar function called bridging can be found on the Network Access Layer of the Internet Model or the Data Link Layer of the OSI/RM, it is assumed that all physical segments interconnected using bridging are "almost" homogeneous (why they are "almost" homogeneous is discussed in Chapter 2). Unlike routing, the other function of IP—congestion control—is found on nearly every layer of the Internet Model. Congestion control on the Internet Layer is called *basic congestion control* because it is really primitive compared to the congestion control performed by TCP. However, the main function of IP is routing—that is, delivering datagrams from the source to the destination, possibly across multiple heterogeneous intermediate networks.

When the hosts are located on the same physical network, they can communicate using only the routing services provided by their own IP modules. However, when the hosts are separated by multiple intermediate networks, special devices called *routers* become necessary.

Routers are network nodes with multiple network interfaces that receive datagrams from the networks to which they are directly attached and that, depending on the destination address, route them via the appropriate interfaces.

NOTE: *Notice that routers are not the only network nodes that can have multiple network interfaces. Hosts are also allowed to have multiple network interfaces, in which case they are called multihomed hosts. However, multihomed hosts are not allowed to route datagrams.*

A perfect example of IP routers is Cisco routers. However, Cisco routers are not limited to routing IP only. Cisco routers are *multiprotocol routers*, which means that they can act as routers for many other protocols, such as IPX, AppleTalk, DECNET, CLSN, and so on. Cisco routers can also act as bridges (devices that operate on the Network Access Layer). Because bridging can greatly affect the operation of IP routing, it is covered in Chapter 2.

TCP/IP Protocol Suite

The set of protocols designed around the two main protocols, TCP and IP, is often called the *TCP/IP protocol suite*. Figure 1.5 gives a graphical representation of the relation between some protocols of the TCP/IP protocol suite.

As Figure 1.5 shows, IP has quite a unique position in the TCP/IP protocol suite. It is the only Internet Layer protocol that carries out the functions found on the Internet Layer. There are some other auxiliary protocols not depicted in Figure 1.5 that also operate on the Internet Layer, but none of them provides services for the protocols of the Transport Layer, such as TCP or UDP. Examples of these protocols are ICMP, IGRP, EIGRP, and so on.

The unique service provided by IP to the Transport Layer protocols hides the details of the underlying technologies operating on the Network Access Layer, thereby creating an illusion that the hosts are separated by homogeneous "one-hop" media. This service is really all that the Transport Layer protocols expect from IP. Therefore, as long

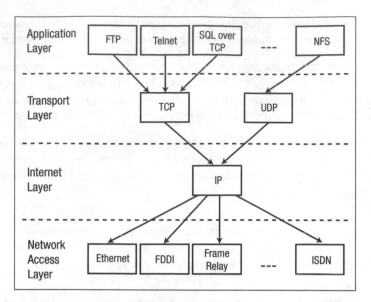

Figure 1.5   The TCP/IP protocol suite.

as it suffices, the Transport Layer protocols should not require an additional Internet Layer protocol.

IP Service Characteristics

The IP routing function performs the service of delivering the datagrams from the source to the destination. This service has three conceptual characteristics, which are beyond the scope of the Internet Model but are inherent to IP. These characteristics are very important for understanding the behavior of IP routing in various scenarios:

- *Connectionless*—The service delivers each datagram absolutely independently of all other datagrams. The datagrams can be sent along different paths, they can arrive out of sequence, and so on.

- *Unreliable*—The service does not guarantee that every single datagram will be delivered to the destination or arrive intact. The datagrams can get lost or can become corrupted en route to the destination.

- *Best-effort*—The service uses its "best-effort" to deliver the datagrams. IP only discards the datagrams if it is forced to because it is running low of resources, such as buffers, or because underlying network components, such as network hardware or drivers, are causing errors.

Being a protocol, IP defines the format of the IP datagrams. From our earlier discussion, we know that the datagrams being processed by the intermediate routers are recreated. The new datagrams receive the data portion intact, unless fragmentation is necessary. Their headers also inherit most fields from the headers of the original datagrams unchanged, although some fields are changed. We also know that all of the changes, as well as fragmentation, are performed by the routers. Now we will examine the process of datagram transmission between the source and destination.

Operation Of IP Routing At A Glance

The Internet Model, unfortunately, does not address some size issues of the PDUs on different layers. Let's take a closer look at the encapsulation process and try to imagine what would happen if the protocol implementation blindly followed the Internet Model. (In all fairness, it's important to note that this shortcoming is not limited to the Internet Model; the OSI/RM, as well as any other "pure" layered model, is not free from it.)

TCP is not supposed to know anything about the MTU size of the network on which the host resides because this information exists only on the Network Access Layer and TCP belongs to the Transport Layer. Obviously, IP can't know anything about the MTU of the network for the same reason.

If TCP did not make any assumptions about the MTU size of the network, it would simply create the biggest possible segment in order to decrease the overhead associated with the TCP header. It would then pass this segment to IP, which would have to encapsulate it into an IP datagram. When IP would try to pass this IP datagram to the network adapter driver, there would be a good chance that it would fail, simply because the underlying physical network cannot carry frames big enough to encapsulate the datagram.

Therefore, although it may seem like a violation of the principles of the layering, the Transport Layer protocols and IP must have some idea at least about the MTU size of the directly connected networks, because segments created on the Transport Layer should fit into datagrams, which in turn should fit into physical frames. Theoretically, the fragmentation function of IP can be used to break large IP datagrams into pieces, each of which fits into a physical frame. In practice, however, such a use of the fragmentation function is not feasible for two reasons. First, the fragmentation function is a means to overcome the difference in the MTU sizes of the intermediate networks, and therefore it's normally only implemented on the routers. Although the hosts are allowed to perform fragmentation, they are not required to. Second, as we'll see shortly, fragmentation always leads to performance degradation, and therefore unjustified use of it should be avoided whenever possible.

Suppose that the Transport Layer protocols and IP are aware of the MTU sizes of the directly attached networks. Also suppose that they use this knowledge when creating their respective PDUs, so that the encapsulation into a physical frame won't fail. What happens if there is an intermediate network between the source and destination with an MTU size smaller than that of the directly attached networks?

Let's consider the situation depicted in Figure 1.6.

Host H1 sends a datagram to host H2. Host H1 is aware of the MTU size of the physical network on which it resides—in this case, 1,500 bytes. However, it doesn't know anything about the intermediate network N3 and its MTU size. Therefore, the TCP module creates a segment with a size that is adequate only for network N1. When the network adapter on the host H1 sends the corresponding frame over the physical media, the frame's size is 1,500 bytes. Host H1 knows, however, that the destination is not on the same physical network and that it should then use router R1 to deliver the data to the final destination host H2. Host H1 sends the physical frame to router R1. When router R1 receives this frame, it extracts the datagram and discovers that the datagram size does not allow it to send the datagram

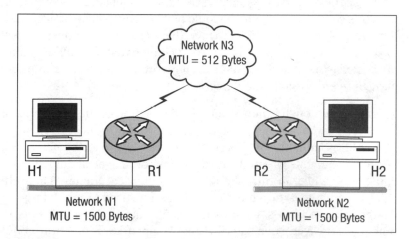

Figure 1.6   Datagrams become fragmented when they traverse networks with an MTU size smaller than that of the network from which the datagrams originate.

over network N3 without fragmentation. Therefore, router R1 breaks the datagram into four pieces called *fragments* (we'll find out shortly why it is broken into four), each of which is encapsulated separately into physical frames of network N3. Router R1 then sends them to router R2. After router R2 receives all four pieces, it understands that all of them should be sent to the destination over network N2 and that all of them are parts of one bigger datagram. The MTU size of network N2 is large enough to accommodate the original datagram, so router R2 faces the dilemma of either reassembling the datagram at this point or leaving this work for the destination. The IP specification requires routers to leave the reassembling work for the final destination. Thus, router R2 sends all four fragments separately over network N3 to the destination. Host H2, the final destination, receives all four pieces and reassembles the original datagram. The reassembling process takes place inside the IP module. The TCP module on host H2 is unaware of the fragmentation because it receives exactly the same TCP segment created by the TCP module on host H1.

During the process of fragmentation, the original datagram sent by host H1 has undergone critical changes. Not only have some fields in its header been changed, but the datagram itself has been broken into fragments to satisfy the intermediate network MTU size. However, the Transport Layer protocol—in this case, TCP—at host H2 does not notice any change in the segment created by its peer at host H1. The whole process was handled by the IP modules of the network nodes involved in the transmission totally transparently to the Transport Layer protocol.

Let's now examine the contents of the datagram and see how it's changed during the transmission process.

IP Datagrams

An IP datagram consists of the header and the payload. The *payload* is the data that the IP module receives from the upper layer protocols, such as TCP or UDP, during the encapsulation process. The *header* is auxiliary data created by the IP module that is used only by IP to route the datagram to the final destination. We know from our earlier discussion that IP service is connectionless. Therefore, the datagram header is designed so that it contains enough information to make all routing decisions for each individual datagram independently.

Figure 1.7 shows the format of an IP datagram.

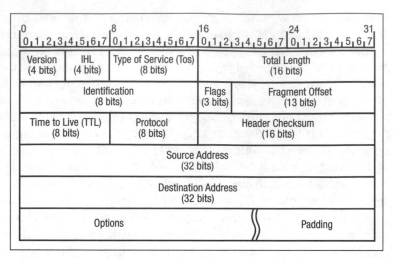

Figure 1.7   IP datagram format.

Version

The Version field has four bits and contains the IP version number. The current IP version is 4.

IP Header Length (IHL)

The IP Header Length (IHL) field is the size of the datagram header expressed in 32-bit words. As we'll see later, the Options field is optional, which makes the size of the datagram header variable. The typical header has no options. It has a size of 20 bytes and a header length value of 5.

Type Of Service (ToS)

The Type of Service (ToS) field specifies how the datagram should be handled. It has several subfields, each specifying a certain desired way of handling the datagram (see Figure 1.8).

The Precedence field is the first Type of Service subfield. It indicates the importance of the datagram—the higher the value of the Precedence field, the more important the datagram is. This field is 3 bits long, and there can be eight different values of precedence (see Table 1.1).

The other three fields—labeled *D* (for *delay*), *T* (for *throughput*), and *R* (for *reliability*) in Figure 1.8—are used to specify the desired characteristics of the path along which the datagram is sent. As Figure 1.8 shows, these fields all are only 1 bit long; hence, they can be either cleared or set. If bit D is set, the datagram is sent over a path with a low delay. If bit T is set, the datagram is sent over a path with a high throughput. Finally, if bit R is set, the datagram is sent over a path

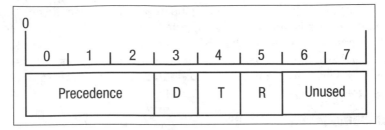

Figure 1.8   Type of Service subfields.

Table 1.1   Precedence values.

Decimal	Binary	Description
7	111	Network Control
6	110	Internetwork Control
5	101	CRITIC/ECP
4	100	Flash Override
3	011	Flash
2	010	Immediate
1	001	Priority
0	000	Routine (Normal)

with high reliability. If any of these fields is cleared, the respective characteristic is not requested.

Conceptually, Type of Service is a robust idea. If a router has more than one path to the destination, it can choose the one that satisfies the requested characteristics. For instance, if you use Telnet to communicate with a remote host, you expect a quick response from the host. Therefore, you may require setting bit D of all the Telnet sessions datagrams to force the connection to be carried over a path with a low delay. On the contrary, if you want to download a large file using FTP, you don't care about the response time, but you do care about how quickly the file gets downloaded. In this case, you may require setting bit T to request a higher throughput for the FTP connection.

Unfortunately, the Type of Service is not guaranteed. The routers are not required to meet the requested Type of Service and, in many cases, physically can't.

Total Length

The total length is the size of the datagram measured in octets—that is, 8-bit bytes. The Total Length field is 16 bits long, which theoretically allows creating datagrams up to 65,535 octets long. As we know, such large datagrams will probably be dropped because the network adapter driver is not able to encapsulate them into the physical network frames. The size of the real datagrams must not be larger than the MTU size of the physical networks over which the datagrams are sent. Nevertheless, all hosts and routers are required to accept datagrams with a size of 576 octets or less.

Identification

The Identification field, along with the following two fields, are used to facilitate datagram fragmentation and reassembling processes. Before describing this and the other fields, it's important to note that the fragments of the datagrams are also datagrams. Their structure is the same as the structure of the regular IP datagrams.

The Identification field has 16 bits and is used during a datagram reassembling process to identify the arriving fragments that constitute the datagram. Each time the source host creates a datagram, it uses a unique number for the datagram Identification field. When a router decides that it needs to fragment a datagram, it copies most of the fields from the header of the original datagram to the headers of the fragments. The Identification field is also copied, thereby providing the destination host with a way of recognizing the fragments as parts of the original datagram.

Flags

The Flags field has 3 bits and is solely used for fragmentation purposes. Each bit is interpreted independently as follows:

- Bit 0 is reserved.

- Bit 1 is also called DF bit, which stands for "Don't Fragment." When cleared, it indicates that the datagram can be fragmented. When set, it indicates that the datagram cannot be fragmented.

- Bit 2 is also called MF bit, which stands for "More Fragments." When set, it indicates that this is not the last fragment of the original datagram. When cleared, it indicates that this is the last fragment. (Obviously, if a datagram was not fragmented, this bit is cleared).

Fragment Offset

The Fragment Offset field has 13 bits and specifies which part of the original datagram payload that the fragment carries. The number that it represents is the offset of the fragment payload measured in units of eight octets from the beginning of the original datagram payload.

Figure 1.9 shows how the original datagram becomes fragmented prior to being sent over network N3, as well as the datagram and fragment headers and payloads. Only the datagram header fields that participate in the fragmentation process are shown.

To understand better how the fragmentation is performed and which fields are modified during the fragmentation, let's look at the example in Figure 1.6. Suppose that router R1 receives datagrams with a size of 1,460 bytes from host H1. Router R1 has to fragment these datagrams to satisfy network N3 MTU size, which is 512 bytes. Suppose that the Network Access Layer protocol operating on network N3 takes 32 bytes off the frames for its own purposes, thereby leaving only 480 bytes for IP.

Obviously, fragmentation does not facilitate the efficiency of the transmission. If the fragments have to traverse another intermediate network whose MTU size is larger than the size of the fragments, the

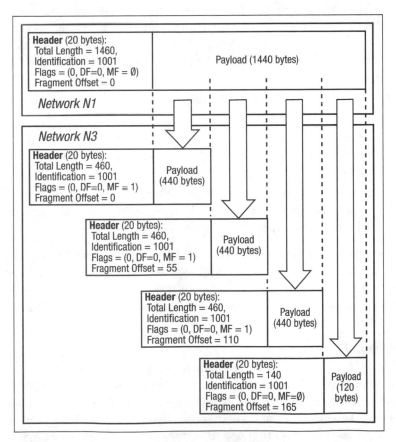

Figure 1.9   Fragmentation process at router R1 shown in Figure 1.6.

fragments will only use a part of that. For example, in Figure 1.6 router R2 will have to send the small fragments it receives from router R1 over network N2 whose MTU size is at least three times larger than the size of the fragments. Quite often, the last fragment turns out to be much smaller than what the MTU of the physical network allows. In our example, the MTU size of network N3 is 512 bytes, which allows the maximum size of the datagram to be 480 bytes. However, the last fragment has only 120 bytes of data. During fragmentation, the original header is replaced with several new headers that create additional overhead. In our example, the original header is replaced with four new ones. In addition, some inefficiency may be introduced because the payload of a fragment must be measured in units of 8 bytes, which can leave some unused space in the physical frame. In our example, the maximum datagram size on network N3 is 480 bytes, whereas the fragments use only 460.

Time To Live (TTL)

The Time to Live field reflects how long the datagram can exist before the intermediate routers drop it as expired. The name *Time to Live* is a bit misleading because it is not really expressed in units of time, such as seconds. Routers calculate the Time to Live field as follows:

1. When a router receives a datagram, it decrements the value of Time to Live by one.

2. If the value is 0, the router drops the datagram; otherwise, it forwards the datagram either to the next-hop router or to the final destination.

3. If the router is forced to store the datagram in its memory for more than 1 second, it decrements the value of the Time to Live field by one each second.

The primary purpose of the Time to Live field is to avoid network congestion in routing loops. Let's imagine a datagram that has been sent along a route, which eventually brings it back. If Time to Live did not exist, the datagram would end up being forwarded an unlimited number of times.

Protocol

The Protocol field is used to identify the protocols that should receive the payload of the datagram. It's 1 byte long, so it is possible to have 255 different protocols using IP service. Table 1.2 shows some protocol field values and their respective protocols. Interestingly enough, the protocols that use IP service do not necessarily have to be on the Transport Layer. Some auxiliary protocols, such as ICMP or IP EIGRP, can also use IP service.

Header Checksum

This 16-bit field contains the header checksum. The checksum is calculated only for the header of a datagram and not for the payload. If the payload arrives corrupted, the IP module will not detect it. The upper layer protocol for which the data is destined should have its own data integrity verification methods and should request retransmission if the data arrives corrupted.

Source And Destination Addresses

The source and destination addresses represent the IP addresses of the host that sent the datagram and the host that is to receive the datagram.

The structure of IP addresses is thoroughly described in the "IP Addresses" section.

Options And Padding

Options are fields that can be used for debugging purposes. Because these fields are usually not particularly helpful, they are rarely used.

The Padding field is used to pad the options on a 32-bit boundary.

IP Addresses

Almost everyone who works with computers has heard about and probably even used IP addresses. But what is an IP address? Is it a way to identify a host on a TCP/IP-compliant network? What if a host

Table 1.2   Some protocols and their corresponding numbers.

Protocol Number (Hexadecimal)	Protocol Number (Decimal)	Protocol Name
6	6	Transmission Control Protocol (TCP)
11	17	User Datagram Protocol (UDP)
1	1	Internet Control Message Protocol (ICMP)
9	9	Cisco Interior Gateway Routing Protocol (IGRP)
58	88	Cisco Extended Interior Gateway Routing Protocol (EIGRP)
59	89	Open Shortest Path First (OSPF)

has several network adapters? Such hosts should have several IP addresses, one for each network card. Is it then a way to identify a network adapter on a host on a TCP/IP-compliant network?

We assume that an IP address belongs to IP (the Internet protocol), which resides on the Internet Layer. In that case, what does an IP address have to do with a network card, which clearly belongs to the Network Access Layer?

There is no clear explanation why it was decided to use a separate IP address for each network adapter of an IP host. Nevertheless, because a host has a separate IP address for each network adapter if it has multiple network adapters, the host itself gets several identities.

The IP addresses also identify the networks on which the hosts reside. The IP address itself has a fixed length of 32 bits. However, the IP address is divided into two variable length parts—the network ID and the host ID—that together constitute the 32 bits of the IP address. The *network ID* uniquely identifies the physical segment to which the host is attached. The *host ID* uniquely identifies the host on that segment.

The notation used to specify the IP addresses in the human readable form is called *dotted decimal notation*. In dotted decimal notation, the 32 bits of an IP address are represented as four decimal numbers separated by periods. For example,

```
IP address in binary:     11010000100000010000000111000011
Dotted decimal notation:  208.129.1.195
```

Evolution Of IP Address Design

The original design of the TCP/IP protocol suite assumed that the majority of IP communications would be *unicast*—that is, a single host would communicate with a single host. Nevertheless, its designers assumed that some communications would be required to be *multicast*—that is, a single host would need to send data destined for multiple hosts. Therefore, the whole address space was divided into three unequally sized categories: unicast addresses, multicast addresses, and reserved address space. The biggest part of the IP address space—unicast addresses—was subdivided into three non-overlapping groups ("non-overlapping" means that the same IP address can only belong to one group). These groups defined which part of the IP address should be interpreted as the network ID and which as the host ID. Since the multicast addresses represent a group of hosts, they do not have network and host IDs.

The unicast groups, the multicast addresses, and the reserved space were collectively called *network classes* and named A, B, C, D, and E, respectively. However, the word *network* is normally omitted when referring to an individual IP address (for example, class A IP address) to avoid confusion.

The bit pattern of the first byte determines to which network class an IP address belongs. Figure 1.10 shows how the bit patterns are used to determine to which class an IP address belongs.

There are some deviations from this scheme in the form of functional addresses. These deviations are described in the Internet standard, "Internet Assigned Numbers" (RFC 1700).

The network ID consisting of all 0s designates *this network* (as per RFC 1700). Obviously, this is a class A address; however, it cannot be assigned to any host. It can only be used to refer to a particular host on *this network*, as long as *this network* can be interpreted unambiguously. The network ID consisting of all 0s can only appear as a source address.

The IP address consisting of all 0s—that is, 0.0.0.0—identifies *this host* on *this network*. Again, it can only appear in unambiguous context and only as a source address.

Both forms of *this* addresses are primarily used when the hosts don't yet know their network IDs and, possibly, their host IDs.

A whole IP address consisting of all 1s (in binary)—for example, 255.255.255.255—is called a *local broadcast*. It addresses all hosts on a segment and can only appear as a destination address.

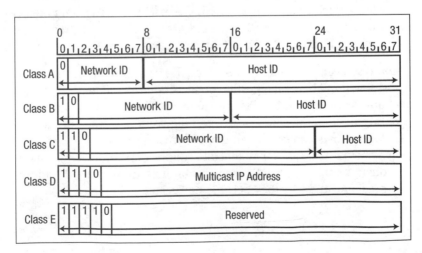

Figure 1.10   IP Network classes.

The class A network address 127.0.0.0 is called a *loopback address*. It means that when the IP software module receives a datagram destined for an IP address from that network address—for example, 127.0.0.1—it docs not attempt to pass the packet to the network driver. Instead, it considers the packet destined for the local machine and passes it back to the appropriate Transport Layer protocol. These addresses are widely used for testing purposes.

In addition, there are two reserved host IDs for each network ID. The first host ID consists of all 0s. This host ID is used to address the network itself. For instance, using dotted decimal notation address 10.0.0.0 addresses the whole class A network, not an individual host. The address with the host ID consisting of all 0s is called a *network address*. The host ID consisting of all 1s is used to address all hosts on a given network. If the network ID belongs to one of the three unicast classes and the host ID consists of all 1s, the IP address is called a *directed broadcast*.

The purpose of having three classes of unicast IP addresses is to accommodate physical networks that have different numbers of hosts. Given the number of the bits reserved for the network ID in each class and keeping in mind the functional addresses just described, the following is true:

- Class A yields 2^7 - 2 or 126 networks, where each network can have up to 2^{24} - 2 or 16,777,214 hosts. Class A defines the range of IP network addresses 1.0.0.0 through 126.0.0.0.

- Class B yields 2^{14} - 1 or 16,383 networks, where each network can have up to 2^{16} - 2 or 65,534 hosts. Class B defines the range of IP network addresses 128.0.0.0 through 191.255.0.0.

- Class C yields 221 - 1 or 2,097,151 networks, where each network can have up to 2^8 - 2 or 254 hosts. Class C defines the range of IP network addresses 192.0.0.0 through 223.255.255.0.

Our discussion thus far has described the very first official IP addressing scheme. Many changes have since been made, and all of these changes are, to a certain extent, incompatible with each other. Fortunately, most of the changes affected the routers instead of the hosts, so older hosts can still communicate with newer ones, provided the intermediate routers implement all versions of IP addressing. The subsequent paragraphs briefly discuss major changes to the IP addressing scheme and why they became necessary.

The invention of the TCP/IP protocol suite marked the beginning of the Internet, a worldwide public network. As the popularity of the Internet grew, more companies chose TCP/IP as their primary corporate networking standard. Very soon, the number of TCP/IP deployments exceeded the number of the networks based on all other protocols. Moreover, most companies wanted to be connected to the Internet, which made the Internet the biggest network in the world. Although the popularity of TCP/IP revealed that its design was so robust and interoperable that it could handle the unprecedented amount of communications involving a huge number of networks, hosts, equipment, and software by different vendors, nevertheless the flexibility of the original IP addressing was missing.

Very early in the course of the Internet evolution, it became clear that the original IP addressing scheme wasn't acceptable anymore simply because few physical networks consisted of more than a thousand hosts. In other words, most of the class A and B address space was wasted. On the other hand, the class C addresses quite often did not provide a sufficient number of hosts, which sometimes created an obstacle when it was necessary to expand existing networks.

The original IP address design soon was expanded by the addition of *subnetting*. Subnetting is a complementary concept that extends the classful version of the IP address space by dividing the classful network addresses into smaller groups of addresses. Thus, the original host ID was divided into a *subnet ID* used to identify the subnet and the *host ID* used, as before, to identify the host. The original relation between a network ID and a physical segment was also revised. The subnet ID was used to uniquely identify a physical network, and the network ID was used to designate a group of networks under the same authority.

Unlike network classes, subnetting does not have predefined boundaries for the subnet IDs and host IDs. Moreover, pure subnetting allows for non-contiguous subnet and host IDs. The dividing is performed by using an additional component called a *subnet mask*. A subnet mask is a 32-bit pattern applied to an IP address to determine which bits belong to the subnet ID and which to the host ID. If a bit in the subnet mask is set, the corresponding bit in the IP address is considered part of the subnet ID. If a bit in the subnet mask is cleared, the corresponding bit in the IP address is considered part of the host ID. Subnet masks are also often written using dotted decimal notation—for example, 255.255.255.0.

A subnet mask is not part of the IP address; it is a rule applied to the IP addresses of all hosts on a segment. As mentioned earlier, a subnet ID is used to identify a physical segment. Because a subnet mask is used to define the subnet ID, it cannot be a part of individual host addresses.

The additions of subnetting introduced two extra functional addresses. Both of these addresses are described in RFC 1700. The first functional address consists of a valid network ID, valid subnet ID, and all 1s as the host ID. This address is called a *subnet directed broadcast*, and it addresses all hosts on the specified subnet. The second functional address consists of a valid network ID and all 1s at the subnet ID and host ID. It is referred to as a *directed broadcast* to all subnets of a specified subnetted network. Both of these addresses can only appear as the destination address.

Although not clearly mentioned in the "Internet Assigned Numbers," the address consisting of a valid network ID, valid subnet ID, and the host ID consisting of all 0s may be very handy when it is necessary to refer to a particular subnet of a subnetted network. For instance, suppose that network 10.0.0.0 is subnetted using subnet mask 255.255.0.0. It is very convenient to refer to a particular subnet as 10.5.0.0, as opposed to specifying the network ID and subnet ID separately (for example, network ID 10, subnet ID 5). The combination of the network ID and the subnet ID is often called a *subnet address*. This notation and term is used throughout this book.

The first edition of subnetting did not extend to the classful network ID. In other words, the meaning of the subnet mask bits corresponding to the bits of the network ID was not defined. This approach to subnetting is called *classful*. Later, when allocation of the new addresses became very tight, it was decided that the classful approach was no longer satisfactory. The new approach, called *classless*, put an end to the unicast network classes and demanded that all classless TCP/IP implementations use the subnet masks to assign the network IDs and host IDs. Reminiscent of legacy classful IP addressing, the network prefixes that combine multiple classful network addresses are sometimes called *supernets*. For example, network address 193.0.0.0 with subnet mask 255.0.0.0 is a supernet, and it is legitimate only in the classless version of IP addressing.

As mentioned before, the new requirements hardly affected the hosts. However, the routers were required to implement new classless routing algorithms in order to be classless compliant. The differences between the classful and classless routing algorithms are discussed in Chapter 3.

Subnetting

Subnetting turned out to be one of the most important concepts of IP addressing, although at first it appeared to be more like a patch for the shortcomings of the original addressing design. Unfortunately, by being a patch, it inherited the nature of a patch. The history of IP addressing is somewhat similar to the history of the Intel x86 processors. The design of the original processor had very strong memory limitations, which later made the life of the engineers at Intel very difficult as they tried to work around those limitations. The limitations of the original IP addressing forced IP designers to introduce subnet masks. Later, as the Internet grew and the IP address allocation was almost brought to the limit, the consequences of subnetting followed. Some of the major issues associated with the subnetting are Variable Length Subnet Masks (VLSM), classful and classless routing protocols, and related interoperability problems. Fortunately, most of these only affect the routers, not the hosts.

To configure the routers to accommodate different subnetting strategies, we need to consider a few additional concepts related to the subnetting.

As mentioned before, subnet masks can be contiguous or non-contiguous. Contiguous subnet masks start with 1s, and the first 0 can only be followed by 0s. Figure 1.11 gives an example of an IP address and a contiguous subnet mask.

Using dotted decimal notation, the IP address and the subnet mask in Figure 1.11 is written as 67.240.1.3 and 255.255.240.0, respectively.

If one or several 1s appear after any instance of 0 in a subnet mask, the subnet mask is called non-contiguous. Figure 1.12 gives an example of a non-contiguous subnet mask.

Using dotted decimal notation, the IP address and subnet mask in Figure 1.12 is written as 67.240.1.3 and 255.252.31.0, respectively.

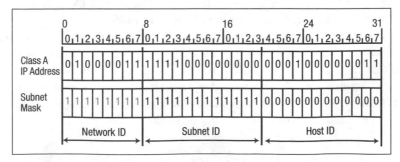

Figure 1.11   Classful contiguous subnet example.

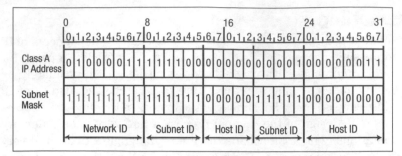

Figure 1.12   Classful non-contiguous subnet example.

Non-contiguous masks are very rare (in fact, I do not know of any TCP/IP deployments where non-contiguous masks were used). The reason is that manageability of the address space with non-contiguous subnet masks is very low. With non-contiguous subnet masks, neither the host ID nor the subnet ID can be represented by contiguous bit fields. For now, it is enough to say that it's important because the routing algorithms become a lot less predictable when they have to consider the presence of non-contiguous subnet and host IDs. Also, it becomes particularly difficult for users to extract the subnet IDs and host IDs from the IP addresses if non-contiguous subnet masks are used. For instance, the range of IP addresses defined in Figure 1.11 is from 67.240.0.1 to 67.240.15.255. This makes it easy and convenient to assign IP addresses to the hosts located on that network. On the contrary, the non-contiguous subnet mask in Figure 1.13 makes it practically impossible to specify the range of available IP addresses using such a simple notation. Thus, the administration effort associated with assigning IP addresses from subnets with non-contiguous subnet masks to the hosts becomes very high.

Unlike non-contiguous subnet masks, contiguous subnet masks are used in almost all TCP/IP deployments. An interesting feature of contiguous subnet masks is that they can be uniquely identified just by specifying the number of the set bits. This feature can be quite useful if used as an alternative notation for the subnet masks. For instance, the subnet mask in Figure 1.12 can be written as 20 instead of 255.255.240.0 as in classic dotted decimal notation. Usually, if this alternative notation is used, the number of set bits is written after the "/" character—for example, /20. This alternative notation is called *bit-count*. It is also convenient to use the bit-count notation along with the address itself—for example, 67.240.1.3/20.

NOTE: *Throughout the rest of this book, I will use the bit-count notation for the subnet masks, unless it's necessary to use the dotted decimal notation. I will also refer to contiguous subnet masks simply as subnet masks, because non-contiguous subnet masks do not have any practical use.*

In addition, because of this feature of the contiguous subnet masks and because the non-contiguous subnet masks at some point were called illegal, the subnet IP addresses were alternatively called network prefixes. Likewise, the subnet masks were called network prefix lengths. These new terms are getting used more often then their older twins in technical discussions about IP routing.

NOTE: *Throughout the rest of this book, I will use the terms network prefix and network prefix length when talking about IP routing. I will still use the terms subnet address and subnet mask in all other situations. In reality, these are the same things.*

There is a direct relation between the length of a subnet mask and the number of hosts that it makes available. Thus, the primary purpose of subnetting is to divide the assigned network address into smaller subnets depending on the number of hosts located on each individual segment.

The formula for calculating the number of hosts given the length of the subnet mask is fairly simple: Since the length of the subnet mask is the number of set bits, the number of cleared bits (designating the host ID) is 32 minus the length of subnet mask. The number of host IDs available is equal to the total of all combinations of 1s and 0s in the bits belonging to the host ID minus the broadcast address and the subnet address. Therefore, the formula is

$$N = 2^{(32 - L)} - 2$$

where N is the number of hosts and L is the length of the subnet mask.

Let's consider several examples.

subnet mask /30
Using the formula for subnet mask /30, we'll get the following:

$$N = 2^{32 - 30} - 2 = 2^2 - 2 = 2$$

subnet mask /24
Using the formula for subnet mask /24, we'll get the following:

$$N = 2^{32 - 24} - 2 = 2^8 - 2 = 256 - 2 = 254$$

This subnet mask is default for class C networks. Therefore, it's not surprising that the number of hosts it yields is equal to the number of hosts defined by a class C network.

subnet mask /31

Using the formula for subnet mask /31, we'll get the following:

$$N = 2^{32-31} - 2 = 2^1 - 2 = 2 - 2 = 0$$

In other words, subnet mask /31 is illegal because it does not produce a valid individual IP address. This is quite understandable because subnet mask /31 leaves only one bit for the host ID. The host ID consisting of all 0s is the subnet ID. The host ID consisting of all 1s is the subnet directed broadcast. However, one bit can only have two values—1 and 0—which are already used.

subnet mask /32

Using the formula for subnet mask /32, we'll get the following:

$$N = 2^{32-32} - 2 = 2^0 - 2 = 1 - 2 = -1$$

It appears that subnet mask /32 is also illegal. Theoretically, it should be illegal, but as an exception, it is used to specify an individual host address, which is not a part of any subnet. We'll return to this subnet mask and its usage in the chapters devoted to routing protocols.

The deduced formula is not particularly useful, because in real life the task is reversed. We are given the number of hosts and must deduce the length of the subnet mask. Unfortunately, the reversed formula

$$L = 32 - \log_2(N + 2)$$

is rather complex. It's much easier to use a precalculated table than this formula to calculate the lengths of subnet masks. Because physical networks containing more than a thousand hosts are rare, the table is not too large.

The precalculated values of subnet mask lengths are shown in Table 1.3.

Let's calculate the subnet masks for the example shown in Figure 1.13.

Suppose branches A and B have equal requirements for the maximum number of hosts, which is 100, including the router connections.

Table 1.3 **The relation between the length of subnet masks and the number of hosts that the subnet mask allows.**

Number of Hosts	Subnet Length	Subnet Mask
up to 2	/30	255.255.255.252
up to 6	/29	255.255.255.248
up to 14	/28	255.255.255.240
up to 30	/27	255.255.255.224
up to 62	/26	255.255.255.192
up to 126	/25	255.255.255.128
up to 254	/24	255.255.255.0
up to 510	/23	255.255.254.0
up to 1022	/22	255.255.252.0
up to 2046	/21	255.255.248.0

Suppose the number of hosts connected to the FDDI ring at the headquarters is less than 1,000. There are two physical networks between the routers at the branches and headquarters, and the number of hosts on both these networks is two—that is, one for each router. The following subnet masks will be used with the hosts located on the respective networks:

- The FDDI ring should have subnet mask /22.
- The two Ethernet segments located at branches A and B should use subnet mask /25.
- The connections between the routers should use subnet mask /30.

Unfortunately, in real life, it's not enough to only calculate the subnet masks. The calculated subnet masks do not guarantee that the address ranges we allocate will not overlap, nor do they guarantee that the available address space is not wasted. This subject is beyond the scope of this chapter, but will be discussed in Chapter 4 in the section on dividing the allocated address space for use with VLSM.

Internet Control Message Protocol

The Internet Control Message Protocol (ICMP) is an integral part of IP. Although it is a separate protocol and uses IP transmission services, ICMP resides on the same layer as IP and does not provide any services for the Transport Layer protocols.

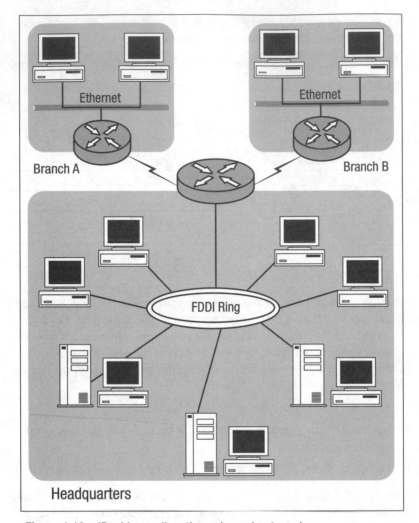

Figure 1.13   IP address allocation using subnet masks.

ICMP is primarily used to report error conditions that IP may experience in transmitting datagrams. Typically, ICMP messages are generated by the routers on the way to the destination. However, some
ICMP messages can also be sent by the hosts. ICMP is also used to
send certain control messages. Thus, the packets that ICMP generates are often called *error* or *control messages*.

ICMP Control Messages

ICMP control messages are sent encapsulated in IP datagrams as the
payload, just as the PDUs of the other protocols that rely on IP are
sent. Since ICMP resides on the Internet Layer, the transmission of

ICMP control messages is not guaranteed. They can get lost or become corrupted enroute to the destination.

If ICMP is used to report an error, the corresponding ICMP message is sent to the IP address that appears as the source address in the header of the datagram causing the error. No message is sent to the destination of the datagram. The IP module on the source machine, on receipt of an ICMP error message, should take appropriate steps to notify the upper layer protocols of the error condition. The network node, whose ICMP module generated the error message, does not try to correct the problem.

Each individual ICMP message has its own format. Nevertheless, all ICMP messages have a common part consisting of three fields located at the beginning of the ICMP message. These fields are as follows:

- An 8-bit TYPE field, which identifies the message.

- An 8-bit CODE field, which provides further information on the message.

- A 16-bit CHECKSUM field, which is used to verify the integrity of the whole ICMP message.

In addition, the ICMP messages that report errors always include the header and the first 64 bits of the payload of the datagram that caused the error.

Table 1.4 provides information on possible values for the TYPE field.

We will examine only the types of ICMP messages as they are discussed in subsequent chapters. For those interested in the details of all ICMP messages, I recommend checking the ICMP specification (RFC 792) and the latest "Assigned Numbers" document (RFC 1700 when this book was written).

Table 1.4   ICMP message types.

TYPE Field	Type Description
0	Echo Reply
1	Unassigned
2	Unassigned
3	Destination Unreachable
4	Source Quench
5	Redirect
6	Alternate Host Address

(continued)

Table 1.4   ICMP message types (continued).

TYPE Field	Type Description
7	Unassigned
8	Echo
9	Router Advertisement
10	Router Selection
11	Time Exceeded
12	Parameter Problem
13	Timestamp
14	Timestamp Reply
15	Information Request
16	Information Reply
17	Address Mask Request
18	Address Mask Reply
19	Reserved (for Security)
20-29	Reserved (for Robustness Experiment)
30	Traceroute
31	Datagram Conversion Error
32	Mobile Host Redirect
33	IPv6 Where-Are-You
34	IPv6 I-Am-Here
35	Mobile Registration Request
36	Mobile Registration Reply
37-255	Reserved

Echo And Echo Reply

The Echo and Echo Reply messages are control messages. They are used only for testing host reachability through the network. A host, on receiving an ICMP Echo message, should reply using an ICMP Echo Reply message. An ICMP Echo message can contain optional data. In that case, the corresponding ICMP Echo Reply message should contain the same data. The CODE field always contains 0.

A very popular network debugging tool called *ping* uses ICMP Echo messages. Unlike most network applications that require both communicating hosts to have software modules responsible for receiving and sending data, ping uses the "built-in" replying capability of IP. In other words, ping can always be used to check the reachability of IP hosts—no matter what software is installed on them.

Destination Unreachable

Destination Unreachable is an error message that is sent back to the source host when the datagram cannot be delivered to the destination as requested.

The CODE field is used to indicate why the datagram cannot be delivered. Table 1.5 shows the values that the CODE field can have. Most of them are self-explanatory.

Depending on the value of the CODE field, the ICMP Destination Unreachable message can be sent by either an intermediate router or the final destination. For instance, the message with CODE = 0, "Net Unreachable," is only sent by an intermediate router if it doesn't know a route to the destination. However, the message with CODE = 3, "Port Unreachable," is sent by the destination host itself if the upper layer protocol port, for which the data is destined, is not available.

Source Quench

The Source Quench message is used when IP needs to perform congestion control. An intermediate router or the destination host usually sends an ICMP Source Quench message for every datagram that it has to drop. The source, on receiving the Source Quench message, lowers the rate at which it sends the datagrams. It keeps lowering the rate as long as it receives the Source Quench messages. Since there is

Table 1.5   The CODE values of the ICMP Destination Unreachable error message.

CODE	Description
0	Net Unreachable
1	Host Unreachable
2	Protocol Unreachable
3	Port Unreachable
4	Fragmentation Needed and DF (Don't Fragment) Bit Was Set
5	Source Route Failed
6	Destination Network Unknown
7	Destination Host Unknown
8	Source Host Isolated
9	Communication with Destination Network Is Administratively Prohibited
10	Communication with Destination Host Is Administratively Prohibited
11	Destination Network Unreachable for Type of Service
12	Destination Host Unreachable for Type of Service

1. The Layered Communication Model And Internet Protocol

no ICMP message to indicate that the originator of the Source Quench messages is relieved, the host begins increasing the rate when it stops receiving the Source Quench messages. It continues to do so until it either reaches the maximum rate or starts receiving the Source Quench messages again.

Redirect

When more than one router is available, the ICMP Redirect message is used by one of them to inform the source of the datagram which has a better route to the destination. The message contains the IP address of the best router en route to the destination and the first 64 bits of the datagram. Even though the router sends an ICMP Redirect message, it routes the datagram.

Although Redirect messages appear to be a good idea, they have a major shortcoming. If an intermediate router receives a datagram from another router instead of from the source, and a better route to the destination exists through some other router, it sends the ICMP Redirect message to the source and not to the "confused" router. The reason for that is that ICMP operates on the Internet Layer, and therefore it can't use the MAC address of the gateway from which it received the datagram (it is stripped off by the driver of the NIC, an entity that operates on the Network Access Layer, in the course of the encapsulation process). On the other hand, the datagram only contains the IP addresses of the source and destination, and thus provides no means of knowing from which intermediate router it was received. Hence, the ICMP redirect messages turn out to be useless, unless they are issued by the first router en route to the destination back to the source of the original datagram.

Time Exceeded

The ICMP Time Exceeded message is sent by an intermediate gateway if it discovers that the TTL (Time To Live) field has reached 0. The intermediate gateway drops the datagram and issues an ICMP Time Exceeded message back to the source of the datagram.

IP And Network Access Layer Technologies

As we already know, IP depends on the Network Access Layer technologies for delivering the datagrams via the physical networks. However, we do not know how IP communicates its needs, such as the hardware address of the destination or next-hop router, to the network adapter and its driver.

Before learning how IP communicates with the Network Layer technologies, let's look at the Network Access Layer technologies and try to categorize them in some way.

The Network Access Layer technologies are probably better known as Data Link Layer technologies. However, the LAN hardware addresses often burned into the ROM of the network adapters are often called *MAC addresses*, for the Media Access Control sublayer of the Data Link Layer. (I will refer to the hardware addresses of the network adapters as *MAC addresses*, because unfortunately the Internet Model does not provide a distinct name for them.) Furthermore, I will refer to Network Access Layer PDUs as *frames*, as it became a *de facto* name for the Network Access Layer PDUs—for example, an Ethernet frame, an HDLC frame, and so on. I will refer to physical networks as *segments* for the same reason.

The Network Access Layer technologies can be categorized into three groups as follows:

- *Broadcast networks*—Allow addressing of all nodes of a network segment. In other words, it is possible to send a frame destined for all nodes on a segment. Examples of broadcast networks are most LANs, such as Ethernet, TokenRing, FDDI, and so on.

- *Point-to-point networks*—Assume there are only two interconnected devices. Examples of point-to-point networks are leased lines, circuit switched connections, and so on.

- *Non-Broadcast Multiple Access (NBMA) networks*—Allow interconnecting multiple devices; however, they do not provide for sending packets destined for all nodes. Examples of NBMA networks are frame relay and X.25.

From a Network Access Layer perspective, segments connected with routers are, in fact, disconnected. The Internet Layer functionality must be involved to forward a piece of data from one segment to another. Therefore, the Network Access Layer broadcasts do not propagate beyond the segment boundaries.

Interlayer Addressing And IP Routing

How does IP know how to send a datagram to the next-hop router using Network Access Layer technologies? The IP module receives the destination IP address from the higher layers. However, it does not receive the MAC of the next-hop router. If there is no next-hop router, how does the network adapter and its driver know the MAC address of the destination node? Or, if there is a next-hop router, then how does the network adapter and its driver know the MAC address of its interface?

As we learned in previous sections in this chapter, TCP and UDP use the IP address of the source host to identify the connection to avoid ambiguity. Neither the TCP nor the UDP header contains any information about the IP addresses of the source and destination hosts. The IP header is stripped off the payload before the TCP or UDP gets it. So, how does the TCP or UDP on the destination host know the IP address of the source host?

To answer these questions, let's start with the highest layer—the Application Layer—and try to understand how the whole process works.

As we know, an Application Layer module, such as telnet.exe, uses the network Application Programming Interface to establish communication with the TCP module on the local machine. The Application Layer module then passes the destination IP address to the appropriate procedure that establishes a connection with the destination host. That's how the TCP or UDP module on the local machine knows the destination IP address. The TCP or UDP module passes the destination IP address to the IP module again as the parameter using SAP of the Internet Protocol. Until this point, the operation appears to be seamless.

At the IP level, however, the process gets complicated. First, the IP module must decide if it can send the datagram directly to the destination or if it should use an intermediate router. Second, the IP module must somehow figure out how to tell the network driver which MAC address it should use to send the frame either to the destination or to the next-hop router. However, the network driver is located at the Network Access Layer and does not know anything about IP addressing; therefore, the destination IP address is useless for the network driver.

These issues are resolved using two concepts at the core of IP operation—IP routing and IP address resolution.

IP Routing

An IP host uses IP routing to figure out how to send the datagrams to a destination. IP routing uses the IP routing algorithm to understand if communication with the destination can be done directly or if it requires the aid of intermediate routers. If intermediate routers are needed, the IP routing algorithm helps choose the best route to the destination.

Although IP routing may seem simple at first, it is not. Complications arise when the route to the destination travels through multiple networks interconnected with multiple routers. The routers must somehow know about the networks to which they are not directly connected and must be able to calculate the best routes to all possible destinations. The networks involved must also be able to handle potential changes, such as failures, modifications, expansions, and so on, and the routers must then be able to adapt to these changes and recalculate the routes accordingly. The level of complexity increases dramatically when networks consisting of individual segments are interconnected.

The IP routing algorithm is based on a single principle that does not change even if IP routing function itself gets enhanced. The principle states:

The datagrams are routed based on the network portions of the destination addresses—not on the individual host addresses.

Further details of IP routing will be discussed in detail in the "In Brief" section of Chapter 3.

Address Resolution

Address resolution is a technique that IP uses to map IP addresses to the corresponding Network Access Layer addresses, such as MAC addresses. However, it's important to note that a Network Access Layer address has a rather broad meaning; we'll see some interesting examples in the "Immediate Solutions" section in this chapter. IP addresses, however, should only be mapped to the Network Access Layer addresses for the hosts on directly attached networks, because hosts that are not on directly attached networks are considered unreachable from the Network Access Layer perspective.

IP can find the mappings in two ways: by learning which MAC address corresponds to which IP address or by configuring the mappings manually.

Normally, IP can learn the mappings between the IP addresses and the Network Access Layer addresses on directly attached broadcast networks, such as LANs, using the following procedure: Suppose a host wants to send data to another host on the same physical network but does not know the other host's MAC address. The host assumes that this other host will always receive a frame destined for the broadcast address. Thus, the first host sends a broadcast frame in which it specifies that it wants the MAC address of the host with a certain IP address. All hosts on that physical network receive the frame, but only the one with the specified IP address answers.

The implementation of this idea was embodied in a special protocol called *Address Resolution Protocol*, or *ARP*. ARP is an auxiliary protocol used only by IP. Like ICMP, it resides on the Internet Layer and does not provide any services for the Transport Layer protocols. However, unlike ICMP, ARP PDUs are not encapsulated into IP datagrams. ARP PDUs are encapsulated directly into LAN frames.

The operation of ARP is simple. It maintains a table of mappings between the IP addresses and MAC addresses called an *ARP table*. When the host is first booted, the ARP table is empty. When IP needs to send a datagram to a host on a directly connected network, it invokes the ARP module to determine the MAC address by the destination's IP address. ARP first tries to locate the IP address in the ARP table. If it does not find an entry for the IP address, it performs MAC address lookup via the network. Because ARP does not know anything about the host but its IP address, it sends out a packet called an *ARP request*, using the MAC broadcast address as the destination address. The ARP request contains the IP address of the host. Because of the nature of the broadcast address, all hosts on that network receive the ARP request, and the one whose IP address corresponds to the IP address in the ARP request replies. This reply, called an *ARP reply*, is sent directly to the requesting host using its MAC address. When ARP receives the ARP reply, it adds the pair of the MAC address and IP address into the ARP table and notifies IP of the found mapping. If the IP address is not used for a certain period, the corresponding entry is removed from the ARP table to avoid outdated MAC addresses—for example, a Mac address of a host may change if the network adapter in the host is replaced.

When ARP or similar technology is not available, manual mappings can be used. Manual mappings may be necessary if the underlying network technology does not support broadcast addressing—for example, ISDN.

Filtering Packets

Packet filtering is a technology that allows PDUs to be dropped that do not meet certain conditions. In the case of IP, packet filtering allows datagrams that do not meet certain conditions to be dropped.

The implementation of packet filtering in Cisco IOS is based on logical expressions called *access-lists*. An access-list specifies the conditions that a datagram must meet and the action that is taken if the datagram meets the conditions.

We'll discuss this and other uses of access-lists in Chapter 6.

Useful Tools

I have found several tools that are very useful and that I mention throughout this book. A brief explanation of these may be helpful.

The first is the Cisco IOS **debug** command. Quite often, this is the best tool for determining what the router is doing, what packets it is receiving, and so on. However, I would advise against using this tool in production environments, because enabling the debug feature on a heavily loaded Cisco router often leads to a serious impact on the router performance. If this is the case, the router probably won't be able to process any command line input and will have to be reloaded, which is generally unacceptable.

The Microsoft Network Monitor is a very basic LAN analyzer, but its functionality is often enough for both troubleshooting and testing purposes. It is usually more available than other LAN analyzers, such as Network Associates Sniffer. However, tools such as Sniffer are definitely more desirable if they are available. Nevertheless, the use of network analyzers in this book is kept to minimum.

Some other tools are available from Tsunami Computing's site at http://www.hugewave.com/blackbook. Check back occasionally; this collection will be expanded in the future.

Immediate Solutions

I assume that most readers are familiar with the Cisco IOS command line interface and its basic features. Thus, I will skip the obvious steps in most examples.

Also, I use the full commands instead of abbreviated versions. However, I would encourage you to use the abbreviated versions when doing a real configuration, as it saves a lot of time.

Finally, the examples in this section are not intended to teach you how to configure Cisco router's interfaces. Their purpose is to demonstrate some important features of IP discussed in the "In Brief" sections of this chapter and to create a foundation for the material to be discussed in the rest of this book.

When explaining the format of various commands I will stick to the notation that is very similar to the one used in the Cisco documentation. The notation is as follows:

- **Boldface** is used to denote mandatory command elements that must be entered as shown.

- *<Italics in angle brackets>* are used to denote the mandatory command elements that supply values. Values have no predefined format and can consist of characters, digits, and maybe some other characters.

- [Text in square brackets] is used to denote optional command elements.

- Bolded words in curved brackets separated by vertical bars, such as **{Choice1|Choice2|Choice3}**, are used to indicate mandatory elements of the command, which consist of choices—the words. In this example, there are three choices—Choice1, Choice2, and Choice3—one of which must be entered as a part of the command.

- If the previous element is shown in square brackets and is not bolded, such as [{Choice1|Choice2|Choice3}], this will indicate an optional command element consisting of choices.

As you can see, the only difference between the Cisco notation and the one used in this book is that the latter uses angle brackets in addition to italicized text to denote the command elements that supply values. I believe it's important to emphasize the functional role of these elements in a clearer way.

Using IP Over LAN: ARP And ProxyARP

Configuring a LAN interface on a router is probably one of the easiest configuration tasks. Let's examine what needs to be done on a router to enable Ethernet and TokenRing interfaces for IP routing.

The first step is to assign an IP address and subnet mask to the interface. The next step is to bring the interface up.

Suppose the address and subnet mask that we assign is 10.1.0.1/24. Listing 1.1 shows the steps, which should be taken to assign the IP address on an Ethernet interface.

Listing 1.1   Assigning the IP address to the Ethernet 0 interface and bringing it up.

```
Router (config)#interface ethernet 0
Router (config-if)#ip address 10.1.0.1 255.255.255.0
Router (config-if)#no shutdown
```

A TokenRing interface requires one extra step—assigning the ring speed—shown in Listing 1.2.

Listing 1.2   Assigning the IP address to the TokenRing 0 interface and bringing it up

```
Router (config)#interface tokenring 0
Router (config-if)#ip address 10.1.0.1 255.255.255.0
Router (config-if)#ring-speed 16
Router (config-if)#no shutdown
```

If there is no physical problem, the interface should now be up and ready for use. To use the router, the hosts on the Ethernet or TokenRing segment must have a route that points to the IP address that we just assigned.

The most common route found on the hosts is the *default gateway route*. The default gateway route is only used when a host or router cannot find a network address match in the routing table. Interestingly enough, the default gateway route provides a route for network 0.0.0.0, which is the so-called *this network* address, as we know from the "In Brief" section of this chapter. Nevertheless, there is a logical explanation why this address is used. First, this address is not allowed to appear as the destination address. Therefore, no host will ever try to send a real datagram destined for that address. Second, this is a legal unicast address. Hence, if we give this address a special meaning that it is a match for an otherwise unsuccessful lookup in the routing table, we have a perfect candidate for a default gateway route.

The IP address of the router that appears in the default gateway route is often referred to as a *default gateway* or *default router*.

Obviously, a subnet address cannot exist without the subnet mask. Therefore, if subnetting is used, the routing table should contain the subnet masks. The point is that the subnet mask used with the default gateway route by definition consists of all 0s—that is, 0.0.0.0—thereby reducing the actual network address to nothing. Theoretically, it doesn't matter which address is used for the default gateway route, as long as the subnet mask consists of all 0s.

Let's now consider the situation depicted in Figure 1.14.

The Ethernet interfaces on router R are configured as shown in Listing 1.3.

Listing 1.3   Router R's configuration.

```
interface Ethernet0
 ip address 10.1.0.1 255.255.255.0

interface Ethernet1
 ip address 10.1.0.1 255.255.255.0
```

Both workstations H1 and H2 use the incorrect subnet mask /8, which is the default for network class A. Assuming host H1 is a Windows NT workstation, the TCP/IP configuration dialog box from the Network Properties should look like the one in Figure 1.15.

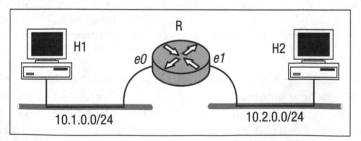

Figure 1.14   The workstations are configured with the "wrong" subnet mask /8.

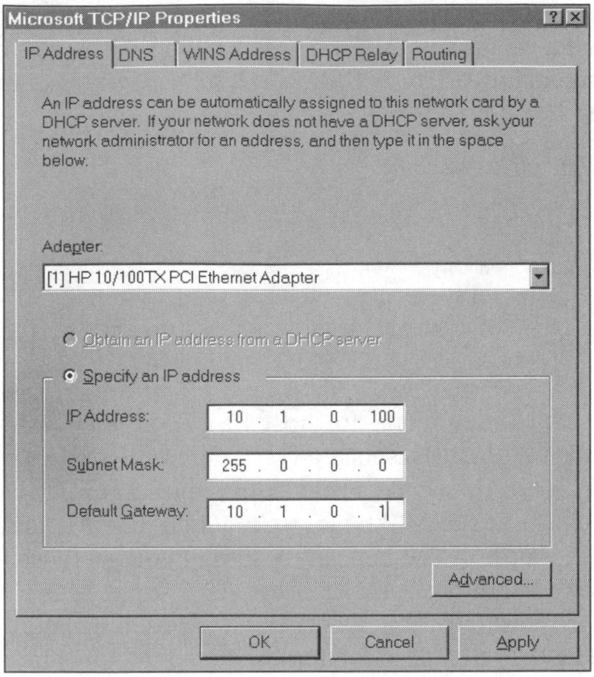

Figure 1.15   Implicit ProxyARP configuration in Windows NT 4.0.

The question is, will host H1 be able to communicate with host H2 via IP? Theoretically, the answer is no. Host H1 considers host H2 to be on the same directly connected network. Therefore, it uses ARP to resolve host H2's IP address to the corresponding MAC address. However, in reality, host H2 is located on a separate segment. Hence, the ARP request sent by host H1 will time out. The IP will return an error indicating that communication is not possible.

If we try this configuration, however, we will be surprised to see that it works perfectly. For instance, if we try to **ping** host H2 from host H1, we will see the output shown in Listing 1.4.

Listing 1.4   The output of ping indicates the reachability of host H2 from host H1.

```
C:\>ping 10.2.0.100

Pinging 10.2.0.100 with 32 bytes of data:

Reply from 10.2.0.100: bytes=32 time=10ms TTL=253
Reply from 10.2.0.100: bytes=32 time=10ms TTL=253
Reply from 10.2.0.100: bytes=32 time=10ms TTL=253
Reply from 10.2.0.100: bytes=32 time=10ms TTL=253
```

The fact that host H1 sees replies from host H1 means that somehow host H1 received a reply to its ARP request for the host H2's IP address. If we examine the ARP table on host H1, we will see the output shown in Listing 1.5.

Listing 1.5   The ARP table of host H1.

```
C:\>arp -a

Interface: 10.1.0.100 on Interface 2
  Internet Address      Physical Address      Type
  10.1.0.1              00-e0-b0-64-50-63     dynamic
  10.2.0.100            00-e0-b0-64-50-63     dynamic
```

The ARP table contains an entry for host H2's IP address, which shouldn't make sense. Host H2 is located on a different physical network and, therefore, cannot reply to the ARP requests sent by host H1. If we look closer at the ARP table, we'll notice that it contains another entry for router R. The MAC addresses of both of these entries are identical. Therefore, we can conclude that the router answered the ARP request on behalf of host H2. This obscure feature of IP is called *ProxyARP*. It is described in the Cisco documentation, but it has somehow been omitted in most the documentation of most host implementations of IP.

The idea behind ProxyARP is simple. If a router receives an ARP request for an IP address that belongs to a network different than the one from which the request was received, the router may choose to answer the request with its own MAC address if it knows the route to the destination. However, the router will not answer all such requests. The router only answers requests with a source address that belongs to the same network as the IP address of the interface on which the request was received. For instance, if the IP address in Figure 1.15 was 10.1.1.100 instead of 10.1.0.100, the router would ignore the ARP request, and host H1 would not be able to communicate with host H2.

The only difference between the configuration that uses ProxyARP and one that does not is the subnet mask configured on the hosts. It should be shorter (because it's contiguous we can call it "shorter") than the "actual" subnet mask, which is the one configured on the routers.

Let's call this an *implicit* Proxy ARP configuration. It is also possible to enable Proxy ARP explicitly. Figure 1.16 shows an *explicit* ProxyARP configuration. It is the same TCP/IP configuration dialog box from the Network Properties as shown in Figure 1.15, but the IP

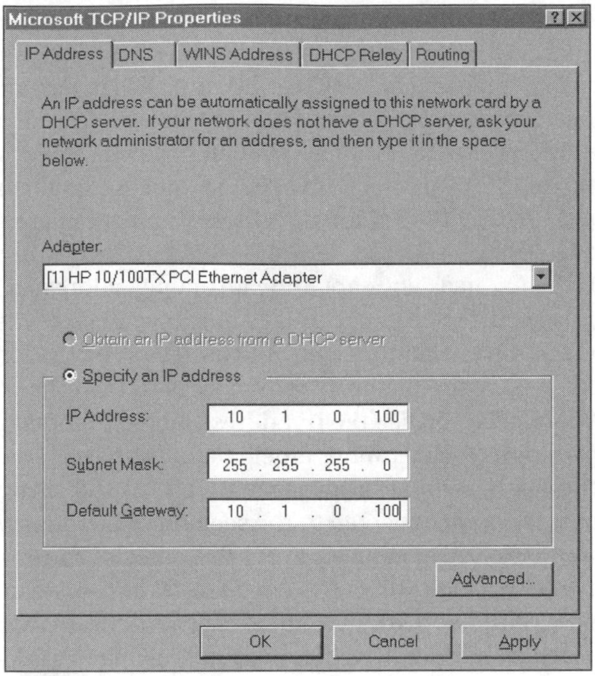

Microsoft TCP/IP Properties   `? X`

| IP Address | DNS | WINS Address | DHCP Relay | Routing |

An IP address can be automatically assigned to this network card by a
DHCP server. If your network does not have a DHCP server, ask your
network administrator for an address, and then type it in the space
below.

Adapter:

[1] HP 10/100TX PCI Ethernet Adapter   ▾

　　○ Obtain an IP address from a DHCP server

　　● Specify an IP address

　　IP Address:　　　　10 . 1 . 0 . 100

　　Subnet Mask:　　　255 . 255 . 255 . 0

　　Default Gateway:　　10 . 1 . 0 . 100|

Advanced...

| OK | Cancel | Apply |

Figure 1.16　Explicit ProxyARP configuration in Windows NT 4.0.

address of the default gateway is equal to the IP address of the network adapter. Making this change enables one host to communicate
with another host, regardless on which network the second host's IP
address resides, provided the intermediate router supports ProxyARP.

ProxyARP allows changing the IP address of the router used as the
default gateway without reconfiguring the workstation. Also, if there
is more than one router on a segment, all routers may be used as the
default gateway by the hosts configured for Proxy ARP. Theoretically,
the least busy router can issue an ARP reply first, thereby allowing it
to share the load of the traffic between the routers. In practice, this
may not happen, because if the network consists of several segments
connected with bridges, the least busy router may reside on a segment behind a bridge. Therefore, its reply may be delayed by the bridge
long enough for the busier routers to issue their ARP replies. The
ProxyARP-enabled networks can also be used in conjunction with
so-called *classful dynamic routing protocols*, such as RIP or IGRP.
These protocols cannot tolerate more than one subnet mask per
classful network address. However, if it is necessary to have a network segment with a subnet mask shorter than the one used with the

classful routing protocol, it can be accomplished by means of ProxyARP. We'll study these protocols further in Chapter 4. Using Proxy ARP may sometimes seem justified, although it is in fact undesirable. Let's consider the situation shown in Figure 1.17. The subnet mask used with RIP, a classful dynamic routing protocol, is /25. For correct operation of RIP, all participating routers must be configured with the /25 mask on all RIP-enabled interfaces. Suppose there is a site with only one physical segment, and the number of hosts on this segment is 200. The /25 mask does not allocate enough addresses for 200 hosts. Suppose you decide to use the /24 mask on all hosts, keep the /25 mask on the router's interface e0, and use the ProxyARP feature of the router to provide the hosts with access to the other networks. For now, suppose you use the IP address labeled "primary IP address" for the interface Ethernet 0, labeled e0. From the router's perspective, the hosts with IP addresses of 10.1.0.130 through 10.1.0.254 are now illegally connected to the segment. The router will not issue ARP replies on ARP requests from these hosts. To resolve the problem, a technique known as a *secondary IP address* can be used. The secondary IP address is an additional IP address, which can be assigned on an interface. It may or may not belong to a subnet different from the one to which the first IP address belongs. The first IP address is known as the *primary IP address*.

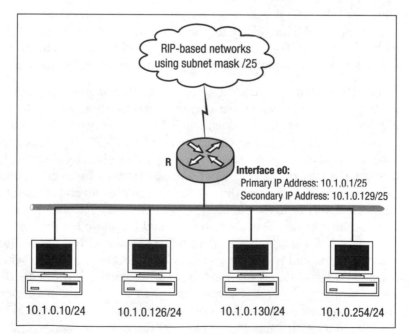

Figure 1.17   *Using Proxy ARP in conjunction with classful routing protocols and secondary IP addresses.*

The configuration of interface Ethernet 0 is shown in Listing 1.6.

Listing 1.6   The configuration of the Ethernet 0 interface of router R.

```
interface Ethernet 0
 ip address 10.1.0.129 255.255.255.128 secondary
 ip address 10.1.0.1 255.255.255.128
```

The proposed solution is quite inconsistent from the IP addressing point of view. The hosts "believe" they are located on subnet 10.1.0.0/24. The router "believes" it has two logical networks connected to its single interface. Because of RIP operation, the other routers perceive this site's network as two networks.

Involvement of Proxy ARP also leads to excessive broadcast traffic. In a normal routed environment, the hosts use the router's MAC address for external access, producing a single entry in their ARP table corresponding to the router's MAC and IP addresses. The entry is created with a single ARP request and should not expire as long as the hosts are using the router. In ProxyARP-enabled environments, the hosts use ARP for some, or maybe all, IP addresses that they otherwise would access through the router's IP address. This results in multiple ARP table entries for different IP addresses, but they all point to the router's MAC address. Each entry was created by an unnecessary ARP request.

Given all of the shortcomings of ProxyARP, how can you disable generating ProxyARP replies on the router? Luckily, that's easy. If we examine the commands available under a LAN interface command mode, we'll see that the command **ip proxy-arp** enables ProxyARP. This command is on by default and is not displayed in the configuration of the router (this may change in the future releases of Cisco IOS). To turn the command off, we just enter **no ip proxy-arp**. Listing 1.7 shows how the configuration of the interface has changed.

Listing 1.7   The updated ProxyARP-disabled configuration of the Ethernet 0 interface of router R.

```
interface Ethernet0
 ip address 10.1.0.1 255.255.255.0
 no ip proxy-arp
```

If interface Ethernet 0 in Figure 1.14 was configured this way, host H1 could not communicate with host H2.

In general, turning off the ProxyARP feature on the Cisco routers may not be necessary, as long as the hosts do not rely on it. It may be helpful for troubleshooting if some hosts are wrongly configured with a default subnet mask instead of a specific subnet mask.

Configuring Serial Interface

The serial interface on the Cisco routers is used in a variety of configurations. The way in which a Cisco router interprets the data sent to and received from a serial interface depends on the encapsulation type defined on that interface. If you type **encapsulation ?**, you'll see the output shown in Listing 1.8.

Listing 1.8   Encapsulation types available on a serial interface.

```
R(config-if)#encapsulation ?
  atm-dxi         ATM-DXI encapsulation
  bstun           Block Serial tunneling (BSTUN)
  frame-relay     Frame Relay networks
  hdlc            Serial HDLC synchronous
  lapb            LAPB (X.25 Level 2)
  ppp             Point-to-Point protocol
  sdlc            SDLC
  sdlc-primary    SDLC (primary)
  sdlc-secondary  SDLC (secondary)
  smds            Switched Megabit Data Service (SMDS)
  stun            Serial tunneling (STUN)
  x25             X.25
```

Let's consider two of the most common encapsulation types: HDLC and frame relay. Some people may say PPP is also quite common. That's true, but PPP is more often used with dialup connections, such as ISDN, and is discussed in the section "Configuring IP Over ISDN," later in this chapter.

Using HDLC Encapsulation

HDLC, or *High-Level Data Link Control*, is a general-purpose protocol developed by ISO that operates on the Data Link Layer of OSI/RM or on the Network Access Layer of the Internet Model. Being a general-purpose protocol, HDLC does not provide a complete ready-to-implement specification, but rather serves as a foundation for several other protocols, such as Logical Link Control (LLC), Link Access Procedure Balanced (LAPB), and Link Access Procedure for the ISDN D channel (LAPD). For serial connections, Cisco Systems completed the HDLC specification to their proprietary version and referenced it in their documentation as HDLC.

Configuring a serial interface with the HDLC encapsulation is really simple. The HDLC encapsulation is the default for a serial interface, which means that nothing needs to be done.

A serial interface with HDLC encapsulation is a point-to-point type of network. There is no common automatic method of establishing a relation between the IP addresses and the corresponding Network Access Layer addresses on point-to-point networks. Luckily, Cisco's implementation of HDLC protocol provides all of the necessary functionality to perform this mapping. It is automatic and is on by default, so we are spared from doing anything manually.

Therefore, configuring a serial interface with HDLC encapsulation is simply assigning the IP address and enabling the interface, as shown in Listing 1.9.

Listing 1.9   *Configuring a serial interface for HDLC encapsulation and IP is accomplished by simply assigning it an IP address.*

```
R(config)#interface serial 1
R(config-if)#ip address 10.1.0.1 255.255.255.0
R(config-if)#no shutdown
```

Configuring IP Over Frame Relay: Static Mapping And InverseARP

The serial interfaces of Cisco routers are most commonly used today to connect the routers to the frame relay networks.

Frame relay is a packet switching technology that operates on the Network Access Layer. Frame relay defines two types of nodes: Data Terminal Equipment (DTE) and Data Communication Equipment (DCE). DTE nodes are the user devices, such as routers, bridges, and hosts, whereas DCE nodes are the devices that constitute frame relay networks, such as frame relay switches.

The transmission service provided by frame relay is optimized for speed. To facilitate speed optimization, the frame relay switches only detect errors in frames; they do not attempt to retransmit the corrupted frames. Like in IP, this function is left for the upper layer protocols.

Frame relay allows multiplexing multiple logical connections called *virtual circuits* over a single physical connection. Currently, frame relay defines *permanent virtual circuits* (PVCs), which are statically configured in a frame relay network. *Switched virtual circuits* (SVCs) are in a proposed state. Frame relay uses numeric Data Link Circuit Identifiers (DLCIs) to identify the PVCs. Interestingly enough, from the IP point of view, DLCIs are simply Network Access Layer addresses.

Frame relay also defines Local Management Interface (LMI). LMI is used to exchange the management information between the frame relay DTE and DCE. An example of management information is the status of a certain PVC. LMI uses a predefined PVC so that both the DTE and DCE can exchange the management information even when no PVC has been administratively defined. There are different versions of LMI. Cisco IOS supports three: Cisco, ANSI Annex D, and ITU-T Q.933 Annex A. For example, the default LMI, called Cisco LMI, uses PVC 1023.

How are IP addresses mapped to the appropriate DLCIs? Frame relay is an NBMA type of network; thus, pure ARP is not going to work. Nevertheless, a modification of ARP called *Inverse ARP*, or *InARP*, is available and supported by Cisco IOS. InARP performs a function very similar to ARP; the only difference is that it maps IP addresses to DLCIs as opposed to LAN MAC addresses. Another way to establish mapping between IP addresses and DLCIs is to configure them manually.

There are two ways to configure a serial interface for frame relay. One way is to perform all configuration under the serial interface itself. The other way is to define only the encapsulation and optional LMI type under the interface itself and then use subinterfaces. A *subinterface* is essentially a logical interface, which inherits most parameters, such as encapsulation, from its parent interface. From an IP perspective, a subinterface is not different from a regular interface.

There are two types of subinterfaces: point-to-point and multipoint. A point-to-point subinterface can be configured with only one PVC. A multipoint subinterface can be configured with multiple PVCs. The point of having subinterfaces will become clear in later chapters where we'll discuss dynamic routing protocols. For now, we'll just examine how to configure the subinterfaces.

A basic configuration of a serial interface for frame relay without subinterfaces consists of the following steps:

1. Configure the frame relay encapsulation using the command **encapsulation frame-relay**.

2. Optionally specify the LMI type, using the command **frame-relay lmi-type** *<lmi-type>*.

3. Assign an IP address, using the command **ip address** *<IP address> <subnet-mask>*.

4. Enable the interface, using the command **no shutdown**.

Let's consider the situation shown in Figure 1.18.

Notice in Figure 1.18 that both the LMI type and DLCIs are different on both sides of the connection through the frame relay network. This is possible because they both have a local significance between the DTE, the routers in our case, and DCE, the frame relay switches (not shown). Using the configuration guidelines just defined, the configuration of the two routers will include those shown in Listings 1.10 and 1.11.

Listing 1.10   Router R1's configuration.

```
interface Serial0
 ip address 10.1.1.1 255.255.255.0
 encapsulation frame-relay
```

Listing 1.11   Router R2's configuration.

```
interface Serial0
 ip address 10.1.1.2 255.255.255.0
 encapsulation frame-relay
 frame-relay lmi-type ansi
```

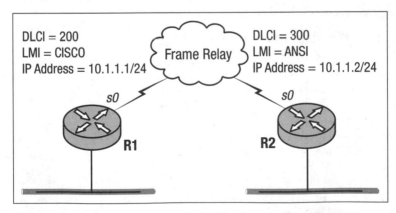

Figure 1.18   Two routers connected over a frame relay network.

The configuration of the serial interface on router R2 differs from that on router R1 because of the command **frame-relay lmi-type ansi**. As we remember, router R1 uses Cisco LMI , which is the default LMI type, so we don't have to enter it.

To configure a serial interface for frame relay encapsulation and to define subinterfaces, perform the following steps:

1. Configure frame relay encapsulation on the appropriate serial interface, using the command **encapsulation frame-relay**.

2. Optionally specify the LMI type for the whole interface, using the command **frame-relay lmi-type** *<lmi-type>*.

3. Define one or several subinterfaces either point-to-point or multipoint, using the command **subinterface point-to-point** or **subinterface multipoint**.

4. For point-to-point subinterfaces, assign an IP address. The subinterface should be ready to use. Use the command **ip address** *<IP address> <subnet-mask>*.

5. For multipoint subinterfaces, choose whether the interface uses InARP or static mapping for address resolution. For InARP, use the command **frame-relay interface-dlci** *<DLCI>*. To define static mapping, use the command **frame-relay map ip** *<remote IP address> <DLCI>*. This command can be optionally followed by the keyword **broadcast**, which allows sending datagrams destined for the IP broadcast address.

Figure 1.19 shows an example of a frame relay–based network that uses subinterfaces. Listings 1.12 through 1.14 show the interface configurations of all three routers.

Listing 1.12   Router R1's configuration.

```
interface Serial0
 no ip address
 encapsulation frame-relay

interface Serial0.1 multipoint
 ip address 10.1.0.1 255.255.255.0
 frame-relay map ip 10.1.0.2 200 broadcast

interface Serial0.2 multipoint
 ip address 10.2.0.1 255.255.255.0
 frame-relay interface-dlci 100
```

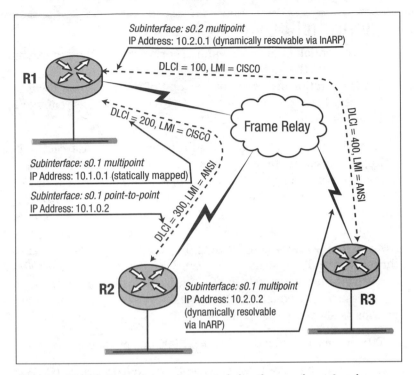

Figure 1.19   *Multiple routers connected via a frame relay network using subinterfaces.*

Listing 1.13   *Router R2's configuration.*

```
interface Serial0
 no ip address
 encapsulation frame-relay
 frame-relay lmi-type ansi

interface Serial0.1 point-to-point
 ip address 10.1.0.2 255.255.255.0
 frame-relay interface-dlci 300
```

Listing 1.14   *Router R3's configuration.*

```
interface Serial0
 no ip address
 encapsulation frame-relay
 frame-relay lmi-type ansi

interface Serial0.1 multipoint
 ip address 10.2.0.2 255.255.255.0
 frame-relay interface-dlci 400
```

Configuring IP Over ISDN

ISDN is essentially a digital telephone service and is another example of how diverse the underlying physical networks can be. The details of ISDN operation are beyond the scope of this book, but I will provide a very basic coverage of the ISDN technology, just enough for our purposes.

The smallest connection in digital telephony, called a *channel*, is 64Kbps. This connection is enough to pass exactly one voice channel using a digitizing technique called *pulse code modulation*, or *PCM*. Why the connection is 64Kbps is simple. PCM uses 8-bit patterns, or *samples*, to modulate the amplitude of a voice at any given moment. Most human voice energy and intelligence is in the frequency range from 30 to 3100Hz, which, for the purposes of PCM, is rounded as 0 through 4KHz. The so-called *voice-grade channel* is therefore defined as the frequency band of 4KHz. To digitize the voice-grade channel, it is necessary to produce 8,000 samples per second, which produces 64Kbps as shown in the calculation below:

8,000 samples per second × 8-bits = 64,000 bits per second, or 64Kbps

There are two types of ISDN service: Basic Rate Interface (BRI) and Primary Rate Interface (PRI). The BRI service provides two 64Kbps channels called *B-channels* that can be used for either voice or data, and one 16Kbps channel called a *D-channel* used solely for signaling.

The PRI service exists in two versions. The one used in North America and Japan offers 23 B-channels and one 64Kbps D-channel. The other used in Europe, Australia, and other parts of the world offers 30 B-channels and one 64Kbps D-channel.

In this book, we discuss only BRI service. However, the principles explained can also be used with PRI service.

In ISDN, the Network Access Layer address is the digital phone number used for dialing. The mapping between the remote IP address and the ISDN number must be done manually.

There are some other specifics of ISDN that must be considered when establishing a connection via ISDN. Normally, the ISDN connections are paid on a per-connection time basis. In other words, the longer the connection, the more it costs. To avoid excessive telecommunication bills, some precautions should be taken when working with

ISDN connections. In Cisco IOS, these precautions are covered by using *interesting traffic*. Interesting traffic is the administratively defined type of traffic that is permitted to bring an ISDN connection up. If no interesting traffic is defined, an ISDN connection will not be established even if there is data that needs to be transmitted over ISDN. Once an ISDN connection is established, both interesting and "uninteresting" traffic can be transferred through it. When the interesting traffic stops being transmitted via the ISDN connection, a timer is started. Each time the interesting traffic appears in the ISDN connection, the timer is reset. If the timer expires, the ISDN connection is dropped. The time after which the timer expires is administratively definable.

Another optional precaution is authentication of the calling party. Because the ISDN connections in most cases go through a public ISDN provider, an unauthorized person may try to connect via ISDN to a private network. To prevent such situations, many types of authentication are available. In the example at the end of this chapter, we'll discuss the *ppp chap* authentication.

We'll cover some additional ISDN configuration guidelines in Chapter 7. For now, we'll confine our discussion of ISDN to the example shown in Figure 1.20 and the configuration of the routers shown in Listings 1.14 and 1.15.

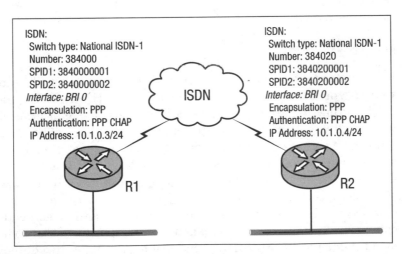

Figure 1.20   Two routers connected via an ISDN public network.

Listing 1.15   Router R1's configuration.

```
username g4 password 0 tsunami
isdn switch-type basic-ni1

interface BRI0
 ip address 10.1.0.3 255.255.255.0
 encapsulation ppp
 isdn spid1 3840000001
 isdn spid2 3840000002
 dialer map ip 10.1.0.4 name g4 broadcast 384020
 dialer-group 1
 ppp authentication chap

dialer-list 1 protocol ip permit
```

Listing 1.16   Router R2's configuration.

```
username g3 password 0 tsunami
isdn switch-type basic-ni1

interface BRI0
 ip address 10.1.0.4 255.255.255.0
 encapsulation ppp
 isdn spid1 3840200001
 isdn spid2 3840200002
 dialer map ip 10.1.0.3 name g3 broadcast 348000
 dialer-group 1
 ppp authentication chap

dialer-list 1 protocol ip permit
```

In the router configurations just shown, the lines that start with **isdn switch-type** define the type of ISDN switches used by the ISDN provider. The lines that start with **dialer map** are very similar in terms of functionality to **frame-relay map** statements found in Listings 1.12 through 1.14. These lines actually define the mapping between the IP address and the Network Access Layer address, the ISDN number in that case. The lines **encapsulation ppp**, **ppp authentication chap**, and **username** *<remote-router-name>* **password** *<encryption-type>* *<password>* define the encapsulation type and the desired authentication, which in our case are **ppp** and **chap**, respectively. The command **dialer-list 1 protocol ip permit** defines the interesting traffic. Finally, the pairs of commands that start with **isdn spid**<SPID#> are specific to the ISDN switch type and are special values used when the router makes a connection to the ISDN switch. Some switches do not require these.

## Chapter 2

Bridging With Cisco Routers

If you need an immediate solution to:	See page:
Configuring Transparent Bridging	72
Using A Single Bridge Group On A Single Router	73
Using Multiple Bridge Groups	75
Configuring Mixed-Media Transparent Bridging	77
Bridging Over HDLC	78
Bridging Over Frame Relay	79
Bridging Over ISDN	83
Configuring Concurrent Routing And Bridging	86
Configuring Integrated Routing And Bridging	87
Tuning The Spanning Tree Parameters	89
Configuring Source-Route Bridging	97
Using Pure Source-Route Bridging	97
Configuring Remote Source-Route Bridging	98
Configuring Source-Route Translational Bridging And Transparent Bridging	100

In Brief

Bridges are devices that operate on the Network Access Layer of the
Internet Model. The Internet model does not provide sufficiently detailed functional specification for the Network Access Layer and its
entities. OSI/RM, however, not only provides such a specification but
also has two layers—the Physical Layer and the Data Link Layer—
instead of a single Network Access Layer. In fact, the specification
provided for the Data Link Layer is so comprehensive that it actually
breaks the Data Link Layer into two sublayers: the Logical Link Control (LLC) sublayer and the Media Access Control (MAC) sublayer.

The details of these two sublayers are beyond the scope of this book.
Nevertheless, one aspect of the MAC sublayer—MAC addressing—is
crucial for understanding how bridging works.

For the purposes of this book, I will use the term *Data Link Layer*
when referring to the devices covered by the Network Access Layer
of the Internet Model. In addition, I will call the segments that do not
contain bridges *LAN segments*, and a group of such segments interconnected with bridges a *Bridged LAN*.

MAC Address

Similar to the Internet datagram, the MAC frame or PDU created by
an entity operating on the Data Link Layer, contains address information about the source and the destination. This address information
is often referred to as the *MAC address*.

The structures of the MAC addresses used in most LAN technologies
are very similar. The most popular LAN technologies are Ethernet,
TokenRing, FDDI, and variations, such as Fast Ethernet, but we will
examine only Ethernet and TokenRing MAC addresses.

MAC addresses are typically used to address the nodes located on
the network segments. Normally, such addresses are burned into the
Read Only Memory (ROM) located on the network interface card
(NIC). Both Ethernet and TokenRing MAC addresses are 48-bits long
and have two bits that are assigned special meaning, which we'll discuss shortly. The major difference between Ethernet and TokenRing

MAC addresses is the bit order within the individual bytes. The following example of the same MAC address shows that the TokenRing has a reversed bit order:

```
Ethernet:    00000000.11001100.10101111
TokenRing:   00000000.00110011.11110101
```

If an Ethernet or TokenRing MAC address consists of only 1s, that address is *broadcast*, that is, it addresses all nodes on a network segment.

The two special bits mentioned earlier are the last two bits of the first byte of an Ethernet MAC address or the first two bits of the first byte of a TokenRing MAC address, as shown in Figure 2.1.

These two special bits are called *Group/Individual* and *Global/Local*, respectively. If the Group/Individual bit is cleared, the MAC address refers to an individual node. Otherwise, the address refers to a certain logical group of nodes. The MAC addresses in which the Group/Individual bit is set are called *multicast MAC addresses*. Except for one case, which we'll discuss in the "Configuring Source-Route Bridging" section later in this chapter, the multicast MAC addresses must not appear as the source MAC addresses in the frame headers.

The Global/Local bit specifies whether the MAC address was assigned by IEEE, the global authority that distributes MAC addresses, or locally. Organizations that want to have their own MAC addresses—for example, for the purposes of manufacturing NICs—can purchase a block of addresses from IEEE. These addresses always have the Global/Local bit cleared, whereby indicating that part of the address, namely the first three octets, was officially assigned to a certain organization. The remaining three octets can only be assigned by this organization. Contrary to that, if the Global/Local bit is set, these addresses can be used freely without any constraints.

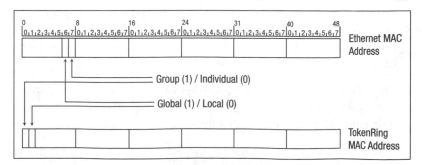

Figure 2.1   Special bits in the Ethernet and TokenRing MAC addresses.

Transparent Bridging

The transparent bridging operation is totally transparent for the nodes connected to a bridged LAN. (The formal specification of the transparent bridging operation is contained in the IEEE 802.1D standard.)

Transparent bridging operates based on several rules:

- A bridge can have multiple ports. Ports can be either in a forwarding or blocking state. A port in a forwarding state can send and receive frames, whereas a port in a blocking state cannot. The purpose of putting some ports into a blocking state is to avoid frame duplication caused by active redundant data paths.

- To minimize the amount of traffic on a bridged LAN, the bridges maintain a filtering database that specifies which MAC addresses appear on which bridge ports. When a bridge has to forward a frame, it looks up the destination MAC address in the filtering database and forwards the frame through the appropriate port only if it finds a match.

- A frame containing a destination MAC address that is not found in the filtering database is flooded through all bridge ports in a forwarding state, with the exception of the port on which the frame has been received.

- A frame destined for the multicast or broadcast address is flooded through all bridge ports in a forwarding state, with the exception of the port on which the frame has been received.

- The bridges use a special bridge protocol to exchange the topology information and to put the ports into either a blocking or a forwarding state. This bridge protocol is based on the spanning tree algorithm, discussed in the next section.

Spanning Tree Algorithm

The spanning tree algorithm is a way to define a topology over a bridged LAN composed of LAN segments arbitrarily connected by bridges, so that the topology is loop-free, and there is always a path between any two LAN segments of the bridged LAN.

The topology established as the result of the spanning tree algorithm operation is called the *spanning tree topology*. The spanning tree topology is enforced by putting appropriate ports into a blocking state.

The spanning tree algorithm allows the bridged LAN to be dynamically modified either by adding additional LAN components—such as segments, bridges, or nodes—or by removing them. It also handles the changes caused by failures of any of these LAN components and uses any redundant paths to preserve the overall loop-free connectivity. If any of these events occurs, the spanning tree algorithm takes the necessary steps to establish a new spanning tree topology, a process known as *spanning tree recalculation*. Spanning tree recalculation usually takes less than one minute to complete.

The spanning tree algorithm works as follows: In any bridged LAN, a single bridge is elected as the *root bridge*. All other bridges determine which of their ports provides the shortest path to the root bridge. This port is known as the *root port* and is put into a forwarding state. For every LAN segment, the bridges connected to it determine which one of them is closest to the root bridge. This bridge is called the *designated bridge* for this LAN segment, and only this bridge forwards the packets from the LAN segment toward the root bridge and from the direction of the root bridge onto that LAN segment. The designated bridge chooses a single port connected to this LAN segment, known as the *designated port*, to actually perform the forwarding. The root bridge is the designated bridge for all segments to which it is connected. Finally, all ports of all bridges that are neither root ports nor designated ports, including the root bridge, are put into a blocking state.

The following example demonstrates how the spanning tree algorithm works. The physical layout of the bridged LAN that we will consider is shown in Figure 2.2.

Assuming bridge B1 is the root bridge candidate, the spanning tree recalculation leads to the spanning tree topology shown in Figure 2.3. The ports that are in a forwarding state are shown using thick lines, and the root ports are labeled with the letters *RP* in a circle.

As the result of this Spanning Tree Algorithm operation, bridges B2 and B4 have become the designated bridges for segment 4 and segment 5, respectively. Bridge B3 then puts its two ports connected to these segments into a blocking state. Apparently, root bridge B1 is the designated bridge for all the segments to which it is connected.

There are two obvious results of the Spanning Tree Algorithm operation. First, the overall connectivity is preserved so that every single node on the bridged LAN can communicate with every other node. Second, the created logical topology is completely free of loops, which guarantees that no data packet is duplicated or, even worse, multiplied.

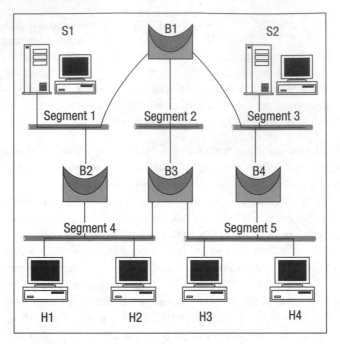

Figure 2.2   The physical layout of a bridged LAN.

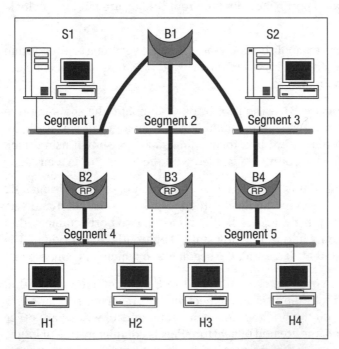

Figure 2.3   Spanning tree topology of the bridged LAN.

However, the spanning tree topology may not produce optimal data paths. For example, if hosts H1 and H3 are needed for communication, their traffic would have to traverse bridges B2, B1, and B4, instead of going directly through bridge B3.

What if one of the bridges fails? For example, if bridge B4 fails, the Spanning Tree Algorithm recalculates and creates a new spanning tree topology, as shown in Figure 2.4. Bridge B3 becomes the designated bridge for segment 5, thereby preserving the overall loop-free connectivity.

The Spanning Tree Algorithm works even if the root bridge fails. Figure 2.5 shows the spanning tree topology produced as the result of root bridge B1 failure. Bridge B2 becomes the root bridge, and bridges B3 and B4 adjust for that accordingly. Bridge B3 becomes the designated bridge for segments 2 and 5, and bridge B4 becomes the designated bridge only for segment 3. As before, the overall loop-free topology is preserved.

Obviously, these examples do not cover all possible scenarios, but they do demonstrate the key features of the Spanning Tree Algorithm:

2. Bridging With Cisco Routers

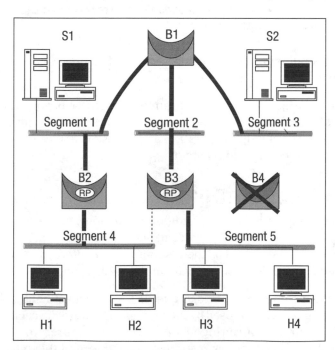

Figure 2.4 *Spanning tree topology after spanning tree recalculation caused by bridge B4 failure.*

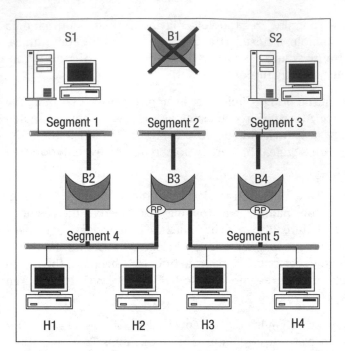

Figure 2.5   Spanning tree topology after spanning tree recalculation caused by the root bridge B1 failure.

preserving overall connectivity, using redundant connections, and keeping the logical topology loop-free.

The details of the spanning tree algorithm operation are beyond the scope of this book. However, the most important parameters involved in the spanning tree algorithm operation are discussed in the "Immediate Solutions" section of this chapter.

Source-Route Bridging

Source-route bridging is another bridging technology that was designed by IBM specifically for TokenRing networks. All operation of source-route bridging is based on the assumption that interconnected segments are either TokenRing, or can emulate TokenRing.

The idea behind source-route bridging is that each packet contains routing information, which is used by the bridges to forward the packet through the source-route bridged LAN from the source to the destination. The source node is responsible for inserting this information into the header of the packet. In addition, the source-route bridging assumes that each node is aware of source-route bridging and locally stores the routing information. This storage capability is what makes source-route bridging very different from transparent bridging, in which none of the nodes knows of the underlying bridging infrastructure.

The source-route bridged LAN must meet the following requirements:

- Each ring should be assigned a unique number.
- Each bridge should be assigned a number unique within each ring to which it is connected.
- Each "pure" source-route bridge cannot connect more than two rings.

The routing information is stored in the header of the TokenRing frames in the *routing information field*, or *RIF*. The format of RIF is shown in Figure 2.6.

The presence of a RIF field is indicated by setting the group/individual bit in the source address. The frame containing RIF does not have to be a special TokenRing frame; it can be a regular broadcast frame containing a fully functional, upper layer protocol PDU, such as an ARP request.

The broadcast bits indicate whether the frame is an *all routes broadcast*, a *single route broadcast*, or a specific route frame. The respective values of this route control subfield are shown in Table 2.1.

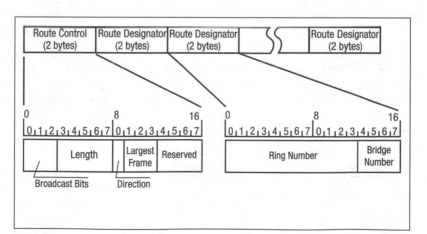

Figure 2.6   The structure of RIF field.

Table 2.1   The meaning of the broadcast bits.

Broadcast Bits	Description
000	Specific route (non broadcast)
100	All routes broadcast
110	Single route broadcast

The length field indicates the total length of RIF in bytes. Only even numbers between 2 and 30 are allowed. According to the IBM specification, the maximum number of bridges that a frame can traverse is limited to seven.

The direction field indicates in which direction the route designators should be interpreted. When set, the direction field requires the bridges to start interpretation from the last route designator and move toward the first one.

The largest frame field specifies the MTU supported by all bridges along the route contained in RIF. Table 2.2 shows the possible values for this field and the respective frame MTUs and maximum IP datagram sizes.

Obviously, the source node needs to know the route to the destination. The source node can discover a route to the destination using either *all route explorers* or *single route explorers*.

The source node uses *all route explorer* packets, or simply an *all routes explorer*, which is flooded by the bridges throughout the source-route bridged LAN. In order to indicate that the packet is an all routes explorer, the source node sets RII and creates RIF, which only contains a route control field. The broadcast bits field contains value 100, the all routes broadcast. As they forward the explorer packet, the bridges append the records containing the ring number from which the packet

Table 2.2   The relation between largest frame values, the frame MTUs, and maximum IP datagram sizes.

Largest Frame Size	Frame MTU	Maximum IP Datagram Size
000	552	508
001	1064	1020
010	2088	2044
011	4136	4092
100	8232	8188

arrived and their own bridge number to RIF. The bridges do not forward the explorer to the next ring if the ring number has already been recorded in RIF. If multiple routes to the destination exist, the destination node receives multiple instances of the explorer, each containing an individual route. The destination normally replies to all explorers that it receives. Usually, the source chooses the route from the first reply on the original explorer.

The other way to discover the route to the destination is based on *single route explorers*, or *spanning explorers*. The operation of the route discovery process using spanning explorers is similar to the one that uses all routes explorers, with a few exceptions. When the node creates RIF, it sets the broadcast bits field to value 110, the single route broadcast. The bridges append the route designators in exactly the same way as they do when processing the all routes explorers, but they do not flood the explorer over all possible routes. Instead, the bridges only forward the spanning explorer along routes that are either administratively or dynamically assigned for single route broadcast forwarding. The destination node replies in the same way as before.

As mentioned earlier, the source-route bridging operation is not transparent for the nodes. The TokenRing NIC driver interface provides all necessary source-route bridging functionality to the upper layer protocols. The upper layer protocol chooses whether to use source-route bridging and which type to use.

The RFC 1042 document specifies how IP and ARP should work in source-route bridging environments. In brief, the document states:

- IP and ARP are both required to use the source-route bridging functionality.

- When ARP is used to resolve an IP address to an appropriate MAC address, it should first use an *all stations broadcast*—that is, a frame that is destined for the broadcast address but does not contain RIF (RII = 0). If a reply is not received within a reasonable time, ARP should try either an all routes explorer or a single route explorer.

- IP broadcasts should be sent using only spanning explorers.

Immediate Solutions

Configuring Transparent Bridging

Routing and bridging do similar things—packet forwarding. Nevertheless, they follow different algorithms, which often contradict each other, making it practically impossible to simultaneously use both bridging and routing on the same device. Over the years, Cisco engineers have come up with several brilliant ideas on how to implement routing and bridging within a single router. These ideas were embodied as three different approaches to configuring Cisco routers for bridging. These approaches are not equal; they actually replace each other, every time providing more features than the previous version.

Originally, transparent bridging and IP routing could not coexist on the same Cisco router because bridging of IP traffic was allowed only if IP routing was turned off. To address this problem of not being able to bridge and route IP (as well as other protocols) simultaneously, in IOS version 11.0, Cisco developed *concurrent routing and bridging*, or *CRB*. CRB allows routing and bridging IP at the same time, but only on different interfaces. However, the interfaces configured for bridging IP cannot possibly pass even a tiny bit of traffic to the interfaces configured for routing IP. In other words, if you configure a Cisco router for concurrent bridging and routing IP, you basically end up with two separate devices—a bridge and an IP router—in the same box. This solution was simply not good enough. Finally, in IOS version 11.2, Cisco created a better solution: *integrated routing and bridging*, or *IRB*. IRB allows IP (as well as many other protocols) traffic to be passed between the routing process and bridging process on the same Cisco router.

Luckily, both CRB and IRB add only a few new commands to what is available with the plain old "bridge only or die" functionality. The next sections describe the guidelines for bridging-only configurations, for CRB, and for IRB.

Using A Single Bridge Group On A Single Router

The most primitive bridging configuration requires that IP routing functions are turned off. Therefore, all configurations, except those for CRB and IRB, share the same command—**no ip routing**.

Take the following steps to configure a Cisco router purely for transparently bridging IP:

1. Disable IP routing using the command **no ip routing** in the global configuration mode.

2. Create a bridge group using the command **bridge** *<group number>* **protocol** *<protocol>* in the global configuration mode. Parameter *group number* allows defining several bridge groups within the same router, where each bridge group behaves as a separate bridge. The protocol provides a choice of three bridging protocols: **ieee**, **dec**, and **ibm**. The first, **ieee**, is the IEEE 802.1D–compliant bridging protocol. The second, **dec**, is the original spanning tree protocol developed at Digital Equipment Corporation, on which the IEEE 802.1D is based. The last, **ibm**, is the IBM version of spanning tree protocol used in source-route bridging environments.

3. Assign the appropriate interfaces to the created bridge group using the command **bridge-group** *<group number>*.

WARNING! *The command ip routing does not appear in the router configuration, which facilitates forgetting its reversal using the command no ip routing. Its presence, however, makes bridging IP impossible (unless CRB or IRB is used). Unfortunately, the router will not produce any error or warning message indicating that you forgot to turn off IP routing, and therefore bridging IP cannot be performed. When IP traffic, which is supposed to be bridged, reaches the router, the router will still try to route it. Obviously, it will fail. However, even now the router will not produce any visible indication of misconfiguration.*

Figure 2.7 shows a router that is used to bridge IP traffic between two segments.

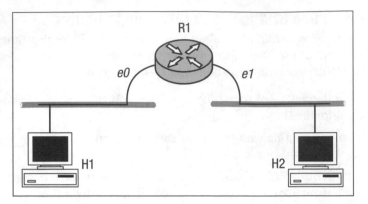

Figure 2.7   Using a single router as a bridge between two Ethernet segments.

The router from Figure 2.7 is configured as shown in Listing 2.1.

Listing 2.1   Router R1.

```
no ip routing

bridge 1 protocol ieee

interface Ethernet0
 bridge-group 1

interface Ethernet1
 bridge-group 1
```

Although separated by a router, hosts H1 and H2 should be configured with the same subnet address.

As discussed in the "In Brief" section of this chapter, the bridges maintain the filtering database. A router allows you to display the filtering database using the command **show bridge** *<group number>*. The *group number* can be omitted, in which case the router displays the filtering databases for each defined bridge group.

The example shown in Listing 2.2 demonstrates the output of the **show bridge** command entered on router R1 from Figure 2.7.

Listing 2.2   Router R1 configuration.

```
R1#show bridge

Total of 300 station blocks, 295 free
Codes: P - permanent, S - self
```

```
Bridge Group 1:

    Address      Action    Interface   Age    RX count   TX count
0260.8c4c.1132   forward   Ethernet1   3            41         32
0060.5cc4.f4c5   forward   Ethernet0   0           475          0
0060.b01a.9e1c   forward   Ethernet0   3           500        202
```

The field **Age** indicates the number of minutes since a frame was last
sent from or received at the corresponding MAC address. Fields **RX
count** and **TX count** specify the number or frames received from
and transmitted to the MAC address.

TIP: *Although the routing is turned off, individual interfaces can still be assigned IP addresses
using the command **ip address** <ip address> <subnet mask>, thereby making the router
accessible via telnet or other remote access commands. The IP address must belong to the
subnet address used by the hosts on the segments connected with the router.*

Using Multiple Bridge Groups

It is possible to configure multiple bridge groups on a single Cisco
router. As mentioned in the previous section, multiple Ethernet groups
behave as separate bridges.

Take the following steps to configure a Cisco router for multiple bridge
groups:

1. Disable IP routing using the command **no ip routing** in the
   global configuration mode.

2. Create multiple bridge groups using the command **bridge**
   <group number> **protocol** *<protocol>* the necessary number
   of times with different group numbers.

3. Assign the interfaces to the appropriate bridge groups using the
   command **bridge-group** *<group number>*.

Let's consider the situation shown in Figure 2.8 as an example.

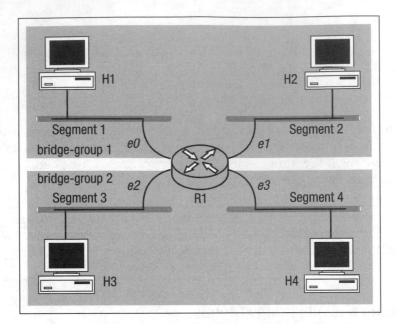

Figure 2.8 A single router configured with multiple bridge groups.

Router R1 is configured as shown in Listing 2.3.

Listing 2.3 Router R1 configuration.

```
no ip routing

bridge 1 protocol ieee
bridge 2 protocol ieee

interface Ethernet0
 bridge-group 1

interface Ethernet1
 bridge-group 1

interface Ethernet2
 bridge-group 2

interface Ethernet3
 bridge-group 2
```

Although all four segments are connected via a single router, there can be no communication between the segments 1 and 2 pair and the segments 3 and 4 pair. Even if all hosts use IP addresses from the same subnet address, hosts H1 or H2 cannot communicate with either hosts H3 or H4.

If the command **show bridge** is used on router R1 without parameters, it displays two filtering databases, as shown in the Listing 2.4.

Listing 2.4   The filtering databases of router R1.

```
R1#show bridge

Total of 300 station blocks, 295 free
Codes: P - permanent, S - self

Bridge Group 1:

      Address      Action   Interface  Age  RX count  TX count
0260.8c4c.1132  forward  Ethernet1  3         41        32
0060.5cc4.f4c5  forward  Ethernet0  0        475         0
0060.b01a.9e1c  forward  Ethernet0  3        500       202

Bridge Group 2:

0060.97fb.566a  forward  Ethernet3  0          5         4
0260.8ca3.28cd  forward  Ethernet2  0         41        10
```

Configuring Mixed-Media Transparent Bridging

It's possible to configure bridging over non-LAN types of media or between two different LAN types, such as Ethernet and TokenRing.

There are two primary purposes for configuring bridging over non-LAN types of media. The first is to provide a Data Link Layer network connection for protocols that cannot be routed, such as NetBEUI or LAT. The other is to provide redundant paths for higher speed primary bridged media, such as Ethernet.

Unlike bridging over non-LAN types of media, the bridging between dissimilar LAN types, especially TokenRing and Ethernet, does not have a strong justification. Transparent bridging between TokenRing and Ethernet has a lot in common with so-called translational bridging between TokenRing and Ethernet, and these are discussed at the end of this chapter.

Bridging Over HDLC

The easiest way to configure bridging over non-LAN media is to do it over an HDLC connection. In fact, it is the same as the method used to configure either single group or multiple groups bridging over LAN connections.

Figure 2.9 shows an example of how two Cisco routers can be used to bridge traffic between two Ethernet segments over a serial link.

The configuration commands shown in Listings 2.5 and 2.6 are used on both routers.

Listing 2.5   Router R1 configuration.

```
no ip routing
bridge 1 protocol ieee

interface Ethernet0
 bridge-group 1

interface Serial0
 bridge-group 1
```

Listing 2.6   Router R2 configuration.

```
no ip routing
bridge 1 protocol ieee
```

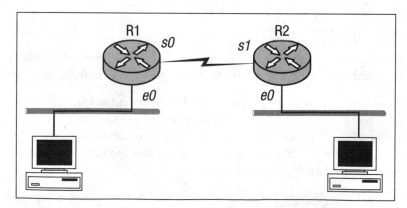

Figure 2.9   Bridging two Ethernet segments using two routers connected via a serial link configured with HDLC encapsulation.

```
interface Ethernet0
 bridge-group 1

interface Serial1
 bridge-group 1
```

The **show bridge** commands entered on either router produce typical output; however, instead of pointing to a LAN interface, they point to a serial interface.

Listing 2.7   The filtering database of Router R1.

```
R1#show bridge

Total of 300 station blocks, 296 free
Codes: P - permanent, S - self

Bridge Group 1:

    Address        Action  Interface  Age  RX count  TX count
0260.8c4c.1132  forward  Serial0    0         15         4
0060.b01a.9e1c  forward  Ethernet0  0         10        10
00e0.b064.30a9  forward  Ethernet0  1         30         0
0260.8ca3.28cd  forward  Serial0    0         42         4
```

Listing 2.8   The filtering database of Router R2.

```
R2#show bridge

Total of 300 station blocks, 296 free
Codes: P - permanent, S - self

Bridge Group 1:

    Address        Action  Interface  Age  RX count  TX count
0260.8c4c.1132  forward  Ethernet0  0         19         6
0060.b01a.9e1c  forward  Serial1    0         12        11
00e0.b064.30a9  forward  Serial1    1         30         0
0260.8ca3.28cd  forward  Ethernet0  0         42         4
```

Related Solution:	Found on page:
Using HDLC Encapsulation	52

Bridging Over Frame Relay

Unlike HDLC, other types of serial interface encapsulations, such as frame relay, require a little bit more involvement from the network administrator in terms of configuration effort.

Take the following steps to configure an interface with the frame relay encapsulation for bridging:

1. Disable IP routing using the command **no ip routing** in the global configuration mode.

2. Create a bridge group using the command **bridge** <*group number*> **protocol** <*protocol*> in the global configuration mode.

3. Configure a serial interface for frame relay using the command **encapsulation frame-relay** and, if necessary, **frame-relay lmi-type** <*LMI type*>. It's entirely up to you whether to use subinterfaces. If you use subinterfaces, they can be either point-to-point or multi-point, whichever is more suitable for your needs.

4. Using the command **bridge-group**, assign the bridge group on all involved interfaces, including any frame relay subinterfaces.

5. If you use multi-point subinterfaces or no subinterfaces, use the command **frame-relay map bridge** <*DLCI*> **broadcast** to map the bridging function to the appropriate frame relay DLCI (it's done automatically for point-to-point subinterfaces).

NOTE: *The keyword broadcast should be used to allow bridges to exchange special packets called BPDUs (which stands for Bridge Protocol Data Units).*

The example in Figure 2.10 shows how two routers can be used to bridge IP traffic between two Ethernet segments over a frame relay PVC.

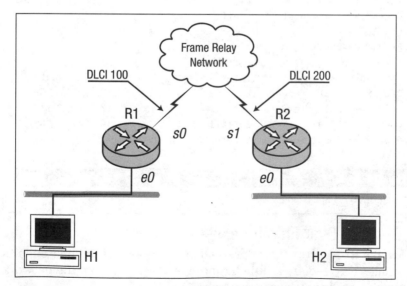

Figure 2.10   Bridging two Ethernet segments using two routers connected via a frame relay network.

Listings 2.9 and 2.10 show how routers can be configured for bridging using subinterfaces.

Listing 2.9   Router R1 configuration.

```
no ip routing
bridge 1 protocol ieee

interface Ethernet0
 bridge-group 1

interface Serial0
 encapsulation frame-relay
 frame-relay lmi-type ansi

interface Serial0.1 multipoint
 frame-relay map bridge 100 broadcast
 bridge-group 1
```

Listing 2.10   Router R2 configuration.

```
no ip routing
bridge 1 protocol ieee

interface Ethernet0
 bridge-group 1

interface Serial1
 encapsulation frame-relay
 frame-relay lmi-type ansi

interface Serial1.1 multipoint
 frame-relay map bridge 200 broadcast
 bridge-group 1
```

Alternatively, point-to-point subinterfaces can be used, in which case the configuration of the routers is as shown in Listings 2.11 and 2.12.

Listing 2.11   Router R1 configuration.

```
no ip routing
bridge 1 protocol ieee

interface Serial0
 encapsulation frame-relay
 frame-relay lmi-type ansi

interface Serial0.1 point-to-point
 frame-relay interface-dlci 100
 bridge-group 1
```

Listing 2.12   Router R2 configuration.

```
no ip routing
bridge 1 protocol ieee

interface Serial1
 encapsulation frame-relay
 frame-relay lmi-type ansi

interface Serial1.1 point-to-point
 frame-relay interface-dlci 200
 bridge-group 1
```

The output of the command **show bridge** on both routers is shown in
Listings 2.13 and 2.14. As you might expect, some of the lines point to
subinterfaces instead of LAN interfaces.

Listing 2.13   The filtering database of Router R1.

```
R1#show bridge

Total of 300 station blocks, 296 free
Codes: P - permanent, S - self

Bridge Group 1:
```

Address	Action	Interface	Age	RX count	TX count
0260.8c4c.1132	forward	Serial0.1	2	11	4
0060.97fb.566a	forward	Ethernet0	0	73	4
0060.b01a.9e1c	forward	Ethernet0	0	39	9
0260.8ca3.28cd	forward	Serial0.1	0	36	10

Listing 2.14   The filtering database of Router R2.

```
R2#show bridge

Total of 300 station blocks, 296 free
Codes: P - permanent, S - self

Bridge Group 1:
```

Address	Action	Interface	Age	RX count	TX count
0260.8c4c.1132	forward	Ethernet0	0	12	4
0060.97fb.566a	forward	Serial1.1	0	73	4
0060.b01a.9e1c	forward	Serial1.1	0	34	9
0260.8ca3.28cd	forward	Ethernet0	0	36	10

Related Solution:	*Found on page:*
Configuring IP Over Frame Relay: Static Mapping and InverseARP	53

Bridging Over ISDN

Configuring a BRI ISDN interface for bridging is somewhat similar to configuring a multi-point subinterface with frame relay encapsulation for bridging. The whole process consists of an ISDN-specific part and mapping of the bridging function to the appropriate ISDN counterpart. Let's have a look at all of these steps:

1. Disable IP routing using the command **no ip routing** in the global configuration mode.

2. Create a bridge group using the command **bridge** *<group number>* **protocol** *<protocol>* in the global configuration mode.

3. Assign an appropriate ISDN switch type using the command **isdn switch-type** *<switch type>* in the global configuration mode.

4. Define interesting traffic using the command **dialer-list** *<list number>* **protocol bridge [permitl list** *<Ethernet-typecode access-list number>*] in the global configuration mode.

5. Define an appropriate encapsulation, such as PPP or HDLC, on the BRI interface. If you use authentication, you also have to perform authentication-specific configuration. This involves defining users using the command **username** *<user name>* **password** *<password>* in the global configuration mode and choosing the appropriate authentication type using the command **ppp authentication [chaplpap]** in the interface configuration mode. Depending on the version of IOS installed on your routers, you may also need to perform certain version-specific authentication configuration tasks. Refer to the Cisco documentation.

6. Assign an appropriate dialer group on the BRI interface using the command **dialer-group** *<dialer group>*. The dialer group should match the dialer list number.

7. If necessary, configure ISDN-specific features, e.g., ISDN SPIDs in the interface configuration mode.

8. Assign the BRI interface to the defined bridge group using the command **bridge-group** *<group number>*.

9. Finally, map the bridging function to the ISDN counterpart
    router using the command **dialer map bridge….** This com-
    mand accepts various parameters. For information on these
    parameters, refer to the Cisco documentation.

Figure 2.11 shows an example of how two Cisco routers can be used
to bridge IP traffic between two Ethernet segments over an ISDN connection. It is assumed that the ISDN switch type is *National ISDN-1*.

Listings 2.15 and 2.16 show the configuration of the routers.

Listing 2.15   Router R1 configuration.

```
username R2 password cisco
no ip routing
isdn switch-type basic-ni1
dialer-list 1 protocol bridge permit
bridge 1 protocol ieee

interface Ethernet0
 bridge-group 1

interface BRI0
 encapsulation ppp
 isdn spid1 3840000001
 isdn spid2 3840000002
```

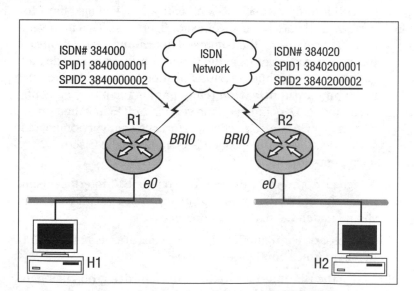

*Figure 2.11   Bridging two Ethernet segments using two routers connected
via an ISDN network.*

```
dialer map bridge name R2 broadcast 384020
dialer-group 1
ppp authentication chap
bridge-group 1
```

Listing 2.16   Router R2 configuration.

```
username R1 password cisco
no ip routing
isdn switch-type basic-ni1
dialer-list 1 protocol bridge permit
bridge 1 protocol ieee

interface Ethernet0
 bridge-group 1

interface BRI0
 encapsulation ppp
 isdn spid1 3840200001
 isdn spid2 3840200002
 dialer map bridge name R1 broadcast 384000
 dialer-group 1
 ppp authentication chap
 bridge-group 1
```

The output of the command **show bridge** shown in Listings 2.17 and 2.18 now contains lines pointing to the BRI interface.

Listing 2.17   The filtering database of Router R1.

```
R1#show bridge

Total of 300 station blocks, 296 free
Codes: P - permanent, S - self

Bridge Group 1:

    Address       Action   Interface   Age  RX count  TX count
0260.8c4c.1132  forward   BRI0        1          5         4
0060.97fb.566a  forward   Ethernet0   0          6         0
0060.b01a.9e1c  forward   Ethernet0   0          5         5
0260.8ca3.28cd  forward   Ethernet0   0          2         0
```

Listing 2.18   The filtering database of Router R2.

```
R2#show bridge

Total of 300 station blocks, 297 free
Codes: P - permanent, S - self
```

```
Bridge Group 1:

        Address        Action   Interface   Age  RX count  TX count
    0260.8c4c.1132   forward   Ethernet0   0         5         4
    0060.b01a.9e1c   forward   BRIO        0         5         5
    0260.8ca3.28cd   forward   BRIO        3         1         0
```

Related Solution:	Found on page:
Configuring IP Over ISDN	58

Configuring Concurrent Routing And Bridging

Concurrent Routing and Bridging, or CRB, allows the configuration of a router to route and bridge IP traffic simultaneously. CRB is enabled using the command **bridge crb** in the global configuration mode. After that, the command **no ip routing** is no longer necessary. With IP routing on and CRB enabled, some interfaces on a router can be configured for routing IP, and some can be configured for bridging. The guidelines for configuring bridging are the same as described in the "Configuring Transparent Bridging" section but without the **no ip routing** command.

Figure 2.12 shows a router configured to bridge IP traffic between segments 1 and 2 and to route IP traffic between segments 3 and 4.

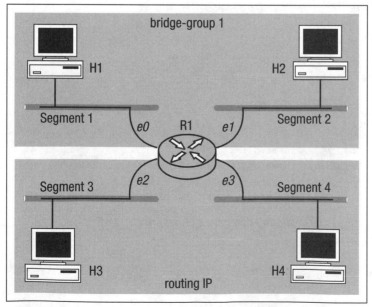

Figure 2.12   Enabling CRB on a router allows IP traffic to be bridged and routed independently.

Router R1 has the configuration shown in Listing 2.19.

Listing 2.19   Router R1 configuration.

```
bridge crb
bridge 1 protocol ieee

interface Ethernet0
 bridge-group 1

interface Ethernet1
 bridge-group 1

interface Ethernet2
 ip address 10.0.1.1 255.255.255.0

interface Ethernet3
 ip address 10.0.2.1 255.255.255.0
```

TIP: *When you use the command **bridge crb**, all protocols including IP are bridged on the interfaces configured for bridging. To re-enable routing IP on the interfaces configured for bridging, use the command **bridge** <group number> **route ip**. After that, all interfaces are configured with this bridge group route IP.*

Configuring Integrated Routing And Bridging

Integrated Routing and Bridging, or IRB, not only allows simultaneous bridging and routing IP, but also makes it possible for IP traffic to be passed between the bridging and routing processes within the same router. The latter is done by means of introducing a special virtual interface that represents the whole bridge group. This interface is called a *bridge virtual interface.*

IRB is enabled using the command **bridge irb** in the global configuration mode. This command also makes bridge virtual interfaces available for configuration. You can configure a bridge virtual interface using the command **interface BVI** *<bridge group number>*. This type of interface represents the whole bridge group whose number matches that of the bridge virtual interface. The interface can be assigned an IP address from the subnet used by the hosts connected to the segments serviced by the router interfaces configured with this bridge group. The hosts can use this IP address as their default gateway to communicate with the rest of the network.

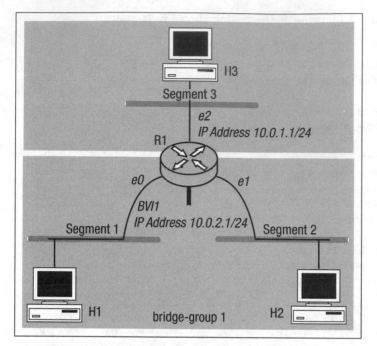

Figure 2.13   Router R1 is configured for Integrated Routing and Bridging, which allows routing between bridged groups and single interfaces within the same router.

Figure 2.13 shows a configuration in which router R1 is used to route IP traffic between segment 3 and two bridged segments 1 and 2.

Route R1 has the configuration shown in Listing 2.20.

Listing 2.20   Router R1 configuration.

```
interface Ethernet0
 bridge-group 1

interface Ethernet1
 bridge-group 1

interface Ethernet2
 ip address 10.0.1.1 255.255.255.0

interface BVI1
 ip address 10.0.2.1 255.255.255.0
```

```
bridge irb
bridge 1 protocol ieee
 bridge 1 route ip
```

NOTE: *IRB requires the command **bridge** <group number> **route ip** in order to pass the bridged traffic to the corresponding BVI interface. Without this command, the router will not attempt to route IP traffic to or from the bridge group.*

Tuning The Spanning Tree Parameters

The bridges implement the Spanning Tree Algorithm using a nameless bridge protocol. The bridge protocol can be either IEEE 802.1D compliant or DEC compliant.

Both implementations use special packets called *BPDUs* to communicate the topology information. The BPDUs are sent to a special multicast MAC address reserved only for the bridges. This address is 0180.C200.0000 (this notation is used by Cisco IOS to denote the values of MAC addresses). The BPDUs are used to maintain the spanning tree topology intact.

The bridges themselves have certain parameters that affect how the spanning tree protocol recalculates. Among these parameters, the most important are the bridge ID and the paths costs associated with the individual bridge ports. The bridge with the smallest ID becomes the root bridge. The path cost value determines which ports are put into a blocking state and which are put into a forwarding state.

The bridge ID consists of two parts: the MAC address of the bridge and the *bridge priority*. The bridge priority is administratively assigned and is more significant than the bridge MAC address. The bridge IDs are compared by first comparing the bridge priorities. The smaller priority designates the smaller bridge ID. If the priorities are equal, which may be the case if they are left at the default values, the MAC addresses are compared. MAC addresses are guaranteed to be unique, and, therefore, the MAC address with the smaller value determines the smaller bridge ID.

Let's take the configuration depicted in Figure 2.14 as an example and examine how the spanning tree recalculates by default and how we can improve that by tuning the discussed bridge parameters.

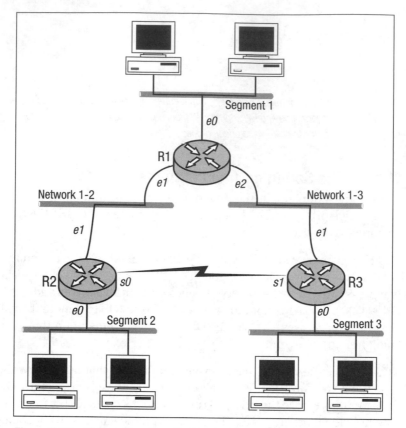

Figure 2.14   *Bridged topology built using three Cisco routers configured for bridging IP.*

The routers have the configurations shown in Listings 2.21 through 2.23.

Listing 2.21   Router R1 configuration.

```
no ip routing
bridge 1 protocol ieee

interface Ethernet0
 bridge-group 1

interface Ethernet1
 bridge-group 1

interface Ethernet2
 bridge-group 1
```

Listing 2.22   Router R2 configuration.

```
Router R2

no ip routing
bridge 1 protocol ieee

interface Ethernet0
 bridge-group 1

interface Serial0
 bridge-group 1

interface Ethernet1
 bridge-group 1
```

Listing 2.23   Router R3 configuration.

```
no ip routing
bridge 1 protocol ieee

interface Ethernet0
 bridge-group 1

interface Serial1
 bridge-group 1

interface Ethernet1
 bridge-group 1
```

So far, we have not examined the spanning tree topology defined as the result of the Spanning Tree Algorithm operation. One reason for not doing this was that the configurations we examined consisted of a maximum of two bridges connected via a single link. All ports on such bridges should be put into a forwarding state. However, now we have three bridges (actually routers configured for bridging IP), each connected to two other ones. At least one port on one of the bridges must be put into a blocking state.

The command that is used to examine the spanning tree topology as it is perceived by a single bridge is **show spanning-tree** <*bridge group number*>. You can use a simplified version of this command, **show spanning-tree**, to display the spanning tree topology for all defined bridge groups.

Entering this command on the routers from Figure 2.14 yields the output shown in Listings 2.24 through 2.26 (because this output is quite long, I have italicized some key parts).

**Listing 2.24   The output of the command show spanning-tree entered on
router R1.**

```
R1#show spanning-tree 1

Bridge Group 1 is executing the IEEE compatible Spanning Tree
protocol
  Bridge Identifier has priority 32768, address 0010.1111.1111
  Configured hello time 2, max age 20, forward delay 15
  Current root has priority 32768, address 0000.0000.1000
  Root port is 7 (Ethernet1), cost of root path is 100
  Topology change flag not set, detected flag not set
  Times:   hold 1, topology change 30, notification 30
           hello 2, max age 20, forward delay 15, aging 300
  Timers: hello 0, topology change 0, notification 0

Port 6 (Ethernet0) of bridge group 1 is forwarding
  Port path cost 100, Port priority 128
  Designated root has priority 32768, address 0000.0000.1000
  Designated bridge has priority 32768, address 0010.1111.1111
  Designated port is 6, path cost 100
  Timers: message age 0, forward delay 0, hold 0

Port 7 (Ethernet1) of bridge group 1 is forwarding
  Port path cost 100, Port priority 128
  Designated root has priority 32768, address 0000.0000.1000
  Designated bridge has priority 32768, address 0000.0000.1000
  Designated port is 2, path cost 0
  Timers: message age 0, forward delay 0, hold 0

Port 8 (Ethernet2) of bridge group 1 is blocking
  Port path cost 100, Port priority 128
  Designated root has priority 32768, address 0000.0000.1000
  Designated bridge has priority 32768, address 0000.0000.2000
  Designated port is 2, path cost 100
  Timers: message age 2, forward delay 0, hold 0
```

**Listing 2.25   The output of the command show spanning-tree entered on
router R2.**

```
R2#show spanning-tree 1

Bridge Group 1 is executing the IEEE compatible Spanning Tree
protocol
  Bridge Identifier has priority 32768, address 0000.0000.1000
  Configured hello time 2, max age 20, forward delay 15
  We are the root of the spanning tree
  Topology change flag not set, detected flag not set
```

```
Times:   hold 1, topology change 30, notification 30
         hello 2, max age 20, forward delay 15, aging 300
Timers: hello 1, topology change 0, notification 0

Port 2 (Ethernet0) of bridge group 1 is forwarding
Port path cost 100, Port priority 128
Designated root has priority 32768, address 0000.0000.1000
Designated bridge has priority 32768, address 0000.0000.1000
Designated port is 2, path cost 0
Timers: message age 0, forward delay 0, hold 0

Port 4 (Serial0) of bridge group 1 is forwarding
Port path cost 100, Port priority 128
Designated root has priority 32768, address 0000.0000.1000
Designated bridge has priority 32768, address 0000.0000.1000
Designated port is 4, path cost 0
Timers: message age 0, forward delay 0, hold 0

Port 3 (Ethernet1) of bridge group 1 is forwarding
Port path cost 100, Port priority 128
Designated root has priority 32768, address 0000.0000.1000
Designated bridge has priority 32768, address 0000.0000.1000
Designated port is 3, path cost 0
Timers: message age 0, forward delay 0, hold 0
```

Listing 2.26   *The output of the command* **show spanning-tree** *entered on router R3.*

```
R3#show spanning-tree 1

Bridge Group 1 is executing the IEEE compatible Spanning Tree
protocol
  Bridge Identifier has priority 32768, address 0000.0000.2000
  Configured hello time 2, max age 20, forward delay 15
  Current root has priority 32768, address 0000.0000.1000
  Root port is 5 (Serial1), cost of root path is 100
  Topology change flag not set, detected flag not set
  Times:   hold 1, topology change 30, notification 30
           hello 2, max age 20, forward delay 15, aging 300
  Timers: hello 0, topology change 0, notification 0

Port 2 (Ethernet0) of bridge group 1 is forwarding
Port path cost 100, Port priority 128
Designated root has priority 32768, address 0000.0000.1000
Designated bridge has priority 32768, address 0000.0000.2000
Designated port is 2, path cost 100
Timers: message age 0, forward delay 0, hold 0
```

```
Port 5 (Serial1) of bridge group 1 is forwarding
  Port path cost 100, Port priority 128
  Designated root has priority 32768, address 0000.0000.1000
  Designated bridge has priority 32768, address 0000.0000.1000
  Designated port is 4, path cost 0
  Timers: message age 1, forward delay 0, hold 0

Port 3 (Ethernet1) of bridge group 1 is forwarding
  Port path cost 100, Port priority 128
  Designated root has priority 32768, address 0000.0000.1000
  Designated bridge has priority 32768, address 0000.0000.2000
  Designated port is 3, path cost 100
  Timers: message age 0, forward delay 0, hold 0
```

Let's assume that router R1 is the most powerful of all three routers, and we want the majority of traffic to go through this router. In other words, we want R1 to become the root bridge. Remember that the root bridge is the designated bridge for all segments to which it is attached and more likely to forward the majority of bridged traffic.

However, line 4 of the output received on router R2 tells us that R2 is the root bridge. Why? Because we did not change the default bridge priorities, the bridges used their MAC addresses to decide which should become the root bridge. Router 2 has a MAC address equal to 0000.0000.1000. Routers R1 and R2 have MAC addresses equal to 0010.1111.1111 and 0000.0000.2000, respectively. R2's MAC address has the smallest value, and thus R2 became the root bridge.

In addition, we might not like the fact that both serial interfaces on routers R2 and R3 are in a forwarding mode, whereas the Ethernet 2 interface on router R1 is in a blocking mode. Notice also that the path cost configured on both serial interfaces is equal to 100. The same value of path cost can be found on all of the Ethernet interfaces. Thus, simply because the serial interface on R3 provides the shortest (in terms of path cost) path to the root bridge, it is put into forwarding mode.

The easiest way to change the produced spanning tree topology is to set an appropriate bridge priority value on R1. The default value of the bridge priority is set to the maximum. Therefore, setting it to anything except the maximum forces the bridge to become the root bridge.

The command used to change the bridge priority is **bridge** *<group number>* **priority** *<priority>*. This command changes the bridge priority only for the corresponding bridge group.

Let's examine what happens when we change the bridge priority on router R1 to the value of 1000. Listings 2.27 through 2.29 show the state of routers after the spanning tree recalculated with this new parameter. To make the output more readable, I omitted the lines that we do not examine.

Listing 2.27 *The output of the command **show spanning-tree** entered on router R1.*

```
R1#show spanning-tree 1

Bridge Group 1 is executing the IEEE compatible Spanning Tree
protocol
 Bridge Identifier has priority 1000, address 0010.1111.1111
 ...
We are the root of the spanning tree
 ...

Port 6 (Ethernet0) of bridge group 1 is forwarding
 ...

Port 7 (Ethernet1) of bridge group 1 is forwarding
 ...

Port 8 (Ethernet2) of bridge group 1 is forwarding
 ...
```

Listing 2.28 *The output of the command **show spanning-tree** entered on router R2.*

```
R2#show spanning-tree 1

Bridge Group 1 is executing the IEEE compatible Spanning Tree
protocol
 Bridge Identifier has priority 32768, address 0000.0000.1000
 ...
 Current root has priority 1000, address 0010.1111.1111
 Root port is 2 (Ethernet0), cost of root path is 100
 ...

Port 2 (Ethernet0) of bridge group 1 is forwarding
 ...

Port 4 (Serial0) of bridge group 1 is forwarding
 ...

Port 3 (Ethernet1) of bridge group 1 is forwarding
 ...
```

Listing 2.29   The output of the command *show spanning-tree* entered on router R3.

```
R3#show spanning-tree 1

Bridge Group 1 is executing the IEEE compatible Spanning Tree
protocol
 Bridge Identifier has priority 32768, address 0000.0000.2000
 ...
 Current root has priority 1000, address 0010.1111.1111
 Root port is 2 (Ethernet0), cost of root path is 100
 ...

Port 2 (Ethernet0) of bridge group 1 is forwarding
 ...

Port 5 (Serial1) of bridge group 1 is blocking
 ...

Port 3 (Ethernet1) of bridge group 1 is forwarding
 ...
```

Now the spanning topology reflects what we want. R1 is the root bridge, and only the Ethernet ports are in forwarding mode. Nevertheless, in many cases you may want to set the adequate path cost values on all of the ports involved in the spanning tree operation. Ideally, the path cost value should reflect the bandwidth of the segment. Suppose the bandwidth of the serial connection is about one-third of the Ethernet bandwidth. In this case, we may set the serial interface path cost value to 300. The command used to set the path cost value is **bridge-group** *<group number>* **path-cost** *<cost>*.

TIP: *It is possible (although undesirable) to change the burned MAC address of an Ethernet interface on a Cisco router. To do this, you have to use the command **mac-address** <new MAC address> in the interface configuration mode.*

NOTE: *The MAC address values that appeared in the **show spanning-tree** command output were assigned using the **mac-address** command. This was done to simplify the explanation of the spanning tree recalculation process. In addition, the path cost value on the serial interfaces was changed from its default value using the command **bridge-group** <group number> **path-cost <100>** to force the interface into a forwarding state (for the purposes of the discussion). Although the default path-cost value on a serial interface is higher than that on an Ethernet interface, it may not adequately reflect the actual bandwidth of the serial interface and, therefore, may require adjusting.*

Configuring Source-Route Bridging

Source-route bridging is another type of bridging. It really serves the same purpose—forwarding PDUs among LAN segments of the same type. Nevertheless, it is based upon the ideas completely different from those used in transparent bridging.

Using Pure Source-Route Bridging

Pure source-route bridges cannot have more than two ports; however, this requirement is too strict for the real world. The designers of the Cisco IOS overcame this restriction by introducing a *virtual ring*. From the source-route bridging perspective, the virtual ring appears to be a normal ring. It has a number, and it is referenced in the route stored in the source-route bridged frames. The ring, however, is only logically defined within the router, which is why it is virtual. The router itself appears as multiple source-route bridges, each with only two ports and each connected to the virtual ring. This is reflected in the source-route bridged frames that traverse the router in the form of two route designators both inserted by a single router.

Take the following steps to configure source-route bridging of an IP on a Cisco router:

1. Disable IP routing using the command **no ip routing** in the global configuration mode.

2. Define a virtual ring using the command **source-bridge ring-group** *<ring-number>* in the global configuration mode.

3. Assign ring numbers to the individual TokenRing interfaces and bridge numbers to the logical bridges connecting the physical rings to the virtual ring using the command **source-bridge** *<physical ring number> <bridge number> <virtual ring number>* in the interface configuration mode.

4. Use the command **multiring ip** to enable source-route bridging of the MAC frames containing IP datagrams on that interface.

Listing 2.30 gives an example of a configuration that enables source-route bridging of IP traffic on a router with three TokenRing interfaces.

Listing 2.30   Basic source-route bridging configuration.

```
no ip routing
source-bridge ring-group 1000
```

```
interface TokenRing0
 ring-speed 16
 source-bridge 110 1 1000
 multiring ip

interface TokenRing1
 ring-speed 16
 source-bridge 120 2 1000
 multiring ip

interface TokenRing2
 ring-speed 16
 source-bridge 130 3 1000
 multiring ip
```

Configuring Remote Source-Route Bridging

Like transparent bridging, source-route bridging can also be used over non-LAN or non-TokenRing networks. This form of source-route bridging is called *remote source-route bridging*, or *RSRB*.

Unlike transparent bridging, the RSRB configuration does not map the bridging service directly to the non-TokenRing interfaces (because usually non-TokenRing interfaces do not support TokenRing operation required for source-route bridging). Instead, the virtual ring is extended over non-TokenRing interfaces, so that all participating routers appear to be connected to a single virtual ring (TokenRing emulation).

The virtual ring is extended by specifying all remote neighbors that participate in the ring. The command that is used to specify the remote neighbors is **source-bridge remote-peer....** This command takes numerous parameters, the most important of which are the transport type—which can, but doesn't have to, be limited to TCP or frame relay—and the remote peer identification, which is the remote IP address in the case of TCP.

Let's consider the example shown in Figure 2.15. Two routers configured for RSRB perform source-route bridging of IP traffic between two remote TokenRing segments.

Listings 2.31 and 2.32 show the configuration of both routers.

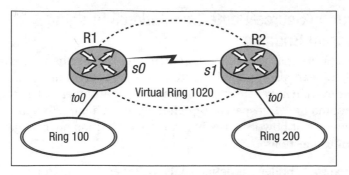

Figure 2.15 *Two routers configured for RSRB are used to source-route bridge IP traffic between two TokenRing segments.*

Listing 2.31 *Router R1 configuration.*

```
no ip routing
source-bridge ring-group 1020
source-bridge remote-peer 1020 tcp 10.1.1.2 local-ack
source-bridge remote-peer 1020 tcp 10.1.1.1

interface Serial0
 ip address 10.1.1.1 255.255.255.0

interface TokenRing0
 ring-speed 16
 multiring ip
 source-bridge 100 11 1020
```

Listing 2.32 *Router R2 configuration.*

```
no ip routing
source-bridge ring-group 1020
source-bridge remote-peer 1020 tcp 10.1.1.1 local-ack
source-bridge remote-peer 1020 tcp 10.1.1.2

interface Serial1
 ip address 10.1.1.2 255.255.255.0

interface TokenRing0
 ring-speed 16
 multiring ip
 source-bridge 200 12 1020
```

Configuring Source-Route Translational Bridging And Transparent Bridging

Transparent bridging is not limited to Ethernet LANs only. Transparent bridging can also be implemented in pure TokenRing environments, or even in mixed TokenRing Ethernet environments. It's easy to understand how transparent bridging works in a pure TokenRing environment, but how it works in a mixed TokenRing environment raises a few questions.

The source-route bridging is defined only for TokenRing environments. Some sophisticated bridges may try to "translate" the source-route bridging specific information into transparent bridging information and vice versa, thus making it possible to merge a transparent bridge LAN with a source-route bridged LAN. This type of bridging is called *source-route translational bridging*. (As mentioned before, the justification for using bridging between such different types of LANs is nearly nonexistent, and the technological aspects of attempting such a configuration are rather problematic.)

First, as discussed in the "In Brief" section, the Ethernet and TokenRing MAC addresses have a different order of bits in bytes. Therefore, a bridge must translate the TokenRing bit order to Ethernet, and vice versa. An example of such a translation is shown in Figure 2.16.

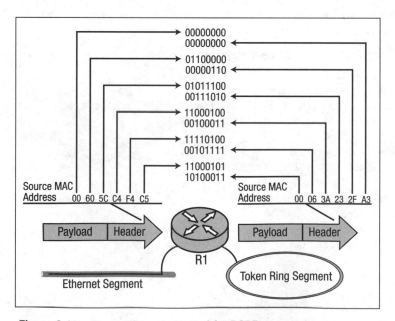

Figure 2.16   Two routers configured for RSRB are used to source-route bridge IP traffic between two TokenRing segments.

The translation itself wouldn't be a big problem if ARP did not save a copy of the source MAC address in its own PDU. From the Data Link Layer perspective, the ARP's PDU is nothing more than a payload of a MAC frame. Therefore, there is no way that a bridge, a device of the Data Link Layer, can look into the payload and translate the copy of MAC address in it as well. The ARP module at the destination uses the copy of the source MAC address as opposed to the translated version in its reply, thereby sending it nowhere. The only way to avoid this problem is to set all of the necessary ARP entries manually, which is obviously too much trouble.

Another problem arises from the different MTU sizes of TokenRing and Ethernet. In the pure Ethernet world, the IP MTU size is 1500 bytes, whereas in the TokenRing world, it is 4096. If a router is used to route IP traffic between a TokenRing segment and an Ethernet segment, the router fragments the large datagrams coming from the TokenRing segment to accommodate the Ethernet MTU size. Unlike routers, bridges do not provide a fragmenting function; therefore, they have to silently drop large frames that cannot be sent over media because the MTU size of the media is too small. Interestingly enough, a communication can usually be started between two stations if one has a connection to a TokenRing segment, the other has a connection to an Ethernet segment, and these segments are bridged. The reason for this is that most protocols don't normally try to make their first PDU the biggest possible size. However, after the first PDU, the protocols usually start gradually increasing the size of subsequent PDUs, trying to reach the MTU size of the underlying physical network. Thus, when the size of the packets created by the protocol entity located on the node connected to the TokenRing segment exceeds the Ethernet MTU size, the packets are dropped by the intermediate bridge. At this point, the connection hangs. The solution is to change the MTU size on every node connected to the TokenRing segment that may potentially need to communicate with a node connected to the Ethernet segment.

Because both types of mixed media bridging are barely useful in the case of IP, I have only provided two sample configurations—one for each type of bridging—for a single router connecting an Ethernet and a TokenRing segment. An example of a physical topology in which these types of bridging can be applied is shown in Figure 2.17.

Listing 2.33 shows a sample router configuration that enables transparent bridging of IP traffic between an Ethernet segment and a TokenRing segment.

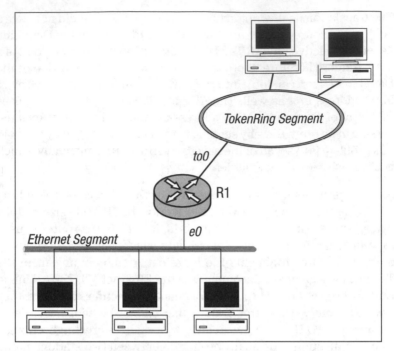

Figure 2.17   A router used to bridge IP traffic between an Ethernet segment and a TokenRing segment.

Listing 2.33   Basic mixed-media transparent bridging configuration.

```
no ip routing
bridge 1 protocol ieee

interface Ethernet0
 bridge-group 1

interface TokenRing0
 ring-speed 16
 bridge-group 1
```

Listing 2.34 gives a sample configuration that enables translational bridging on a router connecting an Ethernet segment and a TokenRing segment.

Listing 2.34   Basic source-route translational bridging.

```
no ip routing
source-bridge ring-group 1000
source-bridge transparent 1000 200 15 1
bridge 1 protocol ieee

interface Ethernet0
 bridge-group 1

interface TokenRing0
 ring-speed 16
 source-bridge 100 1 1000
 multiring ip
```

Chapter 3

Static Routing

If you need an immediate solution to:	See page:
Using Connected Interfaces To Perform Basic Routing	110
Configuring Basic Static Routing	111
Using Metrics With Static Routes	115
Using Output Interface Instead Of Next-Hop Router With Static Routing	119
Configuring Classless Routing	123
Configuring A Default Gateway On A Router	125
Configuring Individual Host Routes	125
Configuring Equal Cost Load Balancing Using Static Routing	126
Configuring Unequal Cost Load Balancing Using Static Routing	132

In Brief

In previous chapters, we examined the principles of protocols layering and details of the Internet Protocol, such as IP addressing, datagram forwarding, fragmentation, and so on. We learned that IP routers are used to forward IP datagrams among multiple diverse networks in order to provide overall connectivity. Now it's time to discuss how IP routers make routing decisions.

Routers forward datagrams among the segments directly attached to them, and they make routing decisions based on network addresses as opposed to host addresses. Somehow, the routers must figure out which network addresses are accessible through which interfaces. Obviously, it's easy if all of the segments are connected to a single router, because the router knows which network addresses are configured on its interfaces. If multiple routers are used to route the traffic between segments and if the traffic must go through more than one hop, making routing decisions becomes more challenging for the router.

The routers face two important challenges. They must:

- Find out which network addresses are available on the segments that are not directly attached to them.

- Have certain rules to resolve potential ambiguities that can arise if the same IP address matches several network addresses. (Remember that network addresses can be either pure network addresses, subnet addresses, individual host addresses, or even supernet addresses in the classless addressing model.)

The routers resolve the first challenge by using a special database that all routers are supposed to maintain, called a *routing table*. The routing table consists of entries called *routes*. A route lists a single network address, or, as it's nowadays often called, a network prefix, which usually contains a network IP address and a subnet mask and one or more references for reaching this network address. Such references normally consist of the next-hop router IP address, which must be accessible directly from one of the local interfaces, and the corresponding interface. However, if the network address belongs to one of the locally attached segments, the next-hop router entry is left blank. The routing table may also contain some auxiliary information such as route metrics, route tags, and so on.

The routers have two approaches for populating the routing table with the routes: *static routing* and *dynamic routing*. Static routing assumes that all necessary routes are entered into the routing table manually by network administrators. Dynamic routing relies on special auxiliary protocols called *dynamic routing protocols*, which automatically discover all necessary routes by means of exchanging special packets called *routing updates* and populate them into the routing table.

This chapter is devoted to static routing and how it can be configured on the Cisco routers. Dynamic routing is discussed thoroughly in the two subsequent chapters.

Before getting down to static routing configuration tasks, let's first consider how routers choose the correct routes from their routing tables. The possibility of the same IP address matching several network addresses is resolved using a set of predefined rules, called the *routing algorithm*, that defines the best network address match for any given destination IP address.

Routing Algorithm

The first version of the routing algorithm was known as "classful" and did not have a written standard. This version was constantly improved until the classless IP addressing scheme was introduced. Details of this "classless" version of the routing algorithm are documented in RFC 1812, "Requirements for IP Version 4 Routers." Our discussion of the routing algorithm is based on the classless version and points out how the classful version differs from the classless.

The routing algorithm operates using two arguments: the destination IP address and the routing table. The output of the algorithm is a single route, which the router uses to forward the datagram.

The simplified version of the classless routing algorithm consists of two steps:

1. *Basic match*—The algorithm keeps only network prefixes that the destination IP address matches and discards all other network prefixes. For example, if the destination address is 10.234.24.194, then the result of the basic match step can contain network prefixes 8.0.0.0/4, 10.0.0.0/8, and 10.234.0.0/16. If the routing table also contains network prefixes 9.0.0.0/8, 10.200.0.0/16, and 146.123.45.0/24, they will be discarded.

2. *Longest match*—From the prefixes left as the result of the basic match step, the algorithm chooses the longest prefix, which is returned as the result of the algorithm operation. However, if the basic match step did not keep any prefixes, the algorithm will indicate that the packet must be dropped. For example, among the network prefixes kept by the basic match step in the previous paragraph, the longest match step will choose 10.234.0.0/16.

These two steps can be combined in one logical function—longest match lookup—but the standard specifies two steps. Using two steps makes it easier to point out the difference between the classful and classless routing algorithms.

The difference only exists at the basic match step. The basic match step in the classful version can be described as follows:

1. *Basic match*—The algorithm first extracts the classful network address from the destination IP address. If the router is directly connected to any subnets that belong to that network address, the algorithm will first select the prefixes that are subnets of the network address (including the prefix, which is equal to the network address itself if such is present in the routing table). Among these prefixes the algorithm will keep only those which match the destination address.

If the router is not connected to any such subnets, the algorithm will keep all prefixes that match the destination IP address.

TIP: *In other words, if a router is connected to any subnets of the classful network address to which the destination IP address belongs, the router will never forward the datagram using supernet routes of the destination address.*

---

2. *Longest match*—The longest match step is the same as that of the classless routing algorithm.

Because the basic match step may sound a bit complicated, let's consider an example, which will demonstrate how it works. Suppose a router has routes for the following prefixes: 10.1.1.0/24, 10.1.2.0/24, 10.2.1.0/24, 10.2.2.0/24, 172.16.0.0/16, and 0.0.0.0/0. Let the router be directly connected to subnets 10.1.1.0/24 and 10.1.2.0/24. A datagram destined for IP address 10.3.1.10 arrives, and the router performs the classful routing algorithm. First, it extracts the network address from the destination IP address—10.0.0.0/8. Second, it selects only the prefixes that are subnets of 10.0.0.0/8; those are 10.1.1.0/24, 10.1.2.0/24, 10.2.1.0/24, and 10.2.2.0/24. None of these prefixes matches the destination IP address, which forces the router to drop the datagram. Pay attention that the classful routing algorithm discarded the default gateway route, 0.0.0.0/0, which would be used by the class-less version.

Load Splitting

When I covered routing table entries, or routes, I pointed out that a single route consists of a network prefix, and one or more references for reaching the destinations matched by the network prefix. If there is only one such reference, the router will simply use it to forward the datagrams to the destination. If, however, there were multiple references, the router will have to decide which one of them it has to use.

The routers can actually use multiple entries simultaneously, thereby utilizing multiple paths for traffic forwarding. This is called *load splitting*, or *load balancing*. In some cases, the routers can even perform so-called *unequal cost load balancing*, whereby the traffic is divided into streams whose sizes are unequal proportionally to the bandwidths of the paths utilized. Another alternative is called *equal cost load balancing*, which operates with equally sized streams taking different paths to the same destination.

NOTE: *Alternatively, you can think that the routing table can contain multiple routes for the same destination, which can be used to load balance the traffic among multiple paths. In that case, the routing algorithm is allowed to return multiple routes as opposed to a single route. I think that these two descriptions are equal; however, personally I like the one given before better, because it appears to be more logical to me.*

In addition, the Cisco routers employ two strategies when deciding which datagram should take which path, if load balancing is available for the destination IP address. These strategies are called *per-destination load balancing* and *per-packet load balancing*. In the case of per-destination load balancing, the router randomly chooses a path for the first datagram to a certain destination, after which it will always use that path to forward all subsequent datagrams to that destination. In the case of per-packet load balancing, the router dispatches all datagrams in a round-robin fashion among all the paths available for the corresponding network prefix.

Because load balancing sometimes is undesirable, the routers provide means to turn it off.

Immediate Solutions

All solutions provided in the following sections assume that all necessary interfaces on the routers have already been configured properly and assigned appropriate IP addresses.

Using Connected Interfaces To Perform Basic Routing

If a single router is used to perform routing among directly attached segments, no extra routing configuration is required because the router automatically adds the IP addresses configured on all active interfaces into the routing table. "Active" means that the corresponding interface is physically and logically up, which can be verified using the command **show ip interfaces** *<interface> <interface number>*. A sample output of this command is shown in Listing 3.1.

*Listing 3.1   The first line of the command **show interfaces ethernet 0** output displays the physical and logical status of the interface.*

```
R1#show interfaces ethernet 0
Ethernet0 is up, line protocol is up
...
```

Ethernet is up means that the interface is physically up, and **line protocol is up** means that the interface is logically up. Suppose the interface is assigned IP address 10.1.1.1. By using the command **show ip route** as shown in Listing 3.2, we can verify that the IP address appears in the routing table.

Listing 3.2   The routing table of router R1.

```
R1#show ip route
...
10.0.0.0/24 is subnetted, 3 subnets
C       10.2.2.0 is directly connected, TokenRing0
C       10.1.1.0 is directly connected, Ethernet0
C       10.0.255.0 is directly connected, Serial1
```

In some cases, an interface can be logically down and physically up at the same time. If this happens, the corresponding IP address is removed from the routing table. For example, if a router uses an Ethernet transceiver to connect to a hub, the corresponding Ethernet interface—for example, Ethernet 0—is always physically up, as long as the transceiver is working properly. If the transceiver is disconnected from the hub, the interface on the router goes logically down, as shown here in the output of the command **show interfaces ethernet 0**:

```
R1#show interfaces ethernet 0
Ethernet0 is up, line protocol is down
```

Even if the interface is only logically down, the network address to which the interface's IP address belongs will not appear in the routing table, which is demonstrated by the output of the command **show ip route** shown in Listing 3.3.

Listing 3.3   The routing table of router R1.

```
R1#show ip route
...
10.0.0.0/24 is subnetted, 2 subnets
C       10.2.2.0 is directly connected, TokenRing0
C       10.0.255.0 is directly connected, Serial1
```

The hosts connected to segments interconnected with a single router must have routes pointing to the IP addresses assigned on the corresponding router interfaces. For example, all such hosts can have a single default-gateway entry pointing to the router's interfaces.

Configuring Basic Static Routing

To configure static routing on a router, perform the following steps:

1. Identify the networks that need to be accessible via the router.

2. Create static route entries for each remote network using the command **ip route** *<remote network address> <subnet mask> <next-hop router>*.

You may encounter a few pitfalls when configuring static routing. First, be sure to consider the traffic going to the destination and also the traffic coming back. This is especially important when configuring a router that routes traffic between the networks, none of which is directly attached to it. Let's consider the example depicted in Figure 3.1.

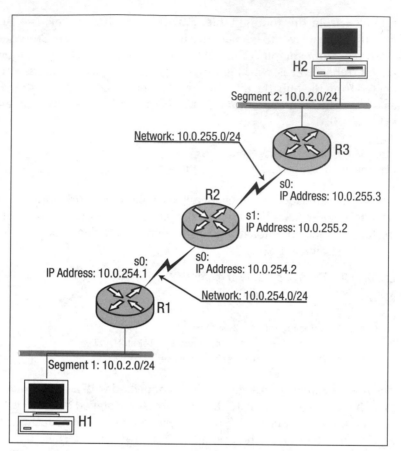

Figure 3.1   A router is used to route traffic between two remote networks.

First, let's assume that router R1 and R3 are configured correctly. Then, assume that host H1 on segment 1 must be able to communicate with host H2 on segment 2. You could add only one static route as follows:

```
R2(config)#ip route 10.0.2.0 255.255.255.0 10.0.255.3
```

This route works when a packet from host H1 destined for host H2 hits router R2. Router R2 then performs a router table lookup that yields next-hop router R3, to which router R2 forwards the packet. After the packet is delivered to host H2, host H2 replies to host H1 with its own packet, which is sent to router R3 for delivery across the intermediate networks.

If router R3 is configured correctly, it forwards the packet to router R2. However, this time router R2 does not know the route to the destination network—that is, segment 1. Therefore, router R2 drops the packet. You can easily correct the situation by adding another route on router R2, as follows:

```
R2(config)#ip route 10.0.1.0 255.255.255.0 10.0.254.1
```

Configurations that require static routing rarely involve only one router. Normally, such configurations are built using two or more routers. Configuring static routing on a single router creates only one-way connectivity. The packet is delivered to the destination, but when the destination replies, the router at the other end won't know the route to the original source. The packet is then simply dropped. For example, suppose that router R1 in Figure 3.2 has the following static routing entry:

```
ip route 10.0.2.0 255.255.255.0 10.0.254.2
```

3. Static Routing

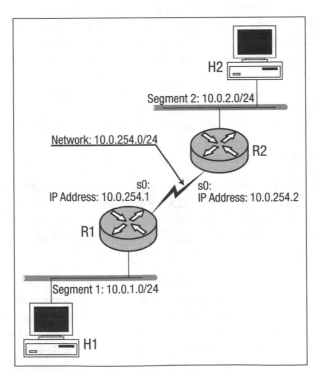

Figure 3.2   Only router R1 is configured with a static route for segment 2.

However, router R2 does not have any static routing entries configured. The communication initiated from host H1 to host H2 fails, because the reply sent by host H2 is dropped by router R2. You can correct this, again, very simply by entering the following command:

```
R2(config)#ip route 10.0.1.0 255.255.255.0 10.0.254.1
```

Interestingly enough, this simple problem can be sometimes difficult to diagnose. If, for example, the **ping** command is used on router R1 to verify host H2's accessibility, host H2 may appear to be perfectly accessible. However, if **ping** is used to verify accessibility of the Ethernet interface on router R1, it times out. At first, such symptoms may look like a one-way connectivity problem—traffic goes from R1 to host H2 normally, but not from H2 back to R1. Because this happens at router R1 and because H2 cannot access anything behind R1, it appears that router R1 is having some sort of a problem. If we think carefully, however, these suspicions will turn out to be groundless. First, **ping** on router R1 shows that host H2 is accessible, which means that **ping** is receiving replies. Thus, we know that it's not a one-way connectivity problem. At the same time, the router uses the closest interface to send the **pings** to the destination, which happens to be interface Serial 0, directly connected to segment 3. Router R2 is also directly connected to segment 3; thus, it has a route to segment 3. When host H2 replies, the replies are sent to the IP address configured on interface Serial 0 of router R1, for which router R2 has the route. If host H2 sends **ping** packets destined for the IP address configured on interface Ethernet 0 of router R1, the packets are dropped because router R2 does not have a route for this network.

This confusion usually happens because an IP address is associated with the router instead of with a particular interface of a router. This usually isn't a problem in the case of hosts because hosts normally don't have multiple interfaces. Remember, however, that routers rarely have a single interface.

Finally, another important consideration is the host configuration. Static routing won't work without an appropriate routing configuration on the hosts. All hosts that rely on routers must have routing entries pointing to the appropriate interfaces of the routers. Incomplete host configuration and incorrect static routing configured on the single closest router frequently go hand in hand. In other words, network administrators configuring static routing often do only half of the job—they only configure a single site, forgetting that this site needs to communicate with other sites.

Using Metrics With Static Routes

The command **ip route** *<remote network address> <subnet mask>*
<next-hop router> can have an optional parameter called *distance*.
This parameter defines which static route is added to the routing table
if there are several static routes for the same destination network.
The smaller the distance, the more preferable the route is. Thus, the
router will add the route with the smallest distance to the routing
table, leaving all other routes behind. The default distance is equal to
1, the highest possible distance for static routes. If the distance is
255, the route is never added to the routing table.

TIP: *Notice that the router will use the distances only if the network prefixes in the static routes are the same. If the network prefixes have different lengths they are considered different. For example, if there are two static routes for network prefixes 10.1.0.0/16 and 10.1.0.0/24, they both will be added to the routing table regardless of the configured distances.*

Why would anyone need routes that are not added to the routing table?
Well, the answer is based on one of the principles of how routes are
added to the routing table. The router does not add a route to the
routing table unless it knows a route to the next-hop gateway. Plus,
the router removes a route from the routing table if the route that
made the next-hop gateway available disappears. Typically, the next-
hop gateway is available through one of the directly connected networks. Thus, if the corresponding interface is up, the router keeps a
route for the network address that corresponds to the IP address assigned on the interface. If the interface goes down, the router immediately removes the route. Any other routes pointing to the next-hop
routers available through that interface are then also removed from
the routing table. However, a static route for the same destination
that has a distance value greater than that of the routes removed is
immediately added to the routing table following the removal of the
route associated with the interface. Such static routes can be used to
unitize alternative routes, in case the primary routes fail.

Static routes that are activated only if all other routes with smaller
distance values disappear are called *floating static routes*.

Floating static routes are often used when it's necessary to provide a
backup for a certain connection. Figure 3.3 shows two routers connected using two serial links going in parallel between a pair of routers R1 and R2.

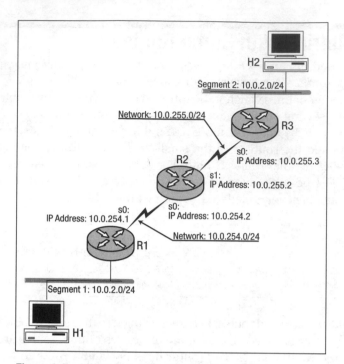

Figure 3.3   *Link 2 is only used when link 1 fails.*

The routers are configured as shown in Listings 3.4 and 3.5.

Listing 3.4   Router R1's configuration.

```
interface Serial0
 ip address 195.0.0.1 255.255.255.0

interface Serial1
 ip address 195.1.0.1 255.255.255.0

interface TokenRing0
 ip address 200.1.0.1 255.255.255.0
 ring-speed 16

ip route 200.2.0.0 255.255.255.0 195.0.0.2
ip route 200.2.0.0 255.255.255.0 195.1.0.2 10
```

Listing 3.5   Router R2's configuration.

```
interface Ethernet0
 ip address 200.2.0.1 255.255.255.0

interface Serial0
 ip address 195.1.0.2 255.255.255.0
```

```
interface Serial1
 ip address 195.0.0.2 255.255.255.0

ip route 200.1.0.0 255.255.255.0 195.0.0.1
ip route 200.1.0.0 255.255.255.0 195.1.0.1 10
```

If we examine the routing table on either router, we'll notice that the route whose distance is 10 was not added (see Listings 3.6 and 3.7).

Listing 3.6   The routing table of router R1.

```
R1#show ip route
...
C    195.1.0.0 is directly connected, Serial1
C    195.0.0.0 is directly connected, Serial0
C    200.1.0.0 is directly connected, TokenRing0
S    200.2.0.0 [1/0] via 195.0.0.2
```

Listing 3.7   The routing table of router R2.

```
R2#show ip route
...
C    195.1.0.0/24 is directly connected, Serial0
C    195.0.0.0/24 is directly connected, Serial1
S    200.1.0.0/24 [1/0] via 195.0.0.1
C    200.2.0.0/24 is directly connected, Ethernet0
```

If we break the connection between interface serial 0 on router R1 and interface serial 1 on router R2, we'll see in Listing 3.8 that the original route disappears along with the route associated with the corresponding interface, and the floating route is added instead.

Listing 3.8   Breaking the connection between routers R1 and R2 makes the corresponding route disappear from the routing table of both routers.

```
R1#
%LINEPROTO-5-UPDOWN: Line protocol on Interface Serial0,
changed state to down
%LINK-3-UPDOWN: Interface Serial0, changed state to down
R1#show ip route
...
C    195.1.0.0 is directly connected, Serial1
C    200.1.0.0 is directly connected, TokenRing0
S    200.2.0.0 [10/0] via 195.1.0.2

R2#
%LINEPROTO-5-UPDOWN: Line protocol on Interface Serial1,
changed state to down
```

3. Static Routing

117

```
%LINK-3-UPDOWN: Interface Serial1, changed state to down
R2#show ip route

...
C    195.1.0.0/24 is directly connected, Serial0
S    200.1.0.0/24 [10/0] via 195.1.0.1
C    200.2.0.0/24 is directly connected, Ethernet0
```

When the line is restored, the original route returns, and the floating route disappears, as shown in Listing 3.9.

Listing 3.9   *When the physical connection is restored, the floating route is superseded by the original "connected" route on both routers.*

```
R1#
%LINK-3-UPDOWN: Interface Serial0, changed state to up
%LINEPROTO-5-UPDOWN: Line protocol on Interface Serial0,
changed state to up
R1#show ip route

...
C    195.1.0.0 is directly connected, Serial1
C    195.0.0.0 is directly connected, Serial0
C    200.1.0.0 is directly connected, TokenRing0
S    200.2.0.0 [1/0] via 195.0.0.2

R2#
%LINK-3-UPDOWN: Interface Serial1, changed state to up
%LINEPROTO-5-UPDOWN: Line protocol on Interface Serial1,
changed state to up
R2#show ip route

...
C    195.1.0.0/24 is directly connected, Serial0
C    195.0.0.0/24 is directly connected, Serial1
S    200.1.0.0/24 [1/0] via 195.0.0.1
C    200.2.0.0/24 is directly connected, Ethernet0
```

There is a relation between the distance and the routes labeled connected in the routing table. When an IP address is assigned to an active interface, the router actually adds a form of a static route into the routing table. Because the interface is connected to that network directly, the router assigns the highest possible distance to that route—0—which denotes the best route to that network. If, for example, you try to overwrite this route with a static route for that network, it will fail because the highest possible distance for a static route is 1, which is greater than 0.

Using Output Interface Instead Of Next-Hop Router With Static Routing

To configure a static route pointing to an interface, use the command **ip route** *<remote network address> <subnet mask> <output interface>*.

From the routing concept standpoint, using an interface instead of a next-hop router may seem strange. How does the router using such a route know which next-hop router to choose?

The answer can be found rather easily, if we take a closer look at the connected routes in the routing table. These routes actually point to interfaces, not to next-hop routers. In the case of connected routes, it's perfectly understandable because the router itself is the last step to these networks. No other router is needed. As discussed in an earlier chapter, when the last-hop router needs to deliver a datagram to the final destination, it tries to resolve the destination's IP address to the corresponding Network Access Layer address, such as a MAC address in the case of LANs. If it succeeds, the router sends the datagram directly to the destination.

Static routes pointing to interfaces actually behave as connected routes. The router assumes that these networks are directly connected and that all traffic destined for them terminates on the segment to which the router's corresponding interface is connected. Therefore, the router does not try to find a next-hop router—it considers itself the next- and the last-hop router. The router tries to resolve the final destination's IP address to the appropriate Network Access Layer address using available methods, such as ARP in the case of LANs. For the sake of simplicity, I call such static routes *pseudo-connected*.

The problem is that although a pseudo-connected static route behaves just like a regular connected route, the router does not actually have an IP address on this "connected" network. Obviously, if some host does have an address on this network, it can't use this router as the default gateway because the router doesn't have an IP address. In other words, the router can deliver packets to the destination network, but it cannot receive the packets from this network because it does not have an IP address on that network. However, if the destination host relies on ProxyARP, it does not need the default gateway or some other type of a route. It can use a router, which has only a pseudo-connected static route for that network.

Alternatively, instead of a ProxyARP-enabled host, another router can pick up the first router's ARP request and reply with its own MAC address. This new router can serve as the ProxyARP server for the first router, and it can potentially route the packet farther toward the actual destination. This is possible because a static route for a certain network pointing to an interface does not assume that this network must be assigned on the interfaces of the hosts located on the corresponding segment. From the first router's perspective, however, the traffic still terminates on that segment.

For example, two routers in Figure 3.4 are interconnected with a TokenRing segment. They are configured with pseudo-connected static routes for the networks located behind each other and pointing to their respective TokenRing interfaces.

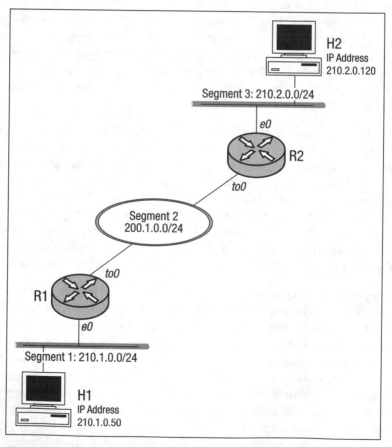

Figure 3.4   *Two routers use static routes pointing to their TokenRing interfaces to forward the packets exchanged by hosts H1 and H2.*

Listings 3.10 and 3.11 show the configurations of both routers.

Listing 3.10 Router R1's configuration.

```
interface Ethernet0
 ip address 210.1.0.1 255.255.255.0

interface TokenRing0
 ip address 200.1.0.1 255.255.255.0
 ring-speed 16

ip route 210.2.0.0 255.255.255.0 TokenRing0
```

Listing 3.11 Router R2's configuration.

```
interface Ethernet0
 ip address 210.2.0.1 255.255.255.0

interface TokenRing0
 ip address 200.1.0.2 255.255.255.0
 ring-speed 16

ip route 210.1.0.0 255.255.255.0 TokenRing0
```

The routing table on the routers is shown in Listings 3.12 and 3.13.

Listing 3.12 The routing table of router R1.

```
R1#show ip route

...
C    200.1.0.0 is directly connected, TokenRing0
S    210.2.0.0 is directly connected, TokenRing0
C    210.1.0.0 is directly connected, Ethernet0
```

Listing 3.13 The routing table of router R2.

```
R2#show ip route

...
C    200.1.0.0/24 is directly connected, TokenRing0
C    210.2.0.0/24 is directly connected, Ethernet0
S    210.1.0.0/24 is directly connected, TokenRing0
```

Notice how the real connected routes differ from the pseudo-connected static routes. The real connected routes are labeled with the letter "C," which stands for connected, whereas the pseudo-connected routes are still labeled with the letter "S," which stands for static.

Suppose the **ping** command is used to verify reachability of host H2 from host H1. If you enter the **debug arp** command on router R1, the output of which is shown in Listing 3.14, you should be able to see how the routers handle their mutual ProxyARP "relationship."

*Listing 3.14   The output of the command **debug arp** entered on router R1.*

```
R1#debug arp
ARP packet debugging is on
R1#
IP ARP: creating incomplete entry for IP address: 210.2.0.120
IP ARP: sent req src 200.1.0.1 0007.0d26.0a46,
               dst 210.2.0.120 0000.0000.0000 TokenRing0
IP ARP: rcvd rep src 210.2.0.120 0007.0d26.0c15,
 dst 200.1.0.1 TokenRing0
IP ARP: rcvd req src 200.1.0.2 0007.0d26.0c15,
 dst 210.1.0.50 TokenRing0
IP ARP: creating entry for IP address: 200.1.0.2,
 hw: 0007.0d26.0c15
IP ARP: sent rep src 210.1.0.50 0007.0d26.0a46,
               dst 200.1.0.2 0007.0d26.0c15 TokenRing0
```

First, router R1 uses ARP to resolve host H2's IP address to the MAC address. Router R2 replies with its TokenRing MAC address. The original **ping** packet that caused this exchange of ARP requests/replies is then delivered to host H2, and host H2 sends a reply. Router R2 now needs to know host H1's MAC address so it uses ARP. Router R1 becomes the ProxyARP server and replies with router R1's TokenRing MAC address.

There is a similarity between the pseudo-connected static routes and the secondary IP addresses that can be assigned on a router interface. Both create routes for the corresponding network address in the routing table, which appear to be connected—that is, both point to an interface instead of to a next-hop router. The difference between pseudo-connected static routes and secondary IP addresses is that the secondary IP address is an IP address; therefore, it can be used by other devices connected to the segment as the default gateway or somehow else. Pseudo-connected routes do not create appropriate IP addresses; the router is connected to a network for which it has a route, but no IP address from that network.

Using pseudo-connected routes should generally be considered as a temporary measure. They lead to excessive broadcast traffic on the segments referenced in the pseudo-static routes and make overall configuration much more complex and prone to problems. This is also the case with secondary IP addresses.

Configuring Classless Routing

Classless routing is enabled on the Cisco routers by entering the command **ip classless** in the global configuration mode. This command makes the router use the best available supernet address if the following applies:

- One or more router's interfaces are configured with an IP address from the subnets of the network address to which the destination IP address belongs.

- The destination IP address belongs to a subnet for which the router does not have a route.

- The routing table of the router does not have a route for the whole network.

- The routing table of the router contains one or more routes for supernets to which the destination IP address belongs.

Without the **ip classless** command, the router drops the packet destined for an IP address that meets these conditions. If this command is used and if one or more supernet routes matches the destination IP address, the router forwards the datagram.

Let's consider the example shown in Figure 3.5.

Router R1 does not have an individual route for network 150.1.2.0/24. Instead, it is configured with static supernet route 150.0.0.0/8. See Listings 3.15 and 3.16.

Listing 3.15   Router R1's configuration.

```
interface Ethernet0
 ip address 150.1.1.1 255.255.255.0

interface Serial0
 ip address 150.1.254.1 255.255.255.0

ip route 150.0.0.0 255.0.0.0 150.1.254.2
```

Listing 3.16   Router R2's configuration.

```
interface Ethernet0
 ip address 150.1.2.1 255.255.255.0

interface Serial1
 ip address 150.1.254.2 255.255.255.0

ip route 150.1.1.0 255.255.255.0 150.1.254.1
```

3. Static Routing

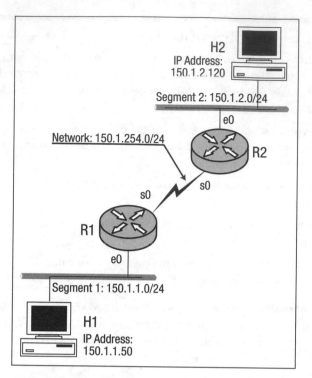

Figure 3.5   Router R1 is only configured with supernet route 150.0.0.0/8 for segment 2.

At this point, router R1 does not have the command **ip classless** in its configuration. If you try to **ping** host H2 from host H1, you will see the **ping** output similar to the one shown in Listing 3.17.

Listing 3.17   Classful routing algorithm does not allow using the supernet route for address 150.0.0.0/8.

```
C:\>ping 150.1.2.120

Pinging 150.1.2.120 with 32 bytes of data:

Reply from 150.1.1.1: Destination host unreachable.
Reply from 150.1.1.1: Destination host unreachable.
Reply from 150.1.1.1: Destination host unreachable.
Reply from 150.1.1.1: Destination host unreachable.
```

After you enter the command **ip classless** on router R1, the output of the **ping** command shown in Listing 3.18 indicates that communication is possible.

Listing 3.18   When the routing algorithm is changed from classful to classless, the connectivity becomes established.

```
C:\>ping 150.1.2.120

Pinging 150.1.2.120 with 32 bytes of data:

Reply from 150.1.2.120: bytes=32 time=40ms TTL=126
Reply from 150.1.2.120: bytes=32 time=30ms TTL=126
Reply from 150.1.2.120: bytes=32 time=30ms TTL=126
Reply from 150.1.2.120: bytes=32 time=30ms TTL=126
```

NOTE: *Despite the description of the command **ip classless** that you can find in the Cisco documentation (which states that this command is always disabled by default), some later versions of the Cisco IOS have this command enabled by default.*

Configuring A Default Gateway On A Router

A default gateway is a supernet route that is used when no other route matches the destination IP address. By definition, the default gateway is represented in the routing table as the route for network prefix 0.0.0.0/0.

To configure a default gateway on a router, the command **ip route 0.0.0.0 0.0.0.0** *<next-hop router>* should be used in the global configuration mode. The command should be used in conjunction with the command **ip classless**.

Configuring Individual Host Routes

Using the command **ip route** *<IP address>* **255.255.255.255** *<next-hop router>*, you can configure an individual host route. The IP address used in the command does not have to be a host's IP address—for example, it can be one of a router's IP addresses.

The router configured in Listing 3.19 has an individual host route for 200.2.0.120.

3. Static Routing

Listing 3.19   Router R1's configuration.

```
interface Serial0
 ip address 195.0.0.1 255.255.255.0

interface Serial1
 ip address 195.1.0.1 255.255.255.0

ip route 200.2.0.0 255.255.255.0 195.0.0.2
ip route 200.2.0.120 255.255.255.255 195.1.0.2
```

Notice in the routing table in Listing 3.20 that the router uses two different interfaces for routing traffic to a host whose address is 200.2.0.120 and to the other hosts on network 200.2.0.0/24.

Listing 3.20   The routing table of router R1.

```
R1#show ip route
...
C    195.1.0.0/24 is directly connected, Serial1
C    195.0.0.0/24 is directly connected, Serial0
C    200.1.0.0/24 is directly connected, TokenRing0
     200.2.0.0/24 is variably subnetted, 2 subnets, 2 masks
S       200.2.0.120/32 [1/0] via 195.1.0.2
S       200.2.0.0/24 [1/0] via 195.0.0.2
```

Individual host routes are generally used either for debugging purposes or in emergencies when the main route to a certain network is no longer available.

Configuring Equal Cost Load Balancing Using Static Routing

A router performs load balancing if it has up to six static routes going to the same destination. (The number of routes over which a router can perform load balancing may change in future releases of the Cisco IOS.) The router assumes that all routes have the same bandwidth regardless of what the actual bandwidths are. Therefore, the router distributes the outgoing traffic among multiple routes equally. As it was explained in this chapter's "In Brief" section, this type of load balancing is called *equal cost* load balancing.

NOTE: *Notice that load balancing is only performed over the outgoing traffic. The router has no control over the incoming traffic, which can arrive on a single interface.*

To configure load balancing, you must enter several statements containing the same destination network but pointing to different next-hop routers or different interfaces.

For example, in Figure 3.6, routers R1 and R2 are interconnected with two serial connections going in parallel.

Listings 3.21 and 3.22 show the configurations of these two routers.

Listing 3.21   Router R1's configuration.

```
interface Serial0
  ip address 195.0.0.1 255.255.255.0
```

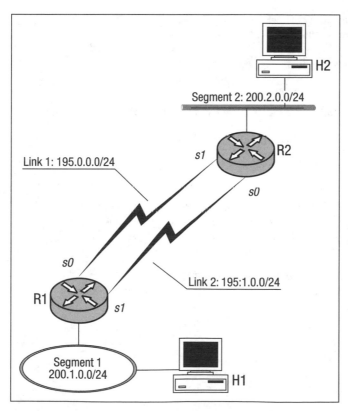

Figure 3.6   Two routers perform load balancing over two parallel serial connections.

```
interface Serial1
 ip address 195.1.0.1 255.255.255.0

interface TokenRing0
 ip address 200.1.0.1 255.255.255.0
 ring-speed 16

ip route 200.2.0.0 255.255.255.0 195.0.0.2
ip route 200.2.0.0 255.255.255.0 195.1.0.2
```

Listing 3.22   Router R2's configuration.

```
interface Ethernet0
 ip address 200.2.0.1 255.255.255.0

interface Serial0
 ip address 195.1.0.2 255.255.255.0

interface Serial1
 ip address 195.0.0.2 255.255.255.0

ip route 200.1.0.0 255.255.255.0 195.0.0.1
ip route 200.1.0.0 255.255.255.0 195.1.0.1
```

Listings 3.23 and 3.24 display the routing tables of both routers.

Listing 3.23   The routing table of router R1.

```
R1#show ip route
...
C    195.1.0.0 is directly connected, Serial1
C    195.0.0.0 is directly connected, Serial0
C    200.1.0.0 is directly connected, TokenRing0
S    200.2.0.0 [1/0] via 195.0.0.2
               [1/0] via 195.1.0.2
```

Listing 3.24   The routing table of router R2.

```
R2#show ip route
...
C    195.1.0.0/24 is directly connected, Serial0
C    195.0.0.0/24 is directly connected, Serial1
S    200.1.0.0/24 [1/0] via 195.0.0.1
                  [1/0] via 195.1.0.1
C    200.2.0.0/24 is directly connected, Ethernet0
```

Notice how the routers display the presence of two or more routes for the same destination. They do not copy the destination subnet or network address for each route; instead, they leave all of the spaces normally occupied by the destination address blank except for the first line.

Also notice that both routers are configured with two static routes. As mentioned before, configuring multiple static routes on a single router enables load balancing on this router only. If the other router or routers involved are configured with single routes, the traffic is only sent over these single routes.

As it was mentioned in this chapter's "In Brief" section, the Cisco routers can perform load balancing in two modes: *per destination* and *per packet*. The router performs per destination load balancing if it is configured for *fast switching* of IP traffic. Fast switching means that the router maintains a cache of the destination addresses, so that it does not perform a routing table lookup each time that a packet destined for the same address arrives on an interface. As long as an IP address remains in the cache, the router always uses the same output interface when forwarding packets to that address. You can specifically enable fast switching using the command **ip route-cache**. Normally, fast switching is enabled by default, and this command usually does not appear in the router configuration.

NOTE: *The high-end Cisco routers (such as RSM modules in the Catalyst switches) or Cisco series 7500 routers (especially those with VIP modules) have more fast switching modes. For more information on these modes, please refer to the Cisco documentation.*

Per packet load balancing is performed when fast switching is disabled. The router distributes the packets going to the same destination in a round-robin fashion among all output interfaces pointing to that destination. You can disable fast switching using the command **no ip route-cache**. Usually, this is not recommended, because, except for overflowed slow links or heavy traffic bursts, the Cisco routers perform better with fast switching enabled.

Disabling fast switching temporarily may be useful for two practical purposes:

- By using the command **debug ip packet**, you can see how the packets are forwarded. If fast switching is enabled, this command only produces output if the packets either originate from or are destined for the router itself.

- By using **debug ip packet**, you can actually see how the load balancing is performed. For example, if host H1 in Figure 3.6 has

IP address 200.1.0.15 and host H2 IP address 200.2.0.120, the routers produce the output shown in Listings 3.25 and 3.26 when host H1 pings host H2.

Listing 3.25   The output of the command _debug ip packet_ entered on router R1.

```
IP: s=200.1.0.15 (TokenRing0), d=200.2.0.120 (Serial0),
  g=195.0.0.2, len 82, forward
IP: s=200.2.0.120 (Serial0), d=200.1.0.15 (TokenRing0),
  g=200.1.0.15, len 64, forward
IP: s=200.1.0.15 (TokenRing0), d=200.2.0.120 (Serial1),
  g=195.1.0.2, len 82, forward
IP: s=200.2.0.120 (Serial1), d=200.1.0.15 (TokenRing0),
  g=200.1.0.15, len 64, forward
IP: s=200.1.0.15 (TokenRing0), d=200.2.0.120 (Serial0),
  g=195.0.0.2, len 82, forward
IP: s=200.2.0.120 (Serial0), d=200.1.0.15 (TokenRing0),
  g=200.1.0.15, len 64, forward
IP: s=200.1.0.15 (TokenRing0), d=200.2.0.120 (Serial1),
  g=195.1.0.2, len 82, forward
IP: s=200.2.0.120 (Serial1), d=200.1.0.15 (TokenRing0),
  g=200.1.0.15, len 64, forward
```

Listing 3.26   The output of the command _debug ip packet_ entered on router R2.

```
IP: s=200.1.0.15 (Serial1), d=200.2.0.120 (Ethernet0),
  g=200.2.0.120, len 60, forward
IP: s=200.2.0.120 (Ethernet0), d=200.1.0.15 (Serial1),
  g=195.0.0.1, len 60, forward
IP: s=200.1.0.15 (Serial0), d=200.2.0.120 (Ethernet0),
  g=200.2.0.120, len 60, forward
IP: s=200.2.0.120 (Ethernet0), d=200.1.0.15 (Serial0),
  g=195.1.0.1, len 60, forward
IP: s=200.1.0.15 (Serial1), d=200.2.0.120 (Ethernet0),
  g=200.2.0.120, len 60, forward
IP: s=200.2.0.120 (Ethernet0), d=200.1.0.15 (Serial1),
  g=195.0.0.1, len 60, forward
IP: s=200.1.0.15 (Serial0), d=200.2.0.120 (Ethernet0),
  g=200.2.0.120, len 60, forward
IP: s=200.2.0.120 (Ethernet0), d=200.1.0.15 (Serial0),
  g=195.1.0.1, len 60, forward
```

Notice how the routers alternate the serial interfaces when forwarding the packets.

Load balancing does not necessarily require parallel links between two routers. It is possible to configure static routes pointing to different next-hop routers so that load balancing is enabled. However, the more routers and links interconnecting them, the more complex the configurations of individual routers become. Usually, load balancing is automatically achieved using dynamic routing protocols, which can populate all necessary routes to the routing table to achieve optimal performance. Load balancing using static routing is, therefore, usually limited to either parallel links or to very symmetrical configurations such as the one shown in Figure 3.7. It's easy to configure static routes on routers R1 and R4 so that the traffic going between segments 1 and 2 is split equally between two paths going through routers R2 and R3.

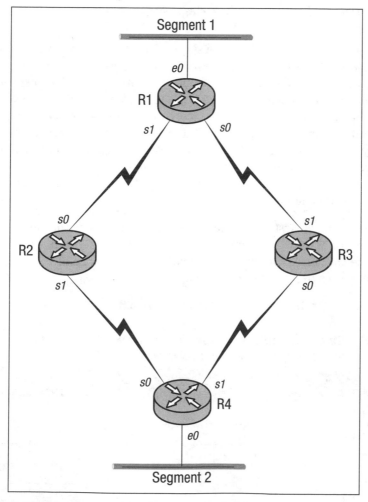

Figure 3.7   Four-router configuration, which enables load balancing of the traffic between segments 1 and 2.

Configuring Unequal Cost Load Balancing Using Static Routing

However improbable it may sound, nevertheless, unequal cost load balancing can be performed using static routing. Unfortunately, such load balancing is fairly limited. Still, the solution demonstrated in this section is rather neat and really unique.

NOTE: *This solution was posted by Steve Kann to the newsgroup called comp.dcom.sys.cisco. Aside from being neat, this helped overcome the stereotypes that we technical "gurus" develop working with the technology and sometimes following the directions given by vendors too blindly, such as "static routing only allows equal cost load balancing." Thank you, Steve!*

This solution is based on a very simple fact that the router actually splits the traffic among the routes for the same destination, not among the interfaces. For example, if a router has three routes for a certain destination pointing to one interface and two routes for the same destination pointing to another interface, the router sends three-fifths of the traffic over the first interface and two-fifths over the other. Obviously, this type of unequal cost load balancing is limited in terms of variety of ratios because the router can split the traffic among not more than six routers. Table 3.1 shows several ratios, which may be useful in some situations.

Probably the easiest way to implement multiple routes for the same destination is by using secondary addresses on the interfaces involved and then setting static routes that point to the primary and secondary IP addresses of the next hop router.

Let's consider the example shown in Figure 3.8.

Table 3.1   Traffic split ratios achievable through varying the number of routes pointing to two different interfaces.

Load Split Ratios	Number of Routes Pointing to Interface 1	Number of Routes Pointing to Interface 2
1/3 and 2/3	1	2
1/4 and 3/4	1	3
1/5 and 4/5	1	4
1/6 and 5/6	1	5
2/5 and 3/5	2	3

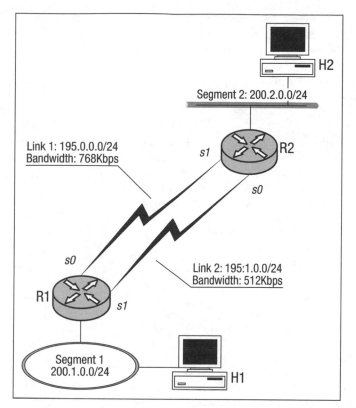

Figure 3.8   The actual bandwidths of the two links between router R1 and R2 are 768Kbps and 512Kbps.

As Figure 3.8 suggests, the link bandwidths are 768Kbps and 512Kbps. These two numbers relate to each other as 3/5 and 2/5. According to Table 3.1, the necessary traffic split ratio can be achieved using three routes pointing to the interfaces connected to the first link and two routes pointing to the interfaces connected to the second link.

Listings 3.27 and 3.28 are two sample configurations that when entered on routers R1 and R2 will perform load splitting with the specified ratio.

Listing 3.27   Router R1's configuration.

```
interface Serial0
 ip address 195.0.0.1 255.255.255.0
 ip address 195.0.0.2 255.255.255.0 secondary
 ip address 195.0.0.3 255.255.255.0 secondary
```

```
interface Serial1
 ip address 195.1.0.1 255.255.255.0
 ip address 195.1.0.2 255.255.255.0 secondary

interface TokenRing0
 ip address 200.1.0.1 255.255.255.0
 ring-speed 16

ip route 200.2.0.0 255.255.255.0 195.0.0.4
ip route 200.2.0.0 255.255.255.0 195.0.0.5
ip route 200.2.0.0 255.255.255.0 195.0.0.6
ip route 200.2.0.0 255.255.255.0 195.1.0.3
ip route 200.2.0.0 255.255.255.0 195.1.0.4
```

Listing 3.28   Router R2's configuration.

```
interface Ethernet0
 ip address 200.2.0.1 255.255.255.0

interface Serial0
 ip address 195.1.0.3 255.255.255.0
 ip address 195.1.0.4 255.255.255.0 secondary

interface Serial1
 ip address 195.0.0.4 255.255.255.0
 ip address 195.0.0.5 255.255.255.0 secondary
 ip address 195.0.0.6 255.255.255.0 secondary

ip route 200.1.0.0 255.255.255.0 195.0.0.1
ip route 200.1.0.0 255.255.255.0 195.0.0.2
ip route 200.1.0.0 255.255.255.0 195.0.0.3
ip route 200.1.0.0 255.255.255.0 195.1.0.1
ip route 200.1.0.0 255.255.255.0 195.1.0.2
```

If you turn off fast switching, you can use the command **debug ip packet** to make sure that the traffic is really split with the necessary ratio. Listing 3.29 shows sample output of the **debug ip packet** command typed in on router R1. Notice how the router alternates the output interface (which is italicized, and the output lines are truncated to make it easier to follow).

Listing 3.29   The output of the command *debug ip packet* entered on router R1.

```
IP: s=200.2.0.120 (Serial0), d=200.1.0.15 (TokenRing0), ...
IP: s=200.2.0.120 (Serial0), d=200.1.0.15 (TokenRing0), ...
IP: s=200.2.0.120 (Serial0), d=200.1.0.15 (TokenRing0), ...
IP: s=200.2.0.120 (Serial1), d=200.1.0.15 (TokenRing0), ...
IP: s=200.2.0.120 (Serial1), d=200.1.0.15 (TokenRing0), ...
IP: s=200.2.0.120 (Serial0), d=200.1.0.15 (TokenRing0), ...
IP: s=200.2.0.120 (Serial0), d=200.1.0.15 (TokenRing0), ...
IP: s=200.2.0.120 (Serial0), d=200.1.0.15 (TokenRing0), ...
IP: s=200.2.0.120 (Serial1), d=200.1.0.15 (TokenRing0), ...
IP: s=200.2.0.120 (Serial1), d=200.1.0.15 (TokenRing0), ...
```

3. Static Routing

Dynamic Routing: Distance Vector Routing Protocols

If you need an immediate solution to:	See page:
Configuring Classful Routing Protocols	148
Configuring RIP	148
Using Individual Host Addresses With RIP	158
Configuring RIP To Originate The Default Route	160
Using RIP In The Presence Of Secondary IP Addresses	161
Preventing RIP From Sending Routing Updates On An Interface	165
Using Unicast Routing Updates With RIP	167
Discriminating Incoming Routing Updates	169
Configuring Equal Cost Load Balancing With RIP	173
Changing RIP Metrics	175
Configuring RIP Over Non-Fully Meshed Frame Relay Networks	177
Configuring IGRP	182
Understanding IGRP Metrics	184
Configuring Equal And Unequal Cost Load Balancing With IGRP	187
Configuring Classless Routing Protocols	192
Dividing IP Address Space For Use With VLSM	192
Configuring RIP Version 2	202
Disabling RIP Version 2 Auto-Summarization	208
Using RIP Version 1 And RIP Version 2 Simultaneously	209
Configuring EIGRP	210
Understanding EIGRP Metrics	213
Disabling EIGRP Auto-Summarization	213
Configuring Route Summarization With EIGRP	214
Configuring EIGRP Over Non-Fully Meshed Frame Relay Networks	216

In Brief

Dynamic routing protocols are special-purpose protocols that are used to maintain the routing table of a router or a regular host. The routing protocols perform the exchange of special packets, called *routing updates*, that contain information used to populate routes to the routing table. The routing updates are specific to a particular routing protocol and cannot be received and interpreted by other routing protocols.

NOTE: *Routing protocols should not be confused with routed protocols. Routed protocols are the protocols that are actually routed by the routers using the information stored in the routing tables. For example, IP and IPX are routed protocols. Different routed protocols in most cases use different routing tables. For example, if a single router is used to route IP and IPX, it will have two separate routing tables—one for IP and one for IPX.*

The routing protocols fall into two categories: *interior routing protocols*, or *IGPs*, and *exterior routing protocols*, or *EGPs*. IGPs are used to route IP traffic within a single *autonomous system*. An autonomous system is, generally speaking, a group of networks under the same administrative authority. Examples of autonomous systems are corporate networks, ISPs' networks, and so on. EGPs are used to route traffic between autonomous systems. The use of EGPs is most often associated with routing in the Internet; however, EGPs can be used to route traffic between autonomous systems that are not connected to the Internet.

IGPs and IP routing within an autonomous system is the primary subject of this book. EGPs and routing in the Internet are very complex and require a separate book for a comprehensive discussion.

Aside from being categorized into IGPs or EGPs, dynamic routing protocols can also be categorized by the type of algorithm on which they are based. Two types of algorithms are used in the dynamic routing protocols: *distance vector* and *link state*. This chapter discusses the distance vector–based routing protocols, commonly referred to as *distance vector protocols*, available on the Cisco routers. The next chapter is devoted to the link state based routing protocols.

Distance Vector Algorithm

The original algorithm on which the distance vector algorithm is based was first invented by Bellman in 1957 and then by Ford and Fulkerson in 1962. For that reason, this algorithm has two names: Bellman-Ford algorithm and Ford-Fulkerson algorithm.

Before we examine the distance vector algorithm itself we need to discuss its specific terminology and assumptions, which are described in the next paragraphs.

Routers that use the same distance vector routing protocol can only exchange routing updates if they are separated by a single physical network. In other words, the routing updates cannot be routed (by intermediate routers), which is perfectly understandable because the routing updates are used to establish routing. The routers that exchange routing updates are called *neighbors*.

The routing information is exchanged in the form of routing updates, which are the PDUs of the respective routing protocol. The routing updates normally contain the network prefixes and protocol-specific metrics of these prefixes. The network prefixes are said to be *advertised* by the router when the router sends them in the routing updates.

The metrics generally reflect how far away from the advertised network prefix the router perceives itself to be. The router uses the metrics to find the best route for each network prefix, which is added to the routing table. All other routing updates advertising that same network prefix are disregarded.

The metrics are really routing protocol specific and can vary greatly from protocol to protocol according to how they are represented and calculated. Nevertheless, all distance vector routing protocols follow these considerations when calculating the metrics:

- Each interface on a router serviced by a certain routing protocol has a cost. The cost is protocol specific.

- When a router receives a routing update, it recalculates the metrics of the advertised network prefix using the cost of the interface, through which it will forward the datagrams destined for that network prefix. In most cases, this interface coincides with the interface on which the routing update was received.

- The new metric that the router calculates must be greater than the one it received in the original routing update, because it must incorporate the cost of the output interface.

- The router advertises the remote network prefixes using the recalculated metrics.

Given these assumptions, the distance vector algorithm boils down to the following. Initially, before a router has received any routing updates, it only advertises the networks to which it is directly connected. As it receives routing updates from other routers on directly connected segments, it recalculates the metrics for the learned network prefixes and starts advertising these network prefixes itself. Eventually all routers on all segments will learn all of the network prefixes used throughout the network.

NOTE: *Notice that the routers that use distance vector protocols have no knowledge of the intermediate networks along the path to the network prefixes that they advertise in the routing updates. Therefore, the distance vector algorithm is sometimes called routing by rumors.*

In a stable network, the routing table of every router should not change after it has been populated by a routing protocol. However, nearly every stable network can temporarily become unstable. In this event, the dynamic routing protocols handle the changes, whether they are caused by additions, removals, or failures of network components.

The distance vector protocols handle the changes using the following two techniques:

- If a new segment is added to a network, the router for the segment being connected starts advertising the network prefix assigned to that segment. This is how the routers on the network learn of the new segment's existence. At the same time, the router sends routing updates about the rest of the network to this new segment. If there are any other routers on this segment, they eventually receive the first router's routing updates, and the first router eventually receives the routing updates from these other routers.

- Network component removals and failures are addressed as follows: First, the routers exchange the routing updates on a regular basis (for example, every 30 seconds). Second, for every route installed in the routing table, the router maintains a special timer. The timer is reset each time the router receives a routing update for that network prefix. If the timer expires, the router removes the route from operation.

NOTE: *The way in which different distance vector routing protocols use the regular updates and timers may not necessarily follow the preceding procedure. Primitive routing protocols, such as RIP or IGRP, exchange routing updates on a regular basis for all network prefixes for which they have routes. More sophisticated routing protocols—for example, EIGRP—do not exchange routing updates regularly. Instead, they exchange small hello messages, which indicate whether the router itself or the segment over which the hello messages are sent is functioning properly. Likewise, the router does not maintain timers for the routes but does keep track of the hello messages. If the router misses a certain number of the hello messages, it declares the respective neighhbor down and recalculates the metrics of the affected routes.*

Distance Vector Algorithm Refinements: Split-Horizon Rule, Holddowns, And Triggered Updates

It takes the routers a certain amount of time to communicate information about network changes with each other. Until the network changes are conveyed to every router, some segments of the network may not be accessible because not all of the routers may have the correct "after-the-change" routes for these segments. The process of making the routing tables of all routers consistent is called *convergence*.

The time during which convergence occurs is called *convergence time*. The convergence time depends on the employed dynamic routing protocol. Different protocols have different convergence times. Regardless of the particular implementation, all routing protocols based on the distance vector algorithm suffer from the same problem known as *counting-to-infinity*.

To understand the counting-to-infinity problem, let's consider the network shown in Figure 4.1

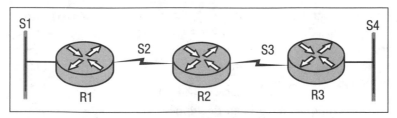

Figure 4.1 *A simple network topology that demonstrates the counting-to-infinity problem.*

Let's suppose all three routers use the same distance vector routing protocol. Also assume that convergence is achieved—that is, all three routers know about all of the networks. As we know, the routers exchange routing updates in case something fails. For example, router R2 advertises segment S1 via both of its interfaces. Router R3, not having a better route for segment S1, picks up router R2's update. Because router R1 is directly connected to segment S1 and therefore has a better metric for segment S1, it ignores router R2's updates for segment S1. Suppose now that segment S2 fails. Router R2 starts a timer for segment S1. Eventually the timer expires, and router R2 stops considering segment S1 as available via router R1. Until this happens, router R2 continues to advertise segment S1, which means that router R3 does not even know that router R2 has stopped receiving updates from router R1. After router R2's timer for segment S1 expires, router R2 considers an alternative route for that segment. Eventually, router R2 gets the update from router R3, with R3's metrics. Router R2 recalculates its own metric for this new route and sends it back to router R3 in the next regular update. Router R3 then sees that the routing updates for segment S1 from router R2 have a worse metric, so router R3 recalculate its own metric which it sends out with the next regular update. Each iteration of this process makes the route to segment S1 worse, although it will never disappear.

The easiest way to solve this problem is to consider any network prefix unreachable if the metric of the route is greater than a certain value. This value is called *infinity*; thus, the problem is called *counting to infinity*. As this value is reached, the corresponding network prefix is declared unreachable.

Although the routers eventually "count to infinity," this process takes time. In addition, during the counting-to-infinity process, the routers believe that a route for the affected network prefix is still available. Because both routers point to each other, this creates a routing loop. Therefore, any traffic destined for the affected network prefix is still forwarded, but because of the loop, the traffic continues to go around totally uselessly, until the time-to-leave field expires. During this period, the links between the routers can become very congested, which in turn makes the routers often delay and even drop the useful traffic destined for the networks.

A few techniques have been developed to eliminate or lessen this counting-to-infinity problem.

Split Horizon

The first technique is called a *split-horizon rule*. This rule forbids a router to advertise a network prefix via the interface from which it learned of the prefix. In our example, the routers would not encounter the counting-to-infinity problem at all if they obeyed the split-horizon rule.

A more aggressive version of the split-horizon rule is known as the *split-horizon with poisoned reverse*. This rule instructs the router to advertise a network prefix via the interface from which it learned of the prefix with the metric set to infinity.

Although the split-horizon rules are very important tools in improving convergence of distance vector algorithms, they may not help in all situations. Let's consider the network shown in Figure 4.2 as an example.

Suppose all routers respect both versions of the split-horizon rule. Segment S2 goes down. Eventually, router R2 times out the route for segment S1 via router R1. Until this happens, router R2 continues to advertise segment S1 to routers R3 and R4 as available. In turn, routers R3 and R4 continue to advertise their routes for segment S1 to each other. As router R2 stops sending updates, routers R3 and R4 start their own timers for the routing update from R2. When these expire, routers R3 and R4 pick up the routes from each other and advertise them back to router R2. This establishes a temporary routing loop.

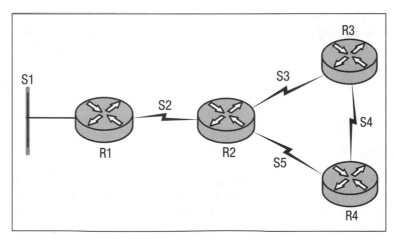

Figure 4.2   *A network topology in which the split-horizon rule will not solve the counting-to-infinity problem.*

Holddowns

Another technique is called *holddowns*. It is even simpler than the split-horizon rule. The route, in addition to the regular route timer, also maintains a *garbage collection timer*. The router starts the garbage collection timer when the regular timer expires. The router also declares the corresponding network prefix unreachable by setting the route's metric to infinity. Until the garbage collection timer expires, the route cannot be removed from the routing table or modified even if another routing update for that network prefix arrives.

The purpose of holddowns is to avoid routing loops, thus preserving the remaining links from congestion.

Triggered Updates

One more technique is called *triggered updates*. This method requires a router to send an update whenever the metrics of any route change. The purpose of triggered updates is to propagate the information about network failures as fast as possible, so that no router mistakenly tries to advertise the network prefix from a failed network segment.

Administrative Distance

A single router may possibly run several IP routing protocols. If so, an ambiguity may arise when two or more routing protocols attempt to install routes for the same destination (expressed as a network prefix) to the routing table. To resolve such ambiguities, a special numeric value called *administrative distance* is associated with each routing protocol, which reflects the level of trust that the router has in the routing information supplied by the respective routing protocol. The lower the administrative distance, the more the protocol is trusted. If, for example, a routing protocol with an administrative distance of 100 tries to establish a route to destination 10.1.0.0/16 and this route has already been established by another protocol with an administrative distance of 70, the new route is discarded. If, however, the first protocol's administrative distance is 50 (as opposed to 100), its route supersedes the existing one.

Because it's very unlikely that separate routing protocols can attempt to install routes for the same destination simultaneously, the router stores the administrative distance of the protocol that successfully installed a route along with the route. Thus, if a protocol tries to install a route for the destination for which another route already exists, the first route will supersede the existing route only if the administrative distance of the protocol submitting it is lower than the stored administrate distance of the protocol that installed the existing route. For that reason, the administrative distance can be associated not only with the routing protocol but also with the routes the protocol installs.

The administrative distance in the Cisco IOS is a positive integer value, ranging from 0 to 255.

In addition to routing protocols, the other two sources of routing information—static routing and connected routes—also have administrative distances. All of these sources have default values for their administrative distances. Table 4.1 shows the default values for all sources of routing information available on the Cisco routers.

The administrative distances of all other routing information sources can be changed from their default. Exceptions are the administrative distances of connected routes, which are always 0, and EIGRP summary routes, which are always 5.

Following is a brief summary of how the routers handle all of the components we have just discussed.

- The router uses the routing metrics only in the scope of a particular dynamic routing protocol. If a router receives multiple routing updates that advertise the same network prefix, the router chooses the one with the best metric. This route is submitted for installation into the routing table.

Table 4.1   The default values for administrative distances.

Route Source	Default Distance
Connected interface	0
Static route	1
Enhanced IGRP summary route	5
External BGP	20
Internal Enhanced IGRP	90
IGRP	100
OSPF	110
IS-IS	115
RIP	120
EGP	140
Internal BGP	200
Unknown	255

4. Dynamic Routing: Distance Vector Routing Protocols

- If more than one source of routing information (for example, dynamic routing protocols, static routing, and connected routes) tries to install routes for the same network prefix into the routing table, the administrative distance of each method is used to resolve the ambiguity. The route whose method has the smallest administrative distance is installed into the routing table; all other routes are ignored.

- The router uses the routing algorithm when making forwarding decisions. It only looks for the longest match in the routing table to find the best route for the destination.

- A distance vector routing protocol does not advertise a route that it did not install into the routing table.

NOTE: *If a distance vector routing protocol receives a routing update but cannot install the corresponding route into the routing table because it has already been installed there with a smaller administrative distance, the routing protocols will not advertise such a route.*

Classful And Classless Routing Protocols

Dynamic routing protocols (whether they are distance vector or link state) can be classful or classless.

Classful dynamic routing protocols strictly follow the rules and restraints of the classful IP addressing scheme. Although all classful protocols support subnet masks, they require that all subnet masks were the same for all IP addresses belonging to the same classful network address. For example, if network address 10.0.0.0 is used and a certain subnet has the subnet mask 255.255.255.0 (or /24), then all other subnets must use the same subnet mask. However, if address 11.0.0.0 is used in the same network, then its subnets can use a different subnet mask, for example 255.255.240.0 (or /20).

An important feature of classful routing protocols is that they cannot pass the subnet mask in their routing updates. Because these protocols assume that the subnet mask will be the same for all subnets of a certain network address, they will take it from interfaces over which they send and receive routing updates.

Classless routing protocols always send the subnet mask along with the advertised subnet addresses. Classless routing protocols may still follow some of the classful restrictions, although this feature can always be turned off administratively. All classless routing protocols always fully support classless routing.

Immediate Solutions

Configuring distance vector routing protocols on the Cisco routers is fairly easy and very uniform. The basic configuration always includes the following two steps regardless of the chosen routing protocol:

1. Define the routing protocol using the command **router** *<routing protocol>* in the global configuration mode. Some protocols also require an autonomous system number be specified, the meaning of which we'll discuss in the sections devoted to IGRP. This command transfers you to the *routing protocol configuration mode*.

2. Specify the network IP addresses, which should be advertised by the routing protocol, using the command **network** *<network IP address>* in the router configuration mode. You can specify any network address using this command; however, the router only advertises the networks to which it is directly connected. In other words, to advertise a network defined using the **network** command, the router should have at least one active interface with an IP address belonging to that network IP address.

NOTE: *Using the **network** command, you can only specify a classful network address—for example, 10.0.0.0, 150.1.0.0, and so on. You cannot specify individual subnets, even if they are defined on the router's interfaces.*

Step 2 requires some explanation. When the first **network** command is entered, the router assigns the interfaces with IP addresses belonging to the network IP address in the **network** command to the corresponding routing process. On those interfaces, the router starts processing incoming routing updates and sending out its own routing updates. As additional **network** statements are entered, the router automatically adds the corresponding interfaces to the routing process. The interfaces with IP addresses not belonging to any network IP address specified using the **network** command are left out of the routing process completely. The router never sends routing updates via these interfaces, and it ignores all incoming routing updates on them.

Configuring Classful Routing Protocols

The classful routing protocols that are available on the Cisco router are RIP and IGRP. Both are based on the distance vector algorithm; therefore, their operation is very similar. There are a few differences, however. Following are some of the most important:

- RIP is a *de facto* standard protocol available virtually on any IP host and router regardless of the vendor, whereas IGRP is a Cisco proprietary protocol available only on the routers running the Cisco IOS.

- RIP uses very simple metrics, represented by positive integers 1 through 16, where the metric of 16 is considered infinity. RIP calculates the metric of a route as the sum of segments composing the route. IGRP metrics are rather complex and calculated using such characteristics of the paths as bandwidth, delay, and so on. Therefore, the network diameter—the maximum number of router hops that a routing protocol can handle—of IGRP is much bigger than that of RIP.

- There can be only one RIP routing process on a router. On the other hand, there can be multiple IGRP routing processes running on a single router, each servicing a separate autonomous system.

- RIP can advertise individual IP addresses, such as 10.1.0.1/32, whereas IGRP cannot.

Configuring RIP

The very basic configuration of RIP is done using the steps defined at the beginning of the "Immediate Solutions" section in this chapter. The command used on the first step is **router rip** without any arguments.

Let's consider the example shown in Figure 4.3.

Listings 4.1 through 4.4 show the configurations of all four routers.

Listing 4.1   Router R1's configuration.

```
interface Ethernet0
 ip address 200.1.0.1 255.255.255.0

interface Serial0
 ip address 200.3.0.2 255.255.255.0

router rip
 network 200.1.0.0
 network 200.3.0.0
```

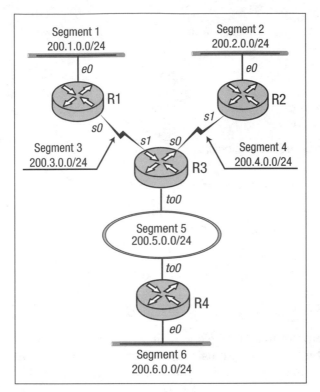

Figure 4.3 *Four routers are configured with RIP to ensure overall connectivity among all six segments.*

Listing 4.2 *Router R2's configuration.*

```
interface Ethernet0
 ip address 200.2.0.1 255.255.255.0

interface Serial1
 ip address 200.4.0.2 255.255.255.0

router rip
 network 200.2.0.0
 network 200.4.0.0
```

Listing 4.3 *Router R3's configuration.*

```
interface Serial0
 ip address 200.4.0.1 255.255.255.0

interface Serial1
 ip address 200.3.0.1 255.255.255.0
```

```
interface TokenRing0
 ip address 200.5.0.1 255.255.255.0
 ring-speed 16

router rip
 network 200.3.0.0
 network 200.4.0.0
 network 200.5.0.0
```

Listing 4.4   Router R4's configuration.

```
interface Ethernet0
 ip address 200.6.0.1 255.255.255.0

interface TokenRing0
 ip address 200.5.0.2 255.255.255.0
 ring-speed 16

router rip
 network 200.5.0.0
 network 200.6.0.0
```

Let's examine router R3. First we'll look at the routing table. As with the static routing, we display it using the command **show ip route**. Router R3's routing table looks like the one shown in Figure 4.4.

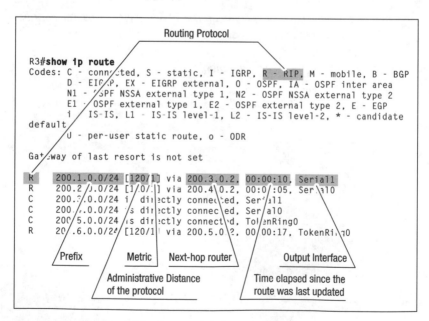

Figure 4.4   Routing table of router R3.

We'll now examine the output of the **show ip route** command. The reason we haven't paid attention to it so far is because we have only used static and connected routes, which are not very diverse, and much of the output of the command does not apply to them. Now, as we start using the dynamic routing protocols, we need to examine the routing table in more detail.

This list describes the key elements of the output of the command **show ip route**:

- The output of the command **show ip route** always begins with six lines of the legend for the first letter that always precedes each line of the routing table. This part of the command output always remains the same, and I will skip over it in subsequent examples.

- The next line indicates whether the gateway of last resort is set. If it is, the line includes its IP address. *Gateway of last resort* is Cisco's name for the default router.

  The rest of the output contains the actual routing table entries. Each entry begins with a letter, which specifies the source of the routing information that established this particular route in the routing table. In Figure 4.4, this letter is "R", which means that the route was learned via routing protocol RIP. The static routes begin with the letter "S".

- The next field in the routing table entry is the network prefix. The way it is displayed depends on the version of IOS that the router is running. The latest versions specify the length of the prefix preceded with the "/" character. Older versions show the prefix followed by the subnet mask in the dotted decimal notation, or the prefix is not displayed at all if the mask is the default (for example, address 150.1.0.0's default mask is 255.255.0.0). Although this can be changed for the duration of a session using the command *terminal ip netmask-format bit-count*, or permanently for a specific terminal line using the command *ip netmask-format bit-count* in the line configuration mode.

- The next two fields are displayed in brackets separated by the "/" character. The first field is the administrative distance of the routing information-source, and the second one is the routing information source-specific metric of the route. In our example, the administrative distance of RIP is 120, and the metric of the route is 1.

- The next field is the next-hop router for that route.

- The next field is the time elapsed since the route was last updated.

- The last field displayed is the output interface.

(This is not the most comprehensive description of the output of the command **show ip route**, but it is enough for our discussion. We will return to it often as we progress through the book.)

RIP uses very simple metrics for the routes. RIP assumes that every network segment has the cost of 1. Thus, it calculates the cumulative cost of a path to the destination simply as the number of the individual segments constituting the path. In the example shown in Figure 4.3, all routes learned via RIP have a metric of 1, which is perfectly understandable. None of them is more than one hop away from router R3. However, if we display the routing table on router R4 (shown in Listing 4.5), the metrics are slightly more diverse.

Listing 4.5   The routing table of router R4.

```
R4#show ip route
...
R    200.1.0.0 [120/2] via 200.5.0.1,00:00:21, TokenRing0
R    200.2.0.0 [120/2] via 200.5.0.1,00:00:21, TokenRing0
R    200.3.0.0 [120/1] via 200.5.0.1,00:00:21, TokenRing0
R    200.4.0.0 [120/1] via 200.5.0.1,00:00:22, TokenRing0
C    200.5.0.0 is directly connected,TokenRing0
C    200.6.0.0 is directly connected,Ethernet0
```

Of course, the route metrics in our example are not very diverse because the diameter of the network is rather small. In real life, however, the metrics can be much larger.

We will now use the command **debug ip rip** to examine how RIP sends and receives the routing updates. Entering this command on router R3 displays the output shown in Listing 4.6.

*Listing 4.6   The output of the command **debug ip rip** demonstrates how router R3 sends and receives RIP routing updates.*

```
R3#debug ip rip
RIP protocol debugging is on
R3#
RIP: received v1 update from 200.3.0.2 on Serial1
     200.1.0.0 in 1 hops
RIP: received v1 update from 200.4.0.2 on Serial0
     200.2.0.0 in 1 hops
RIP: received v1 update from 200.5.0.2 on TokenRing0
     200.6.0.0 in 1 hops
RIP: sending v1 update to 255.255.255.255 via Serial0
(200.4.0.1)
     network 200.1.0.0, metric 2
     network 200.3.0.0, metric 1
```

```
      network 200.5.0.0, metric 1
      network 200.6.0.0, metric 2
RIP: sending v1 update to 255.255.255.255 via Serial1
(200.3.0.1)
      network 200.2.0.0, metric 2
      network 200.4.0.0, metric 1
      network 200.5.0.0, metric 1
      network 200.6.0.0, metric 2
RIP: sending v1 update to 255.255.255.255 via TokenRing0
(200.5.0.1)
      network 200.1.0.0, metric 2
      network 200.2.0.0, metric 2
      network 200.3.0.0, metric 1
      network 200.4.0.0, metric 1
```

WARNING! *Avoid using the command* debug ip rip *or other processing-intensive debug commands on the production routers. This is especially crucial if the routers are processing many routing updates. In most cases, entering such commands will cause the router to be unable to process any terminal access and will greatly degrade its performance. If this happens, only a cold restart will release the router from the lockup.*

Most debug commands are only good for lab experiments. The reason that I use the debug commands in this book is to show what the router actually does and to explain some seemingly difficult cases.

The output is pretty much self-explanatory. Each routing update, either received or sent, is preceded with a line that begins with the words **RIP: sending....** This line is followed by the individual routing entries. Each routing update in RIP can contain up to 25 routing entries.

One interesting observation can be made using the output of the command **debug ip rip** shown in Listing 4.6. The absence of the routes with the metric set to infinity (which is 16 in RIP) indicates that the Cisco's version of RIP uses the simple split-horizon rule as opposed to the split-horizon with poisoned reverse rule.

So far, we have used class C network addresses with the default subnet masks. This is a fairly vanilla configuration, and everything from the routing perspective has gone as expected. Let's now replace some of the class C networks with subnets from class A network 10.0.0.0. Figure 4.5 shows the changes made to the original configuration.

Listings 4.7 through 4.9 show the revised configurations of the routers affected by the addressing change.

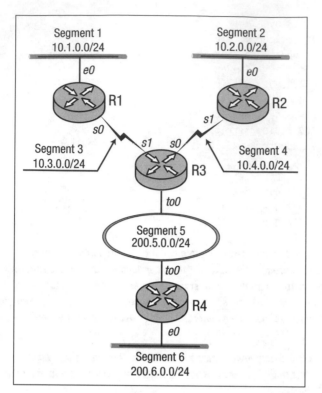

Figure 4.5   Segments 1 through 4 are now configured as subnets of network 10.0.0.0. Segments 5 and 6 retain their original addresses.

Listing 4.7   Router R1's configuration.

```
interface Ethernet0
 ip address 10.1.0.1 255.255.255.0

interface Serial0
 ip address 10.3.0.2 255.255.255.0

router rip
 network 10.0.0.0
```

Listing 4.8   Router R2's configuration.

```
interface Ethernet0
 ip address 10.2.0.1 255.255.255.0

interface Serial1
 ip address 10.4.0.2 255.255.255.0

router rip
 network 10.0.0.0
```

Listing 4.9   Router R3's configuration.

```
interface Serial0
  ip address 10.4.0.1 255.255.255.0

interface Serial1
  ip address 10.3.0.1 255.255.255.0

interface TokenRing0
  ip address 200.5.0.1 255.255.255.0
  ring-speed 16

router rip
  network 10.0.0.0
  network 200.5.0.0
```

As expected, routers R1 and R2 now have only one **network** statement corresponding to the whole class A network 10.0.0.0. Router R3 has two **network** statements: one for network 10.0.0.0 and the other for network 200.5.0.0.

Listing 4.10 shows the routing table of router R1.

Listing 4.10   The routing table of router R1.

```
R1#show ip route

...
     10.0.0.0/24 is subnetted, 4 subnets
R       10.2.0.0 [120/2] via 10.3.0.1, 00:00:23, Serial0
C       10.3.0.0 is directly connected, Serial0
C       10.1.0.0 is directly connected, Ethernet0
R       10.4.0.0 [120/1] via 10.3.0.1, 00:00:23, Serial0
R    200.5.0.0/24 [120/1] via 10.3.0.1, 00:00:23, Serial0
R    200.6.0.0/24 [120/2] via 10.3.0.1, 00:00:23, Serial0
```

The output of the command **show ip route** indicates that network 10.0.0.0 is subnetted and that router R1 knows four subnets of network 10.0.0.0. The rest of the output lines show these four subnets—two directly connected and the other two learned via RIP. Router R1 also learned of networks 200.5.0.0 and 200.6.0.0 via RIP.

Listing 4.11 shows the routing table of router R4.

Listing 4.11   The routing table of router R4.

```
R4#show ip route

...
R    10.0.0.0 [120/1] via 200.5.0.1, 00:00:08, TokenRing0
C    200.5.0.0 is directly connected, TokenRing0
C    200.6.0.0 is directly connected, Ethernet0
```

4. Dynamic Routing: Distance Vector Routing Protocols

155

Now we have a problem. Router R4 has no idea that network 10.0.0.0 is subnetted. Moreover, router R4 thinks that the whole network 10.0.0.0 is just one RIP metric unit away. Why?

The explanation is with router R3. It is the only router that separates router R4 from network 10.0.0.0. To understand what happens at router R3, let's first examine its routing table (shown in Listing 4.12), and then see the routing updates it generates and sends out (shown as the output of the command **debug ip rip** in Listing 4.13).

Listing 4.12   The routing table of router R3.

```
R3#show ip route
...
     10.0.0.0/24 is subnetted, 4 subnets
R       10.2.0.0 [120/1] via 10.4.0.2, 00:00:04, Serial0
C       10.3.0.0 is directly connected, Serial1
R       10.1.0.0 [120/1] via 10.3.0.2, 00:00:02, Serial1
C       10.4.0.0 is directly connected, Serial0
C    200.5.0.0/24 is directly connected, TokenRing0
R    200.6.0.0/24 [120/1] via 200.5.0.2, 00:00:04, TokenRing0
```

Router R3 still knows everything about the subnets of network 10.0.0.0. Listing 4.13 shows the routing updates sent out by router R3.

Listing 4.13   The output of the command *debug ip rip*.

```
R3#debug ip rip
RIP protocol debugging is on
R3#
RIP: sending v1 update to 255.255.255.255 via Serial0 (10.4.0.1)
     subnet  10.3.0.0, metric 1
     subnet  10.1.0.0, metric 2
     network 200.5.0.0, metric 1
     network 200.6.0.0, metric 2
RIP: sending v1 update to 255.255.255.255 via Serial1 (10.3.0.1)
     subnet  10.2.0.0, metric 2
     subnet  10.4.0.0, metric 1
     network 200.5.0.0, metric 1
     network 200.6.0.0, metric 2
RIP: sending v1 update to 255.255.255.255 via TokenRing0
(200.5.0.1)
     network 10.0.0.0, metric 1
```

Here's what is happening. Through the TokenRing interface, router R3 sends an update with only one routing entry for network 10.0.0.0 marked as one hop away. Nevertheless, router R3 sends fully qualified routing updates via both Serial 0 and Serial 1 interfaces.

The explanation for this behavior of router R3 is simple. RIP, being a classful routing protocol, does not pass the subnet masks along with network prefixes in the routing updates. Therefore, RIP can only "guess" what the subnet mask is for any specific route that it receives in incoming routing updates. RIP does this guessing by applying the mask defined on the interface through which the update was received for the routes to the subnets from the same network IP address to which the interface's IP address belongs. If the update also contains routes to IP addresses that do not belong to the interface's network address, RIP assumes that they are either the classful network addresses or individual host addresses if any of the host bits are set. Likewise, the router advertises subnets out of an interface only if the subnets are from the same network as the interface's IP address. Otherwise, the subnets are replaced with the network addresses to which they belong, which are advertised out of the interface with metric 1. This process is called *auto-summarization*.

Obviously, the IP address interface of TokenRing 0 does not belong to network 10.0.0.0. That's why router R3 summarized all subnets of network 10.0.0.0 into one route for network 10.0.0.0 itself, which was advertised via interface TokenRing 0 with metric 1.

The auto-summarization feature is not unique to RIP. Every classful routing protocol performs auto-summarization in routing updates when they cross corresponding network boundaries. As with RIP, this is because classful routing protocols do not pass the subnet masks along with network prefixes.

The fact that classful routing protocols must perform auto-summarization when routing updates that they generate cross classful network boundaries has the following very important side effect:

The classful dynamic routing protocols only work correctly if the IP address space remains contiguous for each individual classful network address.

In other words, a group of subnets belonging to network A cannot be separated by other than A networks from another group of subnets of network A. This means that the example shown in Figure 4.6 will not work because the two groups of network 10.0.0.0 subnets are separated by the link with a network IP address of 200.1.0.0/24.

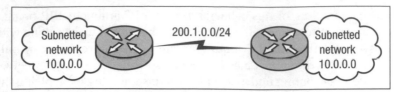

Figure 4.6   Two groups of network 10.0.0.0 subnets are separated by a link with a network IP address of 200.1.0.0.

In this situation, the hosts located on the segments from the left cloud will be unable to communicate with the hosts located on the segments from the right cloud. The situation changes, however, if there is a path between the left and right clouds via segments with network IP addresses that are subnets of network 10.0.0.0. For example, in Figure 4.7, there is another pair of routers connecting the two clouds via a link with a network IP address of 10.255.1.0/24.

Using Individual Host Addresses With RIP

As mentioned in the previous section, RIP can pass individual host addresses in the routing updates. The behavior of individual host addresses is identical to the behavior of subnet routes; therefore, they only operate properly in the contiguous address space.

If the condition of contiguous address space is met, the individual host addresses are configured using the following procedure:

1. Define a *loopback* interface using the command **interface loopback** *<number>* in the global configuration mode.

2. Assign an IP address to the loopback interface using the command **ip address** *<IP address>* **255.255.255.255**.

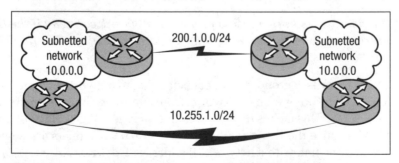

Figure 4.7   An alternative link having a network IP address that is a subnet of network 10.0.0.0 solves the overall connectivity problem.

If the IP address assigned on the loopback interface belongs to one of the networks defined using the **network** statement under the **router rip** configuration, RIP advertises this address as an individual host address.

For example, let's add loopback addresses on routers R1, R2, and R3 and assign them IP addresses of 10.0.0.1/32, 10.0.0.2/32, and 10.0.0.3/32, respectively. Now we should be able to see these addresses as individual host addresses in the router's routing table. For example, let's examine router R3's routing table shown in Listing 4.14.

Listing 4.14   The routing table of router R3.

```
R3#show ip route
...
     10.0.0.0/8 is variably subnetted, 7 subnets, 2 masks
R       10.0.0.2/32 [120/1] via 10.4.0.2, 00:00:17, Serial0
R       10.2.0.0/24 [120/1] via 10.4.0.2, 00:00:17, Serial0
C       10.0.0.3/32 is directly connected, Loopback0
C       10.3.0.0/24 is directly connected, Serial1
R       10.0.0.1/32 [120/1] via 10.3.0.2, 00:00:11, Serial1
R       10.1.0.0/24 [120/1] via 10.3.0.2, 00:00:11, Serial1
C       10.4.0.0/24 is directly connected, Serial0
C     200.5.0.0/24 is directly connected, TokenRing0
R     200.6.0.0/24 [120/1] via 200.5.0.2, 00:00:01, TokenRing0
```

If we examine the contents of the routing updates sent by router R3 using the command **debug ip rip**, we'll see the individual host routes in them. (In the output shown in Listing 4.15, those routes are italicized.)

*Listing 4.15   The output of the command **debug ip rip** shows how the router sends individual host IP addresses in RIP routing updates.*

```
R3#debug ip rip
...
RIP: sending v1 update to 255.255.255.255 via Serial0
(10.4.0.1)
     host    10.0.0.3, metric 1
     subnet  10.3.0.0, metric 1
     host    10.0.0.1, metric 2
     subnet  10.1.0.0, metric 2
     network 200.5.0.0, metric 1
     network 200.6.0.0, metric 2
...
```

Configuring RIP To Originate The Default Route

To make a router advertise the default route—that is, a route for network 0.0.0.0/0—the command **default-information originate** should be entered under the **router rip** configuration.

For example, let's assume that router R4 in Figure 4.5 is also connected to the Internet. Let's also assume that we want to allow every host at every location to access the Internet. It then makes sense to force router R4 to advertise the default route.

Listing 4.16 shows the changed configuration of router R4.

Listing 4.16   Router R4's configuration.

```
interface Ethernet0
 ip address 200.6.0.1 255.255.255.0

interface TokenRing0
 ip address 200.5.0.2 255.255.255.0
 ring-speed 16

router rip
 network 200.5.0.0
 network 200.6.0.0
 default-information originate
```

Let's have a look at the routing table of router R3 shown in Listing 4.17.

Listing 4.17   The routing table of router R3.

```
R3#show ip route
10.0.0.0/24 is subnetted, 4 subnets
...
R       10.2.0.0 [120/1] via 10.4.0.2, 00:00:12, Serial0
C       10.3.0.0 is directly connected, Serial1
R       10.1.0.0 [120/1] via 10.3.0.2, 00:00:27, Serial1
C       10.4.0.0 is directly connected, Serial0
C    200.5.0.0/24 is directly connected, TokenRing0
R    200.6.0.0/24 [120/1] via 200.5.0.2, 00:00:09, TokenRing0
R*   0.0.0.0/0 [120/1] via 200.5.0.2, 00:00:09, TokenRing0
```

Notice that the routing table of router R3 now contains an entry for the default route. In addition to the letter "R", indicating that the route was learned via RIP, there is an asterisk, which suggests that the route is a *candidate default route*.

4. Dynamic Routing: Distance Vector Routing Protocols

NOTE: *Although recommended, the command **ip classless** is not required in the described configuration. Without this command, the router assumes that if it is connected to a subnet of a certain classful network address it will also know how to communicate with the whole classful network. This is true in the case of classful dynamic routing protocols because their operation requires that the classful address space be kept contiguous.*

Using RIP In The Presence Of Secondary IP Addresses

RIP advertises secondary IP addresses if they are configured on any interfaces and if the networks to which they belong are specified under the **router rip** configuration using the **network** statement.

The router uses the following rules when forming and sending the routing updates sent via an interface with secondary IP addresses.

- The router sends multiple copies of the same routing update over an interface configured with secondary IP addresses. The number of copies sent is equal to the number of classful network addresses configured on the interface, regardless of whether the networks are subnetted. Each copy of the update is sent as though it originates from the respective network address.

- For each network, the router takes the first IP address from those configured on the interface and falling into that network. The IP addresses configured on the interface are processed in the order in which they appear in the router configuration. This address is used as the source address in the IP datagram carrying the respective copy of the routing update.

- None of the network and subnet addresses—whether primary or secondary—appear in the copies of the routing update sent via the interface. All copies of the same update will be identical.

These rules may sound complicated. To understand the rules better, let's modify the configuration shown in Figure 4.5. On routers R3 and R4, we will assign secondary IP addresses as shown in their changed configuration (see Listings 4.18 and 4.19).

Listing 4.18   Router R3's configuration.
```
interface Serial0
 ip address 10.4.0.1 255.255.255.0

interface Serial1
 ip address 10.3.0.1 255.255.255.0
```

```
interface TokenRing0
 ip address 172.16.1.20 255.255.255.0 secondary
 ip address 172.16.1.15 255.255.255.0 secondary
 ip address 210.1.0.1 255.255.255.0 secondary
 ip address 172.16.10.20 255.255.255.0 secondary
 ip address 172.16.10.15 255.255.255.0 secondary
 ip address 172.16.10.10 255.255.255.0 secondary
 ip address 200.5.0.1 255.255.255.0
 ring-speed 16

router rip
 network 10.0.0.0
 network 200.5.0.0
 network 172.16.0.0
 network 210.1.0.0
```

Listing 4.19   Router R4's configuration.

```
interface Ethernet0
 ip address 200.6.0.1 255.255.255.0

interface TokenRing0
 ip address 172.16.1.120 255.255.255.0 secondary
 ip address 172.16.1.115 255.255.255.0 secondary
 ip address 210.1.0.2 255.255.255.0 secondary
 ip address 172.16.10.120 255.255.255.0 secondary
 ip address 172.16.10.115 255.255.255.0 secondary
 ip address 172.16.10.110 255.255.255.0 secondary
 ip address 200.5.0.2 255.255.255.0
 ring-speed 16

router rip
 network 200.5.0.0
 network 200.6.0.0
 network 172.16.0.0
 network 210.1.0.0
```

The TokenRing interfaces on both routers now have a number of secondary IP addresses. All of the IP addresses—secondary and primary—fall into three networks: 172.16.0.0/16, 200.5.0.0/24, and 210.1.0.0/24. Therefore, three copies of the same routing update should be sent over the TokenRing interface by each router.

Let's see if this is true. As before, we'll use the command **debug ip rip** to see which routing updates are sent by the routers. Listing 4.20 shows the output of this command used on router R4.

*Listing 4.20   The output of the command **debug ip rip** entered on router R4.*

```
R4#debug ip rip
RIP protocol debugging is on
R4#
RIP: sending update to 255.255.255.255 via Ethernet0
(200.6.0.1)
      network 10.0.0.0, metric 2
      network 172.16.0.0, metric 1
      network 200.5.0.0, metric 1
      network 210.1.0.0, metric 1
RIP: sending update to 255.255.255.255 via TokenRing0
(200.5.0.2)
      network 200.6.0.0, metric 1
RIP: sending update to 255.255.255.255 via TokenRing0
(172.16.1.120)
      network 200.6.0.0, metric 1
RIP: sending update to 255.255.255.255 via TokenRing0
(210.1.0.2)
      network 200.6.0.0, metric 1
RIP: received update from 200.5.0.1 on TokenRing0
      10.0.0.0 in 1 hops
RIP: received update from 172.16.1.20 on TokenRing0
      10.0.0.0 in 1 hops
RIP: received update from 210.1.0.1 on TokenRing0
      10.0.0.0 in 1 hops
```

The output of the **debug ip rip** command in Listing 4.20 confirms that three copies of the same routing update are sent over the TokenRing interface by each router and demonstrates how the rules work. Both routers send exactly three copies of the same routing update over their respective TokenRing interfaces. None of the copies contains any network and subnet addresses configured on the TokenRing interfaces. The addresses that were used to send the copies of the routing updates from network 172.16.0.0/16 are as follows: 172.16.1.20 on router R3 and 172.16.1.120 on router R4. These addresses appear first for network 172.16.0.0 in the TokenRing interfaces configurations of both routers.

WARNING!   Although network 172.16.1.120 was subnetted, only the first subnet was used to send a copy of the routing update. Hosts on any other subnets that are listening to RIP will only receive routing updates with incorrect source IP addresses. In this case, the hosts have to ignore the information in the routing updates, because they don't know how to communicate with the advertising router, which should become the next-hop router in the routes that the hosts establish for the advertised network prefixes. (The reason why the hosts will receive RIP routing updates is because by default RIP sends updates to the local broadcast address, that is, 255.255.255.255.)

The routing tables on both routers were also changed by the presence of the secondary IP addresses (shown in Listings 4.21 and 4.22).

Listing 4.21   The routing table of router R3.

```
R3#show ip route

...
     10.0.0.0/24 is subnetted, 4 subnets
R       10.2.0.0 [120/1] via 10.4.0.2, 00:00:15, Serial0
C       10.3.0.0 is directly connected, Serial1
R       10.1.0.0 [120/1] via 10.3.0.2, 00:00:06, Serial1
C       10.4.0.0 is directly connected, Serial0
     172.16.0.0/24 is subnetted, 2 subnets
C       172.16.10.0 is directly connected, TokenRing0
C       172.16.1.0 is directly connected, TokenRing0
C    200.5.0.0/24 is directly connected, TokenRing0
R    200.6.0.0/24 [120/1] via 200.5.0.2, 00:00:06, TokenRing0
                  [120/1] via 172.16.1.120, 00:00:06, TokenRing0
                  [120/1] via 210.1.0.2, 00:00:06, TokenRing0
C    210.1.0.0/24 is directly connected, TokenRing0
```

Listing 4.22   Routing table of router R4.

```
R4#show ip route

...
R       10.0.0.0 [120/1] via 200.5.0.1, 00:00:13, TokenRing0
                  [120/1] via 172.16.1.20, 00:00:13, TokenRing0
                  [120/1] via 210.1.0.1, 00:00:13, TokenRing0
     172.16.0.0 255.255.255.0 is subnetted, 2 subnets
C       172.16.10.0 is directly connected, TokenRing0
C       172.16.1.0 is directly connected, TokenRing0
C    200.5.0.0 is directly connected, TokenRing0
C    200.6.0.0 is directly connected, Ethernet0
C    210.1.0.0 is directly connected, TokenRing0
```

The lines that are italicized in Listings 4.21 and 4.22 indicate that the router performs load balancing over multiple paths. Notice, however, that all routes point to the same interface. Obviously, it does not make sense to perform load balancing if all "load balanced" traffic is sent over the same media to the same next-hop router. Thus, we conclude that in our case the load balancing is faked. The reason is that the routers receive multiple routing updates, which advertise the same network prefixes—10.0.0.0/8 and 200.6.0.0/24—with the same metric. We'll examine how Cisco's implementation of RIP affects load balancing shortly; for now, it's enough to know that the necessary conditions were met. The only outcome of this occurrence is to confuse the network administrator.

WARNING! *If secondary IP addresses are used with the dynamic routing protocols, all routers connected to the same segment should have exactly the same network and subnet addresses configured on their respective interfaces. Failure to meet this condition can potentially lead to routing loops.*

In addition, the order in which the subnets of the same network appear in the interface configurations of the routers is also crucial. Only the first IP address for each classful network address is used as the source address in the datagrams carrying the copies of the routing updates allegedly originating from that network. Therefore, if the order in which the subnets of the same network appear in the interface configurations varies from router to router, the routing updates formed by different routers will traverse different subnets.

By now, you should be convinced that secondary IP addresses are very undesirable in the production environment. The behavior of the routers configured with secondary IP addresses and dynamic routing is sometimes unpredictable, the rules that the routers follow to handle the routing updates are complicated, and the configuration of the routers becomes cumbersome and superfluously large. The only valid justification for using secondary IP addresses is as a temporary measure in such situations as migrations, an urgent need to allocate extra IP addresses, and so on.

Preventing RIP From Sending Routing Updates On An Interface

To prevent RIP from sending routing updates on an interface, the command **passive-interface** *<interface>* should be used under the **router rip** configuration. RIP will not send routing updates via the interfaces specified using this command even if their IP addresses fall into the network addresses defined using the **network** command. However, RIP will still process incoming RIP updates on those interfaces.

As an example, let's add **passive-interface TokenRing 0** to the **router rip** configuration at router R4 and see what happens. The other routers are configured in accordance with Figure 4.5 without the loopback interfaces and secondary IP addresses.

Listing 4.23 shows the updated configuration of router R4. The line that we just entered is italicized.

Listing 4.23   Router R4's configuration.

```
interface Ethernet0
 ip address 200.6.0.1 255.255.255.0
```

```
interface TokenRing0
 ip address 200.5.0.2 255.255.255.0
 ring-speed 16

router rip
 passive-interface TokenRing0
 network 200.5.0.0
 network 200.6.0.0
```

As the output of the command **show ip route** (shown in Listing 4.24) suggests, the routing table on router R4 stays unchanged, as we should expect given the functionality of the **passive-interface** statement.

Listing 4.24   The routing table of router R4.

```
R4#show ip route
...
R    10.0.0.0 [120/1] via 200.5.0.1, 00:00:09, TokenRing0
C    200.5.0.0 is directly connected, TokenRing0
C    200.6.0.0 is directly connected, Ethernet0
```

However, Listing 4.25 shows that router R3 is now unable to see the network IP address of the Ethernet segment behind router R4.

Listing 4.25   The routing table of router R3.

```
R3#show ip route
...
     10.0.0.0/24 is subnetted, 4 subnets
R       10.2.0.0 [120/1] via 10.4.0.2, 00:00:02, Serial0
C       10.3.0.0 is directly connected, Serial1
R       10.1.0.0 [120/1] via 10.3.0.2, 00:00:03, Serial1
C       10.4.0.0 is directly connected, Serial0
C    200.5.0.0/24 is directly connected, TokenRing0
```

We can see the routing updates now sent by router R4 if we use the command **debug ip rip** on router R4 (shown in Listing 4.26).

Listing 4.26   The output of the command *debug ip rip*.

```
R4#debug ip rip
RIP protocol debugging is on
R4#
RIP: received update from 200.5.0.1 on TokenRing0
     10.0.0.0 in 1 hops
RIP: sending update to 255.255.255.255 via Ethernet0
(200.6.0.1)
     network 10.0.0.0, metric 2
     network 200.5.0.0, metric 1
```

```
RIP: received update from 200.5.0.1 on TokenRing0
     10.0.0.0 in 1 hops
RIP: sending update to 255.255.255.255 via Ethernet0
(200.6.0.1)
     network 10.0.0.0, metric 2
     network 200.5.0.0, metric 1
```

As expected, router R4 no longer sends any routing updates via the TokenRing 0 interface.

The **passive-interface** statement makes RIP *passive* on an interface. RIP in the passive mode is also often used on the hosts. For example, if there is a Unix workstation that runs **routed** daemon (the BSD Unix implementation of RIP), you should make RIP passive on the workstation's NIC, unless specifically required otherwise. This ensures that the workstation receives the RIP routing updates and also prevents the workstation from "polluting" the network segment with superfluous RIP traffic.

NOTE: *Even if a host that runs a RIP routing process has only a single interface, it still can generate poison reverse updates, thereby creating superfluous RIP traffic.*

Superfluous RIP traffic is especially undesirable because of the broadcast nature of the RIP routing updates. Any broadcast traffic, regardless of which protocol it is destined for, is received by every host on the segment, causing unnecessary processing overhead on the hosts' CPUs, thus degrading their performance. Unless properly controlled, the broadcast traffic can become so heavy that it degrades the hosts' performance beyond an acceptable level. That is why it's important to keep the broadcast traffic to the minimum.

RIP in the passive mode can also be effectively used on the routers. If a certain segment has only one router connection and no hosts are willing to receive RIP routing updates, it certainly makes sense to force RIP to be passive on the router's interface connected to that segment.

Using Unicast Routing Updates With RIP

By examining the output of the **debug ip rip** command, we will notice that all routing updates are destined for the local broadcast address—that is, 255.255.255.255. In some cases, which we'll discuss shortly, we may want to send routing updates using unicast addresses.

The Cisco IOS provides a way to send RIP routing updates to unicast addresses. To do that, the command **neighbor** <*IP address*> should be used under the **router rip** configuration. The presence of this command forces the router to send the routing updates to the address specified in the command.

NOTE: The command neighbor does not prevent the router from sending the routing updates to the local broadcast address.

By entering the command **passive-interface TokenRing 0** on router R4 as configured in the previous section, we will see that all other routers stopped seeing network 200.6.0.0/24. If we now specify the TokenRing interface's IP address of router R3 as the argument for the **neighbor** command, the connectivity should be restored.

Listing 4.27 shows the new configuration of router R4.

Listing 4.27   Router R4's configuration.

```
interface Ethernet0
 ip address 200.6.0.1 255.255.255.0

interface TokenRing0
 ip address 200.5.0.2 255.255.255.0
 ring-speed 16

router rip
 passive-interface TokenRing0
 neighbor 200.5.0.1
 network 200.5.0.0
 network 200.6.0.0
```

After we entered the **neighbor 200.5.0.1** command on router R4, router R3 began to see network 200.6.0.0 again (see Listing 4.28).

Listing 4.28   The routing table of router R3.

```
R3#show ip route
...
     10.0.0.0/24 is subnetted, 4 subnets
R       10.2.0.0 [120/1] via 10.4.0.2, 00:00:12, Serial0
C       10.3.0.0 is directly connected, Serial1
R       10.1.0.0 [120/1] via 10.3.0.2, 00:00:05, Serial1
C       10.4.0.0 is directly connected, Serial0
C    200.5.0.0/24 is directly connected, TokenRing0
R    200.6.0.0/24 [120/1] via 200.5.0.2, 00:00:11, TokenRing0
```

The routing updates sent over the TokenRing interface by router R4 are now destined for the router R3's TokenRing interface's IP address. (In the **debug ip rip** output shown in Listing 4.28, the IP address is italicized.)

*Listing 4.29   The output of the command **debug ip rip**.*

```
R4#debug ip rip
...
RIP: sending update to 255.255.255.255 via Ethernet0 (200.6.0.1)
     network 10.0.0.0, metric 2
     network 200.5.0.0, metric 1
RIP: sending update to 200.5.0.1 via TokenRing0 (200.5.0.2)
     network 200.6.0.0, metric 1
```

Discriminating Incoming Routing Updates

The Cisco IOS provides a way to discriminate and possibly completely ignore routing updates from certain sources. The discrimination is performed by setting specific administrative distances for incoming routing updates, depending on the source or the updates.

To set a new administrative distance for the incoming routing updates, the command **distance** *<new distance> [<source IP address> <wildcard mask>]* should be used under the **router rip** configuration. The *<new distance>* parameter indicates the administrative distance set for the routes to the network prefixes advertised in the routing updates received from the source whose IP address is matched by the parameters *<source IP address>* and *<wildcard mask>*. If the last two parameters are omitted, the new distance is applied to all RIP incoming routing updates. The administrative distance of 255 prevents the routes from being populated into the routing table. In other words, the routes from the specified source are ignored.

4. Dynamic Routing: Distance Vector Routing Protocols

NOTE: *The Cisco documentation uses the rather confusing name IP address mask to denote what is labeled here as <wildcard mask>. The meaning of the <wildcard mask> in the context of the **distance** command is identical to that of the wildcard mask used in the IP access-lists—that is, a bit of the mask set to 1 forces the router to ignore the corresponding bit in the IP address of the source of the routing update. In terms of the bits' meaning, you can think of the wildcard mask as a reversed subnet mask.*

TIP: *You can use several **distance** commands to reflect the level of trust that the router should have in different sources of routing updates.*

Let's assume that we added a new extraneous source of RIP routing updates to the topology used in the previous section in the form of multihomed host H1, which also runs RIP. The new topology is shown in Figure 4.8.

Suppose segment 7 does not belong to the networking infrastructure. Therefore, our task is to ignore the routing updates sent by the extraneous source. Let's extend our task to ignore the routing updates sent not only by host H1, but also by any extraneous source located on TokenRing segment 5. Let's also change the administrative distance of the routing updates received from routers R3 and R4 from the default value—which is 120 in the case of RIP-to 200.

The routing tables on routers R4 and R3 currently look as shown in Listings 4.30 and 4.31.

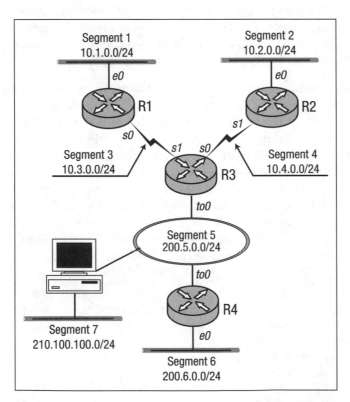

Figure 4.8 *An extraneous source of routing updates advertises a network that does not belong to the networking infrastructure.*

Listing 4.30   The routing table of router R3.

```
R3#show ip route
...
     10.0.0.0/24 is subnetted, 4 subnets
R       10.2.0.0 [120/1] via 10.4.0.2, 00:00:18, Serial0
C       10.3.0.0 is directly connected, Serial1
R       10.1.0.0 [120/1] via 10.3.0.2, 00:00:12, Serial1
C       10.4.0.0 is directly connected, Serial0
C    200.5.0.0/24 is directly connected, TokenRing0
R    200.6.0.0/24 [120/1] via 200.5.0.2, 00:00:24, TokenRing0
R    210.100.100.0/24 [120/2] via 200.5.0.15, 00:00:24, TokenRing0
```

Listing 4.31   The routing table of router R4.

```
R4#show ip route
...
R    10.0.0.0 [120/1] via 200.5.0.1, 00:00:23, TokenRing0
C    200.5.0.0 is directly connected, TokenRing0
C    200.6.0.0 is directly connected, Ethernet0
R    210.100.100.0 [120/2] via 200.5.0.15, 00:00:24, TokenRing0
```

4. Dynamic Routing: Distance Vector Routing Protocols

NOTE: *Although router R4 is configured with the commands **passive-interface TokenRing 0** and **neighbor 200.5.0.1**, it still accepts the routing updates sent by host H1. These two commands cannot be used to make a router ignore the routing updates from extraneous sources.*

Because router R3 is the only source of routing updates that we trust, we can use the IP address of its TokenRing interface along with the wildcard mask 0.0.0.0 as the arguments for the **distance** command. Likewise, we can use address 200.5.0.0 along with the wildcard mask 0.0.0.255 as the arguments for the second **distance** command to indicate that we do not trust the other hosts on TokenRing segment 5.

Listings 4.32 and 4.33 show the updated configurations of routers R3 and R4.

Listing 4.32   Router R3's configuration.

```
interface Serial0
 ip address 10.4.0.1 255.255.255.0

interface Serial1
 ip address 10.3.0.1 255.255.255.0

interface TokenRing0
 ip address 200.5.0.1 255.255.255.0
 ring-speed 16
```

```
router rip
 network 10.0.0.0
 network 200.5.0.0
 distance 200 200.5.0.2 0.0.0.0
 distance 255 200.5.0.0 0.0.0.255
```

Listing 4.33 Router R4's configuration.

```
interface Ethernet0
 ip address 200.6.0.1 255.255.255.0

interface TokenRing0
 ip address 200.5.0.2 255.255.255.0
 ring-speed 16

router rip
 passive-interface TokenRing0
 network 200.5.0.0
 network 200.6.0.0
 neighbor 200.5.0.1
 distance 200 200.5.0.1 0.0.0.0
 distance 255 200.5.0.0 0.0.0.255
```

By examining the routing tables on both routers, we'll see that the routes sent by host H1 disappeared. At the same time, the administrative distance of the routes learned from routers R3 and R4 changed to 200 (these values are italicized in Listings 4.34 and 4.35).

Listing 4.34 The routing table of router R3.

```
R3#show ip route
...
     10.0.0.0/24 is subnetted, 4 subnets
R       10.2.0.0 [120/1] via 10.4.0.2, 00:00:15, Serial0
C       10.3.0.0 is directly connected, Serial1
R       10.1.0.0 [120/1] via 10.3.0.2, 00:00:18, Serial1
C       10.4.0.0 is directly connected, Serial0
C    200.5.0.0/24 is directly connected, TokenRing0
R    200.6.0.0/24 [200/1] via 200.5.0.2, 00:00:16, TokenRing0
```

Listing 4.35 The routing table of router R4.

```
R4#show ip route
...
R    10.0.0.0 [200/1] via 200.5.0.1, 00:00:18, TokenRing0
C    200.5.0.0 is directly connected, TokenRing0
C    200.6.0.0 is directly connected, Ethernet0
```

WARNING! *The order in which the distance commands are entered is crucial. Only the first command whose arguments <source IP address> and <wildcard mask> match the IP address of the source of the routing update is regarded. All subsequent ones are ignored. For example, if in the preceding example, the distance commands were entered in the reversed order, the router would ignore all routing updates regardless of the source. This happens because the distance 255 200.5.0.0 0.0.0.255 matches any IP address on TokenRing segment 5 and, therefore, sets the administrative distance of the routing updates received from that source to 255, ignore.*

NOTE: *The command* **distance** *is routing protocol independent and can be used to influence the behavior of any routing protocol.*

Configuring Equal Cost Load Balancing With RIP

The implementation of RIP found in the Cisco IOS performs load balancing of outgoing traffic over multiple paths to the same destination expressed as a network prefix if all paths have the same metric.

4. Dynamic Routing: Distance Vector Routing Protocols

NOTE: *The router has no control over incoming traffic. Therefore, although the router performs load balancing of outgoing traffic, incoming traffic may return via a single interface.*

Let's consider the network shown in Figure 4.9.

Router R3 has two paths for TokenRing segment 1. These paths are identical to RIP whether they are of equal bandwidth or not and thus are given the same metric of 1. The routing table of router R3 shown in Listing 4.36 confirms this.

Listing 4.36   The routing table of router R3.

```
R3#show ip route
...
C    200.100.0.0/24 is directly connected, Serial1
C    200.101.0.0/24 is directly connected, Serial0
R    200.1.0.0/24 [120/1] via 200.100.0.2, 00:00:05, Serial1
                  [120/1] via 200.101.0.2, 00:00:21, Serial0
C    200.2.0.0/24 is directly connected, Ethernet0
```

The italicized part of the output should now look familiar. It is the same as in Chapter 3 when we configured static routes, which enabled the router to perform load balancing.

Listing 4.37 shows the routing tables on router R1.

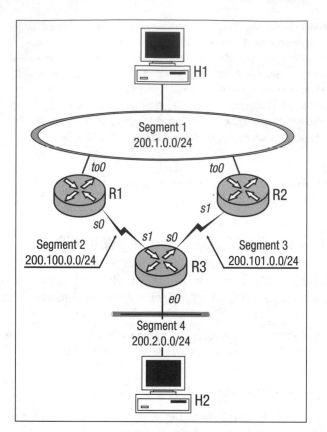

Figure 4.9   Router R3 has redundant paths to TokenRing segment 1.

Listing 4.37   The routing table of router R1.

```
R1#show ip route
...
C   200.1.0.0/24 is directly connected, TokenRing0
R   200.2.0.0/24 [120/1] via 200.100.0.1, 00:00:07, Serial0
C   200.100.0.0/24 is directly connected, Serial0
R   200.101.0.0/24 [120/1] via 200.100.0.1, 00:00:07, Serial0
                    [120/1] via 200.1.0.2, 00:00:05, TokenRing0
```

Router R1 is also willing to perform load balancing. It performs load balancing of traffic destined for the serial link between router R3 and router R2. It's obvious that such load balancing makes little sense, because the bandwidth of the TokenRing segment is much higher than that of the serial link. Thus, if router R1 performs load balancing, the serial link will be overloaded, whereas the TokenRing segment will be nearly empty. Thankfully, it is unlikely that a serious load of traffic will be destined for the serial link or that anyone would send traffic to a segment with only two hosts, both of which are routers, unless that person is driven by some malicious intention.

TIP: *By default, the Cisco routers perform load balancing over up to four paths to the same destination. This value can be changed using the command* **maximum-paths** *<number>, where <number> is an integer in the range from 1 to 6. The value of 1 prevents the router from performing load balancing.*

Changing RIP Metrics

Sometimes, we may want to force RIP to choose one route over another. For example, if there are two parallel links between two routers, one of which has a smaller bandwidth, we may want to make RIP prefer the one with the higher bandwidth. As we know, RIP is not particularly discerning about the network segments on which it works. To RIP, they all have a metric of 1, regardless of their actual characteristics. Therefore, in our example, instead of making the link with the higher bandwidth the only route to the destination, RIP will perform equal cost load balancing over both links, which we may not want. For example, if the bandwidth of the second link is three times smaller than that of the first link, the combined bandwidth is smaller than the bandwidth of the first link alone.

The Cisco IOS provides a very powerful way to change the default metric of 1 that RIP uses for every interface serviced by it. This method is to use the command **offset-list**, available under the **router rip** configuration.

This command does not change the metric of an interface. Instead, it selectively changes the metrics of incoming or outgoing RIP updates by applying a specified offset. I used the word *selectively* because the command allows specifying on which routes we want to change the metrics optionally on a per individual interface basis.

The format of the command is as follows:

offset-list *<access-list>* **{in|out}** *<offset>* [*<Interface>*]

The *<access-list>* parameter can be either 0, a number of a standard IP access-list, or the name of a standard IP access-list. The latter is only available in the versions of Cisco IOS that support named access-lists. If an existing access-list is specified, the offset is only applied to the routes matched by the access-list. If the access-list does not exist or if 0 is used, the offset is applied to all routes. (Access-lists will be thoroughly examined in Chapter 6.)

The second parameter can be either **in** or **out**. If **in** is used, the offset is applied to the routes in the incoming RIP updates. If **out** is used, the offset is applied to the routes in the routing updates created by the router.

The *<Interface>* parameter is optional and specifies an interface to which the operation of the **offset-list** should be limited. If specified, it makes RIP apply the offset only to the routes in the routing updates received from or sent over the respective interface. The logic behind the access-list functionality remains the same.

According to the Cisco documentation, the **offset-list** commands that specify an interface are called *extended offset-lists*. The extended offset-lists take precedence over nonextended offset-lists; therefore, if the same route is matched by both commands, only the offset specified in the extended one is applied.

For each interface, you can have separate **offset-list ... in** and **offset-list ... out** commands. In addition, you can have separate nonextended **offset-list ... in** and **offset-list ... out** commands. If a subsequent **offset-list** command is entered, it overwrites the existing one with the matching {in|out} and *<Interface>* parameters.

For example, let's assume that the bandwidth of segment 3 in Figure 4.9 is three times smaller than that of segment 2. Currently, router R3 performs load balancing over both segments. Our task is to increase the metric RIP that router R3 uses for this segment from the default value of 1 to 3, using the command **offset-list**.

Listing 4.38 shows the modified configuration of router R3.

Listing 4.38   Router R3's configuration.

```
interface Ethernet0
 ip address 200.2.0.1 255.255.255.0

interface Serial0
 ip address 200.101.0.1 255.255.255.0

interface Serial1
 ip address 200.100.0.1 255.255.255.0

router rip
 offset-list 0 in 3 Serial0
 network 200.2.0.0
 network 200.100.0.0
 network 200.101.0.0
```

Listing 4.39 shows the routing table of router R3.

Listing 4.39   The routing table of router R3.
```
R3#show ip route
...
C    200.100.0.0/24 is directly connected, Serial1
C    200.101.0.0/24 is directly connected, Serial0
R    200.1.0.0/24 [120/1] via 200.100.0.2, 00:00:11, Serial1
C    200.2.0.0/24 is directly connected, Ethernet0
```

The evidence of load balancing that we saw in the previous example has disappeared. If we look at the routing updates that router R3 receives on interface Serial 0, we will see that the metric increased by 3 (see Listing 4.40).

*Listing 4.40   The output of the command **debug ip rip**.*
```
R3#debug ip rip
RIP protocol debugging is on
R3#
RIP: received v1 update from 200.101.0.2 on Serial0
     200.1.0.0 in 4 hops
RIP: received v1 update from 200.100.0.2 on Serial1
     200.1.0.0 in 1 hops
```

4. Dynamic Routing: Distance Vector Routing Protocols

Configuring RIP Over Non-Fully Meshed Frame Relay Networks

Configuring all routing protocols over frame relay networks presents a special case, which differs to a certain extent from configuring the same protocols over most other media. The reason is in the NBMA (Non-broadcast Multiple Access) nature of frame relay. Most routing protocols use either broadcast or multicast addresses, which often are not directly supported by frame relay and thus require certain workaround techniques.

These workaround techniques become especially obvious in the case of OSPF, which we'll examine in Chapter 5. Although the distance vector based routing protocols are not as particular with regard to NBMA technologies, such as frame relay, they may still present some surprises, especially in non-fully meshed NBMA networks.

Let's consider the network shown in Figure 4.10.

The routers are interconnected via a non-fully meshed frame relay network. For some unknown reason, router R1 is not allowed to use subinterfaces for the two different PVCs (permanent virtual circuits) going to routers R2 and R3.

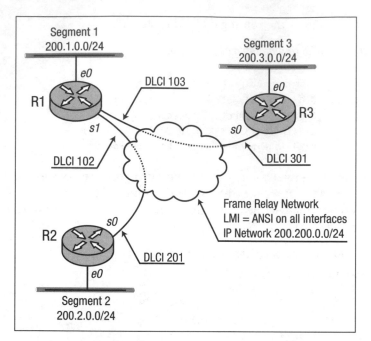

Figure 4.10   *The routers are connected via a non-fully meshed frame relay network.*

All three routers are configured with RIP. According to what we know, RIP will be unable to establish overall connectivity in the network. The split-horizon rule will prevent router R1 from passing the routing updates from router R1 to router R3, and vice versa, because these updates need to be sent over the same interface on which they are received.

Still, let's have a look at what happens in real life. Listings 4.41 through 4.43 show the configurations of all three routers.

Listing 4.41   Router R1's configuration.

```
interface Ethernet0
 ip address 200.1.0.1 255.255.255.0

interface Serial1
 ip address 200.200.0.1 255.255.255.0
 encapsulation frame-relay
 frame-relay map ip 200.200.0.2 102 broadcast
 frame-relay map ip 200.200.0.3 103 broadcast
 frame-relay lmi-type ansi
```

```
router rip
 network 200.1.0.0
 network 200.200.0.0
```

Listing 4.42   Router R2's configuration.

```
interface Ethernet0
 ip address 200.2.0.1 255.255.255.0

interface Serial0
 ip address 200.200.0.2 255.255.255.0
 encapsulation frame-relay
 frame-relay map ip 200.200.0.1 201 broadcast
 frame-relay lmi-type ansi

router rip
 network 200.2.0.0
 network 200.200.0.0
```

Listing 4.43   Router R3's configuration.

```
interface Ethernet0
 ip address 200.3.0.1 255.255.255.0

interface Serial0
 ip address 200.200.0.3 255.255.255.0
 encapsulation frame-relay
 frame-relay map ip 200.200.0.1 301 broadcast
 frame-relay lmi-type ansi

router rip
 network 200.3.0.0
 network 200.200.0.0
```

Router R1 has no problem seeing the IP addresses of the Ethernet segments attached to routers R2 and R3. However, we doubt that router R2 can see the Ethernet segment of router R3, and vice versa.

To see if our suspicion is correct, let's display the routing table on router R2 (shown in Listing 4.44).

Listing 4.44   The routing table of router R2.

```
R2#show ip route
...
C    200.200.0.0/24 is directly connected, Serial0
R    200.1.0.0/24 [120/1] via 200.200.0.1, 00:00:18, Serial0
C    200.2.0.0/24 is directly connected, Ethernet0
R    200.3.0.0/24 [120/2] via 200.200.0.1, 00:00:18, Serial0
```

4. Dynamic Routing: Distance Vector Routing Protocols

Apparently, we were wrong. RIP on router R1 somehow ignores the split-horizon rule and sends the routing updates received from router R3 back to the same interface so that router R1 can see them.

The command **show ip interface** can help explain why this happens. Unlike **show interfaces**, **show ip interface** displays the IP-specific information, which is available on the individual interfaces of the router.

If we use this command on router R1, we will see the output shown in Listing 4.45.

Listing 4.45   The routing table of router R1.

```
R1#show ip interface Serial 1
Serial1 is up, line protocol is up
  Internet address is 200.200.0.1/24
  Broadcast address is 255.255.255.255
  Address determined by non-volatile memory
  MTU is 1500 bytes
  Helper address is not set
  Directed broadcast forwarding is enabled
  Multicast reserved groups joined: 224.0.0.9
  Outgoing access list is not set
  Inbound  access list is not set
  Proxy ARP is enabled
  Security level is default
  Split horizon is disabled
  ICMP redirects are always sent
  ICMP unreachables are always sent
  ICMP mask replies are never sent
  IP fast switching is enabled
  IP fast switching on the same interface is enabled
  IP multicast fast switching is disabled
  Router Discovery is disabled
  IP output packet accounting is disabled
  IP access violation accounting is disabled
  TCP/IP header compression is disabled
  Probe proxy name replies are disabled
  Gateway Discovery is disabled
  Policy routing is disabled
  Network address translation is disabled
```

The italicized line shows the part of the output in which we are interested. Because the split horizon is disabled, RIP on router R1 ignores the rule.

This is not a coincidence. The Cisco IOS always disables the split-horizon rule for IP routing protocols on the interfaces configured for frame relay.

We'll come across another surprise if we try to **ping** the Ethernet interface on router R3 from router R2. The results are shown in Listing 4.46.

*Listing 4.46   The command **ping 200.3.0.1** issued on router R2 gets timed out.*

```
R2#ping 200.3.0.1

Type escape sequence to abort.
Sending 5, 100-byte ICMP Echos to 200.3.0.1, timeout is 2
seconds:
.....
Success rate is 0 percent (0/5)
```

For some reason, the **ping** does not go through. We'll find out why if we turn on **debug ip packet** on router R2 (see Listing 4.47).

*Listing 4.47   The output of the command **debug ip route** explains the behavior of **ping**.*

```
R2#debug ip packet
IP packet debugging is on
R2#ping 200.3.0.1

Type escape sequence to abort.
Sending 5, 100-byte ICMP Echos to 200.3.0.1, timeout is 2 seconds:

IP: s=200.200.0.2 (local), d=200.3.0.1 (Serial0)...
IP: s=200.200.0.2 (local), d=200.3.0.1 (Serial0)...
IP: s=200.200.0.2 (local), d=200.3.0.1 (Serial0)...
IP: s=200.200.0.2 (local), d=200.3.0.1 (Serial0)...
IP: s=200.200.0.2 (local), d=200.3.0.1 (Serial0)...
Success rate is 0 percent (0/5)
```

The italicized part shows the source IP address that router R2 places in the datagrams carrying the ping packets. Router R3 simply does not know how to get to address 200.200.0.2. As we remember from Chapter 1, the **frame-relay map ip** command establishes the mapping of an IP address to the corresponding Network Access Layer address, which is DLCI for frame relay. Neither router R2 nor router R3 has this command for each other's IP addresses assigned to their serial interfaces connected to the frame relay network.

Configuring IGRP

Configuring IGRP is very similar to configuring RIP. We will use the same network topology as we used for RIP (shown in Figure 4.3) to examine basic IGRP configuration. Then I will point out which features of the two protocols are the same. After that we'll examine the important features of IGRP that are not available with RIP.

Configuring IGRP consists of the same steps as configuring RIP. The only difference is in the command **router igrp** *<AS Number>*. The *<AS Number>* parameter specifies an autonomous system number that is serviced by this IGRP process.

In our example, we'll use autonomous system 10.

Listings 4.48 through 4.51 show the modified configurations of all four routers from Figure 4.3.

Listing 4.48   Router R1's configuration.
```
interface Ethernet0
 ip address 200.1.0.1 255.255.255.0

interface Serial0
 ip address 200.3.0.2 255.255.255.0

router igrp 10
 network 200.1.0.0
 network 200.3.0.0
```

Listing 4.49   Router R2's configuration.
```
interface Ethernet0
 ip address 200.2.0.1 255.255.255.0

interface Serial1
 ip address 200.4.0.2 255.255.255.0

router igrp 10
 network 200.2.0.0
 network 200.4.0.0
```

Listing 4.50   Router R3's configuration.
```
interface Serial0
 ip address 200.4.0.1 255.255.255.0

interface Serial1
 ip address 200.3.0.1 255.255.255.0
```

```
interface TokenRing0
 ip address 200.5.0.1 255.255.255.0
 ring-speed 16

router igrp 10
 network 200.3.0.0
 network 200.4.0.0
 network 200.5.0.0
```

Listing 4.51   Router R4's configuration.

```
interface Ethernet0
 ip address 200.6.0.1 255.255.255.0

interface TokenRing0
 ip address 200.5.0.2 255.255.255.0
 ring-speed 16

router igrp 10
 network 200.5.0.0
 network 200.6.0.0
```

The **debug** command available for IGRP is **debug ip igrp transactions**, which produces output similar to **debug ip rip**. Listing 4.52 shows the output of this command on router R3.

Listing 4.52   The output of the command debug ip igrp transactions.

```
R3#debug ip igrp transactions
IGRP protocol debugging is on
R3#
IGRP: received update from 200.4.0.2 on Serial0
      network 200.2.0.0, metric 8576 (neighbor 1100)
IGRP: received update from 200.5.0.2 on TokenRing0
      network 200.6.0.0, metric 1163 (neighbor 1100)
IGRP: received update from 200.3.0.2 on Serial1
      network 200.1.0.0, metric 8576 (neighbor 1100)
IGRP: sending update to 255.255.255.255 via Serial0
(200.4.0.1)
      network 200.1.0.0, metric=8576
      network 200.3.0.0, metric=8476
      network 200.5.0.0, metric=688
      network 200.6.0.0, metric=1163
IGRP: sending update to 255.255.255.255 via Serial1
(200.3.0.1)
      network 200.2.0.0, metric=8576
      network 200.4.0.0, metric=8476
```

4. Dynamic Routing: Distance Vector Routing Protocols

```
        network 200.5.0.0, metric=688
        network 200.6.0.0, metric=1163
IGRP: sending update to 255.255.255.255 via TokenRing0
(200.5.0.1)
        network 200.1.0.0, metric=8576
        network 200.2.0.0, metric=8576
        network 200.3.0.0, metric=8476
        network 200.4.0.0, metric=8476
```

The other commands used by RIP that are also available with IGRP and have the same functionality are **neighbor**, **distance**, and **passive-interface**.

Following are the differences between RIP and IGRP:

- The command **router igrp** *<AS Number>* allows multiple IGRP processes to run on a single router as opposed to the command **router rip** which can only start a single RIP process. The IGRP processes are distinguished by the autonomous systems numbers specified in the **router igrp** *<AS Number>* commands. Separate IGRP processes do not pass the routing information among each other. In other words, the routes established by one IGRP process are not advertised by any other IGRP process.

- Individual host addresses cannot be advertised using IGRP. Unlike RIP, IGRP always summarizes routing updates on the classful boundary.

- Unlike RIP, IGRP does not send routing updates for the secondary IP addresses configured on any interface. The router always sends a single routing update only using the primary address. This routing update does not contain the primary IP address of the interface or any of the secondary ones. (Obviously, Cisco learned the lesson with RIP well. The way in which IGRP handles secondary IP addresses in real environments could probably not be any better.)

Understanding IGRP Metrics

Someone gave IGRP a very apt name—*muscle RIP*—which is true for many reasons. One of these reasons is the IGRP metrics, which allow for much larger network diameters than the RIP metrics do.

Unlike RIP, IGRP uses rather complex metrics that allow IGRP to distinguish between physically unequal paths, which to RIP may appear to be the same. Understanding IGRP metrics is important because some features of IGRP, such as unequal cost load balancing, are based on the metrics.

The metric that IGRP uses for each route is calculated using the following formula:

$$M_{IGRP} = k1*B_{IGRP} + \frac{k2*B_{IGRP}}{256-L} + k3*D_{IGRP} * \frac{k5}{R+k4}$$

B_{IGRP} is the IGRP bandwidth of the path, which is calculated using the following formula:

$$B_{IGRP} = \frac{10^7}{B_{MIN}}$$

where B_{MIN} is the minimum logical bandwidth of the path expressed in kilobits per second (Kpbs). Logical bandwidth is a static parameter configurable on an interface using the command **bandwidth** in the interface configuration mode. Notice however, that this value becomes B_{MIN} for a specific path only if it is the minimum among the logical bandwidths of all of the segments constituting this path. For each interface, there is a default value, which usually reflects the actual bandwidth of the interface. However, this parameter always defaults to 1544 for serial interfaces; therefore, you should adjust the logical bandwidth for serial interfaces using the **bandwidth** command.

4. Dynamic Routing: Distance Vector Routing Protocols

NOTE: *The **bandwidth** command does not change the actual bandwidth of the interface. It only changes the logical value associated with the interface, which is used by the routing protocols, such as IGRP, EIGRP, OSPF, and so on, when calculating route metrics, and some other processes.*

*If the **bandwidth** command is used, you should usually use this command on all interfaces of all routers connected to the same segment. For example, if the logical bandwidth of a serial connection between two routers needs to be adjusted, it should be adjusted on the interfaces of both routers.*

The current bandwidth configured on an interface (as well as the other values used by IGRP in metric calculations) can be displayed using the command **show interfaces** (see Listing 4.53).

Listing 4.53 **The fourth line of the command *show interfaces Serial 1* output displays the logical values used by IGRP in metric calculations.**

```
R3#show interfaces Serial 1
Serial1 is up, line protocol is up
  Hardware is HD64570
  Internet address is 200.100.0.1/24
```

```
   MTU 1500 bytes, BW 1544 Kbit, DLY 20000 usec, rely 255/255,
load 1/255
 . . .
```

The first italicized number is the value of the logical bandwidth configured on interface Serial 1.

D_{IGRP} is the IGRP delay of the path, which is equal to the sum of the delays of all segments along the path expressed in 10-microsecond units. This value is also a static parameter configurable on an interface using the command **delay** in the interface configuration mode. Just as with the current logical bandwidth of an interface, the current delay value can be examined using the command **show interfaces**. For example, in Listing 4.53 the second italicized number is the current delay value of interface Serial 1.

The router stores and communicates the value of the delay as a 32-bit variable. The value of 0xFFFFFFFF is used to designate inaccessible routes.

L is the IGRP load of the corresponding interface. This parameter is measured dynamically by IGRP and is expressed as an integer value in the range from 1 to 255; 1 is the minimally loaded interface, and 255 is the 100 percent loaded interface.

R is the IGRP reliability of the segment to which the corresponding interface is attached. This is another parameter measured dynamically by IGRP itself. Similar to L, R is expressed as an integer value in the range from 1 to 255; 1 is the minimally reliable segment, and 255 is the 100 percent reliable segment.

IGRP does not change parameters L and R abruptly to ensure more stable operation of routing. Abrupt changes of these parameters can be caused by a burst of traffic; if IGRP reacts too soon, it may cause certain routes to be put in holddown.

Both L and R parameters currently defined for an interface can be displayed using the same **show interfaces** command. In Listing 4.53, these are shown in the two last italicized numbers.

Parameters *k1*, *k2*, *k3*, *k4*, and *k5* are administratively configurable weights. Their default values are shown in Table 4.2.

Table 4.2   The default values of IGRP weights.

Weight	Default Value
k1	1
k2	0
k3	1
k4	0
k5	0

When applied, the default values of the weights reduce the formula for calculating the IGRP metrics to the following:

$$M_{IGRP} = B_{IGRP} + D_{IGRP}$$

For example, let's calculate the metric with which IGRP advertises the network connected through interface Serial 1, as shown in Listing 4.53.

$$M_{IGRP} = \frac{10^7}{1544} + \frac{20000}{10} = 6476 + 2000 = 8476$$

If we use the command **debug ip igrp transactions**, we'll be able to verify whether our calculations are correct (see Listing 4.54).

Listing 4.54   The output of the command debug ip igrp transactions.

```
R3#debug ip igrp transactions
IGRP protocol debugging is on
R3#
IGRP: sending update to 255.255.255.255 via Ethernet0 (200.2.0.1)
      network 200.100.0.0, metric=8476
      network 200.101.0.0, metric=8476
      network 200.1.0.0, metric=8539
```

The italicized part of the output confirms that our calculations are correct.

Configuring Equal And Unequal Cost Load Balancing With IGRP

Just as with RIP, IGRP performs load balancing over the equal cost paths by default.

For example, let's use IGRP instead of RIP on the network routers shown in Figure 4.9. The configuration of the routers will change as shown in Listings 4.55 through 4.57.

Listing 4.55   Router R1's configuration.

```
interface Serial0
 ip address 200.100.0.2 255.255.255.0

interface TokenRing0
 ip address 200.1.0.1 255.255.255.0
 ring-speed 16

router igrp 10
 network 200.1.0.0
 network 200.100.0.0
```

Listing 4.56   Router R2's configuration.

```
interface Serial1
 ip address 200.101.0.2 255.255.255.0

interface TokenRing0
 ip address 200.1.0.2 255.255.255.0
 ring-speed 16

router igrp 10
 network 200.1.0.0
 network 200.101.0.0
```

Listing 4.57   Router R3's configuration.

```
interface Ethernet0
 ip address 200.2.0.1 255.255.255.0

interface Serial0
 ip address 200.101.0.1 255.255.255.0

interface Serial1
 ip address 200.100.0.1 255.255.255.0

router igrp 10
 network 200.2.0.0
 network 200.100.0.0
 network 200.101.0.0
```

If we display the routing table now, we will see the output shown in Listing 4.58.

Listing 4.58   The routing table of router R3.

```
R3#show ip route
...
C  200.100.0.0/24 is directly connected, Serial1
C  200.101.0.0/24 is directly connected, Serial0
```

```
I    200.1.0.0/24 [100/8539] via 200.100.0.2, 00:00:36, Serial1
                  [100/8539] via 200.101.0.2, 00:00:15, Serial0
C    200.2.0.0/24 is directly connected, Ethernet0
```

TIP: *The command **offset-list** is available with IGRP as well. However, with IGRP, it increments the value of the delay carried in either the incoming or outgoing routing updates. It has no influence on the value of the advertised bandwidth. For example, if the command **offset-list 0** in 3 Serial 1 appears under the router igrp 10 configuration of router R3 in the previous example, router R3 will stop performing load balancing. This is because the metric of the routes in the routing updates that it receives on interface Serial 1 increases by three.*

Suppose now that the physical bandwidth of segment 2 is 1,024Kbps, and the physical bandwidth of segment 3 is 512Kbps. From the previous section, we know that we can use the command **bandwidth** to adjust the logical bandwidth value that IGRP uses when calculating the metrics.

Listings 4.59 through 4.61 show how the configuration of the routers will change.

Listing 4.59   Router R1's configuration.

```
interface Serial0
 ip address 200.100.0.2 255.255.255.0
 bandwidth 1024

interface TokenRing0
 ip address 200.1.0.1 255.255.255.0
 ring speed 16

router igrp 10
 network 200.1.0.0
 network 200.100.0.0
```

Listing 4.60   Router R2's configuration.

```
interface Serial1
 ip address 200.101.0.2 255.255.255.0
 bandwidth 512

interface TokenRing0
 ip address 200.1.0.2 255.255.255.0
 ring-speed 16

router igrp 10
 network 200.1.0.0
 network 200.101.0.0
```

4. Dynamic Routing: Distance Vector Routing Protocols

Listing 4.61   Router R3's configuration.

```
interface Ethernet0
 ip address 200.2.0.1 255.255.255.0

interface Serial0
 ip address 200.101.0.1 255.255.255.0
 bandwidth 512

interface Serial1
 ip address 200.100.0.1 255.255.255.0
 bandwidth 1024

router igrp 10
 network 200.2.0.0
 network 200.100.0.0
 network 200.101.0.0
```

The evidence of load balancing now disappears from the routing table of router R3 (see Listing 4.62).

Listing 4.62   The routing table of router R3.

```
R3#show ip route
...
C   200.100.0.0/24 is directly connected, Serial1
C   200.101.0.0/24 is directly connected, Serial0
I   200.1.0.0/24 [100/11828] via 200.100.0.2, 00:00:55,Serial1
C   200.2.0.0/24 is directly connected, Ethernet0
```

Unlike RIP, IGRP is capable of performing *unequal cost load balancing*. With unequal cost load balancing, the router shares the outgoing traffic destined for a network prefix for which there are multiple paths with unequal metrics proportionally to the paths' metrics.

Unequal cost load balancing is not enabled by default. To enable unequal cost load balancing, the command **variance** *<multiplier>* should be entered under the **router igrp** *<AS Number>*. The value of the *<multiplier>* parameter should fall into the range from 1 to 128.

As the **variance** *<multiplier>* command appears under the **router igrp** *<AS Number>* configuration, the routes that meet the following two criteria are added to the routing table:

- The next-hop router along the candidate route should have a route for the destination with a metric better than that of the best local route for the same destination.

- The metric of the candidate route should be less than or equal to the metric of the local best route multiplied by the value of *<multiplier>*.

For example, suppose a router has three routes for network 10.0.0.0/8 with metrics of 6000, 5000, and 7000, respectively. Let's assume that the next-hop routers along these routes have metrics of 3000, 4000, and 6000, respectively. According to the first rule, the router can only perform load balancing over the first two routes because the best route of the third router has a metric that is worse than that of the best local route. Let's assume that **variance 2** is added to the **router igrp 10** configuration. The router performs unequal cost load balancing over the first two routes, because the worse metric (which is 6000) is less than the best metric multiplied by *<multiplier>* (5000*2 = 10000).

Let's try to change the configuration of router R3 from the previous example so that it can perform unequal cost load balancing over segments 2 and 3 of the traffic destined for TokenRing segment 1. Let's first calculate the values of the metrics with which the IGRP process on router R3 sees TokenRing segment 1.

The smallest bandwidth along the route via segment 2 is 1,024Kbps. The delays configured on TokenRing segment 1 and segment 2 are 630 and 20000, respectively. Therefore, the metric of the route for TokenRing segment 1 via segment 2 is as follows:

$$M_1 = \frac{10^7}{1024} + \frac{630+20000}{10} = 9765 + 2063 = 11828$$

The route via segment 3 for TokenRing segment 1 differs from the route via segment 2 only by the value of the smallest bandwidth, which is 512Kpbs in this case. Thus, the metric of this route is as follows:

$$M_1 = \frac{10^7}{512} + \frac{630+20000}{10} = 19531 + 2063 = 21594$$

The ratio between the metric of the best route to the destination and the metric of the candidate route is less than 2; therefore, the command **variance 2** should be enough to enable unequal cost load balancing.

The command **show ip route** on router R3 produces the output shown in Listing 4.63.

4. Dynamic Routing: Distance Vector Routing Protocols

Listing 4.63   The routing table of router R3.

```
R3#show ip route
...
C  200.100.0.0/24 is directly connected, Serial1
C  200.101.0.0/24 is directly connected, Serial0
I  200.1.0.0/24 [100/11828] via 200.100.0.2, 00:00:22,Serial1
               [100/21594] via 200.101.0.2, 00:00:22,Serial0
C  200.2.0.0/24 is directly connected, Ethernet0
```

The italicized numbers confirm our calculations, and the presence of two paths for network 200.1.0.0/24 proves that router R3 performs load balancing for that network.

Configuring Classless Routing Protocols

The subsequent sections discuss the details of configuring two classless distance vector routing protocols available in the Cisco IOS. These two protocols are RIP version 2 and EIGRP.

The biggest difference between these two routing protocols and the other two discussed in previous sections is that they can pass the exact network prefixes in their routing updates, whereby making VLSM (Variable Length Subnet Masks) possible.

Dividing a preallocated IP address space for use with VLSM is often considered a tough task. Therefore, the first section is devoted exclusively to one of the methods of doing this.

Despite the differences between classless and classful routing protocols, many configuration tasks remain the same for both types of routing protocols. Hence I will point out which of those tasks are identical, and will only discuss the ones that are not.

Dividing IP Address Space For Use With VLSM

This task is not directly related to configuring the Cisco routers. Nevertheless, it is very important, so I will include it in our discussion on configuring the Cisco routers for classless routing protocol operation.

The original idea behind the method discussed in this section was first formulated in RFC 950, *Internet Standard Subnetting Procedure*. This RFC document explains what the classful subnets are and lists several hypothetical schemes of representing subnetting. As we know, the subnets are currently represented using dotted decimal notation, just like the IP addresses. This fact actually reflects how the subnet masks are stored in the host's memory. The subnet masks are stored as bit masks, in which the bit values 0 and 1 are used to specify whether the corresponding bits in the IP addresses designate the host IDs or the subnet IDs. Although when RFC 950 was written, the decision had yet to be made on how the subnet masks should be implemented.

Thus, RFC 950 listed the following five methods, which could be used to implement subnetting:

- Variable-width field

- Fixed-width field

- Self-encoding variable-width field

- Self-encoding fixed-width field

- Masked bits

The first three methods involve using a fixed number of bits to perform subnetting. The last one was chosen to implement subnetting and became known as *subnet masks*. However, we are interested in the third one—the self-encoding variable-width field method—for use with VLSM.

4. Dynamic Routing: Distance Vector Routing Protocols

NOTE: *These methods should not be confused with methods of dividing the IP address space into subnets. These methods specify how to implement subnetting itself and how to store the subnet masks in the host's memory. I have included them in this book because I will use an idea from one of them to present an actual method of dividing a range of IP addresses into subnets.*

The idea behind the third method is that the higher-order bits of the IP address can be used to encode the meaning of the remaining lower-order bits, just like the classes of networks A, B, and C are encoded using the highest-order bits.

For example, suppose we are given a class B address 172.16.0.0/16, and we have two types of networks: regular Ethernet segments, each with potentially up to 200 hosts, and point-to-point HDLC links, each with only two hosts. We can use the highest-order bit in the third octet of the given address to designate whether we address the Ethernet segments or point-to-point links as follows:

- If the highest-order bit is cleared (0), the subnet mask will be /24, which yields 254 hosts per subnet, enough to address the hosts on the Ethernet segments. Such dividing will produce a range of addresses 172.16.1.0/24 through 172.16.127.0/24.

- If the highest-order bit is set (1), the subnet mask will be /30, which yields two hosts per subnet, exactly what is needed for the point-to-point links. This will produce a range of addresses 172.16.128.4/30 through 172.16.255.252.

The router will not be confused, because it uses the longest-match rule to route the datagrams. Nor will the hosts be confused, because the highest-order bit in the third octet is the tie-breaker when the hosts must decide whether to send the datagrams locally or to use the router to deliver them.

However, this solution does not produce the optimal use of the allocated address space. The first range allocates 127 subnets for the Ethernet segments, whereas the second range allocates 8,190 subnets for the point-to-point links. If 127 seems more or less realistic, 8,190 is definitely quite an overkill, especially compared to the number of possible Ethernet segments.

But what if we use a bit pattern instead of a single higher-order bit to encode the meaning of the remaining lower-order bit?

For example, let's use a bit pattern consisting of eight zeros at the third octet to indicate that subnet mask /30 will be used. Any other bit pattern at the third octet will assume that subnet mask /24 is used. This time, the scheme allocates 255 subnets for the Ethernet segments and 63 subnets for the point-to-point links. Although not a perfect solution for every case, this method appears to be more reasonable. In addition, it uses the otherwise wasted subnet zero—that is, 172.16.0.0/24.

One of these methods may be better than the other in some respects. However, they are both unsatisfactory because of the sporadic nature of how they were drawn and because there is a lack of methodology.

I propose the following method of dividing a previously allocated address space into subnets whose size will meet the requirements for the number of hosts on the individual segments. This method allows allocating addresses in a very economical way. Its one drawback is that it does not address the usage of subnets whose ID is zero, but adding this functionality appears to make the method more complex.

Before I describe the method, I need to introduce some additional terminology.

- The address space from which the subnets are allocated are denoted as A. A is simply a network prefix and the prefix length or, using the older terminology, a subnet mask. The prefix length of A is denoted as L_A.

- Symbol S is used to denote an individual subnet mask. The quantity of "realistic" subnet masks is shown in Table 4.3.

- The length of subnet S is denoted as L_S. When dividing the given address space, we need to calculate the number of subnets that will use the same subnet mask S. After that, we must find out the number of bits necessary to encode each individual subnet that uses subnet mask S. This number is denoted as N_S and can be obtained from Table 4.4.

Table 4.3   The relation between the length of the subnet mask and the number of hosts that the subnet mask allows.

Number of Hosts	Subnet Length	Subnet Mask
1	/32	255.255.255.255
Up to 2	/30	255.255.255.252
Up to 6	/29	255.255.255.248
Up to 14	/28	255.255.255.240
Up to 30	/27	255.255.255.224
Up to 62	/26	255.255.255.192
Up to 126	/25	255.255.255.128
Up to 254	/24	255.255.255.0
Up to 510	/23	255.255.254.0
Up to 1022	/22	255.255.252.0
Up to 2046	/21	255.255.248.0

Table 4.4   The relation between the number of bits and the number of subnets that it allocates.

Maximum Number of Subnets	Number of Bits
3	2
7	3
15	4
31	5
63	6
127	7
255	8
511	9
1023	10

4. Dynamic Routing: Distance Vector Routing Protocols

With this information, we can now implement the method using the following steps:

1. Estimate the number of subnets that will be required in the future.

2. Estimate the maximum number of hosts on each existing and future subnet. Using this number, determine the necessary subnet mask using Table 4.3.

3. For each subnet mask S, calculate the number of the subnets that will use it. Using Table 4.4, define the lowest number of bits necessary to enumerate all subnets for each individual subnet mask. If only one subnet will use a certain subnet mask, the number of bits will be 0. This number is denoted as N_S.

4. Calculate the total number of bits required for each group of subnets that use the same subnet mask. This number is denoted as T_S. T_S can be calculated using the following formula:

$$T_S = N_S + 32 - L_S$$

If there are two equal T_S values, the N_S of one of the subnet masks should be increased by 1. This process should be repeated until there are no equal T_S values.

5. Determine if all necessary subnets can be allocated from the given address space—that is, A. If

$$max(T_S) + 1 \leq 32 - L_A$$

where $max(T_S)$ is the biggest T_S, it is feasible to allocate all of the subnets; otherwise, A should be expanded until the preceding condition is met.

6. Sort the subnets by T_S in descending order and place them into the table shown in Figure 4.11. The shaded cells in the table denote the host bits. For each subnet, two-line borders are placed between cells $T_S + 1$ and T_S (cell T_S is the cell number T_S counting from the last cell in the row, and cell $T_S + 1$ is the cell right before it). In other words, these borders separate the bits that are used to enumerate the subnets that use subnet mask S and the unused bits.

NOTE: *The last two lines in the table show two specific examples. Subnet mask S_{N-1} is only used by a single subnet; therefore, N_{SN-1} is equal to zero. Subnet mask S_N is /32—that is, it consists of IP addresses for individual hosts and therefore does not have the shaded cells.*

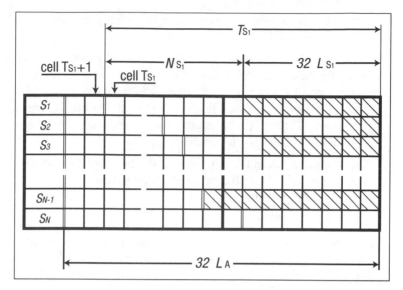

Figure 4.11   *The table used for calculating the subnet masks for use with VLSM.*

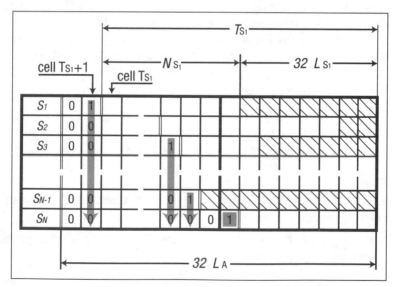

Figure 4.12   *The results of step 7.*

7. For each S, place 1 at the cell $T_s + 1$. Place zero at each cell below cell $T_s + 1$. For each S, there are empty cells between the first cell and cell $T_s + 1$; fill these with zeros. Figure 4.12 shows the results of this process.

The gray arrows show the direction in which zeros are placed under cells $T_S + 1$.

8. The bit pattern between the first cell and cell T_S allows unique identification of all subnets that use subnet mask S. The bits between cell $T_S + 1$ and the shaded cells are used to identify individual subnets. These bits can be assigned in many ways. For example, they can be assigned using the auxiliary table shown in Figure 4.13, in which each row is unique.

The combination of the subnet bits, the bit patterns drawn on step 7, and the bits of the original address range along with the corresponding subnet masks produces the subnet addresses for all future segments.

This procedure may seem complicated, but it's not. To understand better how it works, let's consider the network example shown in Figure 4.14.

Suppose we have a network belonging to the XYZ company. Currently, the company has a headquarters and five branches. The headquarters and all of the branches are located in separate buildings, and each building has a network infrastructure. The network infrastructure at the headquarters consists of an FDDI ring and two Ethernet segments. Each branch has a separate Ethernet segment. The maximum number of hosts on each segment is shown in Figure 4.14.

For simplicity, let's assume that the network is brand new; therefore, no addresses have been assigned. The address space allocated for this network infrastructure is 200.170.176.0/20.

Step 1

The future plans on network expansion are finalized. The plans for network expansion are as follows:

• There will be three extra Ethernet segments at the headquarters, each with up to 200 hosts.

Subnet 1	0	0	1
Subnet 2	0	1	0
Subnet 3	0	1	1
Subnet 4	1	0	0

Figure 4.13   An auxiliary table is used to assign the subnet bits.

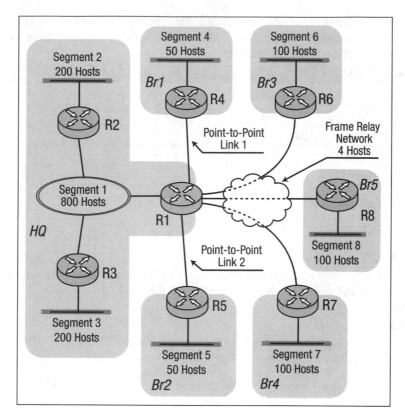

Figure 4.14   Networking infrastructure that requires VLSM.

- The company may add up to seven branches connected over the frame relay network. Each branch will have an Ethernet segment for 100 hosts.

- The company may add up to four branches connected using point-to-point links similar to branches 4 and 5. Each branch will have an Ethernet network for a maximum of 50 hosts.

- The company MIS standards require that each router has an individual IP address. The total number of routers will not exceed 60.

Step 2

The corporate network of company XYZ comprises seven categories of network segments, shown in Table 4.5. The type of network is determined by the maximum number of hosts that the network segments can accommodate.

Table 4.5   Types of network segments of the corporate network of the XYZ company. (Abbreviated names for the network segment types are given in the parentheses.)

Type of Network	Maximum Number of Hosts
FDDI	800
Large Ethernet (LE)	200
Medium-size Ethernet (ME)	100
Small Ethernet (SE)	50
Frame Relay (F/R)	10
Point-to-point links (P2P)	2
Individual IP Addresses (I)	1

Step 3

The data from step 2 is expanded to include information about subnet masks and numbers of segments (see Table 4.6).

Step 4

All of the T_s values for each subnet are calculated. The results of these calculations are shown in Table 4.7.

From Table 4.7 we can see that there are two sets of T_s values that are equal. The T_s values on rows 2 and 3 are equal, as are the T_s values on rows 6 and 7. According to our method for dividing an IP address space into subnets, we can increase the N_s of any of them by 1. Let's increase the N_s of rows 2 and 7 by 1. This will eliminate the ambiguities in the T_s column.

The resulting table will look like that shown in Table 4.8.

Table 4.6   The results of step 3.

Type of Network	Number of Hosts	Necessary Subnet Masks	Number of Segments	32-L_s	N_s
FDDI	800	/22	1	10	0
LE	200	/24	5	8	3
ME	100	/25	10	7	4
SE	50	/26	6	6	3
F/R	10	/28	1	4	0
P2P	2	/30	6	2	4
I	1	/32	60	0	6

Table 4.7 **The T_S values are added, which reveal two ambiguities at lines 2, 3, 6, and 7.**

Type of Network	Number of Hosts	Necessary Subnet Mask	Number of Segments	32-L_S	N_S	T_S
FDDI	800	/22	1	10	0	10
Ethernet	200	/24	5	8	3	11
Ethernet	100	/25	10	7	4	11
Ethernet	50	/26	6	6	3	9
F/R	10	/28	1	4	0	4
P2P	2	/30	6	2	4	6
Individual	1	/32	60	0	6	6

Table 4.8 **Ambiguities resolved. The bolded numbers show the modified N_S values.**

Type of Network	Number of Hosts	Necessary Subnet Mask	Number of Segments	32-L_S	N_S	T_S
FDDI	800	/22	1	10	0	10
Ethernet	200	/24	5	8	**4**	12
Ethernet	100	/25	10	7	4	11
Ethernet	50	/26	6	6	3	9
F/R	10	/28	1	4	0	4
P2P	2	/30	6	2	4	6
Individual	1	/32	60	0	**7**	7

Step 5

We now check to see if the size of the allocated address space is enough to accommodate all subnets. The $max(T_S) + 1$ is equal to 13, and the $32 - L_A$ is equal to 12. The feasibility condition is not met. In this case, the L_A value should be decreased until the condition is met. If L_A becomes 19, the feasibility condition will be met.

Let's assume that the L_A was decreased by 1, and the new address space is 200.170.160.0/19. Now $max(T_S) + 1$ and L_A have equal values; therefore, the feasibility condition is met.

Step 6

The results of step 4 are sorted by the T_S values and placed into a table as shown in Figure 4.15.

/ 24												
/ 25												
/ 22												
/ 26												
/ 32												
/ 30												
/ 28												

Figure 4.15   Subnet masks sorted by T_S are put into a table in accordance with step 6.

/ 24	1											
/ 25	0	1										
/ 22	0	0	1									
/ 26	0	0	0	1								
/ 32	0	0	0	0	0	1						
/ 30	0	0	0	0	0	0	1					
/ 28	0	0	0	0	0	0	0	0	1			

Figure 4.16   The table is filled out with 0s and 1s according to step 7.

Step 7

The cells between the first cell and cell T_S are filled out with appropriate bit values. The results are shown in Figure 4.16.

Step 8

The individual subnets are enumerated using the bits allocated for them, and final IP addresses are drawn. The results of step 8 are shown in Figure 4.17.

Configuring RIP Version 2

RIP Version 2 is not really a separate protocol, but an enhanced version of original RIP routing protocol. RIP version 2 has an important new feature enabling it to send the network prefixes and their lengths in the routing updates. Plus, instead of using the local broadcast address (255.255.255.255), RIP Version 2 uses a special multicast address (224.0.0.9).

To explore the classless nature of RIP Version 2, let's modify the original network that we used for RIP Version 1 (shown in Figure 4.18).

	1	2	3	4	5	6	7	8	9	10	11	12	13	
/ 24	1													
Segment 2	1	0	0	0	1									200.170.177.0/24
Segment 3	1	0	0	1	0									200.170.178.0/24
/ 25	0	1												
Segment 6	0	1	0	0	0	1								200.170.168.128/25
Segment 7	0	1	0	0	1	0								200.170.169.0/25
Segment 8	0	1	0	0	1	1								200.170.169.128/25
/ 22	0	0	1											
Segment 1	0	0	1											200.170.164.0/22
/ 26	0	0	0	1										
Segment 4	0	0	0	1	0	0	1							200.170.162.64/26
Segment 5	0	0	0	1	0	1	0							200.170.162.128/26
/ 32	0	0	0	0	0	1								
Router R1	0	0	0	0	0	1	0	0	0	0	0	0	1	200.170.160.129/32
Router R2	0	0	0	0	0	1	0	0	0	0	0	1	0	200.170.160.130/32
Router R3	0	0	0	0	0	1	0	0	0	0	0	1	1	200.170.160.131/32
Router R4	0	0	0	0	0	1	0	0	0	0	1	0	0	200.170.160.132/32
Router R5	0	0	0	0	0	1	0	0	0	0	1	0	1	200.170.160.133/32
Router R6	0	0	0	0	0	1	0	0	0	0	1	1	0	200.170.160.134/32
Router R7	0	0	0	0	0	1	0	0	0	0	1	1	1	200.170.160.135/32
Router R8	0	0	0	0	0	1	0	0	0	1	0	0	0	200.170.160.136/32
/ 30	0	0	0	0	0	0	1							
P2P Link 1	0	0	0	0	0	0	1	0	0	0	1			200.170.160.68/30
P2P Link 2	0	0	0	0	0	0	1	0	0	1	0			200.170.160.72/30
/ 28	0	0	0	0	0	0	0	0	1					
F/R Network	0	0	0	0	0	0	0	1						200.170.160.16/28

4. Dynamic Routing: Distance Vector Routing Protocols

Figure 4.17   The subnet addresses are computed as a combination of the bits from the assigned bit range and the bits obtained in steps 7 and 8.

Let's also use the VLSM calculation method explained in the previous section to figure out the IP addresses for all the segment of the network. Obviously, we only have to do that for the segments whose IP addresses should be allocated from network 10.0.0.0.

Step 1

We don't have any plans on expansion of this network, do we? In other words, skip step 1.

Step 2

We don't have many categories of network segments. In fact, we have only four real segments and three routers that require individual IP addresses. The results of step 2 are shown in Table 4.9.

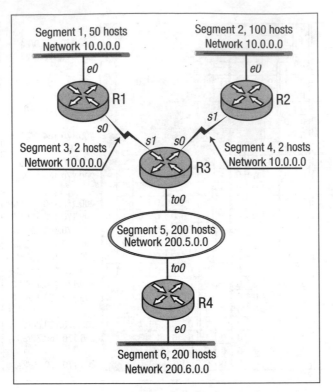

Figure 4.18   The physical network layout with the requirements for the maximum number of hosts on each segment.

Table 4.9   Types of network segments from Figure 4.18.

Type of Network	Maximum Number of Hosts
Segment 2 (LE)	100
Segment 1 (SE)	50
Segments 3 and 4 (P2P)	2
Individual IP addresses (I)	3

Step 3

Using Tables 4.3, 4.4, and 4.9, figure out the necessary values for all of the types of segments that we have (see Table 4.10).

Step 4

Calculate the T_s values for every subnet mask (see Table 4.11).

Since there is no ambiguity in Table 4.11, we can proceed to step 5.

Table 4.10   *Results from step 3.*

Type of Network	Number of Hosts	Necessary Subnet Mask	Number of Segments	$32 - L_s$	N_s
LE	100	/25	1	7	0
SE	50	/26	1	6	0
P2P	2	/30	2	2	2
I	3	/32	3	0	2

Table 4.11   *The T_s values for every subnet mask calculated in step 4.*

Type of Network	Number of Hosts	Necessary Subnet Mask	Number of Segments	$32 - L_s$	N_s	T_s
LE	100	/25	1	7	0	7
SE	50	/26	1	6	0	6
P2P	2	/30	2	2	2	4
I	3	/32	3	0	2	2

Step 5

We were allocated the whole network 10, whose L_A value is 8. Our biggest T_s is 7; therefore, $max(T_s) + 1 = 8$—smaller than $32 - L_s$, which is 24. This means that we have met the feasibility condition.

Steps 6, 7, And 8

Because of the small number of segments, it makes sense to combine steps 6, 7, and 8. The results of these steps are shown in Figure 4.19.

/ 25	1								
Segment 2	1								10.0.0.128/25
/ 26	0	1							
Segment 1	0	1							10.0.0.64/26
/ 30	0	0	0	1					
Segment 3	0	0	0	1	0	1			10.0.0.20/30
Segment 4	0	0	0	1	1	0			10.0.0.24/30
/ 32	0	0	0	0	0	1			
router R1	0	0	0	0	0	1	0	1	10.0.0.5/32
router R2	0	0	0	0	0	1	1	0	10.0.0.6/32
router R3	0	0	0	0	0	1	1	1	10.0.0.7/32

Figure 4.19   *The results of steps 6, 7, and 8.*

4. Dynamic Routing: Distance Vector Routing Protocols

Since we now have all of the network IP addresses, we can figure out the routers' configurations (see Listings 4.64 through 4.67).

Listing 4.64   Router R1's configuration.

```
interface Loopback0
 ip address 10.0.0.5 255.255.255.255

interface Ethernet0
 ip address 10.0.0.65 255.255.255.192

interface Serial0
 ip address 10.0.0.21 255.255.255.252

router rip
 version 2
 network 10.0.0.0
```

Listing 4.65   Router R2's configuration.

```
interface Loopback0
 ip address 10.0.0.6 255.255.255.255
!
interface Ethernet0
 ip address 10.0.0.129 255.255.255.128

interface Serial1
 ip address 10.0.0.25 255.255.255.252

router rip
 version 2
 network 10.0.0.0
```

Listing 4.66   Router R3's configuration.

```
interface Loopback0
 ip address 10.0.0.7 255.255.255.255

interface Serial0
 ip address 10.0.0.26 255.255.255.252

interface Serial1
 ip address 10.0.0.22 255.255.255.252

interface TokenRing0
 ip address 200.5.0.1 255.255.255.0
 ring-speed 16

router rip
 version 2
```

```
network 10.0.0.0
network 200.5.0.0
```

Listing 4.67   Router R4's configuration.

```
interface Ethernet0
 ip address 200.6.0.1 255.255.255.0
 shutdown

interface TokenRing0
 ip address 200.5.0.2 255.255.255.0
 ring-speed 16

router rip
 version 2
 network 200.5.0.0
 network 200.6.0.0
```

If we display the routing table on router R1, we'll see the output shown in Listing 4.68.

Listing 4.68   The routing table of router R1.

```
R1#show ip route
...
     10.0.0.0/8 is variably subnetted, 7 subnets, 4 masks
R       10.0.0.6/32 [120/2] via 10.0.0.22, 00:00:01, Serial0
R       10.0.0.7/32 [120/1] via 10.0.0.22, 00:00:01, Serial0
C       10.0.0.5/32 is directly connected, Loopback0
R       10.0.0.24/30 [120/1] via 10.0.0.22, 00:00:01, Serial0
C       10.0.0.20/30 is directly connected, Serial0
C       10.0.0.64/26 is directly connected, Ethernet0
R       10.0.0.128/25 [120/2] via 10.0.0.22, 00:00:01, Serial0
R    200.5.0.0/24 [120/1] via 10.0.0.22, 00:00:01, Serial0
R    200.6.0.0/24 [120/2] via 10.0.0.22, 00:00:01, Serial0
```

We can see all of the configured subnets with the correct subnet masks. However, if we display the routing table on router R4, we'll see a slightly different picture (shown in Listing 4.69).

Listing 4.69   The routing table of router R4.

```
R4#show ip route
...
C    200.5.0.0/24 is directly connected, TokenRing0
C    200.6.0.0/24 is directly connected, Ethernet0
R    10.0.0.0/8 [120/1] via 200.5.0.1, 00:00:03, TokenRing0
```

Although router R3 is now running a classless routing protocol, it still summarizes the advertised network on the classful boundary if the respective routing updates are sent over interfaces whose IP addresses belong to different classful network IP addresses.

Disabling RIP Version 2 Auto-Summarization

Both versions of RIP perform auto-summarization by default, but in RIP Version 2, this feature can be turned off if required.

NOTE: RIP Version 1 is a classful routing protocol, which forces it to auto-summarize. RIP Version 2, however, is a classless extension of RIP Version 1, which means that it is able to overcome classful restrains, such as auto-summarization.

Because RIP Version 2 is classless, it can send network prefixes and their lengths (also called subnet addresses and subnet masks) in the routing updates.Therefore, RIP Version 2 must be able to send individual subnets even in the routing updates that cross the classful network boundaries.

RIP Version 2 is indeed capable of advertising individual subnets and even supernets, no matter what IP address is configured on the interfaces used to send the respective routing updates. To turn off auto-summarization in RIP Version 2, the command **no auto-summary** should be entered under the **router rip** configuration.

Let's see what happens if we enter the command **no auto-summary** on router R3 from the previous section. We should be able to see individual subnets of network 10.0.0.0 on router R4 (see Listing 4.70).

Listing 4.70   The routing table of router R4.

```
R4#show ip route
...
C   200.5.0.0/24 is directly connected, TokenRing0
C   200.6.0.0/24 is directly connected, Ethernet0
    10.0.0.0/8 is variably subnetted, 7 subnets, 4 masks
R      10.0.0.6/32 [120/2] via 200.5.0.1, 00:00:05, TokenRing0
R      10.0.0.7/32 [120/1] via 200.5.0.1, 00:00:05, TokenRing0
R      10.0.0.5/32 [120/2] via 200.5.0.1, 00:00:05, TokenRing0
R      10.0.0.24/30 [120/1] via 200.5.0.1, 00:00:05, TokenRing0
R      10.0.0.20/30 [120/1] via 200.5.0.1, 00:00:05, TokenRing0
R      10.0.0.64/26 [120/2] via 200.5.0.1, 00:00:05, TokenRing0
R      10.0.0.128/25 [120/2] via 200.5.0.1, 00:00:05,TokenRing0
```

The output of the command **show ip route** entered on router R4 shown in Listing 4.70 proves that auto-summarization is no longer performed by router R3.

I mentioned that RIP Version 2 can even advertise supernets. However, this requires techniques covered in Chapter 6, so we will postpone this discussion until that chapter.

Using RIP Version 1 And RIP Version 2 Simultaneously

Cisco's implementation of RIP allows using both versions simultaneously. Moreover, it can be done on an individual interface basis. Two commands are used to enable processing the desired version of RIP on an interface. The first command is **ip rip send version {1|2}**, which enables sending the desired version of RIP routing updates via the corresponding interface. The second command is **ip rip receive version {1|2}**, which allows the router to receive and process the desired version of RIP routing updates. Both commands should be entered in the interface configuration mode.

TIP: *The full format of the command is **ip rip {receive|send} version {1|2} [{1|2}]**, which allows you to specify exactly which version of RIP you want the router to use when sending and receiving RIP routing updates on a particular interface. The last optional parameter allows using both versions simultaneously. However, exercise care if both versions are specified. The router will double the number of routing updates, because it will have to create a separate routing update for each version.*

No matter which version the **router rip** configuration specifies by means of the command **version**, the command **ip rip {receive|send} version {1|2} [{1|2}]** is still available and takes precedence over the **version** command used under the **router rip** configuration. In other words, the **version** command under the **router rip** configuration specifies the default version, whereas the **ip rip {receive|send} version {1|2} [{1|2}]** specifies the version which should be used on individual interfaces when sending or receiving the RIP routing updates.

Let's modify the original configuration that we considered in the first section devoted to RIP Version 2 so that router R4 is configured with only RIP Version 1 and router R3 uses both versions. Router R3 will send and receive RIP Version 1 updates only on interface TokenRing 0 and RIP Version 2 updates on all other interfaces.

Listing 4.71 shows how the router R3 configuration should be modified.

Listing 4.71   Router R3's configuration.

```
interface Loopback0
 ip address 10.0.0.7 255.255.255.255

interface Serial0
 ip address 10.0.0.26 255.255.255.252

interface Serial1
 ip address 10.0.0.22 255.255.255.252

interface TokenRing0
 ip address 200.5.0.1 255.255.255.0
 ip rip send version 1
 ip rip receive version 1
 ring-speed 16

router rip
 version 2
 network 10.0.0.0
 network 200.5.0.0
```

The routing table on router R4 (shown in Listing 4.72) still includes network 10.0.0.0, which proves that router R3 sends RIP Version 1 routing updates.

Listing 4.72   The routing table of router R4.

```
R4#show ip route
...
C    200.5.0.0/24 is directly connected, TokenRing0
C    200.6.0.0/24 is directly connected, Ethernet0
R    10.0.0.0/8 [120/1] via 200.5.0.1, 00:00:02, TokenRing0
```

Configuring EIGRP

EIGRP is easy to configure and is more robust than any other distance vector routing protocol. The scope of this book does not permit a thorough examination of EIGRP, but it does cover EIGRP's essential features.

Unlike RIP Version 2, which is just an improved version of RIP, EIGRP is a completely different protocol from IGRP. Also, unlike the primitive distance vector routing protocols such as both versions of RIP and IGRP, EIGRP does not send regular routing updates containing the whole routing table. Instead, EIGRP makes the router exchange short *hello* messages with its neighbors. The purpose of the hello messages is to make sure that its neighbors are alive. EIGRP allows the router to send routing updates only when there is a topology change. The router knows about the topology changes in two ways: if a physical interface goes down, or if the router misses three subsequent hello messages from a neighbor, which is then considered to be down. If a topology change is detected, the router uses special algorithms that allow the router to discover alternative routes for the affected network prefixes quickly.

The convergence time of EIGRP is much faster than that of RIP and IGRP. Convergence time is measured in tens of seconds for EIGRP compared to minutes for RIP and IGRP.

Although advanced, EIGRP is still a distance vector routing protocol. Therefore, it uses the same convergence improvement techniques as the other distance vector routing protocols—the split-horizon rule, holddowns, and triggered updates (actually, it only uses triggered updates and it does not use regular routing updates at all).

The basic configuration of EIGRP is essentially the same as that of IGRP. Although EIGRP is a classless routing protocol, the individual interfaces are assigned for servicing by EIGRP in exactly the same way as that used for all other distance vector routing protocols—the command **network**. Just as with all other protocols, the EIGRP version of the command **network** is very classful—it does not accept subnets. Therefore, a combination of the **passive-interface** and **distance** commands should be used to disable EIGRP completely on individual interfaces if necessary.

Commands such as **neighbor**, **distance**, and **passive-interface** are available and have the same functionality as they do in RIP and IGRP.

Let's examine the behavior of EIGRP in a real-life example.

Let's change the routing protocol in the network shown in Figure 4.18 from RIP Version 2 to EIGRP (see Listings 4.73 through 4.76). Because both RIP Version 2 and EIGRP are classless routing protocols, we can keep the existing addressing.

Listing 4.73   Router R1's configuration.

```
interface Loopback0
 ip address 10.0.0.5 255.255.255.255

interface Ethernet0
 ip address 10.0.0.65 255.255.255.192

interface Serial0
```

```
   ip address 10.0.0.21 255.255.255.252

router eigrp 15
   network 10.0.0.0
```

Listing 4.74   Router R2's configuration.

```
interface Loopback0
   ip address 10.0.0.6 255.255.255.255

interface Ethernet0
   ip address 10.0.0.129 255.255.255.128

interface Serial1
   ip address 10.0.0.25 255.255.255.252

router eigrp 15
   network 10.0.0.0
```

Listing 4.75   Router R3's configuration.

```
interface Loopback0
   ip address 10.0.0.7 255.255.255.255

interface Serial0
   ip address 10.0.0.26 255.255.255.252

interface Serial1
   ip address 10.0.0.22 255.255.255.252

interface TokenRing0
   ip address 200.5.0.1 255.255.255.0
   ring-speed 16

router eigrp 15
   network 10.0.0.0
   network 200.5.0.0
```

Listing 4.76   Router R4's configuration.

```
interface Ethernet0
   ip address 200.6.0.1 255.255.255.0

interface TokenRing0
   ip address 200.5.0.2 255.255.255.0
   ring-speed 16

router eigrp 15
   network 200.5.0.0
   network 200.6.0.0
```

Listings 4.77 and 4.78 show the routing tables of routers R1 and R4.

Listing 4.77   The routing table of router R1 demonstrates the presence of the routes learned via EIGRP.

```
R1#show ip route
...
   10.0.0.0/8 is variably subnetted, 7 subnets, 4 masks
D   10.0.0.6/32 [90/2809856] via 10.0.0.22, 00:03:52, Serial0
D   10.0.0.7/32 [90/2297856] via 10.0.0.22, 00:03:52, Serial0
C   10.0.0.5/32 is directly connected, Loopback0
D   10.0.0.24/30 [90/2681856] via 10.0.0.22, 00:03:52, Serial0
C   10.0.0.20/30 is directly connected, Serial0
C   10.0.0.64/26 is directly connected, Ethernet0
D   10.0.0.128/25 [90/2707456] via 10.0.0.22, 00:03:52,Serial0
D 200.5.0.0/24 [90/2185984] via 10.0.0.22, 00:03:52, Serial0
D 200.6.0.0/24 [90/2211584] via 10.0.0.22, 00:03:34, Serial0
```

Listing 4.78   The routing table of router R4.

```
R4#show ip route
...
C   200.5.0.0/24 is directly connected, TokenRing0
C   200.6.0.0/24 is directly connected, Ethernet0
D   10.0.0.0/8 [90/304128] via 200.5.0.1, 00:08:18, TokenRing0
```

Both routing tables look just as they did in case of RIP Version 2, which is no surprise. The only difference is that now the dynamically learned routes are labeled with the letter "D" instead of "R". "D" indicates the routes that were learned with EIGRP.

Understanding EIGRP Metrics

EIGRP uses very similar metrics to those of IGRP. Actually, EIGRP uses the same formula, but it also multiplies IGRP metrics by 256, as follows:

$$M_{EIGRP} = M_{IGRP} * 256$$

Disabling EIGRP Auto-Summarization

Disabling the auto-summarization performed by EIGRP is done in exactly the same way as it was done with RIP. The command **no auto-summary** prevents EIGRP from summarizing the routes on the classful boundary.

If we enter the command **no auto-summary** on router R3 under the **router eigrp 15** configuration and then examine the routing table on router R4, it will look as shown in Listing 4.79.

Listing 4.79   The routing table of router R4.

```
R4#show ip route
...
C 200.5.0.0/24 is directly connected,TokenRing0
C 200.6.0.0/24 is directly connected,Ethernet0
  10.0.0.0/8 is variably subnetted, 7 subnets, 4 masks
D    10.0.0.6/32 [90/231984] via 200.5.0.1,00:00:02,TokenRing0
D    10.0.0.7/32 [90/304128] via 200.5.0.1,00:00:02,TokenRing0
D    10.0.0.5/32 [90/231984] via 200.5.0.1,00:00:02,TokenRing0
D    10.0.0.24/30 [90/218984] via 200.5.0.1,00:00:02,TokenRing0
D    10.0.0.20/30 [90/218984] via 200.5.0.1,00:00:02,TokenRing0
D    10.0.0.64/26 [90/221584] via 200.5.0.1,00:00:02,TokenRing0
D    10.0.0.128/25 [90/221584]via 200.5.0.1,00:00:02,TokenRing0
```

Router R4 now sees the same routes as router R1.

Configuring Route Summarization With EIGRP

A very powerful feature of EIGRP is manual route summarization. To perform manual route summarization, the command **ip summary-address eigrp** <AS Number> <IP Address> <Subnet Mask> should be entered in the interface configuration mode. The router then stops sending regular EIGRP routing updates and instead advertises the summary address as specified in the parameters <IP Address> <Subnet Mask>.

For example, let's change all of the router R1, R2, and R3 addresses (see Figure 4.18) that start with 10, from 10.0.0.X to 210.0.0.X. Afterwards, let's modify the configuration of router R3 as shown in Listing 4.80 (the modified part is italicized).

Listing 4.80   Router R3's configuration.

```
interface Loopback0
 ip address 210.0.0.7 255.255.255.255

interface Serial0
 ip address 210.0.0.26 255.255.255.252

interface Serial1
 ip address 210.0.0.22 255.255.255.252
interface TokenRing0
 ip address 200.5.0.1 255.255.255.0
 ip summary-address eigrp 15 210.0.0.0 255.255.0.0
 ring-speed 16
```

```
router eigrp 15
 network 200.5.0.0
 network 210.0.0.0
```

Listing 4.81 shows the routing table on router R4.

Listing 4.81   The routing table of router R4.

```
R4#show ip route
...
C  200.5.0.0/24 is directly connected, TokenRing0
C  200.6.0.0/24 is directly connected, Ethernet0
D  210.0.0.0/16 [90/304128] via 200.5.0.1,00:01:18,TokenRing0
```

The routing table of router R4 confirms that router R3 performs manual route summarization when sending EIGRP routing updates via interface TokenRing 0.

TIP: *It is a good idea to always accompany manual route summarization with the command* **ip classless**.

If we examine the routing table of router R3, in addition to regular routes, we'll also see the summary that the router advertises (see Listing 4.82). (The parts of the output that are not relevant to the subject were skipped.)

Listing 4.82   The EIGRP summary route in the routing table of router R3.

```
R3#show ip route
...
D    210.0.0.0/16 is a summary, 00:24:13, Null0
```

There are two interesting features of this route. One of these features is obvious—the route points to the Null0 interface. Note that any packet that must be sent out of the null interface is actually dropped (hence, the name of the interface). However, remember that when a router uses the routing table, it first tries to find the longest match. Therefore, a route in the routing table with a longer match than the route that points to the null interface is used instead. Thus, a route that points to the null interface is a perfect candidate for the summary routes. First, a route with a network prefix longer than that of the summary route is used instead; otherwise, the packets are dropped, which means that they will not pollute the network. Second, the presence of such a route in the routing table allows the router to advertise it using the dynamic routing protocol, which created the route.

Another important feature of this route is that the administrative distance of an EIGRP summary route is always 5 and cannot be changed.

Configuring EIGRP Over Non-Fully Meshed Frame Relay Networks

As we know, RIP and IGRP working over a non-fully meshed frame relay network behave in an unexpected way because of the turned-off split horizon. However, EIGRP behaves differently: The routers, not connected with PVC, do not see each other's networks.

For some reason, Cisco decided that it was not necessary to disable the EIGRP split-horizon rule on the interfaces configured with frame relay encapsulation. In addition, the command that enables and disables split horizon for EIGRP is different from the one used for both RIP and IGRP. The EIGRP version is **no ip split-horizon eigrp** *<AS Number>*.

As an example, let's consider the same network used to examine the behavior of RIP over non-fully meshed frame relay networks. Let's return to Figure 4.10. Only this time, we'll use the EIGRP routing protocol.

Listings 4.83 through 4.85 show the new configurations of all three routers.

Listing 4.83   Router R1's configuration.

```
interface Ethernet0
 ip address 200.1.0.1 255.255.255.0

interface Serial1
 ip address 200.200.0.1 255.255.255.0
 encapsulation frame-relay
 frame-relay map ip 200.200.0.2 102 broadcast
 frame-relay map ip 200.200.0.3 103 broadcast
 frame-relay lmi-type ansi

router eigrp 15
 network 200.1.0.0
 network 200.200.0.0
```

Listing 4.84   Router R2's configuration.

```
interface Ethernet0
 ip address 200.2.0.1 255.255.255.0

interface Serial0
```

```
ip address 200.200.0.2 255.255.255.0
encapsulation frame-relay
frame-relay map ip 200.200.0.1 201 broadcast
frame-relay lmi-type ansi

router eigrp 15
 network 200.2.0.0
 network 200.200.0.0
```

Listing 4.85   Router R3's configuration.

```
interface Ethernet0
 ip address 200.3.0.1 255.255.255.0

interface Serial0
 ip address 200.200.0.3 255.255.255.0
 encapsulation frame-relay
 frame-relay map ip 200.200.0.1 301 broadcast
 frame-relay lmi-type ansi

router eigrp 15
 network 200.3.0.0
 network 200.200.0.0
```

Listing 4.86 shows the routing table on router R2.

Listing 4.86   The routing table of router R2.

```
R2#show ip route
...
C   200.200.0.0/24 is directly connected, Serial0
D   200.1.0.0/24 [90/2195456] via 200.200.0.1,00:06:24,Serial0
C   200.2.0.0/24 is directly connected, Ethernet0
```

This output confirms our expectations that the split-horizon rule for EIGRP is still on, even on the serial interfaces configured with frame relay encapsulation.

Let's use the command **no ip split-horizon eigrp 15** under **interface Serial 1** on router R1 to see if it helps. Listing 4.87 shows the revised configuration of router R1 (note the italicized line).

Listing 4.87   Router R1's configuration.

```
interface Ethernet0
 ip address 200.1.0.1 255.255.255.0

interface Serial1
 ip address 200.200.0.1 255.255.255.0
 encapsulation frame-relay
```

```
no ip split-horizon eigrp 15
frame-relay map ip 200.200.0.2 102 broadcast
frame-relay map ip 200.200.0.3 103 broadcast
frame-relay lmi-type ansi

router eigrp 15
 network 200.1.0.0
 network 200.200.0.0
```

The routing table on router R1 shows that all desirable routes are there (see the italicized line in Listing 4.88).

Listing 4.88   The routing table of router R2.

```
R2#show ip route
...
C  200.200.0.0/24 is directly connected, Serial0
D  200.1.0.0/24 [90/2195456] via 200.200.0.1,00:01:09,Serial0
C  200.2.0.0/24 is directly connected, Ethernet0
D  200.3.0.0/24 [90/2707456] via 200.200.0.1,00:00:14,Serial0
```

## Chapter 5

Dynamic Routing: Link State Routing Protocols

If you need an immediate solution to:	See page:
Configuring OSPF With A Single Area	230
Understanding OSPF Costs	234
Configuring OSPF With Multiple Areas	235
Originating Default Information	240
Displaying An OSPF Link State Database	241
Configuring OSPF Stub Areas	242
Using OSPF Virtual Links To Restore A Partitioned Backbone	245
Using OSPF Virtual Links To Connect Remote Areas	255
Configuring OSPF Over NBMA Networks	261
Configuring OSPF Over Fully Meshed NBMA Networks	261
Configuring OSPF Over Non-Fully Meshed NBMA Networks	268

In Brief

Link state protocols represent another breed of dynamic routing protocols based on algorithms completely different from those on which distance vector protocols are based. Unlike distance vector protocols, link state protocols know the complete topology of the whole network in which they operate or, at least, a part that is implemented as a "semi-independent" area.

Link state protocols are represented in the Cisco IOS by the Internet standard protocol OSPF (Open Shortest Path First) and the ISO standard protocol IS-IS (Intermediate System to Intermediate System). The document that describes the latest version of OSPF specification is RFC 2328.

Since its first introduction, OSPF has become one of the most popular dynamic routing protocols. There are many reasons for this—the most important being that it has fast convergence, was specifically designed to work in very large networks, and is an open standard. Although IS-IS also possesses these three qualities, it never received the popularity of OSPF and has rarely been used. In this book, we'll consider only OSPF for this reason.

OSPF

The rest of the "In Brief" section gives a limited overview of OSPF operation, which includes very basic descriptions of most essential OSPF features and how they work. OSPF is a "big" topic, which may be regarded as a science on its own. Probably the best and most comprehensive source of information on OSPF is RFC 2328, entitled "OSPF Version 2."

TIP: *Unfortunately, RFC 2328 is only available in text format. However, one of its predecessors, RFC 1583, now obsolete, is available in PostScript format. The nature of OSPF dictates that the specification should contain many graphs. In RFC 2328 the graphs are presented in the form of tables, whereas in RFC 1583 they are presented in the form of figures. Figures are much easier to understand, and luckily the graphs did not change much in RFC 2328. I personally found it very convenient to study OSPF using RFC 2328 but using the graphs figures from RFC 1583.*

Protocol Overview

OSPF, being a link state protocol, possesses complete topology knowledge of either the entire network or a specific area. Obviously, the routing table alone is not sufficient to sustain such knowledge. Thus, OSPF maintains its own data structure known as a *link state database*. OSPF then uses the link state database to populate the routes to the routing table.

The structure of the link state database is crafted to store the network topology information, whereas the structure of the routing table is designed to facilitate IP address lookup. Therefore, to populate the routing table with information from the link state database, this information should first be converted into the routing table format. OSPF, as well as the other link state protocols, uses the Dijkstra shortest path algorithm to perform this conversion. This algorithm is described in the next section. If the contents of the link state database changes, the router runs the Dijkstra algorithm to re-populate the routing table with updated routes.

The topology information stored in the link state database must be communicated between the routers participating in OSPF routing. The OSPF routers use a communication procedure, which can be briefly described as follows:

1. OSPF routers discover each other using the OSPF HELLO protocol. Afterwards the routers use the OSPF HELLO protocol to monitor each other and the link connecting them.

2. When two OSPF routers discover each other, they synchronize their link state databases. The synchronization consists of finding out and eliminating the discrepancies in the routers' link state databases using the most up-to-date information the two databases contain. (This allows the new routers to quickly learn of the active network topology.)

3. An OSPF router advertises the part of the network topology to which it is directly connected on a regular basis in predefined time intervals (30 minutes) to all its *adjacent* neighbors. Adjacent neighbors will be explained in the section "OSPF Network Types." This router's adjacent neighbors propagate the advertisements to all their adjacent neighbors, and so on. This way all routers discover the topology of the network.

4. Besides the regular OSPF topology advertisements, routers communicate network topology information only if it changes.

OSPF is a truly classless routing protocol. It does not make any assumptions with regard to the IP network classes (that is A, B, and C) and corresponding default subnet masks.

Finally, every OSPF router has a unique number associated with it called *OSPF router ID* or simply *router ID*. If an OSPF autonomous system consists of multiple areas (described in the section "Hierarchical Routing Model" in this chapter), these areas also have unique IDs, called *area IDs*.

Dijkstra's Shortest Path Algorithm

Edsger Dijkstra invented the shortest path algorithm in 1959. Since then, the algorithm has been used in numerous computer and network-related applications; two of which are the spanning tree algorithm and the link state protocols. The algorithm's popularity is due to its efficiency and simplicity.

Following is a brief explanation of the problem the algorithm solves and how it works.

The algorithm operates over a directed graph, consisting of vertices and weighted edges. The problem that the algorithm solves is how to find the shortest path between two vertices of the graph, where the shortest path is defined as the path whose sum of the weights of the edges comprising it is minimal.

During its operation, the algorithm maintains two databases. Both databases have the same structure consisting of two fields: a vertex and the length of the best known path from the source vertex to this vertex. The first database, called *SP* (shortest path), contains the vertices for which the shortest path is already found. The second database, called *CSP* (candidate shortest path), contains the vertices for which the shortest path is not yet finalized. The algorithm starts by putting the source vertex to the SP with the path length 0, leaving the CSP empty. The algorithm recursively cycles through the following steps:

1. It calculates the path lengths for all neighbors of vertex S. (If this is the first iteration of the algorithm, S is equal to the source vertex, otherwise it is passed from the previous step of the algorithm.)

2. It puts all neighbors of vertex S to the CSP. If the CSP already contains some of these vertices, it updates their lengths with the new values only if the new values are better than the existing ones.

3. It chooses the vertex with the smallest path length from among all of the vertices in the CSP and moves it from the CSP to the CS.

4. If the CSP is not empty, the algorithm performs the next iteration (step 1) with this vertex as S, otherwise the algorithm ends.

This more "aggressive" version of the algorithm (which is used in OSPF as well as in the other link state protocols) calculates the shortest paths for all vertices in the graph.

To better understand how the algorithm works, let's consider the graph example shown in Figure 5.1. The vertices are shown as circles with the vertex numbers inside. The edges are shown as lines connecting the vertices. The weights of the vertices are shown in the middle of the corresponding lines.

Figure 5.2 shows all of the steps of the algorithm. The vertices that are added into the CSP are connected with dashed lines. The vertex that is just added to the SP has a thick border. The current lengths of the paths from the source vertex to each individual vertex are shown next to the corresponding vertices.

Several Web-based interactive demos of the pure shortest path algorithm are available, which you may find useful for understanding how the algorithm works. Most of them allow you to modify the graph

5. Dynamic Routing: Link State Routing Protocols

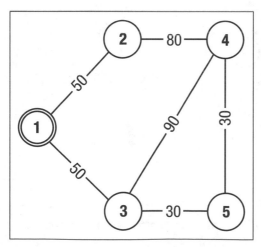

Figure 5.1   An example of a directed graph.

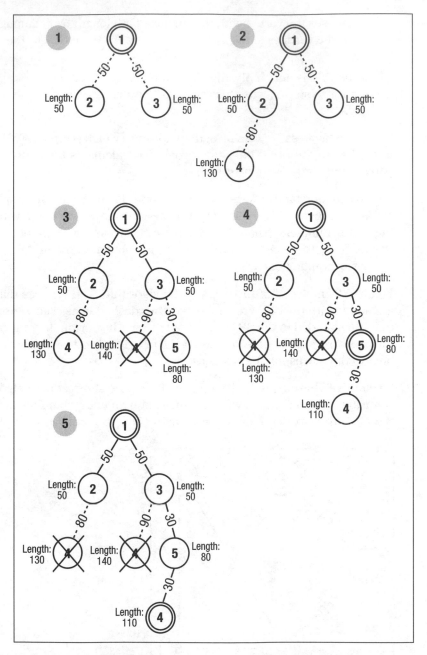

Figure 5.2   *The steps of the algorithm as it calculates the shortest paths to every vertex in the graph.*

parameters, such as the number of vertices, edge weights, and so on, and to choose between continuously running the algorithm or taking one step at a time. One of these interactive demos is implemented as a Java applet and is found at http://carnap.ss.uci.edu/java/dijkstra/DijkstraApplet.html.

OSPF Network Types

Real networks are often very different from the directed graphs over which the Dijkstra shortest path algorithm operates. Therefore, to make the algorithm applicable to real networks, their logical representation, at least in the OSPF data structures, has to be adjusted to accommodate for the algorithm requirements.

The OSPF specification provides the following guidelines for logical representation of the physical network components, such as routers, point-to-point networks, multiaccess networks, and so on:

- OSPF routers are always represented as vertices of a graph.

- Point-to-point links, of course, can be represented as edges of a graph.

- Regular broadcast multiaccess networks (such as LANs) and NBMA networks (such as frame relay) present a problem. Both types of networks allow connecting arbitrary number of routers via a single medium, which cannot be represented as a graph edge.

  OSPF models a broadcast multiaccess network as a graph vertex, to which each individual router (which is also a vertex) is connected via a network interface that becomes a graph edge. Because the network cannot actively participate in OSPF routing, one of the routers takes on the burden of speaking for the network. This router is called a *designated router*. The OSPF specification also requires another router to become a *backup designated router*; it becomes the designated router if the active designated router becomes unavailable.

  The NBMA networks can be represented either as a broadcast multiaccess network, if all routers can directly communicate with each other, or multiple point-to-point networks, if such communication is not an option.

Figure 5.3 shows how different network types are translated into OSPF graphs. Vertices labeled with the letter "R" denote routers; those with the letter "N" denote networks.

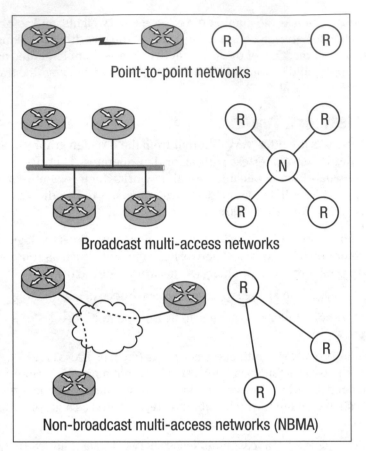

Point-to-point networks

Broadcast multi-access networks

Non-broadcast multi-access networks (NBMA)

Figure 5.3   OSPF representation of a broadcast network.

The operation of OSPF requires that routers form an adjacency in order to communicate. Adjacency is a special relation between two routers that allows logical representation of these two routers as two vertices of a graph connected with an edge. OSPF uses the following rules when creating adjacencies:

- Only those routers that directly reach each other can become adjacent.

- In the case of point-to-point connections, the two routers always become adjacent.

- In the case of broadcast multiaccess networks, every router forms an adjacency with the designated router and backup designated router.

The adjacencies will be used by OSPF routers to propagate the topology information throughout the autonomous system.

Hierarchical Routing Model

As mentioned before, OSPF was specifically designed to serve very large networks. OSPF's ability to perform hierarchical routing is what allows it to address the issues associated with large networks.

Hierarchical routing assumes that a single routing domain, also called an *autonomous system*, is partitioned into smaller areas, each of which performs its own independent routing. From outside, an area is accessible via one or more area summary addresses, which together provide a match for any IP address available within the area. The primary purpose of hierarchical routing is to reduce the size of routing updates exchanged throughout the autonomous system by replacing multiple individual routes in the other areas with much smaller number of summary routes.

To a certain extent, hierarchical routing can be implemented with nearly any routing protocol. For example, even RIP Version 1 replaces individual subnet routes with the classful network route if the corresponding routing update traverses the classful network boundary. This behavior of RIP can be considered to be a sort of primitive hierarchical routing. However, hierarchical routing becomes flexible only if it is implemented using classless routing protocols, such as OSPF, EIGRP, and RIP Version 2. For example, EIGRP provides the command **ip summary-address eigrp** *<AS number> <IP address> <subnet mask>*, which can be used to configure EIGRP for hierarchical routing. However, only OSPF provides comprehensive tools, which greatly simplify the implementation of hierarchical routing.

The OSPF version of hierarchical routing imposes certain requirements, which can briefly be described as follows:

- There must be a single area called a *backbone* with an ID of 0.

- All other areas must be connected to the backbone. No area can be connected to the network via any area except the backbone.

- Routers connected to more than one area must keep a separate link state database for each area. All operations on each individual link state database—such as LSAs flooding, running the shortest path algorithm, and so on—must be performed independently.

The routers that connect areas to the backbone are called *area border routers*, or *ABRs*.

OSPF allows routing information from other protocols to be "redistributed" into OSPF. This redistribution is covered in detail in

Chapter 6, but it is mentioned here because it is required for defining the next OSPF-specific term—*autonomous system boundary routers*, or *ASBRs*. ASBRs are the routers that redistribute the routing information from routing protocols other than OSPF into an OSPF autonomous system.

Link State Advertisements

OSPF routers communicate topology information using data structures called *link state advertisements*, or *LSAs*. LSAs are also entries (or records) in the OSPF link state database.

LSAs contain information about the local state of a router or network. For example, in the case of a router, an LSA describes the state of the router's interfaces and adjacencies. LSAs are originated by OSPF routers and flooded to all router's adjacent neighbors, except the one from which the corresponding LSAs were received. If a router originates an LSA, it floods it to all its adjacent neighbors.

Not all OSPF routers originate all possible LSAs. OSPF has several functionally different LSA types, which are described in Table 5.1.

Table 5.1   OSPF LSA types.

LSA Type	LSA Name	Description
Type 1	Router-LSA	Originated by all routers.
		Describes the states of the router interfaces in the area.
		Flooded throughout the corresponding area only.
Type 2	Network-LSA	Originated for broadcast multiaccess and NBMA networks by their respective designated routers only.
		Contains the list of routers connected to the network.
		Flooded throughout the corresponding area only.
Type 3	Summary-LSA	Originated by ABRs only.
		Describes routes to destination networks outside the area but inside the autonomous system (for example, a summary route for another area).
		Flooded throughout the area only.
Type 4	Summary-LSA	Originated by ABRs only.
		Describes the routes to ASBRs located outside the area.
		Flooded throughout the area only.

(continued)

Table 5.1   OSPF LSA types (continued).

LSA Type	LSA Name	Description
Type 5	AS-external-LSAs	Originated by ASBRs only.
		Describes the external routes and can be used to describe default routes.
		Flooded throughout the autonomous system.

To summarize the information from Table 5.1, the router-LSAs and network-LSAs describe the interconnection of routers and networks within an area, the summary-LSAs describe inter-area routes, and the AS-external-LSAs describe external routes that are injected into an autonomous system.

5. Dynamic Routing: Link State Routing Protocols

Immediate Solutions

Configuring OSPF With A Single Area

To configure OSPF with a single area, follow these comparatively easy steps:

1. Create an OSPF ID by enabling a loopback interface and assigning it an IP address.

NOTE: *This step is optional, although very desirable. If this step is omitted, OSPF chooses the IP address with the highest number among the IP addresses of the active interfaces as its ID. If this interface goes down, OSPF immediately switches its ID over to the remaining IP address with the highest number. However, if there is at least one active loopback interface, OSPF only considers the IP addresses of the loopback interfaces. As before, OSPF chooses the IP address with the highest number, only this time among the IP addresses of the active loopback interfaces.*

It is better to force OSPF to get an ID from a loopback interface because a loopback interface, unlike a physical interface, never goes down.

If this step is omitted and a loopback interface is created after an OSPF configuration has already been entered, OSPF will not automatically switch over its ID to the IP address of the loopback interface. However, if the router is restarted or if the interface with the IP address being used as the OSPF ID is temporarily brought down and then back up, OSPF will switch over to the new ID.

---

2. Using the command **router ospf** *<Process ID>*, create an OSPF process on the routers. The parameter *<Process ID>* is an arbitrary number in the range 1 through 65535.

3. Using the command **network** *<IP Address> <wildcard mask>* **area 0** under the **router ospf** configuration, enable processing of OSPF routing updates on the appropriate interfaces. This OSPF process services only the interfaces with IP addresses matching the parameters *<IP Address>* and *<wildcard mask>*. The parameter *<wildcard mask>* is a bit pattern whose set bits indicate that the corresponding bits in the *<IP address>* parameter must be ignored during comparison of actual IP addresses against the *<IP address>* parameter. The *<wildcard mask>* parameter is written using dotted decimal notation. Notice that unlike subnet masks, which must be contiguous, the *<wildcard mask>* parameter can be an arbitrary bit pattern.

NOTE: *Unlike the commands **router igrp** and **router eigrp**, the command **router ospf** is not followed by an autonomous system number. As previously mentioned in the OSPF configuration guidelines, the command **router ospf** is followed by the OSPF process number, which only allows the router to distinguish between separate OSPF processes in its own memory. This number is not carried in the OSPF PDUs; therefore, the routers that receive these PDUs will not know which OSPF processes on the remote routers created the PDUs. In other words, the commands **router ospf** on the routers that participate in OSPF routing don't have to be configured with the same numbers. However, for purposes of consistency, I recommend that you keep these numbers the same on all routers participating in OSPF routing.*

To see how OSPF works, let's take the same example as we used for RIP Version 2. The network topology is shown in Figure 5.4. The IP addressing is exactly the same as in the "Configuring RIP Version 2" section in Chapter 4.

Listings 5.1 through 5.4 show the configurations of all four routers.

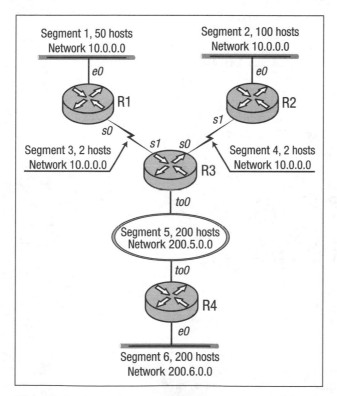

Figure 5.4 All routers are only connected to an OSPF backbone.

Listing 5.1   Router R1's configuration.

```
interface Loopback0
 ip address 10.0.0.5 255.255.255.255

interface Ethernet0
 ip address 10.0.0.65 255.255.255.192

interface Serial0
 ip address 10.0.0.22 255.255.255.252

router ospf 1
 network 10.0.0.0 0.255.255.255 area 0
```

Listing 5.2   Router R2's configuration.

```
interface Loopback0
 ip address 10.0.0.6 255.255.255.255

interface Ethernet0
 ip address 10.0.0.129 255.255.255.128

interface Serial1
 ip address 10.0.0.26 255.255.255.252

router ospf 1
 network 10.0.0.0 0.255.255.255 area 0
```

Listing 5.3   Router R3's configuration.

```
interface Loopback0
 ip address 10.0.0.7 255.255.255.255

interface Serial0
 ip address 10.0.0.25 255.255.255.252

interface Serial1
 ip address 10.0.0.21 255.255.255.252

interface TokenRing0
 ip address 200.5.0.1 255.255.255.0
 ring-speed 16

router ospf 1
 network 10.0.0.0 0.255.255.255 area 0
 network 200.0.0.0 0.255.255.255 area 0
```

Listing 5.4   Router R4's configuration.

```
interface Loopback0
 ip address 200.0.0.1 255.255.255.255
```

```
interface Ethernet0
 ip address 200.6.0.1 255.255.255.0

interface TokenRing0
 ip address 200.5.0.2 255.255.255.0
 ring-speed 16

router ospf 1
 network 200.0.0.0 0.255.255.255 area 0
```

Notice how the command **network** is used in OSPF. The command requires a wildcard mask, which is used to determine which interfaces are serviced by OSPF. However, OSPF doesn't use the wildcard mask to figure out which network prefixes should be advertised. Instead, OSPF takes the IP address and subnet mask from the interfaces to calculate the corresponding network prefix. The command also requires specifying the area to which the corresponding network prefixes belong.

TIP: *For simplicity, you can use host IP addresses to specify the interfaces that you want OSPF to service. To do so, you can use multiple **network** commands followed by the exact IP addresses of the interfaces and the wildcard mask 0.0.0.0. This way, you can enable OSPF on a per interface basis. You also won't have to figure out which wildcard mask to use to cover the necessary interfaces. The tradeoff of this method is that you have to enter a separate **network** command for each OSPF-enabled interface.*

Listing 5.5 shows the output of the command **show ip route** entered on router R4.

Listing 5.5   The routing table of router R4.

```
R4#show ip route
...
   200.0.0.0/32 is subnetted, 1 subnets
C    200.0.0.1 is directly connected, Loopback0
C 200.5.0.0/24 is directly connected, TokenRing0
C 200.6.0.0/24 is directly connected, Ethernet0
   10.0.0.0/8 is variably subnetted, 7 subnets, 4 masks
O   10.0.0.6/32 [110/71] via 200.5.0.1, 01:35:32, TokenRing0
O   10.0.0.7/32 [110/7] via 200.5.0.1, 01:35:32, TokenRing0
O   10.0.0.5/32 [110/71] via 200.5.0.1, 01:35:32, TokenRing0
O   10.0.0.24/30 [110/70] via 200.5.0.1, 01:35:32, TokenRing0
O   10.0.0.20/30 [110/70] via 200.5.0.1, 01:35:32, TokenRing0
O   10.0.0.64/26 [110/80] via 200.5.0.1, 01:35:32, TokenRing0
O   10.0.0.128/25 [110/80] via 200.5.0.1, 01:35:33, TokenRing0
```

First, the routes learned via OSPF are labeled with the letter "O".

Second, in OSPF, router R4 can see all subnets of network 10.0.0.0, although none of its interfaces is assigned an IP address that belongs to network 10.0.0.0. This means that unlike all distance vector protocols available in the Cisco IOS, OSPF does not perform automatic summarization. This is one of the most important features of OSPF.

TIP: *If all interfaces on all routers configured for OSPF belong to the same OSPF area, the area number does not have to be 0. However, it is strongly recommended to use 0 even in the case of a single OSPF area.*

NOTE: *OSPF supports equal cost load balancing in exactly the same way as the other routing protocols and static routing.*

WARNING!   If secondary IP addresses are used on routers configured for OSPF and if they are included in the OSPF operation by means of the network command, they should belong to the same area as the primary IP address.

Understanding OSPF Costs

OSPF uses the costs of the individual interfaces as the weights when running the shortest path algorithm. OSPF costs are calculated using the following formula:

$$C = \frac{10^2}{B}$$

where B is the logical bandwidth of the interface measured in bits per second (bps). The current value of the interface bandwidth can be examined using the command **show interfaces** <*Interface*> <*number*>. The appropriate bandwidth can be set using the command **bandwidth** <*B*> in the interface configuration mode.

NOTE: *The logical bandwidth needs adjustment only on the serial interfaces.*

Related Solutions:	Found on page:
Understanding IGRP Metrics	184
Understanding EIGRP Metrics	213

Configuring OSPF With Multiple Areas

As explained in the "In Brief" section in this chapter, OSPF was specifically designed to meet hierarchical routing requirements. In OSPF, the hierarchy comprises multiple areas connected to a single central area called a *backbone*.

Therefore, before configuring OSPF for multiple areas, we must decide which networks will belong to which areas and then plan the IP addressing accordingly. This planning should include calculating one or more summary addresses for each area. The summary address is a network prefix whose length must be shorter than, or equal to, the shortest network prefix that exists within the area, and it is a match for any IP address defined within the area. For example, suppose an area contains the following addresses: 10.0.128.0/17, 10.0.1.0/24, and 10.0.0.128/25. The area summary could be network prefix 10.0.0.0/16. Its length is shorter than the length of any network prefix that exists within the area, and any IP address defined within the area will be matched by this summary address.

The next step is to configure the routers for the devised IP addressing scheme. Following are the revised guidelines for configuring OSPF with multiple areas:

1. Create an OSPF ID by enabling a loopback interface and assigning it an IP address.

2. Using the command **router ospf** *<Process ID>*, create an OSPF process on the router.

3. Using the command **area** *<area>* **range** *<IP address> <subnet mask>*, define one or more summary addresses for each area on the routers that connect the area to the backbone. This command instructs OSPF to advertise this new network prefix to the backbone area instead of advertising any individual network prefixes.

NOTE: *This command expects a subnet mask, not a wildcard mask as the **network** command does.*

TIP: *Multiple commands **area** <area> **range** <IP address> <subnet mask> entered with the same <area> parameter but different <IP address> <subnet mask> parameters define multiple summary addresses for the same area. All of these network prefixes are advertised by the ABRs on which they were configured into the areas other than <area> instead of any individual network prefixes that exist in the area <area>.*

4. Using the command **network** *<IP Address> <wildcard mask>* **area 0** under the **router ospf** configuration, enable processing of OSPF routing updates on the appropriate interfaces.

Let's modify the network topology used in the previous sections (see Figure 5.5).

The network topology, which previously consisted of a single area, now comprises two areas as shown in Figure 5.5. Remembering the classless nature of OSPF, we can, therefore, define the area summary addresses as follows:

*   Area 0 summary address is 200.0.0.0/8.

*   Area 10 summary address is 10.0.0.0/24.

To better understand what the command **area** *<area>* **range** actually does, let's configure router R3 (which is the only router requiring this command) without it.

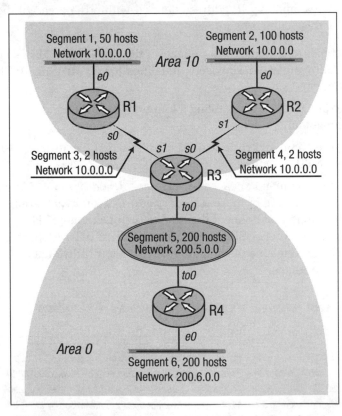

Figure 5.5   The previous network topology now comprises two areas.

Listings 5.6 through 5.8 show the revised configurations of routers R1, R2, and R3. (Router R4 requires no configuration change because it stays in the same area 0.)

Listing 5.6   Router R1's configuration.

```
interface Loopback0
 ip address 10.0.0.5 255.255.255.255

interface Ethernet0
 ip address 10.0.0.65 255.255.255.192

interface Serial0
 ip address 10.0.0.22 255.255.255.252

router ospf 1
 network 10.0.0.0 0.255.255.255 area 10
```

Listing 5.7   Router R2's configuration.

```
interface Loopback0
 ip address 10.0.0.6 255.255.255.255

interface Ethernet0
 ip address 10.0.0.129 255.255.255.128

interface Serial1
 ip address 10.0.0.26 255.255.255.252

router ospf 1
 network 10.0.0.0 0.255.255.255 area 10
```

Listing 5.8   Router R3's configuration.

```
interface Loopback0
 ip address 10.0.0.7 255.255.255.255

interface Serial0
 ip address 10.0.0.25 255.255.255.252

interface Serial1
 ip address 10.0.0.21 255.255.255.252

interface TokenRing0
 ip address 200.5.0.1 255.255.255.0
 ring-speed 16

router ospf 1
 network 10.0.0.0 0.255.255.255 area 10
 network 200.0.0.0 0.255.255.255 area 0
```

5. Dynamic Routing: Link State Routing Protocols

TIP: *We know that the router is ABR because the multiple **network** command shows that at least two have different area numbers.*

To see what transpired after the configurations of routers R1, R2, and R3 were changed, let's examine the output of the command **show ip route** entered on router R4 (shown in Listing 5.9).

Listing 5.9   The routing table of router R4.

```
R4#show ip route
...
   200.0.0.0/32 is subnetted, 1 subnets
C    200.0.0.1 is directly connected, Loopback0
C 200.5.0.0/24 is directly connected, TokenRing0
C 200.6.0.0/24 is directly connected, Ethernet0
   10.0.0.0/8 is variably subnetted, 7 subnets, 4 masks
O IA 10.0.0.6/32 [110/71] via 200.5.0.1, 00:27:11,TokenRing0
O IA 10.0.0.7/32 [110/7] via 200.5.0.1, 00:27:11,TokenRing0
O IA 10.0.0.5/32 [110/71] via 200.5.0.1, 00:27:11,TokenRing0
O IA 10.0.0.24/30 [110/70] via 200.5.0.1, 00:27:11,TokenRing0
O IA 10.0.0.20/30 [110/70] via 200.5.0.1, 00:27:11,TokenRing0
O IA 10.0.0.64/26 [110/80] via 200.5.0.1, 00:27:11,TokenRing0
O IA 10.0.0.128/25 [110/80] via 200.5.0.1,00:27:11,TokenRing0
```

The only change in these configurations is the presence of the letters "IA," which stand for *inter-area*. This only indicates that the corresponding routes are from an area to which this router has no connection, which, in our case, is true. However, if this were the only outcome from having multiple areas, it would not make sense to bother planning the IP addressing for multiple areas and then going through the hassle of configuring the routers.

Let's now add the **area** *<area>* **range** commands to the configuration of router R3. The arguments of these commands should create the summary addresses for the backbone area and area 10, described earlier in this section. Listing 5.10 shows the revised configuration of router R3.

Listing 5.10   Router R3's configuration.

```
interface Loopback0
 ip address 10.0.0.7 255.255.255.255

interface Serial0
 ip address 10.0.0.25 255.255.255.252

interface Serial1
 ip address 10.0.0.21 255.255.255.252
```

```
interface TokenRing0
 ip address 200.5.0.1 255.255.255.0
 ring-speed 16

router ospf 1
 network 10.0.0.0 0.255.255.255 area 10
 network 200.0.0.0 0.255.255.255 area 0
 area 0 range 200.0.0.0 255.0.0.0
 area 10 range 10.0.0.0 255.255.255.0
```

As the **area** *<area>* **range** commands are entered, let's see what's changed in the routing table of router R4. Listing 5.11 shows the output of the command **show ip route** entered on router R4.

*Listing 5.11   The routing table of router R4 after the commands **area** <area> **range** were added to router R3's configuration.*

```
R4#show ip route
...
     200.0.0.0/32 is subnetted, 1 subnets
C     200.0.0.1 is directly connected, Loopback0
C  200.5.0.0/24 is directly connected, TokenRing0
C  200.6.0.0/24 is directly connected, Ethernet0
     10.0.0.0/24 is subnetted, 1 subnets
O IA  10.0.0.0 [110/80] via 200.5.0.1, 00:23:10, TokenRing0
```

This time, going through the processes of hierarchical routing planning and implementation makes sense. Router R4 now only sees a route for the summary address, instead of all of the routes that exist in area 10.

Let's also examine the routing table of router R1 (shown in Listing 5.12).

Listing 5.12   The routing table of router R1.

```
R1#show ip route
...
   10.0.0.0/8 is variably subnetted, 7 subnets, 4 masks
O     10.0.0.6/32 [110/129] via 10.0.0.21, 19:19:57, Serial0
O     10.0.0.7/32 [110/65] via 10.0.0.21, 19:19:57, Serial0
C     10.0.0.5/32 is directly connected, Loopback0
O     10.0.0.24/30 [110/128] via 10.0.0.21, 19:19:57, Serial0
C     10.0.0.20/30 is directly connected, Serial0
C     10.0.0.64/26 is directly connected, Ethernet0
O     10.0.0.128/25 [110/138] via 10.0.0.21, 19:19:57, Serial0
O IA 200.0.0.0/8 [110/80] via 10.0.0.21, 00:25:30, Serial0
```

5. Dynamic Routing: Link State Routing Protocols

Router R1 still sees all of the routes available in area 10 unchanged. However, it can now only see the backbone area via a single route for the backbone area summary address, which is 200.0.0.0/8.

NOTE: *With OSPF, it is strongly recommended that you include the command **ip classless** in the router configuration. This recommendation is explicitly expressed in RFC 1879. The presence of this command brings the router into compliance with RFC 1812, the latest Requirements for IP Version 4 Routers. The latter document is particularly useful in understanding the current routing considerations.*

Originating Default Information

A router can be configured to advertise a default route in OSPF. To do so, the command **default-information originate always** should be used under the **router ospf** configuration.

Let's add this command to router R4's configuration and see what happens to the routing table of router R1 (shown in Listing 5.13).

Listing 5.13   Router R4's configuration.

```
interface Loopback0
 ip address 200.0.0.1 255.255.255.255

interface Ethernet0
 ip address 200.6.0.1 255.255.255.0

interface TokenRing0
 ip address 200.5.0.2 255.255.255.0
 ring-speed 16

router ospf 1
 network 200.0.0.0 0.255.255.255 area 0
 default-information originate always
```

The output of the command **show ip route** entered on router R1 is shown in Listing 5.14.

Listing 5.14   The routing table of router R1.

```
R1#show ip route
...


Gateway of last resort is 10.0.0.21 to network 0.0.0.0
```

```
   10.0.0.0/8 is variably subnetted, 7 subnets, 4 masks
O    10.0.0.6/32 [110/129] via 10.0.0.21, 00:30:51, Serial0
O    10.0.0.7/32 [110/65] via 10.0.0.21, 00:30:51, Serial0
C    10.0.0.5/32 is directly connected, Loopback0
O    10.0.0.24/30 [110/128] via 10.0.0.21, 00:30:51, Serial0
C    10.0.0.20/30 is directly connected, Serial0
C    10.0.0.64/26 is directly connected, Ethernet0
O    10.0.0.128/25 [110/138] via 10.0.0.21, 00:30:51, Serial0
O*E2 0.0.0.0/0 [110/1] via 10.0.0.21, 00:19:27, Serial0
O IA 200.0.0.0/8 [110/80] via 10.0.0.21, 00:19:27, Serial0
```

Notice the two italicized lines in Listing 5.14. The first line indicates that router R1 now knows an IP address of the default gateway, which is 10.0.0.21. The second line is the default route itself. The default route is labeled "E2", which stands for OSPF external route type 2. The meaning of type 1 and type 2 OSPF external routes is explained in Chapter 6.

Displaying An OSPF Link State Database

To display an OSPF link state database on a router, use the command **show ip ospf database**.

Let's examine the output of this command entered on router R4 from Figure 5.5. The output is shown in Listing 5.15.

Listing 5.15   The OSPF database of router R4.
```
R4#show ip ospf database

   OSPF Router with ID (200.0.0.1) (Process ID 1)


          Router Link States (Area 0)

Link ID    ADV Router  Age     Seq#         Checksum Link count
10.0.0.7   10.0.0.7    1627    0x80000003 0x92D8    1
200.0.0.1  200.0.0.1   786     0x80000005 0x70C1    3

          Net Link States (Area 0)

Link ID    ADV Router  Age     Seq#         Checksum
200.5.0.1  10.0.0.7    1627    0x80000001 0xDDA1


          Summary Net Link States (Area 0)
```

```
Link ID   ADV Router   Age    Seq#         Checksum
10.0.0.0  10.0.0.7     1382   0x80000001 0x696E

          Type-5 AS External Link States

Link ID   ADV Router   Age    Seq#         Checksum Tag
0.0.0.0   200.0.0.1    787    0x80000001 0x26C2    1
```

Each area is displayed individually. Router R4 is only connected to the backbone area; therefore, the output of the command **show ip ospf database** only displays the contents of a single link state database that router R4 maintains for the backbone area. The area is shown as sets of LSAs categorized according to the LSA types described in Table 5.1. The output in Listing 5.15 contains all four types of LSAs. Each line describes an individual LSA and consists of the information contained in the LSA: the link ID, the advertising router ID, the link age, the link's sequence number, and the checksum.

For more information on the contents of LSAs, refer to the OSPF specification, RFC 2428.

Configuring OSPF Stub Areas

According to the OSPF specification, some areas can be configured not to receive LSAs type 5. Such areas are called *stub areas*. Instead, these areas receive a default gateway route labeled as an *internal route*. Obviously, the purpose of configuring some areas as stub areas is to reduce the number of LSAs type 5 the routers in such areas have to process.

NOTE: *If an autonomous system does not receive many LSAs type 5, then it is not necessary to make any areas stub. However, if an autonomous system is connected to the Internet and contains routers that run some type of EGP ("exterior gateway protocol"), such as BGP, and these routers redistribute the routes learned via the EGP into OSPF, then it is most certainly worth it to configure some areas as stub.*

To make a certain area stub, all routers in this area must have the command **area** *<area>* **stub** under the **router ospf** configuration. The *<area>* parameter is equal to the area number.

In the network example shown in Figure 5.5, let's make area 10 a stub area. Listings 5.16 through 5.18 show the configurations of routers R1, R2, and R3.

Listing 5.16   Router R1's configuration.

```
interface Loopback0
 ip address 10.0.0.5 255.255.255.255

interface Ethernet0
 ip address 10.0.0.65 255.255.255.192

interface Serial0
 ip address 10.0.0.22 255.255.255.252

router ospf 1
 network 10.0.0.0 0.255.255.255 area 10
 area 10 stub
```

Listing 5.17   Router R2's configuration.

```
interface Loopback0
 ip address 10.0.0.6 255.255.255.255

interface Ethernet0
 ip address 10.0.0.129 255.255.255.128

interface Serial1
 ip address 10.0.0.26 255.255.255.252

router ospf 1
 network 10.0.0.0 0.255.255.255 area 10
 area 10 stub
```

Listing 5.18   Router R3's configuration.

```
interface Loopback0
 ip address 10.0.0.7 255.255.255.255

interface Serial0
 ip address 10.0.0.25 255.255.255.252

interface Serial1
 ip address 10.0.0.21 255.255.255.252

interface TokenRing0
 ip address 200.5.0.1 255.255.255.0
 ring-speed 16

router ospf 1
 network 10.0.0.0 0.255.255.255 area 10
 network 200.0.0.0 0.255.255.255 area 0
 area 0 range 200.0.0.0 255.0.0.0
 area 10 stub
 area 10 range 10.0.0.0 255.255.255.0
```

Notice that the ABR—that is, router R3—only specifies area 10 as a stub area.

NOTE: *If any of the routers within a stub area is not configured with the **area** <area> **stub**, it will not see any routes available via OSPF.*

Let's examine the routing table of router R1 shown in Listing 5.19. Notice that the default route is no longer labeled as an OSPF external route.

Listing 5.19   The routing table of router R1.

```
R1#show ip route
...
Gateway of last resort is 10.0.0.21 to network 0.0.0.0

   10.0.0.0/8 is variably subnetted, 7 subnets, 4 masks
0    10.0.0.6/32 [110/129] via 10.0.0.21, 00:02:35, Serial0
0    10.0.0.7/32 [110/65] via 10.0.0.21, 00:02:35, Serial0
C    10.0.0.5/32 is directly connected, Loopback0
0    10.0.0.24/30 [110/128] via 10.0.0.21, 00:02:35, Serial0
C    10.0.0.20/30 is directly connected, Serial0
C    10.0.0.64/26 is directly connected, Ethernet0
0    10.0.0.128/25 [110/138] via 10.0.0.21, 00:02:35, Serial0
0*IA 0.0.0.0/0 [110/65] via 10.0.0.21, 00:02:35, Serial0
0 IA 200.0.0.0/8 [110/80] via 10.0.0.21, 00:02:35, Serial0
```

The Cisco IOS also provides a way to make an area a *totally stubby area*. Totally stubby areas are a Cisco proprietary definition, which means that the area will not receive any inter-area routes (labeled as "IA" in the output of the command **show ip route**). Instead, such areas receive a single default gateway route for all IP addresses available outside of the area.

TIP: *Configuring some areas as totally stubby allows you to further reduce the numbers of LSAs the routers in this area will have to process.*

To make an area a totally stubby area, the ABR of the area must be configured with the command **area** <area> **stub no-summary**. Listing 5.20 shows the new configuration of router R3.

Listing 5.20   Router R3's configuration.

```
interface Loopback0
 ip address 10.0.0.7 255.255.255.255
```

```
interface Serial0
 ip address 10.0.0.25 255.255.255.252

interface Serial1
 ip address 10.0.0.21 255.255.255.252

interface TokenRing0
 ip address 200.5.0.1 255.255.255.0
 ring-speed 16

router ospf 1
 network 10.0.0.0 0.255.255.255 area 10
 network 200.0.0.0 0.255.255.255 area 0
 area 0 range 200.0.0.0 255.0.0.0
 area 10 stub no-summary
 area 10 range 10.0.0.0 255.255.255.0
```

This time, the routing table of router R1 only contains a single route labeled "IA," which is the default route. The routing table of router R1 is shown in Listing 5.21.

Listing 5.21   The routing table of router R1.

```
R1#show ip route
...
Gateway of last resort is 10.0.0.21 to network 0.0.0.0

     10.0.0.0/8 is variably subnetted, 7 subnets, 4 masks
O       10.0.0.6/32 [110/129] via 10.0.0.21, 00:01:13, Serial0
O       10.0.0.7/32 [110/65] via 10.0.0.21, 00:01:13, Serial0
C       10.0.0.5/32 is directly connected, Loopback0
O       10.0.0.24/30 [110/128] via 10.0.0.21, 00:01:13, Serial0
C       10.0.0.20/30 is directly connected, Serial0
C       10.0.0.64/26 is directly connected, Ethernet0
O       10.0.0.128/25 [110/138] via 10.0.0.21, 00:01:13, Serial0
O*IA 0.0.0.0/0 [110/65] via 10.0.0.21, 00:01:13, Serial0
```

Using OSPF Virtual Links To Restore A Partitioned Backbone

According to the OSPF specification, there can only be a single backbone area, to which all other areas are connected via routers called *ABRs*. Nevertheless, the specification addresses a situation in which the backbone, for some reason, is partitioned. In that case, a special technique called *virtual links* must be used to connect the partitioned parts of the backbone together. Virtual links can be regarded as extensions of the backbone partitions, which merge them into a whole.

To use virtual links, there must a single area between the two backbone partitions. When a common area for both partitions is defined, you have to find two routers connected to this area so that one of them is also connected to the first partition, and the other one is also connected to the second partition. After that, you must use the command **area** *<area>* **virtual-link** *<OSPF ID>* on both routers to restore the backbone integrity. The *<area>* parameter is the number of the common area, and *<OSPF ID>* is the OSPF ID of the counterpart router.

NOTE: *The <OSPF ID> parameter is not an IP address of the counterpart router. It is the OSPF ID of the counterpart router, which, if the loopback interfaces are configured, is equal to the IP address with the highest number among the IP addresses of all loopback interfaces.*

Let's consider the network topology depicted in Figure 5.6.

The OSPF backbone—area 0—is partitioned. However, area 100 is connected to both backbone partitions via routers R1 and R2.

The IP addressing used in this example is derived using the following rules:

- All networks are assigned network prefixes with a length of 24 or longer.

- The area number is encoded in the second octet of all IP addresses defined in the area.

- The IP addresses, with a third octet of 0, can only be assigned to the loopback interfaces of the routers. The last octets of such addresses are equal to the router numbers shown in Figure 5.6.

To see why it is important to preserve the backbone integrity, let's first examine what happens if routers R1 and R2 do not use a virtual link that connects the backbone partitions. Listings 5.22 through 5.27 show the current router configurations.

Listing 5.22 Router R1's configuration.

```
interface Loopback0
 ip address 10.0.0.1 255.255.255.255

interface Ethernet0
 ip address 10.0.1.1 255.255.255.0
```

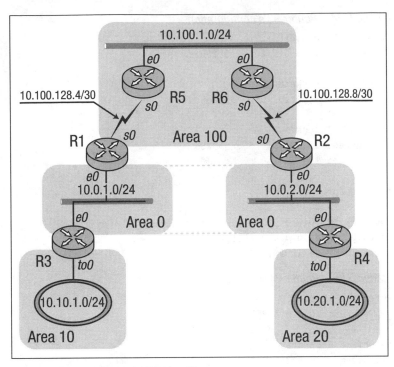

Figure 5.6   Partitioned OSPF backbone.

```
interface Serial0
 ip address 10.100.128.5 255.255.255.252

router ospf 1
 network 10.0.0.0 0.0.255.255 area 0
 network 10.100.0.0 0.0.255.255 area 100
 area 100 range 10.100.0.0 255.255.0.0
```

Listing 5.23   Router R2's configuration.

```
interface Loopback0
 ip address 10.0.0.2 255.255.255.255

interface Ethernet0
 ip address 10.0.2.1 255.255.255.0

interface Serial0
 ip address 10.100.128.9 255.255.255.252

router ospf 1
 network 10.0.0.0 0.0.255.255 area 0
 network 10.100.0.0 0.0.255.255 area 100
 area 100 range 10.100.0.0 255.255.0.0
```

Listing 5.24   Router R3's configuration.

```
interface Loopback0
 ip address 10.0.0.3 255.255.255.255

interface Ethernet0
 ip address 10.0.1.2 255.255.255.0

interface TokenRing0
 ip address 10.10.1.1 255.255.255.0
 ring-speed 16

router ospf 1
 network 10.0.0.0 0.0.255.255 area 0
 network 10.10.0.0 0.0.255.255 area 10
 area 0 range 10.0.0.0 255.255.0.0
 area 10 range 10.10.0.0 255.255.0.0
```

Listing 5.25   Router R4's configuration.

```
interface Loopback0
 ip address 10.0.0.4 255.255.255.255

interface Ethernet0
 ip address 10.0.2.2 255.255.255.0

interface TokenRing0
 ip address 10.20.1.1 255.255.255.0
 ring-speed 16

router ospf 1
 network 10.0.0.0 0.0.255.255 area 0
 network 10.20.0.0 0.0.255.255 area 20
 area 0 range 10.0.0.0 255.255.0.0
 area 20 range 10.20.0.0 255.255.0.0
```

Listing 5.26   Router R5's configuration.

```
interface Loopback0
 ip address 10.100.0.5 255.255.255.255

interface Ethernet0
 ip address 10.100.1.1 255.255.255.0

interface Serial0
 ip address 10.100.128.6 255.255.255.252

router ospf 1
 network 10.0.0.0 0.255.255.255 area 100
```

Listing 5.27   Router R6's configuration.

```
interface Loopback0
 ip address 10.100.0.6 255.255.255.255

interface Ethernet0
 ip address 10.100.1.2 255.255.255.0

interface Serial0
 ip address 10.100.128.10 255.255.255.252

router ospf 1
 network 10.0.0.0 0.255.255.255 area 100
```

Let's display the routing table on router R3. Listing 5.28 shows the output of the command **show ip route**.

Listing 5.28   The routing table of router R3.

```
R3#show ip route
...
   10.0.0.0/8 is variably subnetted, 5 subnets, 3 masks
C     10.10.1.0/24 is directly connected, TokenRing0
C     10.0.0.3/32 is directly connected, Loopback0
O     10.0.0.1/32 [110/11] via 10.0.1.1, 00:14:18, Ethernet0
C     10.0.1.0/24 is directly connected, Ethernet0
O IA 10.100.0.0/16 [110/74] via 10.0.1.1, 00:14:18, Ethernet0
```

It's no surprise that router R3 can't see the whole network. For example, area 20 (with a summary address of 10.20.0.0/16) is not in router R3's routing table. The partitioned OSPF backbone is the reason for this.

Let's restore the backbone by adding the command **area** *<area>* **virtual-link** under the **router ospf 1** configurations of routers R1 and R2. Listings 5.29 and 5.30 show the updated configurations of routers R1 and R2.

Listing 5.29   Router R1's configuration.

```
interface Loopback0
 ip address 10.0.0.1 255.255.255.255

interface Ethernet0
 ip address 10.0.1.1 255.255.255.0

interface Serial0
 ip address 10.100.128.5 255.255.255.252
```

```
router ospf 1
  network 10.0.0.0 0.0.255.255 area 0
  network 10.100.0.0 0.0.255.255 area 100
  area 100 range 10.100.0.0 255.255.0.0
  area 100 virtual-link 10.0.0.2
```

Listing 5.30   Router R2's configuration.

```
interface Loopback0
  ip address 10.0.0.2 255.255.255.255

interface Ethernet0
  ip address 10.0.2.1 255.255.255.0

interface Serial0
  ip address 10.100.128.9 255.255.255.252

router ospf 1
  network 10.0.0.0 0.0.255.255 area 0
  network 10.100.0.0 0.0.255.255 area 100
  area 100 range 10.100.0.0 255.255.0.0
  area 100 virtual-link 10.0.0.1
```

Let's now examine the routing table of router R3. Listing 5.31 shows the output of the command **show ip route** entered on router R3.

Listing 5.31   The routing table of router R3 after the virtual links have been added to the OSPF configuration of routers R1 and R2.

```
R3#show ip route
...
     10.0.0.0/8 is variably subnetted, 9 subnets, 3 masks
C      10.10.1.0/24 is directly connected, TokenRing0
O      10.0.0.2/32 [110/149] via 10.0.1.1, 01:55:46, Ethernet0
O      10.0.2.0/24 [110/158] via 10.0.1.1, 01:55:46, Ethernet0
C      10.0.0.3/32 is directly connected, Loopback0
O      10.0.0.1/32 [110/11] via 10.0.1.1, 01:55:46, Ethernet0
C      10.0.1.0/24 is directly connected, Ethernet0
O      10.0.0.4/32 [110/159] via 10.0.1.1, 01:55:46, Ethernet0
O IA 10.20.0.0/16 [110/164] via 10.0.1.1, 01:55:46, Ethernet0
O IA 10.100.0.0/16 [110/74] via 10.0.1.1, 01:55:46, Ethernet0
```

This time, router R3 can see the summary addresses of all areas.

The command **show ip ospf virtual-links** can be used to check the status of a virtual link. The output of this command entered on router R1 is shown in Listing 5.32.

Listing 5.32 The output of the command *show ip ospf virtual-links* entered on router R1.

```
R1#show ip ospf virtual-links
Virtual Link OSPF_VL0 to router 10.0.0.2 is up
  Run as demand circuit
  DoNotAge LSA allowed.
  Transit area 100, via interface Serial0, Cost of using 138
  Transmit Delay is 1 sec, State POINT_TO_POINT,
  Timer intervals configured, Hello 10, Dead 40, Wait 40,
Retransmit 5
    Hello due in 00:00:07
    Adjacency State FULL (Hello suppressed)
```

The italicized line shows whether the link is up or down. For detailed information on the output of this command, please see the Cisco documentation.

NOTE: *Although virtual links are a part of the OSPF specification, their use is only recommended as a temporary measure in emergency situations or in the early stages of a large-scale network deployment. Virtual links should not be used on a permanent basis.*

Here's an example that shows one of the potential problems that can be associated with virtual links. Perhaps you noticed in the example used in this section (see Figure 5.6) that the summary address for the backbone area was missing in the configurations of routers R1 and R2 (Listings 5.29 and 5.30). Now we'll discover why.

Let's add the summary address to both routers' configurations. Listings 5.33 and 5.34 show the new configurations of routers R1 and R2.

Listing 5.33 Router R1's configuration.

```
interface Loopback0
 ip address 10.0.0.1 255.255.255.255

interface Ethernet0
 ip address 10.0.1.1 255.255.255.0

interface Serial0
 ip address 10.100.128.5 255.255.255.252

router ospf 1
 network 10.0.0.0 0.0.255.255 area 0
 network 10.100.0.0 0.0.255.255 area 100
 area 0 range 10.0.0.0 255.255.0.0
 area 100 range 10.100.0.0 255.255.0.0
 area 100 virtual-link 10.0.0.2
```

5. Dynamic Routing: Link State Routing Protocols

Listing 5.34   Router R2's configuration.

```
interface Loopback0
 ip address 10.0.0.2 255.255.255.255

interface Ethernet0
 ip address 10.0.2.1 255.255.255.0

interface Serial0
 ip address 10.100.128.9 255.255.255.252

router ospf 1
 network 10.0.0.0 0.0.255.255 area 0
 network 10.100.0.0 0.0.255.255 area 100
 area 0 range 10.0.0.0 255.255.0.0
 area 100 range 10.100.0.0 255.255.0.0
 area 100 virtual-link 10.0.0.1
```

Now, let's display the routing table of router R3. Listing 5.35 shows the output of the command **show ip route** entered on router R3.

Listing 5.35   The routing table of router R3.

```
R3#show ip route
...
     10.0.0.0/8 is variably subnetted, 9 subnets, 3 masks
C       10.10.1.0/24 is directly connected, TokenRing0
O       10.0.0.2/32 [110/149] via 10.0.1.1, 00:02:43, Ethernet0
O       10.0.2.0/24 [110/158] via 10.0.1.1, 00:02:43, Ethernet0
C       10.0.0.3/32 is directly connected, Loopback0
O       10.0.0.1/32 [110/11] via 10.0.1.1, 00:02:43, Ethernet0
C       10.0.1.0/24 is directly connected, Ethernet0
O       10.0.0.4/32 [110/159] via 10.0.1.1, 00:02:43, Ethernet0
O IA 10.20.0.0/16 [110/164] via 10.0.1.1, 00:02:43, Ethernet0
O IA 10.100.0.0/16 [110/74] via 10.0.1.1, 00:02:43, Ethernet0
```

The routing table looks suspiciously the same as before. Let's try to **ping** the IP address of the **loopback 0** interface of router R1. Listing 5.36 shows the results of pinging.

Listing 5.36   The output of the command ping 10.0.0.1 entered on router R3.

```
R3#ping 10.0.0.1
Type escape sequence to abort.
Sending 5, 100-byte ICMP Echos to 10.0.0.1, timeout is
2 seconds:
!!!!!
Success rate is 100 percent (5/5), round-trip min/avg/max =
4/4/4 ms
```

So far, everything looks good. Let's now try to **ping** the IP address of the **loopback 0** interface of router R2. Listing 5.37 shows the results of pinging.

*Listing 5.37   The output of the command **ping 10.0.0.2** entered on router R3.*

```
R3#ping 10.0.0.2

Type escape sequence to abort.
Sending 5, 100-byte ICMP Echos to 10.0.0.2, timeout is
2 seconds:
.....
Success rate is 0 percent (0/5)
```

The routing appears to be all right. Router R3's routing table has a route to address 10.0.0.2, and this route points in the right direction. Therefore, the problem is probably not on router R3.

To find out what may be wrong, let's use the command **traceroute** for address 10.0.0.2. Listing 5.38 shows the output of this command entered on router R3.

*Listing 5.38   The output of the command **traceroute 10.0.0.2** entered on router R3.*

```
R3#traceroute 10.0.0.2

Type escape sequence to abort.
Tracing the route to 10.0.0.2

  1 10.0.1.1 4 msec 4 msec 4 msec
  2 10.100.128.6 20 msec 16 msec 20 msec
  3 10.100.128.5 16 msec 20 msec 16 msec
  4 10.100.128.6 32 msec 32 msec 32 msec
  5 10.100.128.5 32 msec 32 msec 32 msec
  6 10.100.128.6 48 msec 44 msec 44 msec
  7 10.100.128.5 44 msec 48 msec 44 msec
  8 10.100.128.6 60 msec 60 msec 60 msec
  9 10.100.128.5 60 msec 60 msec 60 msec
 10 10.100.128.6 76 msec 76 msec 72 msec
...
```

The packets generated by the command **traceroute** appear to be stuck on the serial link between routers R1 and R5. Let's examine the routing table of router R5. Listing 5.39 shows the output of the command **show ip route** entered on router R5.

Listing 5.39   The routing table of router R5.

```
R5#show ip route
...
   10.0.0.0/8 is variably subnetted, 8 subnets, 4 masks
O IA 10.10.0.0/16 [110/80] via 10.100.128.5, 00:50:30,Serial0
O IA 10.0.0.0/16 [110/65] via 10.100.128.5, 00:18:19,Serial0
O IA 10.20.0.0/16 [110/90] via 10.100.1.2, 03:04:14,Ethernet0
O       10.100.0.6/32 [110/11] via 10.100.1.2,03:04:37,Ethernet0
C       10.100.0.5/32 is directly connected, Loopback0
C       10.100.1.0/24 is directly connected, Ethernet0
O       10.100.128.8/30 [110/74] via 10.100.1.2, 03:04:37,
Ethernet0
C       10.100.128.4/30 is directly connected, Serial0
```

The italicized line in Listing 5.39 tells us that router R5 has a single route to the backbone area. Not surprisingly, this route points to router R1, which is closest to router R5 from the backbone area. This means that any packet destined for any address from the whole backbone area router R5 is forwarded to router R1. This creates a routing loop for the IP datagrams that are destined for IP addresses from one of the backbone partitions, but which also have to traverse the other backbone partition. This explains the output of the command **traceroute** (shown in Listing 5.38).

Router R6 is in the same situation; however, its route for the summary address of the backbone area lies through router R2.

If we revert to the configurations of routers R1 and R2 without the backbone area summary address, we'll see that the overall connectivity is restored. For example, if we **ping** the IP address of the **loopback 0** interface of router R2 from router R3, the ping packets will go through. The result of pinging is shown in Listing 5.40.

Listing 5.40   The results of the command **ping 10.0.0.2** after the backbone area summary address is removed from the OSPF configurations of routers R1 and R2.

```
R3#ping 10.0.0.2

Type escape sequence to abort.
Sending 5, 100-byte ICMP Echos to 10.0.0.2, timeout is
2 seconds:
!!!!!
Success rate is 100 percent (5/5), round-trip min/avg/max =
56/61/72 ms
```

Although this change to the configurations of routers R1 and R2 may seem minor, it should not be taken lightly. First, it introduces inconsistency to the routers' configurations. For example, routers R3 and R4 are configured with the backbone area summary address, whereas routers R1 and R2 are not. Second, and even more serious, the removal of the backbone area summary address defeats the purpose of having hierarchical routing. Let's look at router R5's routing table after the backbone area summary address is removed from the configurations of routers R1 and R2. Listing 5.41 shows the output of the command **show ip route** entered on router R5.

Listing 5.41 *The routing table of router R5 after the backbone area summary address is removed from the configurations of routers R1 and R2.*

```
R5#show ip route
...
     10.0.0.0/8 is variably subnetted, 13 subnets, 4 masks
O IA    10.10.0.0/16 [110/80] via 10.100.128.5, 01:14:17, Serial0
O IA    10.0.2.0/24 [110/84] via 10.100.1.2, 00:08:58, Ethernet0
O IA    10.0.0.2/32 [110/75] via 10.100.1.2, 00:08:58, Ethernet0
O IA    10.0.0.3/32 [110/75] via 10.100.128.5, 00:08:58, Serial0
O IA    10.0.1.0/24 [110/74] via 10.100.128.5, 00:08:58, Serial0
O IA    10.0.0.1/32 [110/65] via 10.100.128.5, 00:08:58, Serial0
O IA    10.0.0.4/32 [110/85] via 10.100.1.2, 00:08:58, Ethernet0
O IA    10.20.0.0/16 [110/90] via 10.100.1.2, 03:28:02, Ethernet0
O       10.100.0.6/32 [110/11] via 10.100.1.2, 03:28:24, Ethernet0
C       10.100.0.5/32 is directly connected, Loopback0
C       10.100.1.0/24 is directly connected, Ethernet0
O       10.100.128.8/30 [110/74] via 10.100.1.2, 03:28:24,
Ethernet0
C       10.100.128.4/30 is directly connected, Serial0
```

The backbone area is now represented in router R5's routing table by all of its routes, although router R5 has no direct connection to it. This is because router R1 is no longer configured to summarize the backbone area routes; therefore, it injects all of them into area 100. This renders the hierarchical routing nonexistent.

Using OSPF Virtual Links To Connect Remote Areas

OSPF virtual links can also be used to establish OSPF routing in areas that can only be connected via non-backbone areas. A virtual link can be established between an ABR and a router in the target area, which both have connections to the intermediate area (see Figure 5.7). The

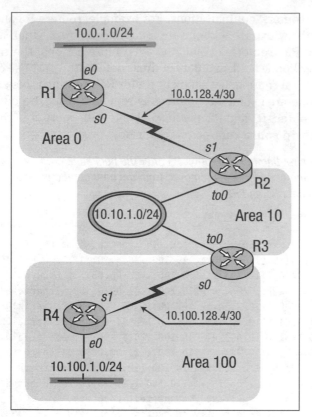

Figure 5.7   Area 100 can only be connected to the backbone area via area 10.

virtual link can thus be regarded as an extension of the backbone area, which makes the router in the target area an ABR.

Area 100 can only be connected to the backbone area via the intermediate area 10.

Let's first examine what happens if we do not configure a virtual link between routers R2 and R3. Listings 5.42 through 5.45 show the configurations of all four routers.

Listing 5.42   Router R1's configuration.

```
interface Loopback0
  ip address 10.0.0.1 255.255.255.255

interface Ethernet0
  ip address 10.0.1.1 255.255.255.0

interface Serial0
  ip address 10.0.128.5 255.255.255.252
```

```
router ospf 1
 network 10.0.0.0 0.0.255.255 area 0
```

Listing 5.43   Router R2's configuration.

```
interface Loopback0
 ip address 10.0.0.2 255.255.255.255

interface Serial1
 ip address 10.0.128.6 255.255.255.252

interface TokenRing0
 ip address 10.10.1.1 255.255.255.0
 ring-speed 16

router ospf 1
 network 10.0.0.0 0.0.255.255 area 0
 network 10.10.0.0 0.0.255.255 area 10
 area 0 range 10.0.0.0 255.255.0.0
 area 10 range 10.10.0.0 255.255.0.0
```

Listing 5.44   Router R3's configuration.

```
interface Loopback0
 ip address 10.10.0.3 255.255.255.255

interface Serial0
 ip address 10.100.128.5 255.255.255.252

interface TokenRing0
 ip address 10.10.1.2 255.255.255.0
 ring-speed 16

router ospf 1
 network 10.10.0.0 0.0.255.255 area 10
 network 10.100.0.0 0.0.255.255 area 100
 area 10 range 10.10.0.0 255.255.0.0
 area 100 range 10.100.0.0 255.255.0.0
```

Listing 5.45   Router R4's configuration.

```
interface Loopback0
 ip address 10.100.0.4 255.255.255.255

interface Ethernet0
 ip address 10.100.1.1 255.255.255.0

interface Serial1
 ip address 10.100.128.6 255.255.255.252
```

```
router ospf 1
network 10.100.0.0 0.0.255.255 area 100
```

Let's display the routing tables on routers R1 and R4. Listings 5.46 and 5.47 show the output of the command **show ip route** entered on these routers.

Listing 5.46   The routing table of router R1.

```
R1#show ip route

...
   10.0.0.0/8 is variably subnetted, 5 subnets, 4 masks
O IA 10.10.0.0/16 [110/71] via 10.0.128.6, 00:13:01, Serial0
O    10.0.0.2/32 [110/65] via 10.0.128.6, 00:13:01, Serial0
C    10.0.1.0/24 is directly connected, Ethernet0
C    10.0.0.1/32 is directly connected, Loopback0
C    10.0.128.4/30 is directly connected, Serial0
```

Listing 5.47   The routing table of router R4.

```
R4#show ip route

...
   10.0.0.0/8 is variably subnetted, 3 subnets, 3 masks
C    10.100.0.4/32 is directly connected, Loopback0
C    10.100.1.0/24 is directly connected, Ethernet0
C    10.100.128.4/30 is directly connected, Serial1
```

Obviously, the routing does not work properly without a virtual link. Router R1 cannot see the whole area 100, and router R4 can only see the directly connected networks.

Let's now add a virtual link between routers R2 and R3. Listings 5.48 and 5.49 show the revised configurations of these routers.

Listing 5.48   Router R2's configuration.

```
interface Loopback0
 ip address 10.0.0.2 255.255.255.255

interface Serial1
 ip address 10.0.128.6 255.255.255.252

interface TokenRing0
 ip address 10.10.1.1 255.255.255.0
 ring-speed 16

router ospf 1
 network 10.0.0.0 0.0.255.255 area 0
 network 10.10.0.0 0.0.255.255 area 10
 area 0 range 10.0.0.0 255.255.0.0
```

```
area 10 range 10.10.0.0 255.255.0.0
area 10 virtual-link 10.10.0.3
```

Listing 5.49 Router R3's configuration.

```
interface Loopback0
 ip address 10.10.0.3 255.255.255.255

interface Serial0
 ip address 10.100.128.5 255.255.255.252

interface TokenRing0
 ip address 10.10.1.2 255.255.255.0
 ring-speed 16

router ospf 1
 network 10.10.0.0 0.0.255.255 area 10
 network 10.100.0.0 0.0.255.255 area 100
 area 10 range 10.10.0.0 255.255.0.0
 area 10 virtual-link 10.0.0.2
 area 100 range 10.100.0.0 255.255.0.0
```

If we display the routing tables on routers R1 and R4 now, they will look as shown in Listings 5.50 and 5.51.

Listing 5.50 The routing table of router R1.

```
R1#show ip route
...
   10.0.0.0/8 is variably subnetted, 6 subnets, 4 masks
O IA 10.10.0.0/16 [110/71] via 10.0.128.6, 00:02:12, Serial0
O    10.0.0.2/32 [110/65] via 10.0.128.6, 00:02:12, Serial0
C    10.0.1.0/24 is directly connected, Ethernet0
C    10.0.0.1/32 is directly connected, Loopback0
O IA 10.100.0.0/16 [110/144] via 10.0.128.6, 00:02:12,Serial0
C    10.0.128.4/30 is directly connected, Serial0
```

Listing 5.51 The routing table of router R4.

```
R4#show ip route
...
   10.0.0.0/8 is variably subnetted, 8 subnets, 4 masks
O IA 10.10.0.0/16 [110/70] via 10.100.128.5, 00:01:58,Serial1
O IA 10.0.0.2/32 [110/71] via 10.100.128.5, 00:01:44,Serial1
O IA 10.0.0.1/32 [110/135] via 10.100.128.5, 00:01:44,Serial1
O IA 10.0.1.0/24 [110/144] via 10.100.128.5, 00:01:44,Serial1
C    10.100.0.4/32 is directly connected, Loopback0
C    10.100.1.0/24 is directly connected, Ethernet0
O IA 10.0.128.4/30 [110/134]via 10.100.128.5,00:01:44,Serial1
C    10.100.128.4/30 is directly connected, Serial1
```

The routing is now working, although it's not perfect. Router R1's routing table is now looking good—it contains a route for the area 100 summary address. However, router R4's routing table still needs improvement. It is populated with every single route that exists in the backbone area, to which router R4 has no direct connection. This can be explained rather easily if we remember that virtual links actually extend the backbone area. In this case, the backbone area was extended to router R3. However, router R3, now connected to the backbone area via the virtual link, does not perform route summarization for the addresses of the backbone area. Our conclusion: The OSPF configuration of router R3 needs the **area 0 range** command.

Let's add this command to router R3's configuration. Listing 5.52 shows the updated configuration of router R3.

Listing 5.52   Router R3's configuration.

```
interface Loopback0
 ip address 10.10.0.3 255.255.255.255

interface Serial0
 ip address 10.100.128.5 255.255.255.252

interface TokenRing0
 ip address 10.10.1.2 255.255.255.0

 ring-speed 16

router ospf 1
 network 10.10.0.0 0.0.255.255 area 10
 network 10.100.0.0 0.0.255.255 area 100
 area 0 range 10.0.0.0 255.255.0.0
 area 10 range 10.10.0.0 255.255.0.0
 area 10 virtual-link 10.0.0.2
 area 100 range 10.100.0.0 255.255.0.0
```

The routing table of router R4 is now correct (see Listing 5.53).

Listing 5.53   The routing table of router R4.

```
R4#show ip route
...
   10.0.0.0/8 is variably subnetted, 5 subnets, 4 masks
O IA  10.10.0.0/16 [110/70] via 10.100.128.5, 00:31:38,Serial1
O IA  10.0.0.0/16 [110/144] via 10.100.128.5, 00:04:38,Serial1
C     10.100.0.4/32 is directly connected, Loopback0
C     10.100.1.0/24 is directly connected, Ethernet0
C     10.100.128.4/30 is directly connected, Serial1
```

Configuring OSPF Over NBMA Networks

Configuring OSPF on the Cisco routers interconnected over NBMA networks, such as frame relay, has always been considered difficult. It will be much less difficult, though, if we remember the basics of the OSPF operation when configuring the routers.

In this section, we'll consider several different approaches for configuring OSPF on the Cisco routers interconnected via frame relay networks.

Configuring OSPF Over Fully Meshed NBMA Networks

The next two sections describe two methods of configuring OSPF on the routers interconnected via fully meshed frame relay networks. Both methods are demonstrated using the network shown in Figure 5.8.

As discussed in the "In Brief" section in this chapter, fully meshed frame relay networks are best represented in the OSPF link state database as broadcast multiaccess networks, such as LANs. In other words, a designated router and backup designated router are elected

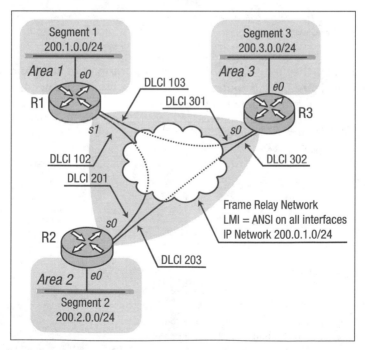

Figure 5.8   Three routers are connected via a fully meshed frame relay network.

on the network and then "speak" on behalf of the network. The network itself is modeled as a graph vertex.

There is, however, a minor problem with using this approach. Normally, OSPF routers employ the HELLO protocol to discover each other and to establish adjacencies. The HELLO protocol uses multicast addressing, which may not be available in NBMA networks. If this is the case, the routers won't be able to establish adjacencies, and the routing won't work. We'll discuss how to address this problem in the next two sections.

Using The neighbor Command

To help OSPF routers connected via an NBMA network establish adjacencies, we can specify the IP addresses of their neighbors connected over the NBMA network. If the routers are specifically configured with the IP addresses of their neighbors, they will no longer rely on multicast addressing to reach these neighbors.

Use the command **neighbor** *<IP address>* under the **router ospf** configuration to specify the neighbors that the router has.

NOTE: Not all neighbors will become adjacencies. This is particularly true if there are more than two routers connected to a single multiaccess network.

Listings 5.54 through 5.56 show the configurations of the routers shown in Figure 5.8. All routers are configured with two neighbors reachable across the frame relay network.

Listing 5.54   Router R1's configuration.

```
ip subnet-zero

interface Loopback0
 ip address 200.0.0.1 255.255.255.255

interface Ethernet0
 ip address 200.1.0.1 255.255.255.0

interface Serial1
 ip address 200.0.1.1 255.255.255.248
 encapsulation frame-relay
 frame-relay map ip 200.0.1.2 102 broadcast
 frame-relay map ip 200.0.1.3 103 broadcast
 frame-relay lmi-type ansi
```

```
router ospf 1
 network 200.0.0.0 0.0.255.255 area 0
 network 200.1.0.0 0.0.255.255 area 1
 neighbor 200.0.1.3
 neighbor 200.0.1.2
 area 0 range 200.0.0.0 255.255.0.0
 area 1 range 200.1.0.0 255.255.0.0

ip classless
```

Listing 5.55   Router R2's configuration.

```
ip subnet-zero

interface Loopback0
 ip address 200.0.0.2 255.255.255.255

interface Ethernet0
 ip address 200.2.0.1 255.255.255.0

interface Serial0
 ip address 200.0.1.2 255.255.255.248
 encapsulation frame-relay
 frame-relay map ip 200.0.1.1 201 broadcast
 frame-relay map ip 200.0.1.3 203 broadcast
 frame-relay lmi-type ansi

router ospf 1
 network 200.0.0.0 0.0.255.255 area 0
 network 200.2.0.0 0.0.255.255 area 2
 neighbor 200.0.1.3
 neighbor 200.0.1.1
 area 0 range 200.0.0.0 255.255.0.0
 area 2 range 200.2.0.0 255.255.0.0

ip classless
```

Listing 5.56   Router R3's configuration.

```
ip subnet-zero

interface Loopback0
 ip address 200.0.0.3 255.255.255.255

interface Ethernet0
 ip address 200.3.0.1 255.255.255.0
```

```
interface Serial0
 ip address 200.0.1.3 255.255.255.248
 encapsulation frame-relay
 frame-relay map ip 200.0.1.1 301 broadcast
 frame-relay map ip 200.0.1.2 302 broadcast
 frame-relay lmi-type ansi

router ospf 1
 network 200.0.0.0 0.0.255.255 area 0
 network 200.3.0.0 0.0.255.255 area 3
 neighbor 200.0.1.1
 neighbor 200.0.1.2
 area 0 range 200.0.0.0 255.255.0.0
 area 3 range 200.3.0.0 255.255.0.0

ip classless
```

NOTE: *All of the preceding configurations contain two commands that have not been used before—**ip classless** and **ip subnet-zero**. From previous chapters, remember that the **ip classless** command is used to change the routing algorithm of the router from classful to classless. We need the classless algorithm because we use supernets such as 200.0.0.0/16 as the area summary addresses. The command **ip subnet-zero** is used to make available the subnets whose IDs consist of only zeros (for example, 10.0.0.0/24, 200.0.1.0/48, and so on). We need this command because address 200.0.1.0/48 is used to address the routers' interfaces connected to the frame relay network.*

The routing table of router R2 should now look as shown in Listing 5.57.

Listing 5.57   The routing table of router R2.

```
R2#show ip route
...
200.0.0.0/32 is subnetted, 3 subnets
O       200.0.0.1 [110/65] via 200.0.1.1, 00:07:55, Serial0
C       200.0.0.2 is directly connected, Loopback0
O       200.0.0.3 [110/65] via 200.0.1.3, 00:07:55, Serial0
C    200.2.0.0/24 is directly connected, Ethernet0
     200.0.1.0/29 is subnetted, 1 subnets
C       200.0.1.0 is directly connected, Serial0
O IA 200.1.0.0/16 [110/74] via 200.0.1.1, 00:07:55, Serial0
O IA 200.3.0.0/16 [110/74] via 200.0.1.3, 00:07:55, Serial0
```

As we may have expected, the router can now see both summary addresses of areas 1 and 3.

We can use the command **show ip ospf neighbor** to verify the availability and the status of the routers' neigbors. Listings 5.58 through 5.60 show the output of that command entered on all three routers.

Listing 5.58   The OSPF neighbors of router R1.

```
R1#show ip ospf neighbor


Neighbor ID   Pri   State       Dead Time  Address     Interface
200.0.0.3      1    FULL/DR     00:01:53   200.0.1.3   Serial1
200.0.0.2      1    FULL/BDR    00:01:49   200.0.1.2   Serial1
```

Listing 5.59   The OSPF neighbors of router R2.

```
R2#show ip ospf neighbor


Neighbor ID   Pri   State        Dead Time  Address     Interface
200.0.0.3      1    FULL/DR      00:01:33   200.0.1.3   Serial0
200.0.0.1      1    FULL/DROTHER 00:01:58   200.0.1.1   Serial0
```

Listing 5.60   The OSPF neighbors of router R3.

```
R3#show ip ospf neighbor


Neighbor ID   Pri   State        Dead Time  Address     Interface
200.0.0.1      1    FULL/DROTHER 00:01:48   200.0.1.1   Serial0
200.0.0.2      1    FULL/BDR     00:01:50   200.0.1.2   Serial0
```

Notice how the output of this command shows the functional role of the neighbor routers. *DR* denotes that the neighbor is the designated router. *BDR* denotes that the neighbor is the backup designated router. *DROTHER* denotes that the neighbor is neither the designated nor the backup designated router. Such routers form adjacencies with both designated and backup designated routers.

NOTE: *For more information on possible states of OSPF neighbor routers, refer to OSPF specification RFC 2328 and the Cisco documentation.*

Using The *ip ospf network broadcast* Command

Although NBMA networks may not support multicast or broadcast addressing on the Network Access Layer, the routers can still perform multicast and broadcast addressing on the Internet Layer.

Notice that the command **frame-relay map ip** *<IP address> <DLCI>* can optionally include the keyword **broadcast**. If it does, the router also sends traffic destined for the broadcast IP address (that is, 255.255.255.255) over the PVC normally used for unicast traffic. If multiple PVCs are configured on the same serial interface or subinterface, this traffic is sent over all PVCs, whose number is followed by the keyword **broadcast** in the command **frame-relay map ip** *<IP address> <DLCI>*.

The command **frame-relay map ip** *<IP address> <DLCI>* alone is not enough for OSPF to start treating the interface as connected to a broadcast multiaccess network. We must also use the command **ip ospf network broadcast** to let OSPF know that the interface will forward the broadcast traffic appropriately.

These two commands eliminate the need to specify explicitly which OSPF neighbors are available over interfaces connected to NBMA networks. Listings 5.61 through 5.63 show the revised configurations of the routers from Figure 5.8.

Listing 5.61   Router R1's configuration.

```
ip subnet-zero

interface Loopback0
  ip address 200.0.0.1 255.255.255.255

interface Ethernet0
  ip address 200.1.0.1 255.255.255.0

interface Serial1
  ip address 200.0.1.1 255.255.255.248
  encapsulation frame-relay
  ip ospf network broadcast
  frame-relay map ip 200.0.1.2 102 broadcast
  frame-relay map ip 200.0.1.3 103 broadcast
  frame-relay lmi-type ansi

router ospf 1
  network 200.0.0.0 0.0.255.255 area 0
  network 200.1.0.0 0.0.255.255 area 1
  area 0 range 200.0.0.0 255.255.0.0
  area 1 range 200.1.0.0 255.255.0.0

ip classless
```

Listing 5.62   Router R2's configuration.

```
ip subnet-zero

interface Loopback0
  ip address 200.0.0.2 255.255.255.255
```

```
interface Ethernet0
 ip address 200.2.0.1 255.255.255.0

interface Serial0
 ip address 200.0.1.2 255.255.255.248
 encapsulation frame-relay
 ip ospf network broadcast
 frame-relay map ip 200.0.1.1 201 broadcast
 frame-relay map ip 200.0.1.3 203 broadcast
 frame-relay lmi-type ansi

router ospf 1
 network 200.0.0.0 0.0.255.255 area 0
 network 200.2.0.0 0.0.255.255 area 2
 area 0 range 200.0.0.0 255.255.0.0
 area 2 range 200.2.0.0 255.255.0.0

ip classless
```

Listing 5.63   Router R3's configuration.

```
ip subnet-zero

interface Loopback0
 ip address 200.0.0.3 255.255.255.255

interface Ethernet0
 ip address 200.3.0.1 255.255.255.0

interface Serial0
 ip address 200.0.1.3 255.255.255.248
 encapsulation frame-relay
 ip ospf network broadcast
 frame-relay map ip 200.0.1.1 301 broadcast
 frame-relay map ip 200.0.1.2 302 broadcast
 frame-relay lmi-type ansi

router ospf 1
 network 200.0.0.0 0.0.255.255 area 0
 network 200.3.0.0 0.0.255.255 area 3
 area 0 range 200.0.0.0 255.255.0.0
 area 3 range 200.3.0.0 255.255.0.0

ip classless
```

The italicized text shows the placement of the commands described in the previous paragraphs.

Listing 5.64 shows the new routing table of router R2, which is the same as the one shown in Listing 5.57.

Listing 5.64   The routing table of router R2.

```
R2#show ip route
...
     200.0.0.0/32 is subnetted, 3 subnets
O       200.0.0.1 [110/65] via 200.0.1.1, 00:07:34, Serial0
C       200.0.0.2 is directly connected, Loopback0
O       200.0.0.3 [110/65] via 200.0.1.3, 00:07:34, Serial0
C    200.2.0.0/24 is directly connected, Ethernet0
     200.0.1.0/29 is subnetted, 1 subnets
C       200.0.1.0 is directly connected, Serial0
O IA 200.1.0.0/16 [110/74] via 200.0.1.1, 00:07:34, Serial0
O IA 200.3.0.0/16 [110/74] via 200.0.1.3, 00:07:34, Serial0
```

Listings 5.65 through 5.67 show the output of the command **show ip ospf neighbor** entered on all three routers.

Listing 5.65   The OSPF neighbors of router R1.

```
R1#show ip ospf neighbor

Neighbor ID Pri  State       Dead Time  Address    Interface
200.0.0.3    1   FULL/DR     00:00:39   200.0.1.3  Serial1
200.0.0.2    1   FULL/BDR    00:00:38   200.0.1.2  Serial1
```

Listing 5.66   The OSPF neighbors of router R2.

```
R2#show ip ospf neighbor

Neighbor ID Pri  State         Dead Time  Address    Interface
200.0.0.1    1   FULL/DROTHER  00:00:39   200.0.1.1  Serial0
200.0.0.3    1   FULL/DR       00:00:36   200.0.1.3  Serial0
```

Listing 5.67   The OSPF neighbors of router R3.

```
R3#show ip ospf neighbor

Neighbor ID Pri  State         Dead Time  Address    Interface
200.0.0.1    1   FULL/DROTHER  00:00:32   200.0.1.1  Serial0
200.0.0.2    1   FULL/BDR      00:00:39   200.0.1.2  Serial0
```

Configuring OSPF Over Non-Fully Meshed NBMA Networks

Configuring OSPF on routers connected over non-fully meshed NBMA networks is in some cases probably the most complex task associated with configuring OSPF on the Cisco routers. However, remembering the basic rules of OSPF operation when performing configurations will make this task much simpler.

The next three sections describe three different methods of configuring OSPF over non-fully meshed frame relay networks. All three sections use the network shown in Figure 5.9 as an example.

Using Subinterfaces

This approach is the easiest—and probably the best. Whether the frame relay network is fully or non-fully meshed, it is always possible to assign individual PVCs connecting the routers to separate subinterfaces on these routers. By doing this, each subinterface is assigned an individual IP address belonging to a separate subnet. Each pair of subinterfaces interconnected via a frame relay PVC from an OSPF standpoint is then considered to be a point-to-point connection.

Listings 5.68 through 5.70 show the configurations of the three routers from Figure 5.9.

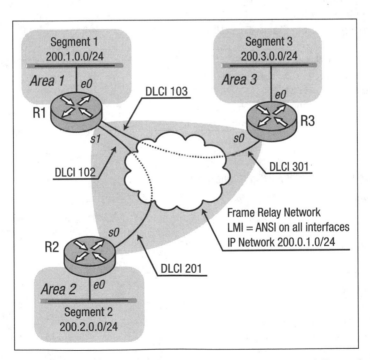

Figure 5.9 *The OSPF backbone consists of a single non-fully meshed frame relay network.*

Listing 5.68   Router R1's configuration.

```
ip subnet-zero

interface Loopback0
 ip address 200.0.0.1 255.255.255.255

interface Ethernet0
 ip address 200.1.0.1 255.255.255.0

interface Serial1
 encapsulation frame-relay
 frame-relay lmi-type ansi

interface Serial1.2 point-to-point
 description connects R1 to R2 via PVC 102
 ip address 200.0.1.1 255.255.255.252
 frame-relay interface-dlci 102

interface Serial1.3 point-to-point
 description connects R1 to R3 via PVC 103
 ip address 200.0.1.5 255.255.255.252
 frame-relay interface-dlci 103

router ospf 1
 network 200.0.0.0 0.0.255.255 area 0
 network 200.1.0.0 0.0.255.255 area 1
 area 0 range 200.0.0.0 255.255.0.0
 area 1 range 200.1.0.0 255.255.0.0

ip classless
```

Listing 5.69   Router R2's configuration.

```
ip subnet-zero

interface Loopback0
 ip address 200.0.0.2 255.255.255.255

interface Ethernet0
 ip address 200.2.0.1 255.255.255.0

interface Serial0
 encapsulation frame-relay
 frame-relay lmi-type ansi

interface Serial0.1 point-to-point
 ip address 200.0.1.2 255.255.255.252
 frame-relay interface-dlci 201
```

```
router ospf 1
 network 200.0.0.0 0.0.255.255 area 0
 network 200.2.0.0 0.0.255.255 area 2
 area 0 range 200.0.0.0 255.255.0.0
 area 2 range 200.2.0.0 255.255.0.0

ip classless
```

Listing 5.70   Router R3's configuration.

```
ip subnet-zero

interface Loopback0
 ip address 200.0.0.3 255.255.255.255

interface Ethernet0
 ip address 200.3.0.1 255.255.255.0

interface Serial0
 encapsulation frame-relay
 frame-relay lmi-type ansi

interface Serial0.1 point-to-point
 ip address 200.0.1.6 255.255.255.252
 frame-relay interface-dlci 301

router ospf 1
 network 200.0.0.0 0.0.255.255 area 0
 network 200.3.0.0 0.0.255.255 area 3
 area 0 range 200.0.0.0 255.255.0.0
 area 3 range 200.3.0.0 255.255.0.0

ip classless
```

Listing 5.71 shows the routing table of router R2. As before, router R2 can see both remote areas; however, this time both areas are available only through a single subinterface, which connects router R2 to router R1.

Listing 5.71   The routing table of router R2.

```
R2#show ip route
...
     200.0.0.0/32 is subnetted, 3 subnets
O       200.0.0.1 [110/65] via 200.0.1.1, 00:12:55, Serial0.1
C       200.0.0.2 is directly connected, Loopback0
O       200.0.0.3 [110/129] via 200.0.1.1, 00:12:55, Serial0.1
C    200.2.0.0/24 is directly connected, Ethernet0
     200.0.1.0/30 is subnetted, 2 subnets
```

```
C       200.0.1.0 is directly connected, Serial0.1
O       200.0.1.4 [110/128] via 200.0.1.1, 00:12:55, Serial0.1
O IA 200.1.0.0/16 [110/74] via 200.0.1.1, 00:12:55, Serial0.1
O IA 200.3.0.0/16 [110/138] via 200.0.1.1, 00:12:55,Serial0.1
```

The output of the command **show ip ospf neighbor** now displays the state of each neighbor as FULL/-. None of the neighbors is a designated or backup designated router, which means that the corresponding link is point-to-point.

Listing 5.72   The OSPF neighbors of router R1.

```
R1#show ip ospf neighbor

Neighbor ID   Pri   State        Dead Time   Address     Interface
200.0.0.2      1    FULL/  -     00:00:30    200.0.1.2   Serial1.2
200.0.0.3      1    FULL/  -     00:00:30    200.0.1.6   Serial1.3
```

Listing 5.73   The OSPF neighbors of router R2.

```
R2#show ip ospf neighbor

Neighbor ID   Pri   State        Dead Time   Address     Interface
200.0.0.1      1    FULL/  -     00:00:35    200.0.1.1   Serial0.1
```

Listing 5.74   The OSPF neighbors of router R3.

```
R3#show ip ospf neighbor

Neighbor ID   Pri   State        Dead Time   Address     Interface
200.0.0.1      1    FULL/  -     00:00:36    200.0.1.5   Serial0.1
```

NOTE: *Multipoint subinterfaces can be used instead of point-to-point subinterfaces. However, multipoint subinterfaces are not automatically treated by OSPF as point-to-point links and therefore require either the appropriate **neighbor** or **ip ospf network broadcast** commands. Later versions of the Cisco IOS also provide the command **ip ospf network point-to-point**.*

Using Command *ip ospf network point-to-multipoint*

The next approach does not require subinterfaces. Nevertheless, the idea on which it is based remains the same—each individual PVC is considered to be a point-to-point connection. Only this time, this connection is not a pair of interfaces or subinterfaces assigned a subnet address. The point-to-point connection now only exists in the OSPF internal data structures.

To make the OSPF process on a router treat a frame relay interface with multiple PVCs as multiple point-to-point connections, enter the command **ip ospf network point-to-multipoint** in the interface configuration mode on every router connected to the frame relay network. The rest of the OSPF configuration remains the same.

Listings 5.75 through 5.77 show the revised configurations of the routers in Figure 5.9.

Listing 5.75   Router R1's configuration.

```
ip subnet-zero

interface Loopback0
 ip address 200.0.0.1 255.255.255.255

interface Ethernet0
 ip address 200.1.0.1 255.255.255.0

interface Serial1
 ip address 200.0.1.1 255.255.255.248
 encapsulation frame-relay
 ip ospf network point-to-multipoint
 frame-relay map ip 200.0.1.2 102 broadcast
 frame-relay map ip 200.0.1.3 103 broadcast
 frame-relay lmi-type ansi

router ospf 1
 network 200.0.0.0 0.0.255.255 area 0
 network 200.1.0.0 0.0.255.255 area 1
 area 0 range 200.0.0.0 255.255.0.0
 area 1 range 200.1.0.0 255.255.0.0

ip classless
```

Listing 5.76   Router R2's configuration.

```
ip subnet-zero

interface Loopback0
 ip address 200.0.0.2 255.255.255.255

interface Ethernet0
 ip address 200.2.0.1 255.255.255.0

interface Serial0
 ip address 200.0.1.2 255.255.255.248
 encapsulation frame-relay
 ip ospf network point-to-multipoint
 frame-relay map ip 200.0.1.1 201 broadcast
 frame-relay lmi-type ansi
```

```
router ospf 1
  network 200.0.0.0 0.0.255.255 area 0
  network 200.2.0.0 0.0.255.255 area 2
  area 0 range 200.0.0.0 255.255.0.0
  area 2 range 200.2.0.0 255.255.0.0
```

```
ip classless
```

Listing 5.77   Router R3's configuration.

```
ip subnet-zero

interface Loopback0
  ip address 200.0.0.3 255.255.255.255

interface Ethernet0
  ip address 200.3.0.1 255.255.255.0

interface Serial0
  ip address 200.0.1.3 255.255.255.248
  encapsulation frame-relay
  ip ospf network point-to-multipoint
  frame-relay map ip 200.0.1.1 301 broadcast
  frame-relay lmi-type ansi

router ospf 1
  network 200.0.0.0 0.0.255.255 area 0
  network 200.3.0.0 0.0.255.255 area 3
  area 0 range 200.0.0.0 255.255.0.0
  area 3 range 200.3.0.0 255.255.0.0
```

```
ip classless
```

Listing 5.78 shows how the routing table of router R2 should now look.

Listing 5.78   The routing table of router R2.

```
R2#show ip route
...
   200.0.0.0/32 is subnetted, 3 subnets
O     200.0.0.1 [110/65] via 200.0.1.1, 00:39:15, Serial0
C     200.0.0.2 is directly connected, Loopback0
O     200.0.0.3 [110/129] via 200.0.1.1, 00:39:15, Serial0
C 200.2.0.0/24 is directly connected, Ethernet0
   200.0.1.0/24 is variably subnetted, 3 subnets, 2 masks
O     200.0.1.1/32 [110/64] via 200.0.1.1, 00:39:15, Serial0
C     200.0.1.0/29 is directly connected, Serial0
O     200.0.1.3/32 [110/128] via 200.0.1.1, 00:39:15, Serial0
```

```
O IA 200.1.0.0/16 [110/74] via 200.0.1.1, 00:38:37, Serial0
O IA 200.3.0.0/16 [110/138] via 200.0.1.1, 00:38:37, Serial0
```

To see the states of the OSPF links interconnecting the routers, let's examine the output of the command **show ip ospf neighbor** on routers R1 and R2 (shown in Listings 5.79 and 5.80).

*Listing 5.79   The output of the command **show ip ospf neighbor** entered on router R1.*

```
R1#show ip ospf neighbor

Neighbor ID Pri  State        Dead Time  Address    Interface
200.0.0.2     1  FULL/  -     00:01:40   200.0.1.2  Serial1
200.0.0.3     1  FULL/  -     00:01:50   200.0.1.3  Serial1
```

*Listing 5.80   The output of the command **show ip ospf neighbor** entered on router R2.*

```
R2#show ip ospf neighbor

Neighbor ID Pri  State        Dead Time  Address    Interface
200.0.0.1     1  FULL/  -     00:01:57   200.0.1.1  Serial0
```

Both outputs indicate that neither of the routers is a designated or backup designated router, which means that the link between them is point-to-point.

NOTE: *This command will work in any NBMA topology. The topology does not have to be similar to the one shown in Figure 5.9, where multiple routers are connected to a single central site router via PVCs.*

Using OSPF Router Priorities

An NBMA network does not have to be treated as having multiple point-to-point connections. Even if an NBMA network is non-fully meshed, it may be possible to make a certain router the designated router for the network.

The main feature of the designated router is that every other router must form an adjacency with it. From that perspective, router R1 in Figure 5.9 is a perfect candidate to be the designated router of the NBMA network.

However, there is one obstacle. The routers connected to the multiaccess networks elect the designated router. In other words, we don't know which of the three routers shown in Figure 5.9 will become the designated router.

Luckily, the OSPF specification addresses this issue by specifying that OSPF routers have priorities, which must be used during the designated router election. The router with the highest priority becomes the designated router on the network. The OSPF specification also requires that router's priorities have to be administratively assignable. The Cisco IOS complies with the OSPF specification providing a special command, which allows us to force the designated router election process in a particular router's favor. This command is **ip ospf priority** *\<priority\>*, available in an interface configuration mode. The router with the highest *\<priority\>* value becomes the designated router. If, however, the *\<priority\>* argument has a value of 0, the router is not allowed to be the designated router on the network connected to this interface. If we assign a value of 0 to routers R2 and R3, this forces the designated router election process in router R1's favor.

Multiaccess networks that do not support broadcasts must specify the OSPF neighbors manually. We do this by using the command **neighbor** in the **router ospf** configuration mode, just as we do when configuring OSPF in fully meshed NBMA networks.

Listings 5.81 through 5.83 show the revised configurations of all three routers.

Listing 5.81   Router R1's configuration.

```
ip subnet-zero

interface Loopback0
 ip address 200.0.0.1 255.255.255.255

interface Ethernet0
 ip address 200.1.0.1 255.255.255.0

interface Serial1
 ip address 200.0.1.1 255.255.255.248
 encapsulation frame-relay
 ip ospf network non-broadcast
 ip ospf priority 10
 frame-relay map ip 200.0.1.2 102 broadcast
 frame-relay map ip 200.0.1.3 103 broadcast
 frame-relay lmi-type ansi

router ospf 1
 network 200.0.0.0 0.0.255.255 area 0
 network 200.1.0.0 0.0.255.255 area 1
 neighbor 200.0.1.2
 neighbor 200.0.1.3
```

```
  area 0 range 200.0.0.0 255.255.0.0
  area 1 range 200.1.0.0 255.255.0.0

ip classless
```

Listing 5.82   Router R2's configuration.

```
ip subnet-zero

interface Loopback0
  ip address 200.0.0.2 255.255.255.255

interface Ethernet0
  ip address 200.2.0.1 255.255.255.0

interface Serial0
  ip address 200.0.1.2 255.255.255.248
  encapsulation frame-relay
  ip ospf network non-broadcast
  ip ospf priority 0
  frame-relay map ip 200.0.1.1 201 broadcast
  frame-relay map ip 200.0.1.3 201 broadcast
  frame-relay lmi-type ansi

router ospf 1
  network 200.0.0.0 0.0.255.255 area 0
  network 200.2.0.0 0.0.255.255 area 2
  area 0 range 200.0.0.0 255.255.0.0
  area 2 range 200.2.0.0 255.255.0.0
  ! neighbor 200.0.1.1  is no longer required.

ip classless
```

Listing 5.83   Router R3's configuration.

```
ip subnet-zero

interface Loopback0
  ip address 200.0.0.3 255.255.255.255

interface Ethernet0
  ip address 200.3.0.1 255.255.255.0

interface Serial0
  ip address 200.0.1.3 255.255.255.248
  encapsulation frame-relay
  ip ospf priority 0
  frame-relay map ip 200.0.1.1 301 broadcast
  frame-relay map ip 200.0.1.2 301 broadcast
  frame-relay lmi-type ansi
```

5. Dynamic Routing: Link State Routing Protocols

```
router ospf 1
 network 200.0.0.0 0.0.255.255 area 0
 network 200.3.0.0 0.0.255.255 area 3
 area 0 range 200.0.0.0 255.255.0.0
 area 3 range 200.3.0.0 255.255.0.0
 ! neighbor 200.0.1.1 is no longer required.

ip classless
```

The output of the command **show ip ospf neighbor** shown in Listings 5.84 through 5.86 indicates that there is no backup designated router. It also indicates that router R1 is the designated router, just as we wanted.

Listing 5.84   *The output of the command show ip ospf neighbor entered on router R1.*

```
R1#show ip ospf neighbor

Neighbor ID Pri  State          Dead Time Address    Interface
200.0.0.2     0  FULL/DROTHER   00:01:45  200.0.1.2  Serial1
200.0.0.3     0  FULL/DROTHER   00:01:47  200.0.1.3  Serial1
```

Listing 5.85   *The output of the command show ip ospf neighbor entered on router R2.*

```
R2#show ip ospf neighbor

Neighbor ID Pri  State          Dead Time Address    Interface
200.1.0.1    10  FULL/DR        00:01:45  200.0.1.1  Serial0
```

Listing 5.86   *The output of the command show ip ospf neighbor entered on router R3.*

```
R3#show ip ospf neighbor

Neighbor ID Pri  State          Dead Time Address    Interface
200.1.0.1    10  FULL/DR        00:01:50  200.0.1.1  Serial0
```

The routing table of router R2 shown in Listing 5.87 indicates overall connectivity, just as it did before.

Listing 5.87   *The routing table of router R2.*

```
R2#show ip route
...
     200.0.0.0/32 is subnetted, 3 subnets
O       200.0.0.1 [110/65] via 200.0.1.1, 00:16:52, Serial0
C       200.0.0.2 is directly connected, Loopback0
O       200.0.0.3 [110/65] via 200.0.1.3, 00:16:52, Serial0
```

```
C     200.2.0.0/24 is directly connected, Ethernet0
      200.0.1.0/29 is subnetted, 1 subnets
C       200.0.1.0 is directly connected, Serial0
O IA 200.1.0.0/16 [110/74] via 200.0.1.1, 00:16:52, Serial0
O IA 200.3.0.0/16 [110/74] via 200.0.1.3, 00:16:52, Serial0
```

Notice that, although area 3 is still available via the same interface as area 2, this time the next-hop router for it is R3, not R1. The reason is that router R1, the designated router, assumes that the network provides direct connectivity among all routers. Therefore, it relays all routes available through router R3 via R3 itself.

Therefore, to make routing work, we have to provide "direct" connectivity between routers R2 and R3. We can do this by entering an additional **frame-relay map ip** *<IP address> <DLCI>* statement under the **Serial 0** interface configuration as in the configurations shown in Listings 5.81 through 5.83.

NOTE: *The last method of configuring OSPF in NBMA networks should never be used in production environments. It violates the OSPF requirements for multiaccess networks, such as direct connectivity among all routers, the necessity of a backup designated router, and so on, and therefore must always be avoided. In this book, I have included it only for educational purposes.*

5. Dynamic Routing: Link State Routing Protocols

Controlling Data Flow And Routing Updates

If you need an immediate solution to:	See page:
Using Access-Lists To Filter Data Traffic	287
Using Standard Access-Lists	287
Using Extended Access-Lists	291
Using Named Access-Lists	293
Controlling Routing Updates	294
Using Redistribution	297
Configuring Basic Redistribution	298
Assigning A Default Redistribution Metric	308
Using One-Way Redistribution	309
Using Access-Lists To Filter Routing Updates During Redistribution	312
Using Route-Maps To Filter Routing Updates During Redistribution	315
Using the **Null** Interface For Route Summarization	318
Using Redistribution With EIGRP	323
Redistributing Between EIGRP And IGRP Configured With The Same AS Number	324
Redistributing Between EIGRP And IGRP Configured With Different AS Numbers	329
Using Redistribution With OSPF	332
Understanding And Configuring ASBRs	333
Understanding And Configuring NSSAs	342

In Brief

Sometimes, it is necessary to run multiple routing protocols on a single router. For example, if two companies merge and one implemented its corporate network using IGRP whereas the other one used RIP, these companies may need to have both protocols on some boundary routers. These routers convert the routing information between the protocols, thereby providing overall network availability. Another example is a network based on IGRP containing some devices, such as Unix servers, that require the exact routing information instead of the default gateway route. Most routing-capable devices support "open" protocols, such as RIP. Hence, the routers connected to the segments on which such devices are located need to convert the routing information from IGRP representation to RIP representation and then advertise it to these devices using RIP.

Simply running multiple routing protocols on the same router is not sufficient for exchanging routing information among these protocols. Generally, the routers do not pass the routing information between multiple routing protocols unless specifically instructed to do so. The reason is that these routing protocols may be used for different purposes (although they are on a single router); therefore, such exchanges of routing information may be undesirable. In addition, different routing protocols use different metric systems, mostly incompatible with each other. For example, RIP relies on simple hop-counts as route metrics, whereas IGRP and EIGRP use complex formulas that operate connection parameters such as bandwidth, delay, and so on, to calculate their respective metrics. Because these metrics are not compatible, passing the routing information between RIP and IGRP requires metric conversion. Another obstacle is that routing protocols can be classful (for example, IGRP) or classless (for example, EIGRP), which makes it very challenging to pass the exact routing information. Passing IGRP routing information to EIGRP may be simple, but the opposite may not be possible at all.

Routing Information Redistribution

The process of converting routing information among different sources of routing information is called *routing information redistribution*, or simply *redistribution*. The sources of routing information are dynamic routing protocols, static routes, and connected routes. Static and connected routes support only redistribution of their routing information into dynamic routing protocol. The reverse process is not available.

The routing information that is passed from one source of routing information into another is said to be *redistributed*. Likewise, the source of the routing information that is redistributed into a dynamic routing protocol is said to be *redistributed* into that protocol.

Redistribution usually involves specifying the source of the routing information to be redistributed, the routing protocol into which the routing information has to be redistributed, and the metric conversion to be used when the routing information is passed to that routing protocol. Redistribution does not necessarily have to be two-way. For example, if routing information from routing protocol A is passed to routing protocol B, the routing information from routing protocol B may not be passed to routing protocol A. It is often desirable to redistribute routing information from only one protocol to another, but not vice versa. When devices such as Unix hosts are present on a network and require the exact routing information, the routing information must be redistributed to the routing protocol that these devices can understand (for example RIP). At the same time, it is usually better to prohibit routers from learning about any routing information that these devices may advertise. If these devices have multiple NICs, they may act as routers (often the default and often overlooked), but because they are not made to be routers, their routing performance is usually rather poor. In some cases, alternative routes advertised by these devices may appear to be better than routes through real routers and may be used instead, which is not desirable.

Metric conversion is another very important process that is performed whenever a route is redistributed into another routing protocol. There are only two routing protocols available in the Cisco IOS that have compatible (that is, can be converted into each other without a loss of accumulated route cost) metrics: *IGRP* and *EIGRP*. The metrics of all other protocols cannot be converted into each other. Except for a special case of redistribution between IGRP and EIGRP, the metric conversion is performed by assigning a new static value for all redistributed routes. In other words, all accumulated route metrics are lost when the routes are redistributed into another routing protocol.

In this book, I will call a contiguous part of a network in which routing information is propagated using a certain routing protocol a *metric domain* of this routing protocol if the metrics of the routes that this routing protocol advertises increase within this part of the network. If metrics are reset to a certain value, this indicates a boundary of the metric domain.

The primary purpose of the term *metric domain* is to denote an area in which the metrics of the routes learned via this routing protocol adequately express the costs of the routes. For example, a number of interconnected networks whose subnet addresses belong to the same classful network address and in which routing information is propagated using a classful routing protocol is the metric domain of this protocol. An OSPF area is another example of a metric domain (of OSPF).

The important feature of redistribution discussed previously can be reformulated as follows:

Except for redistribution between IGRP and EIGRP, metric domains of routing protocols stop at the routers performing redistribution.

Filtering Routing Information While Redistributing

Redistribution must often be performed in a more controlled fashion by specifying which routes are allowed to be passed among the routing protocols. This can be achieved by filtering the routing information as it is passed among the routing protocols based on some criteria. If a route satisfies the criteria it is passed; otherwise, it is not.

Simple filtering is performed by specifying a pattern, which must be matched by the network prefix for the respective route to be passed to another routing protocol. More advanced filtering can also involve comparisons of other route parameters such as metrics, route tags, and so on.

Potential Problems Associated With Redistribution

Although redistribution is unavoidable in many cases, it is undesirable. Multiple problems can arise from routing information redistribution. One of the worst problems is routing loops.

To better understand the issue, let's consider the situation depicted in Figure 6.1.

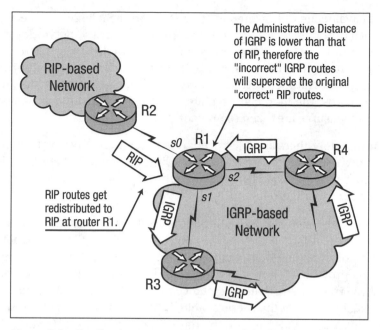

The Administrative Distance of IGRP is lower than that of RIP, therefore the "incorrect" IGRP routes will supersede the original "correct" RIP routes.

RIP-based Network

R2

RIP

s0   R1

IGRP

R4

RIP routes get redistributed to RIP at router R1.

s2

s1

IGRP

IGRP-based Network

IGRP

R3

IGRP

Figure 6.1   Routing loop caused by mutual redistribution of RIP and IGRP.

The network consists of two parts. The first part—*RIP-based network*—uses RIP to propagate routing information. The second part—*IGRP-based network*—uses IGRP to propagate routing information. Suppose router R2 in the RIP-based network uses RIP to exchange routing information with router R1, which then redistributes this information into IGRP and feeds it into the IGRP-based network using IGRP only. If router R2 has more than two connections into the IGRP-based network, a routing loop can potentially emerge. The IGRP routing updates that router R1 sends over one of its links can reach it from one of the other links (as shown in Figure 6.1). Originally, router R1 learned of the routes carried in these updates via RIP; therefore, these routers are present in router R1's routing table with RIP's administrative distance. When router R1 receives the IGRP updates, the routes that they carry will have the administrative distance of IGRP, which is smaller than that of RIP. Thus, these new routes supersede the original routes learned via RIP. At this point, router R1 replaces all of the "correct" RIP-learned routes with the "incorrect" IGRP routes pointing back to the IGRP-based network. After that, the connectivity between the two parts of the network vanishes.

The loop, however, does not stay forever. Eventually, one of the routers increases the metrics of the bogus routes. This event is followed

6. Controlling Data Flow And Routing Updates

by an avalanche of triggered routing updates, which soon make the metrics of the bogus routes infinite. All routes for the network prefixes in the RIP-based network are placed in holddown. When the holddown expires, the connectivity is restored for awhile, until the IGRP updates hit router R1 again and establish a new routing loop. In other words, the loop can oscillate an indefinite number of times, unless measures are taken to prevent this.

Unfortunately, there are other scenarios that potentially lead to routing loops resulting from redistribution. Throughout this chapter, we'll consider several examples of how routing loops can emerge as the result of redistribution.

Interestingly enough, the routing loop does not necessarily emerge right away. In fact, it may never come to existence. The "In Brief" section of Chapter 4 thoroughly discussed the rules that routers and routing protocols follow when advertising routing information. One of these rules stated that if a distance vector routing protocol failed to install a route in the routing table, it does not advertise it. In the situation shown in Figure 6.1, the returning IGRP routing update will probably never reach router R1 over its interface Serial 2. When the one-hop away IGRP routing update reaches router R4, router R4 already has a route for that network prefix learned via IGRP from router R1. Because the existing route has a lower metric than the arriving one, the latter is not installed in the routing table. This should prevent router R4 from advertising the bogus routes to router R1. However, if router R1 "forgets" all of its routes (for example, as the result of a cold restart), it may learn incorrect routes from router R4. If this happens, a routing loop emerges and may not disappear, unless special measures are taken.

Generally speaking, redistribution should be avoided whenever possible. Because redistribution is often unavoidable, however, careful planning should be done before applying redistribution.

Immediate Solutions

Using Access-Lists To Filter Data Traffic

An *access-list* is a logical expression that describes a match condition against which certain characteristics of network traffic are compared. If the condition is matched, the access-list returns one of two results—**permit** or **deny**. These two results should be considered more like logical 1 (true) and 0 (false).

Depending on how access-lists are applied, they can serve different purposes. For example, access-lists can be used to filter user traffic. The IP datagrams carrying user data traffic are dropped if the access-list match condition that matches the datagrams' parameters returns **deny**.

Access-lists can consist of several match conditions, each of which can return either **permit** or **deny**. The router looks through the match conditions until it finds the one that is actually matched. The router uses the result of the match condition as the result of comparison against the access-list as a whole. After the match is found, the router does not look any further through the access-list.

Using Standard Access-Lists

The standard access-lists only allow comparison of the source IP address against a specified pattern.

The standard access-lists for filtering user data traffic are configured using the following two steps:

1. Create an access-list using the command **access-list** *<AL number>* **{permit|deny}** *<source IP address> <wildcard mask>*. The *<AL number>* parameter is the access-list number ranging from 1 to 99. The set bits in the *<wildcard mask>* parameter specify that the corresponding bits in the *<IP address>* parameter will not be compared against the corresponding bits in the source IP address. Alternatively, the last two parameters can be either **host** *<IP address>* or **any**. The first alternative is equal to *<IP address>* **0.0.0.0**, which matches individual IP addresses, and the second one to **0.0.0.0 255.255.255.255**, which matches any IP address.

An access-list can consist of multiple lines, which can be achieved by entering multiple commands **access-list** with the same *<AL number>* parameter. Any access-list contains an implicit **access-list** *<AL number>* **deny any** at the end. This line is always invisible in the router's configuration.

WARNING! *The lines that constitute an access-list cannot be removed individually. If you try to remove an individual line (even if it was the last command that you entered) using the no form of it, you will remove the entire access-list.*

The router looks through an access-list until it finds the first match, after which it stops looking. As the result of looking through the access-list, the router returns the respective **permit** or **deny** condition.

NOTE: *Nonexistent access-lists, if used, always return the **permit** condition. In other words, nonexistent access-lists are equivalent to **access-list** <AL number> **permit any**.*

2. Apply the access-list in the interface configuration mode using the command **ip access-group** *<AL number>* [{in|out}]. If the last optional parameter is **in**, the access-list is called *inbound*, which means that only the source IP addresses of the packets that the router receives through the interface are checked against the access-list. If the last parameter is either blank or **out**, the access-list is called *outbound*, which means that only the source IP addresses of the packets that the router is about to send over the interface are checked against the access-list. If comparing the source IP address against the access-list results in **deny**, the packet is dropped; otherwise, it is forwarded.

NOTE: *You can have separate **ip access-group** <AL Number> **in** and **ip access-group** <AL Number> **out** commands on a single interface.*

TIP: *It makes sense to specify more specific match criteria at the beginning of the access-list. For example, if you want to allow only a single host on a certain subnet to access some service located behind a router, compose the access-list that first specifies the host's IP address with the permit condition, then the subnet address with the deny condition, and then any IP address with the permit condition.*

Let's examine how router R in Figure 6.2 should be configured to allow only host H3 to communicate with host H1.

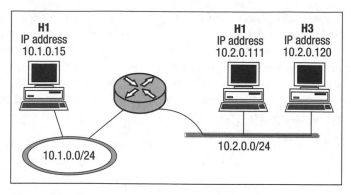

Figure 6.2   Router R only allows host H3 to communicate with host H1.

Listing 6.1 shows the configuration of router R. Pay attention to the order of the conditions in access-list 1. It demonstrates the technique described in the previous tip.

Listing 6.1   Router R1's configuration.

```
interface Ethernet0
 ip address 10.2.0.1 255.255.255.0

interface TokenRing0
 ip address 10.1.0.1 255.255.255.0
 ip access-group 1 out
 ring-speed 16

access-list 1 permit 10.2.0.120
access-list 1 deny   10.2.0.0 0.0.0.255
access-list 1 permit any
```

In this particular configuration, we do not need the last **access-list 1 permit any** line. It was added in case there are other segments connected to router R that may need access to host H1.

The command **ping 10.1.0.15** issued on host H2 fails as shown in Listing 6.2.

*Listing 6.2   The output of the command **ping 10.1.0.15** issued on host H2.*

```
C:\>ping 10.1.0.15

Pinging 10.1.0.15 with 32 bytes of data:

Reply from 10.2.0.1: Destination net unreachable.
Reply from 10.2.0.1: Destination net unreachable.
Reply from 10.2.0.1: Destination net unreachable.
Reply from 10.2.0.1: Destination net unreachable.
```

Interestingly enough, the output of **ping** indicates that the packets are not simply silently dropped by the router (if that were the case, the output would be "Request timed out"). The router returns some type of error packet back to the originator of the ping packets. To see what error packets are sent back by the router, let's use a LAN analyzer on a segment to which host H2 is connected while host H2 is sending the ping packets.

Figure 6.3 shows the main window of Microsoft Network Monitor that was running on host H2 while host H2 was pinging host H1.

Microsoft Network Monitor shows that these error packets are ICMP Destination Unreachable messages. From Chapter 1, we remember that there are several types of ICMP Destination Unreachable messages. The type of an ICMP Destination Unreachable message is defined by specifying the appropriate CODE value. In our case, this value is equal to 0x0D in hexadecimal or 13 in decimal, which does not correspond to any "official" ICMP Destination Unreachable types (see Table 1.5 in Chapter 1).

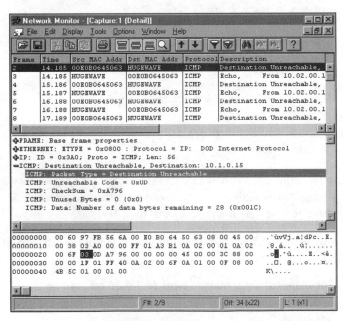

Figure 6.3   *The main window of Microsoft Network Monitor displays the capture of the "destination unreachable" ICMP message sent to host H2 by router R.*

Using Extended Access-Lists

Applying extended access-lists as user data traffic filters allows more flexibility in terms of which characteristics of a datagram should be matched when deciding whether it must be forwarded or dropped. Standard access-lists only provide a way to match the source address of a datagram. Extended access-lists provide a way to match both source and destination addresses; the destination protocol, such as TCP, UDP, ICMP, IGRP, and so on; protocol-specific characteristics, such as TCP or UDP ports; and much more.

The same procedure defined for standard access-lists applies when using extended access-lists for filtering user data traffic. The format of an extended access-list follows:

access-list *<AL number>* **{permit|deny}** *<protocol> <source IP address> <source wildcard mask> <destination IP address> <destination wildcard mask>* [protocol specific parameters]

The parameter *<protocol>* can be either the IP protocol number—that is, the value passed in the Protocol field of an IP datagram header—or the name of a protocol. Some protocol names currently available are shown in Table 6.1.

Table 6.1   Protocol names available with extended access-lists.

Name	Description
ip	Any Internet Protocol (which means that the router will not analyze the Protocol field)
tcp	Transmission Control Protocol (TCP)
udp	User Datagram Protocol (UDP)
icmp	Internet Control Message Protocol
igrp	Cisco's IGRP routing protocol
eigrp	Cisco's EIGRP routing protocol
ospf	OSPF routing protocol
gre	Cisco's GRE tunneling
ipinip	IP in IP tunneling
igmp	Internet Gateway Message Protocol
nos	KA9Q NOS-compatible IP over IP tunneling
ahp	Authentication Header Protocol
esp	Encapsulation Security Payload
pcp	Payload Compression Protocol

Only the protocols that run directly over IP are supported. For example, RIP is not available because it runs over UDP.

As in the case of standard access-lists, the combinations *<source IP address> <source wildcard mask>* and *<destination IP address> <destination wildcard mask>* can be replaced by either **any** or **host** *<IP address>*. The first provides a match for any IP address; the latter, only for individual IP addresses.

For protocol-specific options, see the Cisco documentation.

NOTE: *Like standard access-lists, extended access-lists also contain an implicit* **access-list ip deny ang ang** *at the end.*

Let's modify the user data traffic filtering task for the network in Figure 6.2. This time, we will allow host H1 to access only the Telnet and Daytime services on host H3. All other communication between any two hosts on the network must be fully available.

Listing 6.3 demonstrates one of the ways in which this task can be performed. The last four italicized lines show the extended access-list applied as an inbound user data traffic filter (the first italicized line) on the interface TokenRing 0.

Listing 6.3   Router R's configuration.

```
interface Ethernet0
 ip address 10.2.0.1 255.255.255.0

interface TokenRing0
 ip address 10.1.0.1 255.255.255.0
 ip access-group 100 in
 ring-speed 16

access-list 100 permit tcp any host 10.2.0.120 eq telnet
access-list 100 permit tcp any host 10.2.0.120 eq daytime
access-list 100 deny   ip any host 10.2.0.120
access-list 100 permit ip any any
```

If we try to **ping** host H3 from host H1, **ping** fails (see Listing 6.4).

Listing 6.4   The extended access-list applied as an inbound traffic filter on router R1 prevents host H3 to be pinged from host H1.

```
C:\>ping 10.2.0.120
```

```
Pinging 10.2.0.120 with 32 bytes of data:

Reply from 10.1.0.1: Destination net unreachable.
Reply from 10.1.0.1: Destination net unreachable.
Reply from 10.1.0.1: Destination net unreachable.
Reply from 10.1.0.1: Destination net unreachable.
```

However, if we try to access host H3 from host H1 using **Telnet**, **Telnet** succeeds (see Listing 6.5).

Listing 6.5   The access-list does not block Telnet traffic from host H1 to host H3.

```
C:\>telnet 10.2.0.120
Trying 10.2.0.120...
Connected to 10.2.0.120.  Escape key is Ctrl-].

Welcome to the Telnet Service on THUNDER

Username:
```

Listing 6.6 shows that both **ping** and **Telnet** succeed if they are used to access host H2 from host H1.

Listing 6.6   Neither Telnet nor ping packets are blocked by the access-list if they are destined for host H2.

```
C:\>ping 10.2.0.111

Pinging 10.2.0.111 with 32 bytes of data:

Reply from 10.2.0.111: bytes=32 time<10ms TTL=127
Reply from 10.2.0.111: bytes=32 time<10ms TTL=127
Reply from 10.2.0.111: bytes=32 time<10ms TTL=127
Reply from 10.2.0.111: bytes=32 time<10ms TTL=127

C:\>telnet 10.2.0.111
Trying 10.2.0.111...
Connected to 10.2.0.111.  Escape key is Ctrl-].

Welcome to the Telnet Service on HUGEWAVE

Username:
```

Using Named Access-Lists

In Cisco IOS Version 11.2, a new format of access-lists was introduced. This new format can be called *named access-lists* because a name can be given to an access-list instead of a number. The functionality behind named access-lists remains the same as the functionality of regular standard and extended access-lists.

To create a named access-list, follow these steps:

1. Create an access-list header using the command **ip access-list {standard|extended}** *<AL name>*. After you enter this command, you are transferred in the access-list configuration mode.

2. In the access-list configuration mode, enter one or several match clauses. The format of the match clauses depends on whether the access-list is standard or extended. In both cases, the match clauses have the same format as the part of the regular standard or extended access-list from the word **permit** or **deny** up to the end of the access-list.

NOTE: *A named access-list is terminated with an implicit **deny any** condition at the end.*

Because the functionality of the named access-lists remains the same as the functionality of the regular access-lists, we won't specifically consider how named access-lists can be used to filter user data traffic. However, both named and standard access-lists are used in the remaining examples in this book, so that you can learn how to apply named access-lists.

TIP: *Instead of the <AL name> parameter, you can use a number, just as with regular access-lists. For standard access-lists, the number can be in the range from 1 to 99; for extended access-lists, the number can be in the range from 100 to 199. In this case, however, the router will reformat the access-list from the named access-list format to the regular access-list format in the configuration it stores in the RAM and NVRAM.*

Controlling Routing Updates

Access-lists on the Cisco routers are really a versatile tool. There are numerous ways in which they can be used. We have just considered user data traffic filters. Now we will discuss routing updates filters.

Routing update filters allow filtering routing updates to be sent and received on router interfaces. Before sending or accepting a routing update, the network prefix advertised in the routing update is compared against the access-list. If the result of the comparison is **permit**, the update is sent or accepted. If the result is **deny**, the routing update is discarded. The latter means that if the update is scheduled to be sent, it is not sent; if the update is received, then the routing information in it is ignored.

To configure a routing update filter, follow these steps:

- Create either a standard or extended access-list (see the "Using Access-Lists To Filter Data Traffic" section in this chapter).

- Apply the access-list as the routing update filter using the command **distribute-list** *<AL number>* **{in|out}** *<Interface>* in the routing protocol configuration mode.

  If the parameter **in** is used, than the routing update filter is called *inbound,* and it is applied to the routing updates received on the interface specified using the parameter *<Interface>*. Likewise, if the parameter **out** is used, the routing update filter is called *outbound,* and it is applied to the routing updates sent over the interface.

NOTE: *Outbound routing updates filters cannot be used with the link state routing protocols, such as OSPF. The operation of link state protocols requires the ability to send the entire link state database to the adjacencies. In general, using routing updates filters with link state protocols is undesirable.*

Let's consider the network shown in Figure 6.4.

All routers are configured to run IGRP. Our task is to disallow router R3 to send router R4 routing updates that advertise the network pre-

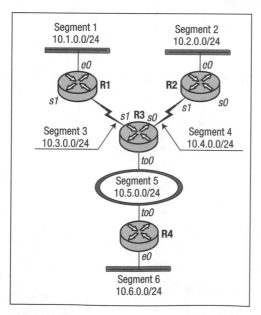

Figure 6.4   Router R3 filters the routing updates for networks 10.3.0.0/24 and 10.4.0.0/24 out.

fixes of the two serial links connecting router R3 to routers R1 and R2. Listings 6.7 through 6.10 show the configurations of all four routers. The italicized lines in Listing 6.9 demonstrate how a routing update filter can be used to accomplish this task.

Listing 6.7   Router R1's configuration.

```
interface Ethernet0
 ip address 10.1.0.1 255.255.255.0

interface Serial0
 ip address 10.3.0.2 255.255.255.0

router igrp 10
 network 10.0.0.0
```

Listing 6.8   Router R2's configuration.

```
interface Ethernet0
 ip address 10.2.0.1 255.255.255.0

interface Serial1
 ip address 10.4.0.2 255.255.255.0

router igrp 10
 network 10.0.0.0
```

Listing 6.9   Router R3's configuration.

```
interface Serial0
 ip address 10.4.0.1 255.255.255.0

interface Serial1
 ip address 10.3.0.1 255.255.255.0

interface TokenRing0
 ip address 10.5.0.1 255.255.255.0
 ring-speed 16

router igrp 10
 network 10.0.0.0
 distribute-list 1 out TokenRing0

access-list 1 deny    10.3.0.0 0.0.255.255
access-list 1 deny    10.4.0.0 0.0.255.255
access-list 1 permit any
```

Listing 6.10   Router R4's configuration.

```
interface Ethernet0
 ip address 10.6.0.1 255.255.255.0
```

```
interface TokenRing0
 ip address 10.5.0.2 255.255.255.0
 ring-speed 16

router igrp 10
 network 10.0.0.0
```

The routing table of router R4 confirms that the router does not receive any routing updates that advertise network prefixes 10.3.0.0/24 and 10.4.0.0/24.

Listing 6.11   The routing table of router R4.

```
R4#show ip route
...
     10.0.0.0/24 is subnetted, 4 subnets
I       10.2.0.0 [100/8639] via 10.5.0.1, 00:00:35, TokenRing0
I       10.1.0.0 [100/8639] via 10.5.0.1, 00:00:35, TokenRing0
C       10.6.0.0 is directly connected, Ethernet0
C       10.5.0.0 is directly connected, TokenRing0
```

If we examine the output of the command **debug ip igrp transactions**, we'll see that router R3 indeed does not advertise those network prefixes over the interface TokenRing 0. Listing 6.12 exhibits the fragment of the command **debug ip igrp transactions** output that shows the routing update sent by router R3 over the interface TokenRing 0.

*Listing 6.12   The output of the command **debug ip igrp transactions** entered on router R3 indicates that network prefixes 10.3.0.0/ 24 and 10.4.0.0/24 are not included in the routing updates sent over the TokenRing 0 interface.*

```
...
IGRP: sending update to 255.255.255.255 via TokenRing0
(10.5.0.1)
      subnet 10.2.0.0, metric=8576
      subnet 10.1.0.0, metric=8576
...
```

Using Redistribution

The way in which redistribution can be performed depends greatly on the redistributed sources of routing information, that is dynamic routing protocols, static, routes, and connected routes. In the remaining sections in this chapter, we'll consider how different types of pro-

6. Controlling Data Flow And Routing Updates

tocols behave when redistributed into each other and how to control routing information during redistribution. We'll also look at some potential problems, such as routing loops, that can emerge solely from redistribution.

Configuring Basic Redistribution

As described in the "In Brief" section of this chapter, redistribution is the process of converting routing information among different sources of routing information, such as dynamic routing protocols, static routes, and connected routes. Static and connected routes can only be redistributed into a dynamic routing protocol; redistribution into static or connected routes is not possible (and meaningless).

A basic form of redistribution is performed using the command **redistribute** *<routing information source>* **metric** *<routing protocol specific metric>* in a routing protocol configuration mode. The *<routing information source>* indicates the source of routing information being redistributed into this routing protocol and accepts the keywords shown in Table 6.2.

NOTE: *The information presented in Table 6.2 was taken from a router running IOS Version 12.0(2a). Depending on the version of IOS that your routers run, some of these keywords may not be available. Future releases of the Cisco IOS may support more keywords.*

Table 6.2 The keywords denoting the souce of routing information in the redistribute command.

Keyword	Description
connected	Connected
static	Static routes
rip	Routing Information Protocol
igrp	Interior Gateway Routing Protocol
eigrp	Enhanced Interior Gateway Routing Protocol
ospf	Open Shortest Path First
bgp	Border Gateway Protocol
egp	Exterior Gateway Protocol
isis	ISO IS-IS
iso-igrp	IGRP for OSI networks
mobile	Mobile routes
odr	On Demand Stub Routes

The *<routing protocol specific metric>* parameter identifies the protocol-specific metric with which all of the redistributed routes will have. This parameter has variable formats depending on the routing protocol into which the routing information is redistributed. For more information about the exact format of this parameter, see the Cisco documentation.

NOTE: *The parameter **metric** <routing protocol specific metric> is optional. If omitted, it defaults to 0, unless the command **default-metric** is used. The command **default-metric** is explained in the next sections.*

Let's examine the network shown in Figure 6.5. Routers R1, R2, and R3 belong to a part of the network called *Routing Domain 1*. Suppose that the routing information in Routing Domain 1 must be propagated using IGRP. Routers R3 and R4 belong to Routing Domain 2, in which the routing information must be propagated using RIP.

Router R3 belongs to both routing domains. Obviously, it must perform a two-way redistribution of routing information between RIP and IGRP to provide overall network connectivity. Listings 6.13

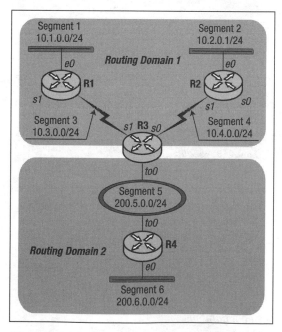

6. Controlling Data Flow And Routing Updates

Figure 6.5   Router R3 performs redistribution of routing information between IGRP used in Routing Domain 1 and RIP used in Routing Domain 2.

through 6.16 show the configurations of all four routers. The italicized lines in Listing 6.15 show the redistribution command used on router R3.

Listing 6.13   Router R1's configuration.

```
interface Ethernet0
 ip address 10.1.0.1 255.255.255.0

interface Serial0
 ip address 10.3.0.2 255.255.255.0

router igrp 10
 network 10.0.0.0
```

Listing 6.14   Router R2's configuration.

```
interface Ethernet0
 ip address 10.2.0.1 255.255.255.0

interface Serial1
 ip address 10.4.0.2 255.255.255.0

router igrp 10
 network 10.0.0.0
```

Listing 6.15   Router R3's configuration.

```
interface Serial0
 ip address 10.4.0.1 255.255.255.0

interface Serial1
 ip address 10.3.0.1 255.255.255.0

interface TokenRing0
 ip address 200.5.0.1 255.255.255.0
 ring-speed 16

router rip
 redistribute igrp 10 metric 1
 network 200.5.0.0

router igrp 10
 redistribute rip metric 10000 1 255 1 1500
 network 10.0.0.0
```

Listing 6.16   Router R4's configuration.

```
interface Ethernet0
 ip address 200.6.0.1 255.255.255.0
```

```
interface TokenRing0
 ip address 200.5.0.2 255.255.255.0
 ring-speed 16

router rip
 network 200.5.0.0
 network 200.6.0.0
```

If we check the routing table of router R4 (Listing 6.17), we'll see a
single route for network 10.0.0.0/8 learned via RIP (because it is labeled "R"). Obviously, this became available as the result of mutual
redistribution between IGRP and RIP performed by router R3.

Listing 6.17 The routing table of router R4.

```
R4#show ip route
...
C  200.5.0.0/24 is directly connected, TokenRing0
C  200.6.0.0/24 is directly connected, Ethernet0
R  10.0.0.0/8 [120/1] via 200.5.0.1, 00:00:10, TokenRing0
```

If we examine the routing table of router R1 (Listing 6.18), we'll see
two routes for networks 200.5.0.0/24 and 200.6.0.0/24 learned via IGRP
(because they are labeled "I"). This is also a result of redistribution
performed by router R3.

Listing 6.18 The routing table of router R1.

```
R1#show ip route
...
10.0.0.0/24 is subnetted, 4 subnets
I     10.2.0.0 [100/10576] via 10.3.0.1, 00:00:04, Serial0
C     10.3.0.0 is directly connected, Serial0
C     10.1.0.0 is directly connected, Ethernet0
I     10.4.0.0 [100/10476] via 10.3.0.1, 00:00:04, Serial0
I  200.5.0.0/24 [100/8539] via 10.3.0.1, 00:00:04, Serial0
I  200.6.0.0/24 [100/8477] via 10.3.0.1, 00:00:04, Serial0
```

The routing table of router R3 (Listing 6.19) indicates that the routes
for all networks are known via their original routing information
sources (that is, IGRP, RIP, and connected).

Listing 6.19 The routing table of router R3.

```
R3#show ip route
...
C  200.5.0.0/24 is directly connected, TokenRing0
R  200.6.0.0/24 [120/1] via 200.5.0.2, 00:00:14, TokenRing0
   10.0.0.0/24 is subnetted, 4 subnets
```

```
I     10.2.0.0 [100/8576] via 10.4.0.2, 00:00:20, Serial0
C     10.3.0.0 is directly connected, Serial1
I     10.1.0.0 [100/8576] via 10.3.0.2, 00:01:00, Serial1
C     10.4.0.0 is directly connected, Serial0
```

TIP: *You can enter multiple commands **redistribute**, each specifying a different source of routing information under the same routing protocol configuration mode.*

Understanding How Routing Loops Can Emerge As The Result Of Redistribution

The "In Brief" section in this chapter provides a description of a typical scenario of how routing loops can emerge because of redistribution of two dynamic routing protocols. Let's now consider a real example and see how routing loop oscillation manifests itself.

Figure 6.6 shows a slightly modified version of the network we have used as an example so far. The only difference between this network and the one shown in Figure 6.5 is that segment 2 is gone. Segment 1 and segment 2 were merged together into a single segment to which

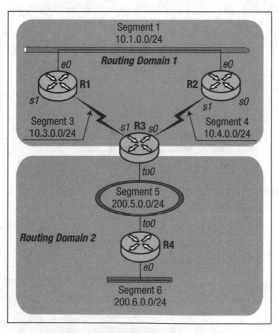

Figure 6.6   If Routing Domain 1 uses IGRP and Routing Domain 2 uses RIP, the IP addresses from Routing Domain 2 won't be accessible from Routing Domain 2 because of a routing loop.

both routers R1 and R2 are now connected. The merged segment inherited the network prefix from the original segment 1.

Because routers R1 and R2 are connected to the same segment, they exchange IGRP routing updates. Router R3 is connected to both routers via segments 3 and 4 (the original names were retained) and exchange IGRP routing updates with them. In addition, router R3 is connected to segment 5. Instead of IGRP routing updates, router R3 now exchanges RIP routing updates with router R4. Router R4 is the only source of the routing updates that advertise segment 6 to router R3. To provide overall connectivity, router R3 performs redistribution of RIP and IGRP. This description gives us enough information to conclude that we have a situation matching the routing loop scenario described in the "In Brief" section in this chapter. Let's see if a routing loop does emerge.

The configurations of router R1, R3, and R4 remain the same as in the previous example. The updated configuration of router R2 is shown in Listing 6.20.

Listing 6.20   Router R2's configuration.

```
interface Ethernet0
  ip address 10.1.0.2 255.255.255.0

interface Serial1
  ip address 10.4.0.2 255.255.255.0

router igrp 10
  network 10.0.0.0
```

Router R1 was first connected to segment 1 and then to segment 3. Thus, it has a chance to first hear a routing update from router R2. If we check the routing table of router R3, shown in Listing 6.21, we'll see signs of a routing loop. The italicized lines show the routes that router R3 has for network prefix 200.6.0.0/24. Notice that the two routes point back to the routers R1 and R2, which are only connected to this network prefix through router R3. Obviously, this is a routing loop.

Listing 6.21   The routing table of router R3 soon indicates the presence of a routing loop.

```
R3#show ip route
...
C  200.5.0.0/24 is directly connected, TokenRing0
I  200.6.0.0/24 [100/10577] via 10.4.0.2, 00:04:43, Serial0
```

```
                    [100/10577] via 10.3.0.2, 00:01:12, Serial1
       10.0.0.0/24 is subnetted, 3 subnets
C        10.3.0.0 is directly connected, Serial1
I        10.1.0.0 [100/8576] via 10.4.0.2, 00:00:30, Serial0
                   [100/8576] via 10.3.0.2, 00:01:13, Serial1
C        10.4.0.0 is directly connected, Serial0
```

The contents of router R3's routing table soon changes, as shown in Listing 6.22. Apparently, one of the routers participating in mutual "cheating" increased the metric of the route to network 200.6.0.0/24, an avalanche of triggered routing updates followed, and the metric was quickly brought down to infinity. The route was put into holddown, which is indicated as "possibly down" in the output of the command **show ip route**.

Listing 6.22   The routing table of router R3 indicates that network 200.6.0.0 is possibly down.

```
R3#show ip route
...
C  200.5.0.0/24 is directly connected, TokenRing0
I  200.6.0.0/24 is possibly down,routing via 10.4.0.2,Serial0
     10.0.0.0/24 is subnetted, 3 subnets
C        10.3.0.0 is directly connected, Serial1
I        10.1.0.0 [100/8576] via 10.4.0.2, 00:00:02, Serial0
                   [100/8576] via 10.3.0.2, 00:00:57, Serial1
C        10.4.0.0 is directly connected, Serial0
```

Let's clear the routing table of router R3. Listing 6.23 shows the command **clear ip route *** followed by the command **show ip route** and its output.

Listing 6.23   The routing table of router R3 after its routing table is flushed.

```
R3#clear ip route *
R3#show ip route
...
C  200.5.0.0/24 is directly connected, TokenRing0
R  200.6.0.0/24 [120/1] via 200.5.0.2, 00:00:07, TokenRing0
     10.0.0.0/24 is subnetted, 3 subnets
C        10.3.0.0 is directly connected, Serial1
I        10.1.0.0 [100/8576] via 10.4.0.2, 00:00:07, Serial0
                   [100/8576] via 10.3.0.2, 00:00:07, Serial1
C        10.4.0.0 is directly connected, Serial0
```

The routing table of router R3 now seems to be back to normal. Even if we watch it for a while, it remains alright, but not for too long.

Listings 6.24 and 6.25 show the routing tables of routers R1 and R2, respectively. Whereas the routing table of router R1 seems to be alright, the routing table of router R2 is certainly not. Currently, the route for network prefix 200.6.0.0/24 is in holddown, although this network prefix is perfectly available via router R3. This is a consequence of the seemingly disappeared routing loop.

Listing 6.24   The routing table of router R1.

```
R1#show ip route
...
     10.0.0.0/24 is subnetted, 3 subnets
C     10.3.0.0 is directly connected, Serial0
C     10.1.0.0 is directly connected, Ethernet0
I     10.4.0.0 [100/8576] via 10.1.0.2, 00:00:17, Ethernet0
I    200.5.0.0/24 [100/8539] via 10.3.0.1, 00:00:35, Serial0
I    200.6.0.0/24 [100/8477] via 10.3.0.1, 00:04:42, Serial0
```

Listing 6.25   The routing table of router R2 indicates that the route for network 200.6.0.0 is in holddown.

```
R2#show ip route
...
     10.0.0.0/24 is subnetted, 3 subnets
I     10.3.0.0 [100/8576] via 10.1.0.1, 00:00:48, Ethernet0
C     10.1.0.0 is directly connected, Ethernet0
C     10.4.0.0 is directly connected, Serial1
I    200.5.0.0/24 [100/8539] via 10.4.0.1, 00:00:12, Serial1
I    200.6.0.0/24 is possibly down,routing via 10.4.0.1,Serial1
```

As soon as the holddown for the route to network prefix 200.6.0.0 on router R2 expires, a positive update is sent from router R2 to router R3, which supersedes the correct RIP-learned route to network 200.6.0.0. This creates a temporary routing loop. The loop exists for a short period until one of the routers decreases the metric of the route to network 200.6.0.0. This event is followed by an avalanche of triggered routing updates, each decreasing the metric until it becomes 4294967295 in decimal, or 0xFFFFFFFF in hexadecimal. As we know from Chapter 4, IGRP uses this metric to indicate infinity. As soon as the metric becomes infinity, the route is put in holddown for 280 seconds. During this time, the router advertises the route with the metric set to infinity and does not accept any positive routing updates for that destination.

NOTE: *A route placed in holddown still exists in the routing table. Therefore, if another protocol whose administrative distance is greater than that of the routing protocol that placed the existing route in holddown attempts to install a possibly correct route for the same destination into the routing table, it will fail.*

Understanding Static And Connected Route Redistribution

Both static and connected routes can be redistributed into a dynamic routing protocol using the commands **redistribute static** or **redistribute connected,** respectively, in the corresponding routing protocol configuration mode.

One special case, however, is represented by the static routes pointing to an interface. These routes are redistributed into dynamic routing protocols if their network prefix is matched by the argument of a **network** statement whether the command **redistribute static** is present or not. If no **network** statement's argument provides a match for such a route, the command **redistribute static** is needed to perform redistribution.

Let's consider the sample network shown in Figure 6.7.

Both routers are configured for IGRP. In addition, router R1 has several static routes as shown in Listing 6.26. Router R2 has a very basic configuration, shown in Listing 6.27.

Listing 6.26   Router R1's configuration.

```
interface Ethernet0
 ip address 10.1.0.1 255.255.255.0

interface Serial0
 ip address 10.3.0.2 255.255.255.0

router igrp 100
 network 10.0.0.0

ip route 10.100.0.0 255.255.255.0 Ethernet0
```

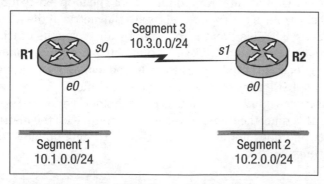

Figure 6.7   A sample network in which router R1 has several static routes, some of which are redistributed into the dynamic routing protocol that the routers are running.

```
ip route 10.110.0.0 255.255.255.0 10.1.0.2
ip route 172.16.1.0 255.255.255.0 Ethernet0
```

Listing 6.27   Router R2's configuration.

```
interface Ethernet0
 ip address 10.2.0.1 255.255.255.0

interface Serial0
 ip address 10.4.0.1 255.255.255.0

interface Serial1
 ip address 10.3.0.1 255.255.255.0

router igrp 100
 network 10.0.0.0
```

The routing table of router R2 only has a route for network prefix 10.100.0.0/24 out of all of the static routes configured on router R1 (see Listing 6.28). This confirms the rule described in the beginning of this section, which states that static routes are redistributed automatically if they are matched by any **network** statement under a routing protocol configuration.

Listing 6.28   The routing table of router R2.

```
R2#show ip route
...
     10.0.0.0/24 is subnetted, 5 subnets
C       10.2.0.0 is directly connected, Ethernet0
C       10.3.0.0 is directly connected, Serial1
I       10.1.0.0 [100/8576] via 10.3.0.2, 00:00:08, Serial1
C       10.4.0.0 is directly connected, Serial0
I       10.100.0.0 [100/8576] via 10.3.0.2, 00:00:08, Serial1
```

If we now add the command **redistribute static metric 10000 1 255 1 1500** under the **router igrp 100** configuration of router R1, we'll see that the routing table of router R2 changes (see Listing 6.29). It now includes all three network prefixes for which router R1 has static routes.

Listing 6.29   The routing table of router R2.

```
R2#show ip route
...
I  172.16.0.0/16 [100/8477] via 10.3.0.2, 00:00:28, Serial1
     10.0.0.0/24 is subnetted, 6 subnets
C       10.2.0.0 is directly connected, Ethernet0
C       10.3.0.0 is directly connected, Serial1
```

```
I       10.1.0.0 [100/8576] via 10.3.0.2, 00:00:29, Serial1
C       10.4.0.0 is directly connected, Serial0
I       10.110.0.0 [100/8477] via 10.3.0.2, 00:00:29, Serial1
I       10.100.0.0 [100/8477] via 10.3.0.2, 00:00:29, Serial1
```

NOTE: *The static routes pointing to an interface are not automatically redistributed into OSPF even if their network prefixes are matched by the OSPF **network** statements.*

Assigning A Default Redistribution Metric

An alternative way to specify a redistribution metric is to set up a default redistribution metric. If the command **redistribute** is used without the **metric** parameter but with the default redistribution metric specified, the redistributed route is assigned the default redistribution metric.

To set up a default redistribution metric, the command **default-metric** *<routing protocol specific metric>* must be used under the routing protocol configuration mode.

Let's change the configuration of router R3 from the network example shown in Figure 6.5 so that it uses a default redistribution metric instead of the **metric** parameter of the command **redistribute**. The modified configuration of router R3 is shown in Listing 6.30.

Listing 6.30   Router R3's configuration.

```
interface Serial0
 ip address 10.4.0.1 255.255.255.0

interface Serial1
 ip address 10.3.0.1 255.255.255.0

interface TokenRing0
 ip address 200.5.0.1 255.255.255.0
 ring-speed 16

router rip
 redistribute igrp 10
 network 200.5.0.0
 default-metric 3

router igrp 10
 redistribute rip
 network 10.0.0.0
 default-metric 10000 1 255 1 1500
```

Listing 6.31 shows the new routing table of router R4. The italicized text shows the new metric of the RIP learned route.

Listing 6.31   The routing table of router R4.

```
R4#show ip route
...
C    200.5.0.0/24 is directly connected, TokenRing0
C    200.6.0.0/24 is directly connected, Ethernet0
R    10.0.0.0/8 [120/3] via 200.5.0.1, 00:00:03, TokenRing0
```

Notice that the metric of the route for network 10.0.0.0/8 is now 3 instead of 1 (see Listing 6.17). Because we don't use the **metric** parameter of the **redistribute** command; the default redistribution metric (in our case, 3) is used instead.

Using One-Way Redistribution

As discussed in the "In Brief" section in this chapter, hosts on a network may occasionally require the exact routing information instead of the default gateway route. Most often, such hosts can run "open" routing protocols, such as RIP. If this is the case and if the routers on the network run an incompatible protocol, such as IGRP, a one-way redistribution is required on those that are connected to the segments on which the hosts reside. A one-way redistribution assumes that only the routes learned via the incompatible routing protocol (such as IGRP) are redistributed into the routing protocols that the hosts can understand (such as RIP), but not vice versa.

If a one-way redistribution is used, it also makes sense to ensure that the routers running the host-compatible routing protocol discard all routing updates that they can potentially receive via this protocol. This can be accomplished using the command **distance 255** in the corresponding routing protocol configuration mode. This is important because, although the network prefixes received in such routing updates are not redistributed into the main routing protocol, the corresponding routes are still added into the routing table of this single router. Thus, it provides access to the advertised networks by all hosts located on the segments to which the router is locally attached.

Let's examine the network topology depicted in Figure 6.8. All routers run IGRP, and multihomed host H1 runs RIP.

This network is very similar to the one that we discussed in Chapter 4, in the "Discriminating Incoming Routing Updates" section. In that network, however, the routers and host H1 were running the same

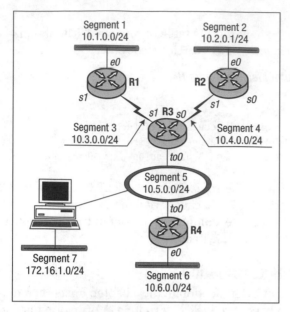

Figure 6.8   Multihomed Host H1 needs exact routing information from the routers connected to segment 5 in the form of RIP routing updates.

routing protocol (RIP), and the task was to continue sending routing updates to the host while ignoring any routing updates that the host may send. In this network, the routers use IGRP to propagate routing information. Multihomed host H1 uses RIP to receive routing information. In addition, host H1 is connected to some test environment consisting of a single segment 7. Somehow, host H1 was configured to forward IP datagrams between its interfaces. Thus, our task is to send host H1 routing updates using RIP, while ignoring its routing updates advertising the network prefix of segment 7.

Listings 6.32 through 6.35 show the revised configurations of all four routers.

Listing 6.32   Router R1's configuration.

```
interface Ethernet0
 ip address 10.1.0.1 255.255.255.0

interface Serial0
 ip address 10.3.0.2 255.255.255.0

router igrp 10
 network 10.0.0.0
```

Listing 6.33   Router R2's configuration.

```
interface Ethernet0
 ip address 10.2.0.1 255.255.255.0

interface Serial1
 ip address 10.4.0.2 255.255.255.0

router igrp 10
 network 10.0.0.0
```

Listing 6.34   Router R3's configuration.

```
interface Serial0
 ip address 10.4.0.1 255.255.255.0

interface Serial1
 ip address 10.3.0.1 255.255.255.0

interface TokenRing0
 ip address 10.5.0.1 255.255.255.0

router rip
 redistribute igrp 10 metric 3
 passive-interface Serial0
 passive-interface Serial1
 network 10.0.0.0
 distance 255

router igrp 10
 network 10.0.0.0
```

Listing 6.35   Router R4's configuration.

```
interface Ethernet0
 ip address 10.6.0.1 255.255.255.0

interface TokenRing0
 ip address 10.5.0.2 255.255.255.0
 ring-speed 16

router rip
 redistribute igrp 10 metric 3
 passive-interface Ethernet0
 network 10.0.0.0

router igrp 10
 network 10.0.0.0
```

6. Controlling Data Flow And Routing Updates

Notice that router R4's **router rip** configuration does not contain the command **distance 255**. That was done on purpose to ensure that router R4 receives the routing updates sent by host H1.

Listing 6.36 shows the routing table of router R4. The italicized line indicates that router R4 does have a route for the network prefix learned via RIP from host H1.

Listing 6.36   The routing table of router R4.

```
R4#show ip route
...
R   172.16.0.0/16 [120/2] via 10.5.0.15, 00:00:07, TokenRing0
     10.0.0.0/24 is subnetted, 6 subnets
I      10.2.0.0 [100/8639] via 10.5.0.1, 00:01:10, TokenRing0
I      10.3.0.0 [100/8539] via 10.5.0.1, 00:01:10, TokenRing0
I      10.1.0.0 [100/8639] via 10.5.0.1, 00:01:10, TokenRing0
C      10.6.0.0 is directly connected, Ethernet0
I      10.4.0.0 [100/8539] via 10.5.0.1, 00:01:10, TokenRing0
C      10.5.0.0 is directly connected, TokenRing0
```

However, the routing table of router R3 (shown in Listing 6.37) does not have any route for network prefix 172.16.0.0/16, because router R3's **router rip** configuration contains the command **distance 255**.

Listing 6.37   The routing table of router R3.

```
R3#show ip route
...
     10.0.0.0/24 is subnetted, 6 subnets
I      10.2.0.0 [100/8576] via 10.4.0.2, 00:01:05, Serial0
C      10.3.0.0 is directly connected, Serial1
I      10.1.0.0 [100/8576] via 10.3.0.2, 00:00:10, Serial1
I      10.6.0.0 [100/1163] via 10.5.0.2, 00:00:08, TokenRing0
C      10.4.0.0 is directly connected, Serial0
C      10.5.0.0 is directly connected, TokenRing0
```

Related Solution:	Found on page:
Discriminating Incoming Routing Updates	169

Using Access-Lists To Filter Routing Updates During Redistribution

In the "In Brief" section in this chapter, it was mentioned that it is sometimes necessary to perform redistribution in a more controlled fashion. For example, it may be necessary to redistribute only certain routes. This task can be performed using access-lists to specify which routes are to be redistributed.

The procedure consists of the following steps:

1. Create an access-list that matches the network prefixes of the routes that must be either included or excluded from redistribution. A route is included if it's matched with the **permit** condition. A route is excluded if it's matched with the **deny** condition, or if it's not matched at all (in which case it is actually matched by the explicit **deny ary** match condition at the end of the access-list).

2. Apply the access-list as a routing update filter using the command **distribute-list** *<AL number>* **out** *<source of routing information>*. The parameter *<source of routing information>* can be **connected**, **static**, or the name of a dynamic routing protocol. Some routing protocols require either the process number or the autonomous system number.

Let's assume that in the network example shown in Figure 6.5, loopback interfaces were added to routers R1 and R2, and these were assigned IP addresses 172.16.1.1 and 172.17.1.1 with subnet mask /24. Routers R1 and R2 are configured to advertise these two new network prefixes to the rest of the network via IGRP. Our task is to filter these two network prefixes on router R3 when redistributing routing information from IGRP to RIP.

Listings 6.38 through 6.41 show the revised router configurations. Notice that a named access-list is now used instead of a regular access-list.

Listing 6.38 Router R1's configuration.

```
interface Loopback0
 ip address 172.16.1.1 255.255.255.0

interface Ethernet0
 ip address 10.1.0.1 255.255.255.0

interface Serial0
 ip address 10.3.0.2 255.255.255.0

router igrp 10
 network 10.0.0.0
 network 172.16.0.0
```

Listing 6.39 Router R2's configuration.

```
interface Loopback0
 ip address 172.17.1.1 255.255.255.0
```

```
interface Ethernet0
 ip address 10.2.0.1 255.255.255.0

interface Serial1
 ip address 10.4.0.2 255.255.255.0

router igrp 10
 network 10.0.0.0
 network 172.17.0.0
```

Listing 6.40   Router R3's configuration.

```
interface Serial0
 ip address 10.4.0.1 255.255.255.0

interface Serial1
 ip address 10.3.0.1 255.255.255.0

interface TokenRing0
 ip address 200.5.0.1 255.255.255.0
 ring-speed 16

router rip
 redistribute igrp 10 metric 1
 network 200.5.0.0
 distribute-list no172 out igrp 10

router igrp 10
 redistribute rip metric 10000 1 255 1 1500
 network 10.0.0.0

ip access-list standard no172
 deny    172.16.0.0 0.15.255.255
 permit any
```

Listing 6.41   Router R4's configuration.

```
interface Ethernet0
 ip address 200.6.0.1 255.255.255.0

interface TokenRing0
 ip address 200.5.0.2 255.255.255.0
 ring-speed 16

router rip
 network 200.5.0.0
 network 200.6.0.0
```

Listing 6.42 shows the routing table of router R4, which does not have a route for either network prefix 172.16.0.0/16 or 172.17.0.0/16.

Listing 6.42   The routing table of router R4.

```
R4#show ip route
...
C    200.5.0.0/24 is directly connected, TokenRing0
C    200.6.0.0/24 is directly connected, Ethernet0
R    10.0.0.0/8 [120/1] via 200.5.0.1, 00:00:05, TokenRing0
```

The routing table of router R3, however, does contain routes for both network prefixes (Listing 6.43). These routers were learned via IGRP.

Listing 6.43   The routing table of router R3.

```
R3#show ip route
...
C    200.5.0.0/24 is directly connected, TokenRing0
R    200.6.0.0/24 [120/1] via 200.5.0.2, 00:00:05, TokenRing0
I    172.17.0.0/16 [100/8976] via 10.4.0.2, 00:01:18, Serial0
I    172.16.0.0/16 [100/8976] via 10.3.0.2, 00:00:09, Serial1
     10.0.0.0/24 is subnetted, 4 subnets
I       10.2.0.0 [100/8576] via 10.4.0.2, 00:01:18, Serial0
C       10.3.0.0 is directly connected, Serial1
I       10.1.0.0 [100/8576] via 10.3.0.2, 00:00:09, Serial1
C       10.4.0.0 is directly connected, Serial0
```

Using Route-Maps To Filter Routing Updates During Redistribution

Another way to filter the routing information during redistribution is based on using special logical expressions called *route-maps*.

A route-map is a logical expression the purpose of which is to modify various characteristics of redistributed routing information based on certain criteria. A route-map consists of one or several clauses, each of which can contain none, one or several match conditions and none, and one or several set actions. The set actions are used to modify routing information characteristics. The match conditions represent the criteria, which must be met in order to modify the routing information characteristics. If one or more match conditions are present in a clause of a route map, and if the parameters of a redistributed route match all of them, the route is redistributed, and its parameters are modified by the set actions contained in the same clause. Otherwise, the router tests the route against the match conditions of the next clause of the route-map. The router continues doing this until it finds a clause, all of whose match conditions are met. If it can't find such a clause, it does not redistribute the route. A route-map clause that contains no match conditions matches all routes.

NOTE: The definition of a route-map given in the previous paragraph represents only a usage of route-maps as routing updates filters. The route-map functionality is not limited to only filtering routing updates. More generic definition, however, would make understanding route-maps more difficult.

By default, each clause of a route-map is considered to return the **permit** result. This can also be specified explicitly. Optionally, a route-map clause can be specified to return the **deny** result. In this case, if a redistributed route's parameters are matched by the match conditions of a **deny** clause, the route is not redistributed, and no further lookup through the route-map is performed.

To configured a route-map-based filtering of routing information during redistribution, follow these steps:

1. Create a route-map clause header using the command **route-map** <RM name> [{permit|deny}] <sequence #>.

2. Add match conditions using the statement **match** followed by specific parameters. A form of the **match** statement that is very frequently used is **match ip address** {<AL number>|<AL name>}. The {<AL number>|<AL name>} parameter is either an access-list number of an access-list name. This form of match condition matches routes whose network prefixes are matched by the access-list. For information on the other available parameters of the **match** statement, see the Cisco documentation.

3. Add set actions using the statement **set** followed by specific parameters (for information on available parameters, see the Cisco documentation).

4. If the route-map consists of multiple clauses, repeat the sequence of Steps 1 through 3 until all clauses are entered. Each time, use the same parameter <RM name> but different <sequence #> parameters. The clauses with the smaller <sequence #> parameters are tested first.

5. Apply the route-map as a routing filter using the parameter **route-map** <RM name> of the command **redistribute**.

Let's modify the configuration of router R3 from the example in the previous section. In this example, router R3 does not filter out the network prefixes 172.16.0.0/16 and 172.17.0.0/16 but keeps them and independently modifies their metrics.

Listing 6.44 shows the revised configuration of router R3. The italicized part of the listing shows how the route-map was applied and the route map itself.

Listing 6.44   Router R3's configuration.

```
interface Serial0
 ip address 10.4.0.1 255.255.255.0

interface Serial1
 ip address 10.3.0.1 255.255.255.0

interface TokenRing0
 ip address 200.5.0.1 255.255.255.0
 ring-speed 16

router rip
 redistribute igrp 10 metric 1 route-map setm172
 network 200.5.0.0

router igrp 10
 redistribute rip metric 10000 1 255 1 1500
 network 10.0.0.0

ip access-list standard net172-16
 permit 172.16.0.0 0.0.255.255

ip access-list standard net172-17
 permit 172.17.0.0 0.0.255.255

route-map setm172 permit 10
 match ip address net172-16
 set metric +5

route-map setm172 permit 20
 match ip address net172-17
 set metric +10
```

Let's examine the routing table of router R4 (shown in Listing 6.45). We can see that routes for both network prefixes are present in router R4's routing table. Notice how the route metrics were modified (the italicized text elements) by the route-map.

Listing 6.45   The routing table of router R4.

```
R4#show ip route
...
C    200.5.0.0/24 is directly connected, TokenRing0
C    200.6.0.0/24 is directly connected, Ethernet0
```

```
R     172.17.0.0/16 [120/10] via 200.5.0.1, 00:00:07, TokenRing0
R     172.16.0.0/16 [120/5] via 200.5.0.1, 00:00:07, TokenRing0
```

TIP: Using the route-map parameter, you can set new metrics for the desired redistributed routes. If, however, the actual route map contains a **match** clause but does not contain a corresponding **set** clause that modifies the metrics of the redistributed routes, these routes are assigned either the default metric or the one specified using the **metric** parameter of the command **redistribute**. If none of these is present in the corresponding routing protocol configuration, the route is redistributed with the metric set to infinity.

Using The **Null** Interface For Route Summarization

Chapter 4 mentioned that it is possible to make RIP Version 2 advertise supernet routes. Unfortunately, Cisco's implementation of RIP Version 2 does not provide a specific method of configuring supernet addresses similar to the OSPF **area** <*area*> **range** command or the EIGRP **ip summary-address eigrp** command. Nevertheless, it is possible. The solution discussed in this section is based on the idea of redistributing a static supernet route into RIP Version 2. RIP Version 2 is the classless routing protocol that can advertise such a route. If a packet arrives that is destined for one of the existing networks matched by the supernet route, it is forwarded to the destination; otherwise, the packet is dropped.

To drop datagrams destined for non-existent network prefixes, which belong to the supernet network prefix, a special logical interface can be used as a parameter of the static route. This logical interface is denoted **Null**. Every packet that must be forwarded via a **Null** interface is dropped.

The proposed solution would be perfect unless RIP Version 2 still advertised the more specific network prefixes along with the redistributed supernet network prefix. The proposed solution does not address filtering out the more specific network prefixes, similar to how the special commands such as the OSPF **area** <*area*> **range** command do. Redistribution means that another network prefix is advertised along with already advertised ones. Therefore, we have to filter out all of the more specific network prefixes so that RIP Version 2 does not advertise them.

How do we filter out all network prefixes and preserve the supernet one? This question is important because the supernet network prefix provides a match for any specific network prefix. On the other hand, if we want to filter out more specific network prefixes, we must use an access-list that matches all of them, which is equal to the supernet network prefix and also matches it. We can do this if we do not assign the supernet network address with a more specific subnet mask to any existing network segment. In that case, we can compose an access-list that filters out more specific network prefixes but preserves the supernet network prefix as follows:

1. The first match condition of the access-list includes the keywords **permit host** followed by the exact supernet address that was used in the static route pointing to the **Null** interface.

2. The second match condition of the access-list consists of the keyword **deny** followed by the supernet address and the wildcard mask equal to the reversed subnet mask of the supernet network prefix.

3. The third match condition of the access-list includes the keywords **permit any**.

NOTE: *In Step 1 when a network prefix is compared against the access-list clauses, the network prefix length is not taken into consideration. Thus, we can use the wildcard 0.0.0.0 to match only the summary network prefix.*

To configure supernet routes for use with RIP Version 2, follow these steps:

1. In the global configuration mode, enter the command **ip classless**.

2. In the **router rip** configuration mode, enter the commands **version 2** and **no auto-summary**.

3. Create a static route pointing to the **Null 0** interface for each supernet network prefix.

4. Create a *single* access-list repeating Steps 1 and 2 of the preceding (match condition) procedure for each supernet network prefix. End the access-list using Step 3 from the preceding procedure.

5. Redistribute static routes into RIP Version 2 using the command **redistribute static**.

6. For each interface through which RIP Version 2 must advertise only the supernet network prefixes, create a routing filter using the command **distribute-list** *<AL number>* **out** *<Interface>*. The parameter *<AL number>* is equal to the access-list created in Step 2 of this procedure, and the parameter *<Interface>* is equal to the interface name.

6. Controlling Data Flow And Routing Updates

7. (This step is optional.) If you don't want the supernet network prefixes to be advertised via the interfaces whose IP addresses are matched by the supernet network prefixes (the *supernets* segments), you must first create a *separate* access-list for each supernet address using the preceding procedure; however, in Step 1, you must replace the keyword **permit** with the keyword **deny**, and vice versa in Step 2. For each interface whose IP address belongs to one of the supernet network prefixes, you must create a routing filter using the command **distribute-list** *<AL number>* **out** *<Interface>*, in which the parameter *<AL number>* references the access-list that denies the corresponding supernet address.

To see how the procedure works, let's consider the network example shown in Figure 6.9.

Router R3 is required to advertise only supernet network prefix 200.0.0.0/8 over its TokenRing 0 interface. Listings 6.46 through 6.49 show the configuration of all four routers. The italicized lines in Listing 6.48 indicate the commands entered as the result of the preceding procedure.

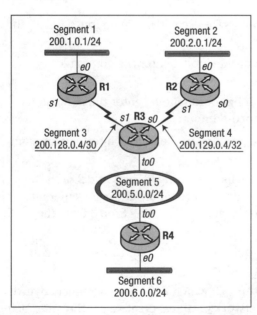

Figure 6.9   Router R3 should only advertise supernet network prefix 200.0.0.0/8 over the TokenRing segment.

Listing 6.46   Router R1's configuration.

```
interface Ethernet0
 ip address 200.1.0.1 255.255.255.0

interface Serial0
 ip address 200.128.0.6 255.255.255.252

router rip
 version 2
 network 200.128.0.0
 network 200.1.0.0
 no auto-summary

ip classless
```

Listing 6.47   Router R2's configuration.

```
interface Ethernet0
 ip address 200.2.0.1 255.255.255.0

interface Serial1
 ip address 200.129.0.6 255.255.255.252

router rip
 version 2
 network 200.129.0.0
 network 200.2.0.0
 no auto-summary

ip classless
```

Listing 6.48   Router R3's configuration.

```
interface Serial0
 ip address 200.129.0.5 255.255.255.252

interface Serial1
 ip address 200.128.0.5 255.255.255.252

interface TokenRing0
 ip address 200.5.0.1 255.255.255.0
 ring-speed 16

router rip
 version 2
 redistribute static metric 1
 network 200.5.0.0
 network 200.128.0.0
```

```
network 200.129.0.0
distribute-list 1 out TokenRing0
distribute-list 2 out Serial0
distribute-list 2 out Serial1
no auto-summary

ip classless

ip route 200.0.0.0 255.0.0.0 Null0

access-list 1 parmit 200.0.0.0 0.0.0.0
access-list 1 deny    200.0.0.0 0.255.255.255
access-list 1 permit any

access-list 2 deny    200.0.0.0 0.0.0.0
access-list 2 permit 200.0.0.0 0.255.255.255
access-list 2 permit any
```

Listing 6.49   Router R4's configuration.

```
interface Ethernet0
 ip address 200.6.0.1 255.255.255.0

interface TokenRing0
 ip address 200.5.0.2 255.255.255.0
 ring-speed 16

router rip
 version 2
 network 200.5.0.0
 network 200.6.0.0
 no auto-summary

ip classless
```

Listing 6.50 shows the routing table of router R4. The routing table only has a route for the supernet network prefix and has no routes for any specific network prefixes available behind router R3.

Listing 6.50   The routing table of router R4.

```
R4#show ip route
...
C    200.5.0.0/24 is directly connected, TokenRing0
C    200.6.0.0/24 is directly connected, Ethernet0
R    200.0.0.0/8 [120/1] via 200.5.0.1, 00:00:25, TokenRing0
```

At the same time, the routing table of router R3 (shown in Listing 6.51) has routes for all specific network prefixes and a route for supernet network prefix 200.0.0.0/8 pointing to the interface **Null 0**.

Listing 6.51 The routing table of router R3.

```
R2#show ip route
...
     200.128.0.0/30 is subnetted, 1 subnets
R       200.128.0.4 [120/1] via 200.129.0.5, 00:00:26, Serial1
     200.129.0.0/30 is subnetted, 1 subnets
C       200.129.0.4 is directly connected, Serial1
R    200.1.0.0/24 [120/2] via 200.129.0.5, 00:00:26, Serial1
C    200.2.0.0/24 is directly connected, Ethernet0
R    200.5.0.0/24 [120/1] via 200.129.0.5, 00:00:26, Serial1
R    200.6.0.0/24 [120/2] via 200.129.0.5, 00:00:26, Serial1
S    200.0.0.0/8 is directly connected, Null0
```

NOTE: *Notice that the route for the summary network prefix pointing to interface Null 0 looks similar to the EIGRP summary route from the "Configuring Route Summarization With EIGRP" section in Chapter 4. Only in this case, the route is labeled "D" instead of "S" and is called a "summary route" instead of "directly connected." Still, both routes point to interface Null 0, which reflects the nature of the routes for the summary network prefixes.*

Using Redistribution With EIGRP

Because EIGRP is an advanced distance vector protocol, it can distinguish between the routes that are originated by an EIGRP process on some router and those that are originated by another routing protocol, such as RIP, and then redistributed into the EIGRP process on another router. EIGRP marks such routes as *EIGRP external routes*, which are labeled "D EX" in the output of the command **show ip route**. The administrative distance of EIGRP external routes is 170, which gives them very low preference compared to the routes learned via other dynamic routing protocols.

There is, however, one case in which EIGRP external routes have a higher preference than other routes for the same destination with a source that has a lower administrative distance than that of EIGRP external routes (170). This case is automatic redistribution between IGRP and EIGRP configured with the same autonomous system number. Commencing with Cisco IOS Version 11.2.X, this rule also applies when IGRP and EIGRP are configured with different autonomous system numbers and redistributed manually using the command **redistribute**.

The next two subsections discuss the two cases of redistributing between IGRP and EIGRP. The first one covers automatic redistribution when IGRP and EIGRP processes run with the same autonomous system number. The second one covers manual redistribution between IGRP and EIGRP processes configured with different autonomous system numbers on routers running Cisco IOS Version 11.1.X or earlier.

Redistributing Between EIGRP And IGRP Configured With The Same AS Number

As mentioned in the previous section, redistribution between IGRP and EIGRP processes configured with the same autonomous system number takes place automatically. In other words, it takes place regardless of whether the command **redistribute** is present in the **router igrp** <*AS number*> and **router eigrp** <*AS number*> configurations where the <*AS number*> parameter is the same.

Another very important feature of this particular redistribution is that it preserves the accumulated metrics of both IGRP and EIGRP routes. The metrics of the routes are not reset to a fixed value when the routes are passed between the two protocols. As we remember from Chapter 4, IGRP and EIGRP metrics are compatible and thus can be converted into each other without a loss of the accumulated distance information. In other words, automatic redistribution between IGRP and EIGRP merges two metric domains of each routing protocol to a single metric domain.

WARNING!   Although the metric domains of the two protocols are preserved, some routes from the EIGRP domain may not be passed to the IGRP domain. All routes for the network prefixes whose prefix lengths are different from the single prefix length available in the IGRP domain cannot survive redistribution into IGRP.

As we know, EIGRP external routes have an administrative distance of 170. IGRP routes have an administrative distance of 100. However, if a single router runs EIGRP and IGRP routing processes with the same autonomous system number, it disregards the lower administrative distance of IGRP if there is an ambiguity between just-submitted and existing IGRP and EIGRP external routes for the same network prefix. Instead, the router compares the metrics of the routes and installs only the route with the better metric, regardless of its administrative distance. Nevertheless, regular EIGRP routes always take precedence over IGRP and EIGRP external routers for the same network prefix.

To better understand how these rules work, let's consider the network example shown in Figure 6.10. This network looks just like the network in Figure 6.6 that was very prone to routing loops (see the "Understanding How Routing Loops Can Emerge As The Result Of Redistribution" section in this chapter).

This time, the IGRP routes redistributed from the IGRP process on router R4 into the EIGRP process on router R4 are given an administrative distance of 170. Thus we may wonder whether a routing loop can emerge when these routes are redistributed to IGRP on router R3 and then advertised to routers R1 and R3 already as IGRP routes— that is, with an administrative distance of 100. What happens if these routes are advertised back to router R3 by routers R1 and R2?

Listings 6.52 through 6.55 show the configurations of all four routers.

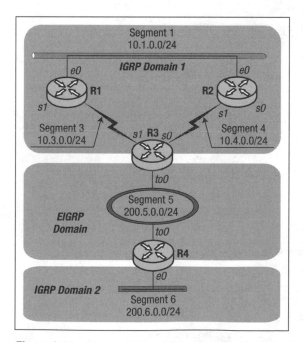

Figure 6.10   *Routers R3 and R4 automatically redistribute routing information between EIGRP and IGRP processes.*

Listing 6.52   Router R1's configuration.

```
interface Ethernet0
 ip address 10.1.0.1 255.255.255.0

interface Serial0
 ip address 10.3.0.2 255.255.255.0

router igrp 10
 network 10.0.0.0
```

Listing 6.53   Router R2's configuration.

```
interface Ethernet0
 ip address 10.1.0.2 255.255.255.0

interface Serial1
 ip address 10.4.0.2 255.255.255.0

router igrp 10
 network 10.0.0.0
```

Listing 6.54   Router R3's configuration.

```
interface Serial0
 ip address 10.4.0.1 255.255.255.0

interface Serial1
 ip address 10.3.0.1 255.255.255.0

interface TokenRing0
 ip address 200.5.0.1 255.255.255.0
 ring-speed 16

router eigrp 10
 network 200.5.0.0

router igrp 10
 network 10.0.0.0
```

Listing 6.55   Router R4's configuration.

```
interface Ethernet0
 ip address 200.6.0.1 255.255.255.0

interface TokenRing0
 ip address 200.5.0.2 255.255.255.0
 ring-speed 16

router eigrp 10
 network 200.5.0.0
```

```
router igrp 10
 network 200.6.0.0
```

If we check the routing table of router R3, we won't see any signs of a routing loop (Listing 6.56).

Listing 6.56   *The routing table of router R3.*

```
R3#show ip route
...
C    200.5.0.0/24 is directly connected, TokenRing0
D EX 200.6.0.0/24 [170/176128] via 200.5.0.2, 00:32:36,
TokenRing0
     10.0.0.0/24 is subnetted, 3 subnets
C        10.3.0.0 is directly connected, Serial1
I        10.1.0.0 [100/8576] via 10.4.0.2, 00:00:54, Serial0
                  [100/8576] via 10.3.0.2, 00:01:03, Serial1
C        10.4.0.0 is directly connected, Serial0
```

Notice how the EIGRP external route to network prefix 200.6.0.0/24 is labeled in the output of the command **show ip route** (the first italicized text element). Also, notice that the administrative distance of that route is 170, the default administrative distance of EIGRP external routes (the second italicized text element in line showing the route for network prefix 200.6.0.0/24).

Let's now see how router R3 processes the IGRP routing updates that it receives from routers R1 and R2. The output of the command **debug ip igrp transactions** is shown in Listing 6.57.

Listing 6.57   *The output of the command* **debug ip igrp transactions.**

```
R3#debug ip igrp transactions
IGRP protocol debugging is on
R3#
...
IGRP: received update from 10.3.0.2 on Serial1
      subnet 10.1.0.0, metric 8576 (neighbor 1100)
      subnet 10.4.0.0, metric 10576 (neighbor 8576)
IGRP: received update from 10.4.0.2 on Serial0
      subnet 10.3.0.0, metric 10576 (neighbor 8576)
      subnet 10.1.0.0, metric 8576 (neighbor 1100)
...
```

Currently, router R3 does not receive any routing updates for network prefix 200.6.0.0/24 from routers R1 and R2.

6. Controlling Data Flow And Routing Updates

What happens if we clear the routing table of router R1? Is router R1 first going to learn a route for network prefix 200.6.0.0/24 from router R2 and then advertise it to router R3, so that the new route supersedes the existing one, which has an administrative distance higher than that of the new one?

Listing 6.58 shows the output of the command **debug ip igrp transactions** entered on router R1, which was quickly followed by the command **clear ip route ***.

**Listing 6.58   The output of the command *debug ip igrp transactions*,
which was quickly followed by the command *clear ip route **.**

```
R1#debug ip igrp transactions
IGRP protocol debugging is on
R1#clear ip route *
R1#
IGRP: broadcasting request on Ethernet0
IGRP: broadcasting request on Serial0
IGRP: received update from 10.1.0.2 on Ethernet0
      subnet 10.1.0.0, metric 1200 (neighbor 1100)
      subnet 10.4.0.0, metric 8576 (neighbor 8476)
      network 200.5.0.0, metric 8639 (neighbor 8539)
      network 200.6.0.0, metric 8639 (neighbor 8539)
IGRP: edition is now 13
IGRP: sending update to 255.255.255.255 via Ethernet0
(10.1.0.1)
      subnet 10.3.0.0, metric=8476
IGRP: sending update to 255.255.255.255 via Serial0
(10.3.0.2)
      subnet 10.1.0.0, metric=1100
      subnet 10.4.0.0, metric=8576
      network 200.5.0.0, metric=8639
      network 200.6.0.0, metric=8639
IGRP: received update from 10.3.0.1 on Serial0
      subnet 10.4.0.0, metric 10476 (neighbor 8476)
      network 200.5.0.0, metric 8539 (neighbor 688)
      network 200.6.0.0, metric 8539 (neighbor 688)
...
```

Router R1 is trying to advertise a bogus route for network prefix 200.6.0.0/24 to router R3, but does router R3 accept it? Let's see. Listing 6.59 shows the output of the command **debug ip igrp transactions** that was entered prior to clearing router R1's routing table.

Listing 6.59 *The output of the command **debug ip igrp transactions** right after the command **clear ip route** * was entered on router R1.*

```
R3#debug ip igrp transactions
IGRP protocol debugging is on
R3#
IGRP: received request from 10.3.0.2 on Serial1
IGRP: sending update to 10.3.0.2 via Serial1 (10.3.0.1)
      subnet 10.4.0.0, metric=8476
      network 200.5.0.0, metric=688
      network 200.6.0.0, metric=688
IGRP: received update from 10.3.0.2 on Serial1
      subnet 10.1.0.0, metric 8576 (neighbor 1100)
      subnet 10.4.0.0, metric 10576 (neighbor 8576)
      network 200.5.0.0, metric 10639 (neighbor 8639)
      network 200.6.0.0, metric 10639 (neighbor 8639)
...
```

Router R3 does receive the routing update that advertises a bogus route for network prefix 200.6.0.0/24. Nevertheless, it does not accept it, and the EIGRP external route remains in the routing table of router R3, which is the same as that shown in Listing 6.56. This confirms that router R3 does not rely on the administrative distances of IGRP and EIGRP external routes to resolve ambiguities. Instead, it uses the metrics of the routes, and the one with the lower metric is installed in the routing table. In our case, the EIGRP external route has a metric of 176128. The IGRP supplies a metric of 10639, which must be multiplied by 256 to be comparable with EIGRP metrics. Thus, the IGRP route has an "EIGRP" metric of 2712945, which is obviously higher than the metric of the original EIGRP external route.

Redistributing Between EIGRP And IGRP Configured With Different AS Numbers

Regardless of the type of redistribution between IGRP and EIGRP (whether it is automatic or manual), the route metrics are always translated instead of being reset to a predefined value, as with other routing protocols. There is, however, a discrepancy in the behavior of manual redistribution between IGRP and EIGRP in Cisco IOS versions before and after Version 11.2.X. In the later versions, the rules for the administrative distances of IGRP and EIGRP external usage are the same for both manual and automatic redistribution between IGRP and EIGRP. In the earlier versions, the manual redistribution between IGRP and EIGRP follows the standard administrative distance rules—that is, if two sources of routing information supply ambiguous routing information, the administrative distance of the sources is used to resolve the ambiguity.

Let's see how it works in real life. The routers in Figure 6.10 run Cisco IOS Version 11.1.24. Listings 6.60 through 6.61 show the configurations of routers R3 and R4.

Listing 6.60 Router R3's configuration.

```
interface Serial0
 ip address 10.4.0.1 255.255.255.0

interface Serial1
 ip address 10.3.0.1 255.255.255.0

interface TokenRing0
 ip address 200.5.0.1 255.255.255.0
 ring-speed 16

router eigrp 200
 redistribute igrp 10
 network 200.5.0.0

router igrp 10
 redistribute eigrp 200
 network 10.0.0.0
```

Listing 6.61 Router R4's configuration.

```
interface Ethernet0
 ip address 200.6.0.1 255.255.255.0

interface TokenRing0
 ip address 200.5.0.2 255.255.255.0
 ring-speed 16

router eigrp 200
 redistribute igrp 10
 network 200.5.0.0

router igrp 10
 redistribute eigrp 200
 network 200.6.0.0
```

Router R4's routing table shows all three routes redistributed from IGRP to EIGRP on router R3. Despite the absence of the redistribution metric, the routes appear with the "translated" metrics in router

R4's routing table (Listing 6.62). As in the case of the same autonomous system number, the mutual metric domain of IGRP and EIGRP extends beyond the redistribution points.

NOTE: *Even if you specify the redistribution metric either using the command **default-metric** or as the **metric** parameter of the **redistribute** command, the IGRP and EIGRP processes preserve the accumulated metrics and translate them instead of resetting them to the specified value.*

Listing 6.62   The routing table of router R4.

```
R4#show ip route

...
     10.0.0.0/24 is subnetted, 3 subnets
D EX 10.3.0.0 [170/176128] via 200.5.0.1,00:08:48,TokenRing0
D EX 10.1.0.0 [170/2211584] via 200.5.0.1,00:08:48,TokenRing0
D EX 10.4.0.0 [170/176128] via 200.5.0.1,00:08:49,TokenRing0
C   200.1.0.0/24 is directly connected, TokenRing0
C   200.5.0.0/24 is directly connected, TokenRing0
C   200.6.0.0/24 is directly connected, Ethernet0
C   200.7.0.0/24 is directly connected, Loopback0
```

Cisco IOS Version 11.1.X and earlier may still suffer from loops emerging because of manual redistribution even between IGRP and EIGRP. Let's have a look at the routing table of router R3 shown in Listing 6.63. The routing just stabilized, and a loop hasn't yet had a chance to emerge. So far, the routing table looks all right.

*Listing 6.63   The routing table of router R3 before the command **clear ip route *** is entered on router R1.*

```
R3#show ip route
...
     10.0.0.0/24 is subnetted, 3 subnets
C       10.3.0.0 is directly connected, Serial1
I       10.1.0.0 [100/8576] via 10.3.0.2, 00:01:08, Serial1
                 [100/8576] via 10.4.0.2, 00:00:25, Serial0
C       10.4.0.0 is directly connected, Serial0
C   200.1.0.0/24 is directly connected, TokenRing0
C   200.5.0.0/24 is directly connected, TokenRing0
D EX 200.6.0.0/24 [170/176128] via 200.5.0.2, 00:03:15,
TokenRing0
```

If we clear the routing table of router R1 using the command **clear ip route ***, router R1 immediately sends out an IGRP request over all of its interfaces on which IGRP is enabled. As before, router R1 will probably hear first from router R2 because these two routers are interconnected via the Ethernet, which is faster than the serial link between routers R1 and R3. As router R1 receives an IGRP routing update from router R2 advertising network prefix 200.6.0.0/24, it installs a route for that network prefix pointing to router R2 as the next-hop router that is available via the interface Ethernet 0. After that, router R1 immediately advertises this network via IGRP over the interface Serial 0 to router R3. As router R3 receives this routing update from router R1, it notices that its administrative distance is lower than that of the existing route for network prefix 200.6.0.0/24, which was installed in the routing table as the EIGRP external route. At this point, router R1 replaces the existing route with the new bogus route, thereby creating a routing loop. The rest of the process develops exactly as it did in the example discussed in the "Understanding How Routing Loops Can Emerge As The Result Of Redistribution" section in this chapter.

Listing 6.64 shows how the routing table of router R3 looks after the command **clear ip route** * is entered on router R1. It now contains the familiar signs of a routing loop, shown in italics.

*Listing 6.64   The routing table of router R3 after the command **clear ip route** * is entered on router R1.*

```
R3#show ip route
...
     10.0.0.0/24 is subnetted, 3 subnets
C       10.3.0.0 is directly connected, Serial1
I       10.1.0.0 [100/8576] via 10.3.0.2, 00:00:30, Serial1
               [100/8576] via 10.4.0.2, 00:00:10, Serial0
C       10.4.0.0 is directly connected, Serial0
C    200.1.0.0/24 is directly connected, TokenRing0
C    200.5.0.0/24 is directly connected, TokenRing0
I    200.6.0.0/24 is possibly down, routing via 10.4.0.2,
Serial0
```

Using Redistribution With OSPF

OSPF goes even further than EIGRP in terms of distinguishing between the routes that are redistributed into OSPF from another protocol. OSPF specifies that these routes can be either type 1 or type 2.

OSPF advertises external routes using type 5 LSAs. As we remember from Chapter 5, type 5 LSAs are flooded throughout the whole autonomous system, except the stub areas.

In addition, type 7 LSAs are available, which allow advertising routing information learned from sources other than OSPF. Type 7 LSAs are not part of RFC 2328, the OSPF specification. Instead, they are specified in a separate document—RFC 1587.

In the subsections of this section, we'll consider how to configure redistribution between OSPF and other routing protocols using both type 5 LSAs and type 7 LSAs. We'll also discuss the differences between these two types of LSAs and their applications.

Understanding And Configuring ASBRs

The routers that perform redistribution between OSPF and other routing protocols are called *ASBRs* (autonomous system boundary routers).

If you need to include routing information from another autonomous system or from the Internet, you must use the regular OSPF external routes advertised using type 5 LSAs.

The following subsections describe how to configure Cisco routers to perform redistribution between OSPF and other routing protocols, so that OSPF uses type 5 LSAs to advertise the redistributed routing information.

Understanding Types 1 And 2 External Metrics

The difference between type 1 and type 2 OSPF external routes is that type 1 routes, propagated by OSPF routers throughout an OSPF autonomous system, receive an increase in metrics with every hop, whereas type 2 routes keep the metrics that they received at the redistribution point.

To configure redistribution between OSPF and another routing protocol, you first need to decide which type of external routes that you want to use. You then use the command **redistribute** to redistribute another routing protocol into OSPF. Optionally, you can specify in which type of OSPF external routes the redistributed routes need to be converted using the parameter **metric-type {1|2}**. If you don't supply this parameter, the default will be type 2.

In addition, you can specify the parameter **subnets** of the **redistribute** command, which allows OSPF to receive specific subnets from another routing protocol. By default, OSPF does not accept subnets during redistribution.

Figure 6.11 shows an OSPF autonomous system consisting of four routers—R1 through R4—and segments interconnecting them and two external routers—R5 and R6. The task is to configure routers R1 and R2 as ASBRs of the autonomous system so that router R1 advertises the external routing information as OSPF external routes type 1, and router R2 as type 2.

Listings 6.65 through 6.70 show the configurations of all six routers.

Listing 6.65   Router R1's configuration.

```
interface Loopback0
 ip address 10.10.0.1 255.255.255.255

interface Ethernet0
 ip address 10.10.1.1 255.255.255.0

interface Serial0
 ip address 10.10.255.6 255.255.255.252

interface Serial1
 ip address 10.203.0.1 255.255.0.0

router eigrp 10
 redistribute ospf 10 metric 10000 1 255 1 1500
 passive-interface Ethernet0
 passive-interface Loopback0
 passive-interface Serial0
 network 10.0.0.0

router ospf 10
 redistribute eigrp 10 metric 10 metric-type 1 subnets
 network 10.10.0.0 0.0.255.255 area 10
 distribute-list 10 out eigrp 10

ip classless

access-list 10 deny    10.10.0.0 0.0.255.255
access-list 10 permit any
```

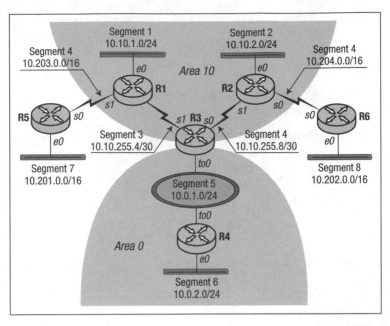

Figure 6.11   External routers R5 and R6 are connected to OSPF ASBRs R1 and R2.

Listing 6.66   Router R2's configuration.

```
interface Loopback0
 ip address 10.10.0.2 255.255.255.255

interface Ethernet0
 ip address 10.10.2.1 255.255.255.0

interface Serial0
 ip address 10.204.0.1 255.255.0.0

interface Serial1
 ip address 10.10.255.10 255.255.255.252

router ospf 10
 redistribute igrp 10 metric 10 subnets
 network 10.10.0.0 0.0.255.255 area 10
 distribute-list 10 out igrp 10

router igrp 10
 redistribute ospf 10 metric 10000 1 255 1 1500
 passive-interface Ethernet0
 passive-interface Loopback0
```

```
 passive-interface Serial1
 network 10.0.0.0

ip classless

access-list 10 deny    10.10.0.0 0.0.255.255
access-list 10 permit any
```

Listing 6.67   Router R3's configuration.

```
interface Loopback0
 ip address 10.0.0.3 255.255.255.255

interface Serial0
 ip address 10.10.255.9 255.255.255.252

interface Serial1
 ip address 10.10.255.5 255.255.255.252

interface TokenRing0
 ip address 10.0.1.1 255.255.255.0
 ring-speed 16

router ospf 10
 network 10.0.0.0 0.0.255.255 area 0
 network 10.10.0.0 0.0.255.255 area 10
 area 0 range 10.0.0.0 255.255.0.0
 area 10 range 10.10.0.0 255.255.0.0

ip classless
```

Listing 6.68   Router R4's configuration.

```
interface Loopback0
 ip address 10.0.0.4 255.255.255.255

interface Ethernet0
 ip address 10.0.2.1 255.255.255.0

interface TokenRing0
 ip address 10.0.1.2 255.255.255.0
 ring-speed 16

router ospf 10
 network 10.0.0.0 0.0.255.255 area 0

no ip classless
```

Listing 6.69   Router R5's configuration.

```
interface Ethernet0
 ip address 10.201.0.1 255.255.0.0

interface Serial0
 ip address 10.203.0.2 255.255.0.0

router eigrp 10
 network 10.0.0.0
```

Listing 6.70   Router R6's configuration.

```
interface Ethernet0
 ip address 10.202.0.1 255.255.0.0

interface Serial0
 ip address 10.204.0.2 255.255.0.0

router igrp 10
 network 10.0.0.0
```

Let's examine the routing table of router R4 shown in Listing 6.71. The OSPF external routes are present in the routing table and are labeled "E1" and "E2"—that is, OSPF external type 1 and type 2 routes respectively.

Listing 6.71   The routing table of router R4.

```
R4#show ip route
...
     10.0.0.0/8 is variably subnetted, 9 subnets, 3 masks
O IA 10.10.0.0/16 [110/80] via 10.0.1.1, 00:21:27, TokenRing0
C    10.0.2.0/24 is directly connected, Ethernet0
O    10.0.0.3/32 [110/7] via 10.0.1.1, 00:21:27, TokenRing0
C    10.0.1.0/24 is directly connected, TokenRing0
C    10.0.0.4/32 is directly connected, Loopback0
O E1 10.201.0.0/16 [110/80] via 10.0.1.1, 00:21:08,TokenRing0
O E1 10.203.0.0/16 [110/80] via 10.0.1.1, 00:21:08,TokenRing0
O E2 10.202.0.0/16 [110/10] via 10.0.1.1, 00:16:31,TokenRing0
O E2 10.204.0.0/16 [110/10] via 10.0.1.1, 00:21:27,TokenRing0
```

Notice the difference between the metrics of OSPF type 1 and type 2 routes. If you check the configuration of routers R1 and R2 (shown in Listings 6.65 and 6.66, respectively), you'll see that the routes were redistributed using the same redistribution metric—10. The type 2 routes kept the metric, whereas the type 1 routes received higher metrics because they had to traverse multiple router hops before they reached router R4.

If you check the configuration of routers R1 and R2, you'll notice that they contain two access-lists, which are used to filter the routing information redistributed from IGRP and EIGRP into OSPF. Why do we need these access-lists?

The explanation is simple. Unlike OSPF, neither IGRP nor EIGRP allows you to specify the exact interfaces on which to process their respective routing updates. All you can do is to use the **network** command followed by a classful network address to specify that all router interfaces with IP addresses belonging to this classful network address are to process the routing updates of the corresponding routing protocol. It also means that the routing process advertises the network prefix configured on this interface out of all of its other interfaces and redistributes it into other routing protocols for which redistribution is configured. The access-lists take care of the latter. They block redistribution of any IP network prefixes that belong to area 10's summary network prefix (10.10.0.0/16) from being redistributed into the OSPF routing process. Such network prefixes are stored as type 5 LSAs and flooded throughout the whole autonomous system except stub areas.

In our case, this use of access-lists is important because OSPF, IGRP, and EIGRP are all enabled on the interfaces with IP addresses belonging to network prefix 10.10.0.0/16. Thus, if the access-lists are not applied, OSPF thinks that the network prefixes configured on these interfaces are both OSPF originated and OSPF external. Within area 10, these routes are placed in the routing tables of the OSPF routers as intra-area OSPF routes. However, unlike all other LSAs, type 5 LSAs are flooded throughout the whole autonomous system; therefore, outside area 10, OSPF routers see these routes as OSPF external routes.

Let's see what happens if we remove the command **distribute-list 10 out eigrp 10** from router R1's configuration. Before we do that, let's have a look at how type 5 LSAs look in router R1's link state database (Listing 6.72).

Listing 6.72   The type 5 LSAs contained in the link state database of router R1.

```
R1#show ip ospf database
...
            Type-5 AS External Link States

Link ID        ADV Router    Age      Seq#         Checksum Tag
10.201.0.0     10.10.0.1     1588     0x80000007 0x4BF0     0
10.202.0.0     10.10.0.2     1314     0x80000001 0xC8F6     0
10.203.0.0     10.10.0.1     1593     0x80000004 0x3904     0
10.204.0.0     10.10.0.2     1672     0x80000002 0xAE0E     0
```

It looks just as we might expect. After the **distribute-list** command is removed from router R1's configuration, this part of the link state database changes as shown in Listing 6.73.

*Listing 6.73   The type-5 LSAs contained in the link state database of router R1 after the command **distribute-list 10 out eigrp 10** is removed from the **router ospf 10** configuration.*

```
R1#show ip ospf database

...

        Type-5 AS External Link States

    Link ID      ADV Router    Age     Seq#          Checksum  Tag
    10.10.0.1    10.10.0.1     5       0x80000001 0x4AB6     0
    10.10.1.0    10.10.0.1     5       0x80000001 0x49B7     0
    10.10.255.4  10.10.0.1     5       0x80000001 0x1AE6     0
    10.201.0.0   10.10.0.1     128     0x80000008 0x49F1     0
    10.202.0.0   10.10.0.2     85      0x80000002 0xC6F7     0
    10.203.0.0   10.10.0.1     130     0x80000005 0x3705     0
    10.204.0.0   10.10.0.2     87      0x80000003 0xAC0F     0
```

Notice the three italicized lines labeled "E1" at the beginning of the output shown in Listing 6.74. These routes are for the network prefixes that are obviously from area 10. However, these routes are also redistributed from EIGRP and thus are stored as type 5 LSAs. As a result, the routing table of router R4, for example, now contains these routes as external. The routing table contains these routes even though all of them are for network prefixes that belong to area 10 that are covered by area 10's summary network prefix (10.10.0.0/16), a route that is also contained in router R4's routing table (the first italicized line).

Listing 6.74   The routing table of router R4.

```
R4#show ip route

...

     10.0.0.0/8 is variably subnetted, 12 subnets, 4 masks
O IA 10.10.0.0/16 [110/80] via 10.0.1.1, 00:32:44, TokenRing0
O E1 10.10.1.0/24 [110/80] via 10.0.1.1, 00:02:28, TokenRing0
O E1 10.10.0.1/32 [110/80] via 10.0.1.1, 00:02:28, TokenRing0
O E1 10.10.255.4/30 [110/80] via 10.0.1.1,00:02:29,TokenRing0
C    10.0.2.0/24 is directly connected, Ethernet0
O    10.0.0.3/32 [110/7] via 10.0.1.1, 00:32:44, TokenRing0
C    10.0.1.0/24 is directly connected, TokenRing0
C    10.0.0.4/32 is directly connected, Loopback0
O E2 10.202.0.0/16 [110/10] via 10.0.1.1, 00:27:48,TokenRing0
O E1 10.203.0.0/16 [110/80] via 10.0.1.1, 00:32:25,TokenRing0
```

6. Controlling Data Flow And Routing Updates

```
O E1 10.201.0.0/16 [110/80] via 10.0.1.1, 00:32:25,TokenRing0
O E2 10.204.0.0/16 [110/10] via 10.0.1.1, 00:32:45,TokenRing0
```

Using The Command summary-address

The primary purpose of the OSPF command **summary-address** is routing information summarization. The command allows you to do the following:

- Summarize OSPF routes for redistribution into another routing protocol

- Summarize external routes injected into an OSPF autonomous system via an ASBR

The command syntax is **summary-address** *<IP address> <subnet mask>*. The parameters *<IP address> <subnet mask>* define the summary network prefix. (This command can accept some additional parameters. For information on these parameters, see the Cisco documentation.)

Let's see how this command can be applied in the situation shown in Figure 6.11. Let's first check router R6's routing table (shown in Listing 6.75). Interestingly enough, we can't see any routes for network prefix 10.0.0.0/16 (area 0's summary address) or for 10.10.0.0/16 (area 10's summary address). This is strange because the network prefix length that IGRP expects is /16, which is exactly what is used with both area summary addresses.

Listing 6.75   The routing table of router R6.

```
R6#show ip route
...
   10.0.0.0/16 is subnetted, 5 subnets
C     10.202.0.0 is directly connected, Ethernet0
I     10.203.0.0 [100/8477] via 10.204.0.1, 00:00:24, Serial0
I     10.201.0.0 [100/8477] via 10.204.0.1, 00:00:24, Serial0
C     10.204.0.0 is directly connected, Serial0
```

Unfortunately, network prefix 10.0.0.0/16 cannot be seen via IGRP because of IGRP's classful nature. IGRP can't use subnet zeros of any classful network address. Because the only areas available are areas 0 and 10 and IGRP can't see the summary address of area 0, the only choice that IGRP has is area 10's summary address. Why does IGRP not see even this summary address?

The answer is simple. Router R2, to which router R6 is connected, is not an ABR and thus does not perform route summarization. Even if it were an ABR, router R6 still would not see the summary address of area 10, because ABRs only perform summarization for OSPF routers. The command **summary-address** should be used on ASBRs to perform summarization for non-OSPF routers.

Listing 6.76 shows the updated configuration of router R4. The italicized line shows how the command **summary-address** is used.

Listing 6.76   Router R2's configuration.
```
interface Loopback0
 ip address 10.10.0.2 255.255.255.255

interface Ethernet0
 ip address 10.10.2.1 255.255.255.0

interface Serial0
 ip address 10.204.0.1 255.255.0.0

interface Serial1
 ip address 10.10.255.10 255.255.255.252

router ospf 10
 summary-address 10.10.0.0 255.255.0.0
 redistribute igrp 10 metric 10 subnets
 network 10.10.0.0 0.0.255.255 area 10
 distribute-list 10 out igrp 10

router igrp 10
 redistribute ospf 10 metric 10000 1 255 1 1500
 passive-interface Ethernet0
 passive-interface Loopback0
 passive-interface Serial1
 network 10.0.0.0

ip classless

access-list 10 deny    10.10.0.0 0.0.255.255
access-list 10 permit any
```

If we now check the routing table of router R6, we'll see that there is a route for the summary address of area 10 (see Listing 6.77).

Listing 6.77   The routing table of router R6.
```
R6#show ip route
...
    10.0.0.0/16 is subnetted, 5 subnets
I    10.10.0.0 [100/8477] via 10.204.0.1, 00:00:24, Serial0
```

```
C    10.202.0.0 is directly connected, Ethernet0
I    10.203.0.0 [100/8477] via 10.204.0.1, 00:00:24, Serial0
I    10.201.0.0 [100/8477] via 10.204.0.1, 00:00:24, Serial0
C    10.204.0.0 is directly connected, Serial0
```

Understanding And Configuring NSSAs

Sometimes an OSPF area, being a perfect candidate for a stub area, requires injection of OSPF external routes in limited amounts. If this area is made a regular area, it receives all of the type 5 LSAs that exist in the autonomous system, which may be very undesirable. Specifically for such situations, a new type of area called a *not-so-stubby area*, or *NSSA*, was introduced along with a new LSA type—type 7 LSA.

An NSSA is very similar to a regular stub area. It is not allowed to receive type 5 LSAs. However, an NSSA can contain routers that perform dynamic routing within the NSSA using routing protocols other than OSPF. The routing information from these routing protocols is redistributed into OSPF, which advertises this routing information using the new type 7 LSAs.

Type 7 LSAs are very similar to type 5 LSAs in that they also describe external routes. However, the following differences exist between type 7 LSAs and type 5 LSAs:

- Type 7 LSAs are only flooded within the NSSA, whereas type 5 LSAs are flooded throughout the autonomous system except the stub areas.

- The NSSA ABRs translate type 7 LSAs into type 5 LSAs, which are flooded throughout the autonomous system.

Figure 6.12 shows an example of a network in which area 10 can be made an NSSA. The most dynamic routing in the area is performed using IGRP. At router R3, IGRP routing information is redistributed into OSPF, which advertises it to the rest of the network via a potentially slow segment 4.

Let's see how the routers must be configured to make area 10 an NSSA. Listings 6.78 through 6.82 show the configurations of all five routers.

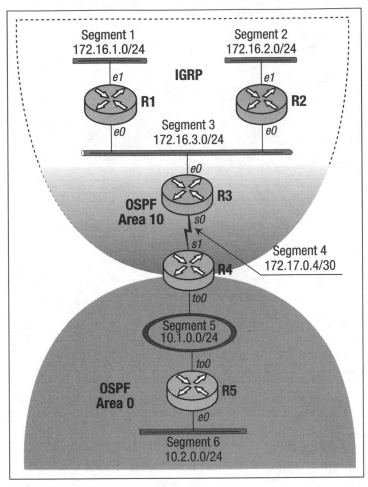

Figure 6.12 *Area 10 is an OSPF NSSA.*

Listing 6.78 *Router R1's configuration.*

```
interface Ethernet0
 ip address 172.16.3.1 255.255.255.0

interface Serial0
 ip address 172.16.1.1 255.255.255.0

router igrp 172
 network 172.16.0.0
```

Listing 6.79   Router R2's configuration.

```
interface Ethernet0
 ip address 172.16.3.2 255.255.255.0

interface Serial0
 ip address 172.16.2.1 255.255.255.0

router igrp 172
 network 172.16.0.0
```

Listing 6.80   Router R3's configuration.

```
interface Loopback0
 ip address 172.17.255.3 255.255.255.255

interface Ethernet0
 ip address 172.16.3.3 255.255.255.0

interface Serial0
 ip address 172.17.0.5 255.255.255.252

router ospf 10
 redistribute igrp 172 metric 10 metric-type 1 subnets
 network 172.17.0.0 0.0.255.255 area 10
 area 10 nssa

router igrp 172
 redistribute ospf 10
 network 172.16.0.0
 default-metric 10000 1 255 1 1500

ip classless
```

Listing 6.81   Router R4's configuration.

```
interface Loopback0
 ip address 10.0.0.4 255.255.255.255

interface Serial1
 ip address 172.17.0.6 255.255.255.252

interface TokenRing0
 ip address 10.1.0.1 255.255.255.0
 ring-speed 16

router ospf 10
 network 10.0.0.0 0.255.255.255 area 0
 network 172.0.0.0 0.255.255.255 area 10
```

```
area 0 range 10.0.0.0 255.0.0.0
area 10 nssa

ip classless
```

Listing 6.82   *Router R5's configuration.*

```
interface Loopback0
  ip address 10.0.0.5 255.255.255.255

interface Ethernet0
  ip address 10.2.0.1 255.255.255.0

interface TokenRing0
  ip address 10.1.0.2 255.255.255.0
  ring-speed 16

router ospf 1
  network 10.0.0.0 0.255.255.255 area 0

ip classless
```

NOTE: *Just like regular OSPF external routes, OSPF NSSA external routes can be type 1 and type 2.*

The routing table of router R3 does not yet show the OSPF external routes (Listing 6.83).

Listing 6.83   *The routing table of router R3.*

```
R3#show ip route
...
O IA 10.0.0.0/8 [110/80] via 172.17.0.6, 00:29:12, Serial0
     172.16.0.0/24 is subnetted, 3 subnets
I      172.16.1.0 [100/8576] via 172.16.3.1, 00:00:42,Ethernet0
I      172.16.2.0 [100/8576] via 172.16.3.2, 00:01:11,Ethernet0
C      172.16.3.0 is directly connected, Ethernet0
     172.17.0.0/16 is variably subnetted, 3 subnets, 3 masks
C      172.17.255.3/32 is directly connected, Loopback0
C      172.17.0.4/30 is directly connected, Serial0
O      172.17.0.0/16 is a summary, 00:01:23, Null0
```

However, router R3's link state database already contains type 7 LSAs (Listing 6.84). Notice that, unlike type 5 LSAs, type 7 LSAs belong to the area in which they were originated.

6. Controlling Data Flow And Routing Updates

Listing 6.84   The part of the OSPF link state database of router R3 that contains information on type 7 LSAs.

```
R3#show ip ospf database

        OSPF Router with ID (172.17.255.3) (Process ID 10)
...
        Type-7 AS External Link States (Area 10)

Link ID       ADV Router      Age    Seq#        Checksum Tag
172.16.1.0    172.17.255.3    1115   0x80000001 0x9051    0
172.16.2.0    172.17.255.3    1115   0x80000001 0x855B    0
172.16.3.0    172.17.255.3    1115   0x80000001 0x7A65    0
```

Let's now examine the routing table of router R4 (Listing 6.85). The three italicized lines show the OSPF NSSA external type 1 routes. Unlike regular OSPF external routes, these are labeled "N1." Likewise, OSPF NSSA external type 2 routes are labeled "N2."

Listing 6.85   The routing table of router R4.

```
R4#show ip route
...
     172.17.0.0/16 is variably subnetted, 2 subnets, 2 masks
O       172.17.255.3/32 [110/65] via 172.17.0.5,00:16:42,Serial1
C       172.17.0.4/30 is directly connected, Serial1
     172.16.0.0/24 is subnetted, 3 subnets
O N1 172.16.1.0 [110/75] via 172.17.0.5, 00:00:48, Serial1
O N1 172.16.2.0 [110/75] via 172.17.0.5, 00:00:48, Serial1
O N1 172.16.3.0 [110/75] via 172.17.0.5, 00:00:48, Serial1
     10.0.0.0/8 is variably subnetted, 4 subnets, 2 masks
O       10.2.0.0/24 [110/16] via 10.1.0.2, 00:16:42, TokenRing0
C       10.1.0.0/24 is directly connected, TokenRing0
C       10.0.0.4/32 is directly connected, Loopback0
O       10.0.0.5/32 [110/7] via 10.1.0.2, 00:16:43, TokenRing0
```

Router R4 is an NSSA ABR for area 10; therefore, it should translate type 7 LSAs into type 5 LSAs, which appear in router R4's link state database (Listing 6.86). Notice that it contains both the original type 7 LSAs and new type 5 LSAs with the same link IDs.

Listing 6.86   The part of the OSPF link state database of router R4 that contains information on type 5 LSAs and type 7 LSAs.

```
R4#show ip ospf database

        OSPF Router with ID (10.0.0.4) (Process ID 10)
...
        Type-7 AS External Link States (Area 10)
```

Link ID	ADV Router	Age	Seq#	Checksum	Tag
172.16.1.0	172.17.255.3	1018	0x80000001	0x9051	0
172.16.2.0	172.17.255.3	1019	0x80000001	0x855B	0
172.16.3.0	172.17.255.3	1019	0x80000001	0x7A65	0

Type-5 AS External Link States

Link ID	ADV Router	Age	Seq#	Checksum	Tag
172.16.1.0	10.0.0.4	970	0x80000001	0x5F3F	0
172.16.2.0	10.0.0.4	970	0x80000001	0x5449	0
172.16.3.0	10.0.0.4	970	0x80000001	0x4953	0

Finally, the routing table of router R5 (shown in Listing 6.87) only contains regular OSPF external routes for the network prefixes that router R3 advertised using type 7 LSAs.

Listing 6.87   The routing table of router R5.

```
R5#show ip route
...
     172.17.0.0/16 is variably subnetted, 2 subnets, 2 masks
O IA 172.17.255.3/32 [110/71]via 10.1.0.1,00:13:48,TokenRing0
O IA 172.17.0.4/30 [110/70] via 10.1.0.1, 00:13:53,TokenRing0
     172.16.0.0/24 is subnetted, 3 subnets
O E1 172.16.1.0 [110/81] via 10.1.0.1, 00:13:47, TokenRing0
O E1 172.16.2.0 [110/81] via 10.1.0.1, 00:13:47, TokenRing0
O E1 172.16.3.0 [110/81] via 10.1.0.1, 00:13:47, TokenRing0
     10.0.0.0/8 is variably subnetted, 4 subnets, 2 masks
C    10.2.0.0/24 is directly connected, Ethernet0
C    10.1.0.0/24 is directly connected, TokenRing0
O    10.0.0.4/32 [110/7] via 10.1.0.1, 00:14:01, TokenRing0
C    10.0.0.5/32 is directly connected, Loopback0
```

We won't see type 7 LSAs in router R5's link state database (the part that contains the LSAs describing external links is shown in Listing 6.88) because this router is located in area 0, whereas the type 7 LSAs originated in area 10.

Listing 6.88   The OSPF link state database of router R5.

```
R5#show ip ospf database
     OSPF Router with ID (10.0.0.5) (Process ID 1)
...
     Type-5 AS External Link States
```

Link ID	ADV Router	Age	Seq#	Checksum	Tag
172.16.1.0	10.0.0.4	913	0x80000001	0x5F3F	0

```
172.16.2.0    10.0.0.4        914      0x80000001 0x5449    0
172.16.3.0    10.0.0.4        914      0x80000001 0x4953    0
```

Using The Command *summary-address* To Summarize External Routes

As mentioned in previous sections, you can use the OSPF command **summary-address** to summarize external routes. Summarizing external routes learned from another autonomous system can be challenging, because it may not be possible to know all of the network prefixes available in other autonomous systems and some network prefixes may be added later. However, NSSAs are parts of the same autonomous system, even though they use routing protocols other than OSPF to perform dynamic routing. Thus, it may often be quite possible to know all of the network prefixes available in NSSAs and, therefore, be able to summarize them.

In the network shown in Figure 6.12, router R3 can perform such summarization for the external routes available in the IGRP domain of area 10 using network prefix 172.16.0.0/16. Listing 6.89 shows the revised configuration of router R3. The italicized line shows the use of the command **summary-address**.

Listing 6.89   *The configuration of router R3, which now performs summarization of the routing information redistributed from IGRP.*

```
interface Loopback0
 ip address 172.17.255.3 255.255.255.255

interface Ethernet0
 ip address 172.16.3.3 255.255.255.0

interface Serial0
 ip address 172.17.0.5 255.255.255.252

router ospf 10
 summary-address 172.16.0.0 255.255.0.0
 redistribute igrp 172 metric 10 metric-type 1 subnets
 network 172.17.0.0 0.0.255.255 area 10
 area 10 nssa

router igrp 172
 redistribute ospf 10
 network 172.16.0.0
 default-metric 10000 1 255 1 1500

ip classless
```

If we now look at router R3's link state database, we'll see only one type 7 LSA, which describes the summary network prefix of all external network prefixes.

Listing 6.90 *The part of the link state database of router R3 that contains type 7 LSAs.*

```
R3#show ip ospf database

     OSPF Router with ID (172.17.255.3) (Process ID 10)
...
               Type-7 AS External Link States (Area 10)

Link ID       ADV Router      Age     Seq#        Checksum Tag
172.16.0.0    172.17.255.3    153     0x80000001 0x9B47    0

          Type-5 AS External Link States

Link ID       ADV Router      Age     Seq#        Checksum Tag
172.17.0.0    172.17.255.3    191     0x80000001 0x5D59    0
```

Likewise, router R4's link state database (the part that describes external LSAs is shown in Listing 6.91) contains a single type 7 LSA and a single type 5 LSA.

Listing 6.91 *The part of the link state database of router R4 that contains LSAs describing external links.*

```
R4#show ip ospf database

     OSPF Router with ID (10.0.0.4) (Process ID 10)
...
Type-7 AS External Link States (Area 10)

Link ID       ADV Router      Age     Seq#        Checksum Tag
172.16.0.0    172.17.255.3    201     0x80000001 0x9B47    0

          Type-5 AS External Link States

Link ID       ADV Router      Age     Seq#        Checksum Tag
172.16.0.0    10.0.0.4        201     0x80000001 0x6A35    0
```

Of course, router R4's routing table (shown in Listing 6.92) only contains one OSPF NSSA external route for the summary network prefix.

Listing 6.92   The routing table of router R4.

```
R4#show ip route
...
     172.17.0.0/16 is variably subnetted, 2 subnets, 2 masks
O     172.17.255.3/32 [110/65] via 172.17.0.5, 00:14:23,
Serial1
C     172.17.0.4/30 is directly connected, Serial1
O N1 172.16.0.0/16 [110/75] via 172.17.0.5, 00:04:22, Serial1
     10.0.0.0/8 is variably subnetted, 4 subnets, 2 masks
O     10.2.0.0/24 [110/16] via 10.1.0.2, 00:14:23, TokenRing0
C     10.1.0.0/24 is directly connected, TokenRing0
C     10.0.0.4/32 is directly connected, Loopback0
O     10.0.0.5/32 [110/7] via 10.1.0.2, 00:14:23, TokenRing0
```

Finally, router R5's routing table (shown in Listing 6.93) now contains a single regular OSPF external route for network prefix 172.16.0.0/16, the summary network prefix of all IGRP-managed network prefixes available in area 10.

Listing 6.93   The routing table of router R5.

```
R5#show ip route
...
     172.17.0.0/16 is variably subnetted, 2 subnets, 2 masks
O IA   172.17.255.3/32 [110/71] via 10.1.0.1, 00:13:56,
TokenRing0
O IA   172.17.0.4/30 [110/70] via 10.1.0.1, 00:13:56,
TokenRing0
O E1 172.16.0.0/16 [110/81] via 10.1.0.1, 00:03:55,TokenRing0
     10.0.0.0/8 is variably subnetted, 4 subnets, 2 masks
C     10.2.0.0/24 is directly connected, Ethernet0
C     10.1.0.0/24 is directly connected, TokenRing0
O     10.0.0.4/32 [110/7] via 10.1.0.1, 00:34:40, TokenRing0
C     10.0.0.5/32 is directly connected, Loopback0
```

## Chapter 7

Special Cases Of Routing

If you need an immediate solution to:	See page:
Configuring Policy-Based Routing	358
Using Policy-Based Routing For Routing Over A Dedicated Link	359
Using Application-Sensitive Policy-Based Routing	365
Configuring Network Address Translation (NAT)	369
Configuring Static Translation Of Inside IP Addresses	369
Configuring Dynamic Translation Of Inside IP Addresses	374
Configuring NAT With Overloading Global Inside IP Addresses	385
Configuring NAT To Translate Between Overlapping Address Spaces	386
Configuring NAT For TCP Load Balancing	390
Configuring Hot Standby Router Protocol (HSRP)	394
Configuring Basic HSRP	394
Using MHSRP For Load Balancing	401
Configuring Dial-On-Demand Routing (DDR)	405
Configuring Snapshot Routing	405
Configuring Dial Backup	411

In Brief

In this chapter, we'll discuss special cases or routing, which are usually considered to be deviations from normal routing procedures. These special cases of routing incorporate policy-based routing, Network Address Translation (NAT), Hot Standby Router Protocol (HSRP), and Dial-On-Demand routing.

Policy-Based Routing

A form of routing in which the datagrams are routed using administratively defined rules that can take into consideration the characteristics of the datagrams other than the destination address when drawing routing decisions is called *policy-based routing*.

NOTE: Although this type of routing is referenced in the Cisco documentation as policy routing, I have chosen to use the term policy-based routing in this book because that term is more widely used.

Policy-based routing can only be static and, if not properly planned and implemented, can adversely affect existing dynamic routing. For example, suppose there is a router configured for policy-based routing. Suppose also the policy-based routing rules dictate to forward certain traffic to a router that perceives the destination network as best available through the router performing policy-based routing. Therefore the second router forwards such traffic back to the first router. Depending on how policy-based routing is implemented, this situation may either lead to superfluous router hops or to routing loops.

Network Address Translation

Network Address Translation (NAT) is a method of replacing original source or destination IP addresses in the IP datagrams crossing a router configured for NAT.

There are three types of problems that can be solved using NAT:

- *Depletion of global IP Network address space*—New IP addresses are becoming more difficult to allocate because the global IP address space is close to capacity. NAT helps solve this problem via reusing of some addresses at multiple locations—for example, it is possible to use private IP addresses (described in RFC 1918, "Address Allocation for Private Internets") on networks that are not accessed from the Internet, such as the segments that constitute corporate intranets.

- *Merger of networks that use overlapped IP address space*—If two companies used private IP addresses, or if one company used IP addresses that officially belonged to another company, and these two companies merge, it may be too costly to readdress the hosts whose addresses overlap. In such situations, NAT can be used to perform IP address translation between the networks whose addresses overlap.

- *Load balancing*—If multiple servers run identical service, such as a Web server, NAT can be used to balance the traffic destined for this service among all servers. To the hosts accessing the service, all servers are known by a single IP address. When the first packet of a connection arrives at the router performing NAT, the destination IP address is translated to the IP address of one of the servers. All subsequent packets belonging to this connection are sent to this server.

NAT is documented in RFC 1631, "The IP Network Address Translator (NAT)." NAT for load balancing is documented in RFC 2391, Load Sharing Using IP Network Address Translation (LSNAT).

NAT Terminology

From the NAT perspective, all networks are divided into two groups: *inside networks* and *outside networks*. The inside networks are networks whose IP addresses are not considerate legitimate and must be translated into legitimate IP addresses. Likewise, the outside networks are networks whose IP addresses are considerate legitimate.

NOTE: *Legitimate in the context of NAT does not always assume officially assigned IP addresses. For example, if two networks both using the same private IP address range are merged, one of these networks becomes an inside network; the other one, an outside network. Hence, the IP addresses of the first network are not legitimate.*

The following terms are used to describe the types of IP addresses used with NAT:

- *Inside local addresses*—IP addresses of hosts connected to inside networks. These addresses are actually configured on the NICs of hosts and must be translated. The inside local addresses do not have to be officially assigned and may not be known in the outside network address space (for example, the routers connected to the outside networks may not have routes for the inside local addresses).

* *Inside global addresses*—IP addresses into which the inside local addresses are translated. Inside global addresses are legitimate and, therefore, must be known in the outside address space. This assumes that the routers connected to the outside networks must know the routes for the inside global addresses.

* *Outside local addresses*—IP addresses in the inside address space under which the hosts connected to the outside networks are known in the inside address space. These addresses may not be legitimate. They must be routable in the inside local address space.

* *Outside global addresses*—IP addresses of the hosts connected to the outside networks. These addresses must be legitimate and must be routable in the outside global address space.

NOTE: Not all of these addresses are used in every NAT configuration.

The routers configured for NAT maintain a table known as a *NAT table*. Each entry of the NAT table contains five fields: protocol, inside local IP address, inside global IP address, outside local IP address, and outside global IP address. The functional role of the latter four fields is to store the corresponding IP addresses. The first field denotes the IP protocol whose connections must be translated using the IP addresses contained in the entry. Depending on the NAT application, these fields may or may not all be used.

The NAT table can be populated with entries in two ways. The first way is called *static NAT*. In static NAT, the entries contained in the NAT table are configured administratively. After the entries are entered on a router, they immediately appear in the NAT table. The second way to populate the NAT table is called *dynamic NAT*. In dynamic NAT, the entries in the NAT table are created dynamically when IP datagrams whose characteristics satisfy administratively configured NAT "rules" reach the router.

Hot Standby Router Protocol

Hot Standby Router Protocol (HSRP) is a Cisco proprietary protocol used to provide a redundant default router (that is, the router to which the default gateway route points) for the hosts that are unable to discover routers dynamically.

NOTE: *It is recommended that HSRP should not be used if the hosts can dynamically discover routers. However, HSRP is so widely used that it is often preferred to the dynamic methods, such as ICMP Router Discovery Protocol (IRDP). The popularity of HSRP can be explained by the fact that it is very easy to configure and it requires no or very little modification to the existing configurations of the hosts.*

HSRP is fully documented in RFC 2281, "Cisco Hot Standby Router Protocol (HSRP)". The status of this document is "informational", which means that HSRP is not an Internet standard protocol.

The idea on which HSRP is based is simple. Suppose there are two or more routes connected to the same segment, and one of these routers serves as the default router for the hosts located on this segment. Obviously, only this router can forward the outbound traffic generated by the hosts on the segment. (The inbound traffic can be forwarded by any of the routers connected to this segment.) Suppose the other routers monitor the default router. If the default router fails, one of the other routers takes over the IP address that was used by the hosts as the default router. The hosts, therefore, will not detect interruption in their intersegment communications.

In HSRP, the router taking over the default router IP address also takes over the MAC address associated with this IP address. This is important, because without this capability, the hosts must first time out the ARP entry for the default router IP address and then use ARP to find out the new MAC address.

The HSRP router currently acting as the default router for the hosts on the segment is called an *active router*. The IP address that the hosts use as the default router is called a *virtual IP address*, which is different from the IP address configured on the corresponding interface of the active router. The MAC address corresponding to the virtual IP address is called a *virtual MAC address*, which may or may not be the MAC address of the interface, depending on the router interface hardware.

In addition to the active router, HSRP also defines a *standby router* as the router that takes over the virtual MAC and IP addresses if the current active router fails. In this case, the standby router becomes the active router. There can be only one active and one standby router on a segment.

HSRP itself is a very simple "hello-like" protocol. The active and standby routers regularly send out HSRP packets destined for all HSRP routers on the segment. The primary purpose of these packets is to notify all of the HSRP routers on the segment of the active and standby routers' presence. If the other HSRP routers do not receive HSRP packets from either the active or standby router for a certain period of time, one of the other HSRP routers is elected as the replacement for the failed router.

The most important information that HSRP packets carry is as follows:

- *Standby priority*—The sending router's standby priority, which is an integer number ranging from 0 to 255 used to determine which HSRP routers become the active and standby routers. The router with the highest standby priority becomes the active router. The router whose standby priority is lower that that of the active router but higher than that of any other HSRP router becomes the standby router.

NOTE: *If two or more HSRP routers have equal standby priorities, the router with the higher number IP address on the HSRP-enabled interface has preference.*

- *Standby group*—The sending router's standby group, which is an integer number ranging from 0 to 2 for TokenRing interfaces and from 0 to 255 for all other media. The routers with the same standby group emulate the virtual MAC address and one or more virtual IP addresses—one primary and all others secondary. Multiple routers connected to the same segment can be configured with multiple, potentially overlapping, standby groups on their interfaces connected to this segment. *Overlapping* means that a single router can have multiple standby groups defined on the same interface. The operation of multiple standby groups is totally independent of each other. In other words, the standby group field in the HSRP packets is used for demultiplexing HSRP packets among multiple standby groups. Each standby group has separate active and standby routers. A single HSRP router may or may not be active or standby router for two different groups.

When HSRP is enabled on a router interface, the router sits on the segment and listens for HSRP packets. If the router finds out that it is the only HSRP router on the segment, it becomes the active router. If there already is an active router whose priority is higher than that of the new router but no standby router, the new router becomes the standby router. If the new router discovers that its priority is higher than that of the active or standby router, it can become the new active or standby router, provided it was configured with the *preempt* capability. The preempt capability is simply a binary value that indicates that if the router has higher priority than that of the current active or standby router, it can supersede them. If the superseded router becomes neither the active nor the standby router, it stops sending out HSRP packets.

HSRP runs on top of UDP. HSRP packets are encapsulated into UDP datagrams, which are sent to the multicast IP address 224.0.0.2, port 1985. The Time To Live (TTL) field of the IP datagrams carrying the UDP datagrams is set to 1. In other words, HSRP packets stay local to the segment on which HSRP is implemented.

Depending on the media type of the interface configured for HSRP, a different MAC address is used as the virtual MAC address. The TokenRing HSRP virtual MAC addresses are C0-00-00-01-00-00, C0-00-00-02-00-00, and C0-00-00-04-00-00, which correspond to groups 0, 1, and 2, respectively. On other media, the virtual MAC addresses must be 00-00-0C-07-AC-XX, where XX corresponds to the HSRP group number. The active router must use the virtual MAC address as the source MAC address in the Data Link Layer frames carrying UDP-encapsulated HSRP packets. Neither the standby nor any other HSRP router can use the virtual MAC address as the source address in any frames. This is necessary because otherwise, HSRP may not work in the presence of transparent bridges.

Dial-On-Demand Routing

Dial-On-Demand routing (DDR) is a huge subject, which deserves a separate book. Here, we'll consider only two configurations, which (I think) are most typical. These configurations are *snapshot routing* and *dial backup*. All necessary information on these two techniques is described in the corresponding subsections of the section "Configuring Dial-On-Demand Routing (DDR)," found at the end of this chapter.

Immediate Solutions

Configuring Policy-Based Routing

Configuring policy-based routing on the Cisco routers is based on route-maps, which are applied as routing policies on the routers' interfaces. Thus, the route-map clauses are applied not to the routing updates (as described in Chapter 6) but to the datagrams received on the interface.

To configure policy-based routing, follow these steps:

1. Create a route-map whose clauses contain the match statements **match ip address** {*<AL number>*|*<AL name>*}, and the actions **set interface** *<Interface>* and **set ip next-hop** *<IP address>*, or **set default interface** *<Interface>* and **set ip default next-hop** *<IP address>*. Use the route-map syntax described in the "Using Route-Maps To Filter Routing Updates During Redistribution" section in Chapter 6.

   The {*<AL number>*|*<AL name>*} parameter is the number or name of an access-list that defines which datagrams must be policy-routed. If the access-list returns **permit**, the **set** actions are applied; otherwise, the datagram's characteristics are compared against the next clause's match conditions.

   The actions **set interface** *<Interface>* and **set ip next-hop** *<IP address>* are used by the router to route the datagrams whose characteristics are matched by the match conditions. These datagrams are routed via the interface *<Interface>* and through the next-hop router whose IP address is *<IP address>*. The set actions contain the keyword **default**, and only the datagrams destined for the IP addresses not having a route in the routing table are routed in accordance with the set actions.

WARNING!   Although you can omit either the set interface <Interface> or set ip next-hop <IP address> action, be sure to use both of them. If either is omitted, the router replaces the missing element with the corresponding information from the routing table. For example, if you omit the set ip next-hop <IP address> action, the router retrieves the next-hop router's IP address from the routing table. However, this IP address may not be available via the interface specified in the set interface <Interface> action. In this case, the policy-routed datagrams are not picked up by any router, and the connection won't be established.

2. Apply the route-map on the appropriate interface using the command **ip policy route-map** *<RM name>*, where the parameter *<RM name>* is the name of the route-map. The datagrams received on this interface are checked against the route-map. If any route-map clause returns **permit**, the datagram is policy-routed as just described. Otherwise, the datagram is routed in accordance with the routing table.

NOTE: *Unlike access-lists, route-maps applied as routing policies can only be inbound.*

Policy routing has a number of applications, which cannot all be discussed in this book. Nevertheless, we'll comprehensively discuss two examples based on the same network topology. The network consists of the headquarters with its own network (the grayed area labeled "HQ") and multiple branches, two of which are shown in Figure 7.1 (the grayed areas labeled "Br.1" and "Br.2"). The topology used is called the *hub-spoke topology*—that is, all branches' networks (the spokes) are interconnected via the central network (the hub).

Nevertheless, two branches have established a sort of "backdoor link" (labeled "segment 7" in Figure 7.1), the purpose of which will be defined for each example separately.

I chose these two examples because (from my personal experience) they seem to be very typical applications of policy-based routing.

Using Policy-Based Routing For Routing Over A Dedicated Link

Suppose that branches Br.1 and Br.2 have some users who have complained that their computers' performance was not acceptable during heavy traffic periods at the headquarters. Suppose also that these users are located in both branches, and they have to communicate with each other. The branches have decided that they will establish a dedicated link between the branches' networks (segment 7) specifically for these users.

Suppose that the users allowed to use segment 7 are all located on segment 1 at branch Br.1 and on segment 3 at branch Br.2.

At first, it may seem that this task can be solved using only static routing. However, if we think more carefully, we'll notice that static routing pays no attention to the source address of the routed datagrams. Thus, static routing will equally route the datagrams originating from segment 1 and segment 2 and destined for segment 3 via

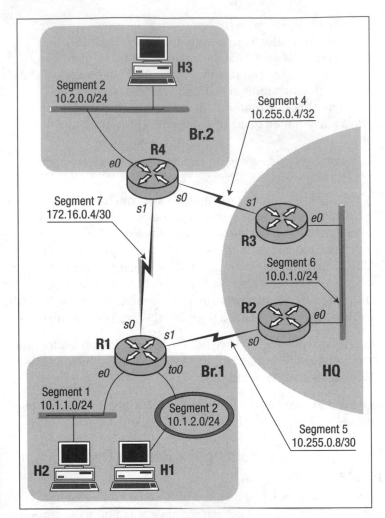

Figure 7.1   The network topology of policy-based routing.

segment 7. However, we want to allow only the datagrams originating from segment 1 and destined for segment 3 to be routed via segment 6. All other traffic must be routed according to the routing table.

The task, however, can be solved easily using policy-based routing. The idea is to define policy-based routing on the Ethernet interfaces of routers R1 and R4 using a route-map matching datagrams destined for segments 1 and 3.

Listings 7.1 through 7.4 show the configurations of all four routers. The policy-based routing is only applied on routers R1 and R4; the policy-based specific configuration is shown using italicized text.

Listing 7.1   Router R1's configuration.

```
interface Loopback0
 ip address 10.0.0.1 255.255.255.255

interface Ethernet0
 ip address 10.1.1.1 255.255.255.0
 ip policy route-map Seg1-Seg6

interface Serial0
 ip address 172.16.0.5 255.255.255.252

interface Serial1
 ip address 10.255.0.10 255.255.255.252

interface TokenRing0
 ip address 10.1.2.1 255.255.255.0
 ring-speed 16

router eigrp 10
 network 10.0.0.0

access-list 100 permit ip any 10.2.1.0 0.0.0.255

route-map Seg1-Seg6 permit 10
 match ip address 100
 set interface Serial0
 set ip next-hop 172.16.0.6
```

Listing 7.2   Router R2's configuration.

```
interface Loopback0
 ip address 10.0.0.2 255.255.255.255

interface Ethernet0
 ip address 10.0.1.1 255.255.255.0

interface Serial0
 ip address 10.255.0.9 255.255.255.252

router eigrp 10
 network 10.0.0.0
```

Listing 7.3   Router R3's configuration.

```
interface Loopback0
 ip address 10.0.0.3 255.255.255.255

interface Ethernet0
 ip address 10.0.1.2 255.255.255.0
```

**7. Special Cases
Of Routing**

```
interface Serial1
 ip address 10.255.0.5 255.255.255.252

router eigrp 10
 network 10.0.0.0
```

Listing 7.4   Router R4's configuration.

```
interface Loopback0
 ip address 10.0.0.4 255.255.255.255

interface Ethernet0
 ip address 10.2.1.1 255.255.255.0
 ip policy route-map Seg6-Seg1

interface Serial0
 ip address 10.255.0.6 255.255.255.252

interface Serial1
 ip address 172.16.0.6 255.255.255.252

router eigrp 10
 network 10.0.0.0

access-list 100 permit ip any 10.1.1.0 0.0.0.255

route-map Seg6-Seg1 permit 10
 match ip address 100
 set interface Serial1
 set ip next-hop 172.16.0.5
```

Although we are interested in policy-based routing applied to the datagrams with specific source addresses, notice that we do not specify these addresses in the access-list (access-list 100 on both routers). This is because the policy-based routing is applied on a per-interface basis. In our case, the datagrams originating from all hosts on the segments connected via the interfaces configured for policy-based routing and destined for a specific address must be policy-routed. Therefore, we can match all of these datagrams, specifying only the destination address pattern in the access-list. If, however, we want to allow only some hosts on, let's say, segment 1 to send traffic to the hosts located on segment 3 via segment 7, we must specify their IP addresses explicitly—that is, instead of the keyword **any**, the access-list must contain a specific IP address pattern.

WARNING! *Although you can use the standard access-lists in route-maps applied as routing policies, you should remember that the standard access-lists allow matching only the source addresses, not the destination ones.*

NOTE: *Policy-based routing is very similar to static routing. Therefore, in most cases, policy-based routing requires that the routers connected to all involved networks must be configured.*

Policy-based routing does not affect the routing table of the routers. Listing 7.5 shows the routing table of router R1.

Listing 7.5   *The routing table of router R1.*

```
R1#show ip route
...
   172.16.0.0/30 is subnetted, 1 subnets
C   172.16.0.4 is directly connected, Serial0
   10.0.0.0/8 is variably subnetted, 10 subnets, 3 masks
D   10.0.0.2/32 [90/2297856] via 10.255.0.9, 06:46:53, Serial1
C   10.1.2.0/24 is directly connected, TokenRing0
D   10.2.1.0/24 [90/2733056] via 10.255.0.9, 06:46:53, Serial1
D   10.0.0.3/32 [90/2323456] via 10.255.0.9, 06:46:53, Serial1
C   10.1.1.0/24 is directly connected, Ethernet0
D   10.0.1.0/24 [90/2195456] via 10.255.0.9, 06:46:53, Serial1
C   10.0.0.1/32 is directly connected, Loopback0
D   10.0.0.4/32 [90/2835456] via 10.255.0.9, 06:46:53, Serial1
D   10.255.0.4/30 [90/2707456] via 10.255.0.9,06:46:53,Serial1
C   10.255.0.8/30 is directly connected, Serial1
```

To verify that policy-based routing works, let's use the command **traceroute** on host H1 for different destinations. (In our example, all hosts are Windows NT workstations, and the version of the command **traceroute** is called **tracert**.)

Listing 7.6 shows the output of the command **tracert -d 10.2.1.120**, where 10.2.1.120 is the IP address of host H3. The command confirms that the packets sent to a host located on segment 3 from a host located on segment 1 do go through segment 7 (notice the italicized line in Listing 7.6).

Listing 7.6   *The output of the command tracert -d 10.2.1.120 entered on host H1.*

```
C:\>tracert -d 10.2.1.120

Tracing route to 10.2.1.120 over a maximum of 30 hops
```

7. Special Cases Of Routing

```
1    20 ms    10 ms    10 ms   10.1.1.1
2    31 ms    20 ms    20 ms   172.16.0.6
3    40 ms    40 ms    40 ms   10.2.1.120
```

Trace complete.

Listing 7.7 shows the output of the command **tracert -d 10.0.1.2**, where 10.0.1.2 is the IP address of router R3's Ethernet 0 interface. This time, the packets are not sent over segment 7, because they are not destined for segment 3.

Listing 7.7   *The output of the command **tracert -d 10.0.1.2** (10.0.1.2 is the IP address of router R3's Ethernet 0 interface) entered on host H1.*

```
C:\>tracert -d 10.0.1.2

Tracing route to 10.0.1.2 over a maximum of 30 hops

1    10 ms    10 ms    10 ms   10.1.1.1
2    10 ms    10 ms    10 ms   10.255.0.9
3    10 ms    10 ms    10 ms   10.0.1.2
```

Trace complete.

Finally, Listing 7.8 shows the output of the command **tracert -d 10.2.1.120**. This time, it was entered on host H2, which is located on segment 2. As the output of the command confirms, the policy-based routing does not apply to the traffic destined for segment 2 but not originated from segment 1.

Listing 7.8   *The output of the command **tracert -d 10.2.1.120** entered on host H2.*

```
C:\>tracert -d 10.2.1.120

Tracing route to 10.2.1.120 over a maximum of 30 hops

1    <10 ms    <10 ms    <10 ms   10.1.2.1
2    <10 ms     10 ms    <10 ms   10.255.0.9
3    <10 ms     10 ms    <10 ms   10.0.1.2
4    <10 ms     10 ms    <10 ms   10.255.0.6
5    <10 ms     11 ms    <10 ms   10.2.1.120
```

Trace complete.

Using Application-Sensitive Policy-Based Routing

Suppose now that branches Br.1 and Br.2 have some network-congestion-sensitive applications (such as real-time databases, and so on) that may not work properly during heavy traffic periods at the headquarters. This time, the branches decided that they would use segment 7 only for the traffic generated by these applications. As before, the applications are located on segment 1 at branch Br.1 and segment 3 at branch Br.2.

For our experiment, the network-congestion-sensitive application is Telnet. Thus, our task is to allow only Telnet traffic initiated by the hosts located on segment 1 and destined for the hosts on segment 3 to traverse segment 7. The returning Telnet traffic must also utilize segment 7. However, the Telnet traffic initiated by the hosts on segment 3 and destined for the hosts located on segment 1 must not be policy-routed.

As we remember from Chapter 1, a Telnet connection is initiated from a Telnet client application, which requests the operating system to allocate an arbitrary unused TCP port to it. This TCP port is used by the client application as the source TCP port in the TCP segments that the application generates for the Telnet connection. These segments are destined for TCP port 23, where the Telnet server application resides. The server application uses port 23 as the source TCP port that it generates for the Telnet connection.

Thus, we have to modify the access-lists on routers R1 and R2 as follows:

- The access-list on router R1 must match the datagrams carrying TCP segments destined for TCP port 23.

- The access-list on router R4 must match the datagrams carrying TCP segments with source TCP port 23.

Listings 7.9 and 7.10 show the revised configurations of routers R1 and R4. The configurations of routers R2 and R3 remain unchanged.

Listing 7.9   Router R1's configuration.

```
interface Loopback0
 ip address 10.0.0.1 255.255.255.255

interface Ethernet0
 ip address 10.1.1.1 255.255.255.0
 ip policy route-map Seg1-Seg6
```

7. Special Cases Of Routing

```
interface Serial0
 ip address 172.16.0.5 255.255.255.252

interface Serial1
 ip address 10.255.0.10 255.255.255.252

interface TokenRing0
 ip address 10.1.2.1 255.255.255.0
 ring-speed 16

router eigrp 10
 network 10.0.0.0

ip access-list extended telnet172
 permit tcp any 10.2.1.0 0.0.0.255 eq telnet

route-map Seg1-Seg6 permit 10
 match ip address telnet172
 set interface Serial0
 set ip next-hop 172.16.0.6
```

Listing 7.10   Router R4's configuration.

```
interface Loopback0
 ip address 10.0.0.4 255.255.255.255

interface Ethernet0
 ip address 10.2.1.1 255.255.255.0
 ip policy route-map Seg6-Seg1

interface Serial0
 ip address 10.255.0.6 255.255.255.252

interface Serial1
 ip address 172.16.0.6 255.255.255.252

router eigrp 10
 network 10.0.0.0

ip access-list extended telnet172
 permit tcp any eq telnet 10.1.1.0 0.0.0.255

route-map Seg6-Seg1 permit 10
 match ip address telnet172
 set interface Serial1
 set ip next-hop 172.16.0.5
```

Notice that named access-lists were used instead of regular extended access-lists. This is optional.

To verify if the policy routing worked, we can no longer use the command **traceroute**. The command **traceroute** sends UDP traffic destined for a nonexistent UDP port. Instead, we can use the command **debug ip policy** to see how the router actually performs policy routing.

Listings 7.11 and 7.12 show the output of the command **debug ip policy** on routers R1 and R4 respectively, after the command **ping 10.2.1.120** is entered on host H1. Because the **ping** traffic is not matched by the access-lists on both routers, it is not policy-routed. (Notice the italicized lines *policy rejected--normal forwarding*).

Listing 7.11   *The output of the command* **debug ip policy** *on router R1 after the command* **ping 10.2.1.120** *is entered on host H1.*

```
R1#debug ip policy
Policy routing debugging is on
R1#
IP: s=10.1.1.10 (Ethernet0), d=10.2.1.120 (Serial1), len 100,
 policy rejected -- normal forwarding
IP: s=10.1.1.10 (Ethernet0), d=10.2.1.120 (Serial1), len 100,
 policy rejected -- normal forwarding
IP: s=10.1.1.10 (Ethernet0), d=10.2.1.120 (Serial1), len 100,
 policy rejected -- normal forwarding
IP: s=10.1.1.10 (Ethernet0), d=10.2.1.120 (Serial1), len 100,
 policy rejected -- normal forwarding
IP: s=10.1.1.10 (Ethernet0), d=10.2.1.120 (Serial1), len 100,
 policy rejected -- normal forwarding
```

Listing 7.12   *The output of the command* **debug ip policy** *on router R4 after the command* **ping 10.2.1.120** *is entered on host H1.*

```
R4#debug ip policy
Policy routing debugging is on
R4#
IP: s=10.2.1.120 (Ethernet0), d=10.1.1.10 (Serial0), len 100,
 policy rejected -- normal forwarding
IP: s=10.2.1.120 (Ethernet0), d=10.1.1.10 (Serial0), len 100,
 policy rejected -- normal forwarding
IP: s=10.2.1.120 (Ethernet0), d=10.1.1.10 (Serial0), len 100,
 policy rejected -- normal forwarding
IP: s=10.2.1.120 (Ethernet0), d=10.1.1.10 (Serial0), len 100,
 policy rejected -- normal forwarding
IP: s=10.2.1.120 (Ethernet0), d=10.1.1.10 (Serial0), len 100,
 policy rejected -- normal forwarding
```

7. Special Cases Of Routing

If, however, we try to Telnet from host H1 to host H3, the output of the command **debug ip policy** on both routers shows that the Telnet traffic is policy-routed (see Listings 7.13 and 7.14).

*Listing 7.13 The output of the command **debug ip policy** on router R1 after the command **telnet 10.2.1.120** is entered on host H1.*

```
R1#debug ip policy
Policy routing debugging is on
R1#
IP: s=10.1.1.10 (Ethernet0), d=10.2.1.120, len 44,
 policy match
IP: route map Seg1-Seg6, item 10, permit
IP: s=10.1.1.10 (Ethernet0), d=10.2.1.120 (Serial0),
 len 44, policy routed
IP: Ethernet0 to Serial0 172.16.0.6
IP: s=10.1.1.10 (Ethernet0), d=10.2.1.120, len 40,
 policy match
IP: route map Seg1-Seg6, item 10, permit
IP: s=10.1.1.10 (Ethernet0), d=10.2.1.120 (Serial0),
 len 40, policy routed
IP: Ethernet0 to Serial0 172.16.0.6
...
```

*Listing 7.14 The output of the command **debug ip policy** on router R4 after the command **telnet 10.2.1.120** is entered on host H1.*

```
R4#debug ip policy
Policy routing debugging is on
R4#
IP: s=10.2.1.120 (Ethernet0), d=10.1.1.10, len 44,
 policy match
IP: route map Seg6-Seg1, item 10, permit
IP: s=10.2.1.120 (Ethernet0), d=10.1.1.10 (Serial1),
 len 44, policy routed
IP: Ethernet0 to Serial1 172.16.0.5
IP: s=10.2.1.120 (Ethernet0), d=10.1.1.10, len 40,
 policy match
IP: route map Seg6-Seg1, item 10, permit
IP: s=10.2.1.120 (Ethernet0), d=10.1.1.10 (Serial1), len 40,
 policy routed
IP: Ethernet0 to Serial1 172.16.0.5
...
```

The output of the command **debug ip policy** is fairly self-explanatory. If you have questions on some particular elements of it, refer to the Cisco documentation.

Another helpful command is **show route-map**. This command not only shows the route-map clauses but also shows the policy-based routing utilization, provided the route-map is applied as the routing policy. The last line of the command output shows how many matches have been encountered and how many traffic bytes were policy-routed.

Sample output of the command **show route-map** is shown in Listing 7.15.

Listing 7.15   *The output of the command show route-map entered on router R4.*

```
R4#show route-map
route-map Seg6-Seg1, permit, sequence 10
  Match clauses:
    ip address (access-lists): telnet172
  Set clauses:
    interface Serial1
    ip next-hop 172.16.0.5
  Policy routing matches: 241 packets, 19386 bytes
```

Configuring Network Address Translation (NAT)

The following sections provide guidelines for configuring various types of NAT on the Cisco routers.

Configuring Static Translation Of Inside IP Addresses

There are several static NAT configurations. Static translation of inside IP addresses is one of these. (The others are performed using the steps defined in this section.)

Static translation of inside IP addresses allows you to configure a router to translate individual local inside IP addresses to global inside IP addresses. The router compares the source IP addresses of the datagrams destined for the global outside IP addresses and received on the interfaces labeled "inside" against the inside local address field of the NAT table entries. If the source IP address matches an entry in the NAT table, it is replaced with the corresponding inside global IP address.

To configure static translation of inside IP addresses, follow these steps:

1. Create NAT mapping between the inside local address and the inside global address using the command **ip nat inside source** *<local IP address> <global IP address>*. The parameter *<local IP address>* is the inside local IP address that is translated into the inside global IP address, which is passed in the parameter *<global IP address>*.

2. Apply NAT on the interfaces connected to the segments with the local inside addresses using the command **ip nat inside** in the interface configuration mode.

3. Apply NAT on the interfaces connected to the segments with the global outside addresses using the command **ip nat outside** in the interface configuration mode.

NOTE: *The global inside addresses must be known in the global addresses space. Moreover, the other routers in the network should perceive the global inside addresses as available via the router performing NAT. This can be achieved either by static routing or by making the router performing NAT advertise this addresses.*

Figure 7.2 shows the example of a network in which router R3 is connected to segment 3, whose network address is not legitimate from the perspective of the rest of the network. Thus, router R3 must perform network address translation to allow host H1 (located on segment 3) to communicate with the rest of the network.

Listings 7.16 through 7.18 show the configurations of all three routers. Notice that only router R3 is configured to perform NAT. The NAT-related commands are shown using italicized text.

Listing 7.16   Router R1's configuration.

```
interface Ethernet0
 ip address 10.1.0.1 255.255.255.0

interface Serial1
 no ip address
 encapsulation frame-relay
 frame-relay lmi-type ansi

interface Serial1.2 point-to-point
 ip address 10.255.0.5 255.255.255.252
 frame-relay interface-dlci 102

interface Serial1.3 point-to-point
 ip address 10.255.0.9 255.255.255.252
 frame-relay interface-dlci 103
```

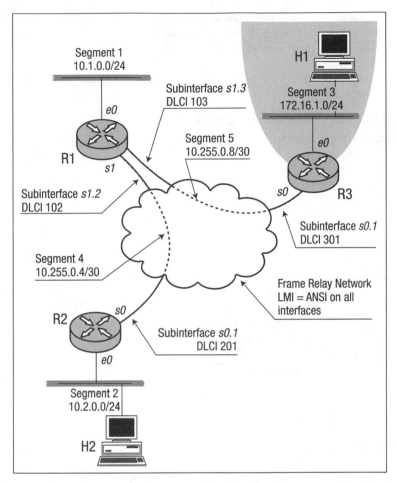

Figure 7.2   The grayed area denotes an illegal address space from the perspective of the rest of the network.

```
router eigrp 10
 network 10.0.0.0
```

Listing 7.17   Router R2's configuration.

```
interface Ethernet0
 ip address 10.2.0.1 255.255.255.0

interface Serial0
 no ip address
 encapsulation frame-relay
 frame-relay lmi-type ansi
```

```
interface Serial0.1 point-to-point
 ip address 10.255.0.6 255.255.255.252
 frame-relay interface-dlci 201

router eigrp 10
 network 10.0.0.0
```

Listing 7.18   Router R3's configuration.

```
interface Loopback0
 ip address 10.100.0.1 255.255.255.0

interface Ethernet0
 ip address 172.16.1.1 255.255.255.0
 ip nat inside

interface Serial0
 no ip address
 encapsulation frame-relay
 frame-relay lmi-type ansi

interface Serial0.1 point-to-point
 ip address 10.255.0.10 255.255.255.252
 ip nat outside
 frame-relay interface-dlci 301

router eigrp 10
 network 10.0.0.0

ip nat inside source static 172.16.1.111 10.100.0.111
```

Listing 7.19 shows that a Telnet session started on host H1 to host H2 succeeds.

Listing 7.19   The Telnet session started from host H1 to host H2 succeeds.

```
C:\>telnet 10.2.0.120

Welcome to the Telnet Service on THUNDER

Username:
```

As expected, the output of the command **netstat -n** entered on host H2 (shown in Listing 7.20) indicates that the Telnet connection is between host H2's IP address and the inside global IP address (10.100.0.111) that we used in static NAT configuration.

Listing 7.20 **Listing 7.20** *The output of the command* ***netstat -n*** *entered on host H2 shows that host H2 has an active Telnet connection with the global inside address 10.100.0.111.*

```
C:\WINDOWS\system32>netstat -n

Active Connections

Proto  Local Address        Foreign Address      State
TCP    10.2.0.120:23        10.100.0.111:1052    ESTABLISHED
TCP    127.0.0.1:1027       127.0.0.1:1028       ESTABLISHED
TCP    127.0.0.1:1028       127.0.0.1:1027       ESTABLISHED
```

A Telnet connection started from host H1 to host H2 also succeeds, as shown in Listing 7.21.

Listing 7.21 *The Telnet session to host H1 initiated from host H2 also succeeds.*

```
C:\>telnet 10.100.0.111

Welcome to the Telnet Service on HUGEWAVE

Username:
```

The output of the command **netstat -n** entered on host H1 (shown in Listing 7.22) indicates that the Telnet connection is between host H1's IP address, which is the inside local IP address, and host H2's IP address, which is the outside global IP address.

Listing 7.22 *The output of the command* ***netstat -n*** *confirms that the router translates the global inside address into the local inside address.*

```
C:\WINDOWS\system32>netstat -n

Active Connections

Proto  Local Address        Foreign Address      State
TCP    127.0.0.1:1026       127.0.0.1:1027       ESTABLISHED
TCP    127.0.0.1:1027       127.0.0.1:1026       ESTABLISHED
TCP    172.16.1.111:23      10.2.0.120:1111      ESTABLISHED

C:\WINDOWS\system32>
```

However, the output of the command **netstat -n** entered on host H2 (shown in Listing 7.23) also shows that the active Telnet connection is between host H2's IP address and the global inside IP address 10.100.0.111.

7. Special Cases Of Routing

Listing 7.23   **The output of the command *netstat -rn* on host H2 shows that**
                   the active connection was made to the global inside address.

```
C:\>netstat -n

Active Connections

  Proto  Local Address        Foreign Address       State
  TCP    10.2.0.120:1111      10.100.0.111:23       ESTABLISHED
  TCP    127.0.0.1:1027       127.0.0.1:1028        ESTABLISHED
  TCP    127.0.0.1:1028       127.0.0.1:1027        ESTABLISHED
```

Configuring Dynamic Translation Of Inside IP Addresses

Dynamic translation of inside IP addresses is one of several dynamic
NAT configurations. (The others are performed using the steps defined in this section.)

The only difference between the operation of dynamic translation of
inside IP addresses and that of static translation of inside IP addresses
is in how the NAT table is populated. In the static version, the NAT
table is populated by administratively entering pairs of IP addresses.
In the dynamic version, the router itself populates the NAT table when
an IP datagram arrives on an interface labeled "inside" and the
datagram's characteristics match certain criteria. The subsequent
datagrams arriving on the router's interfaces labeled "inside" whose
source IP address matches an existing entry in the NAT table are processed in the same way as in the static version.

The criteria that are used to verify a datagram's eligibility to create an
entry in the NAT table are expressed using an access-list. The datagram
should match an entry in the access-list with the **permit** result to be
eligible to create an entry in the NAT table.

Finally, when creating entries in the NAT table, the router uses an
administratively configured pool of inside global addresses. For every new entry, the router picks the next available IP address from the
pool in the ascending order. If the pool no longer contains any IP
addresses, the corresponding entry is not created.

To configure dynamic NAT, follow these steps:

1. Define a pool of global inside IP addresses using the command
    ip nat pool *<name> <start IP address> <end IP address>*
    {**netmask** *<subnet mask>*|**prefix-length** *<prefix length>*} in
    the global configuration mode. The *<name>* parameter is used
    to identify the address pool. The parameters *<start IP address>*
    and *<end IP address>* identify the range of global inside IP

addresses that the router will use when translating the local inside IP addresses. The parameters **netmask** *<subnet mask>* and **prefix-length** *<prefix length>* are two different ways to specify the subnet mask of the network address to which the defined global inside address space belongs.

The described procedure allows you to define a contiguous pool of NAT addresses. If you would like to configure a noncontiguous pool, you must omit the parameters *<start IP address>* *<end IP address>* in the command described. In this case, you enter NAT pool configuration mode and define multiple IP address ranges using the following syntax: **address** *<start IP address>* *<end IP address>*.

2. Define an access-list specifying which traffic arriving on the interfaces labeled "inside" is eligible to create entries in the NAT table.

NOTE: *You can use extended access-lists in this step. Remember, however, that the access-list is only used if the NAT table does not contain an inside local address coinciding with the source IP address of the datagram. If the NAT table already contains such an address, the access-list is no longer used. In this case, the source address of the datagram is translated even though the other characteristics of the datagram may not satisfy the access-list.*

3. Establish an association between the eligible local inside addresses and the pool of global inside addresses using the command **ip nat inside source list {***<AL number>*|*<AL name>***} pool** *<name>*. The parameter *<AL number>* is the name or number of the access-list defined in step 2. The parameter *<name>* is the name of the global inside addresses pool defined in step 1.

4. Apply NAT on the interfaces connected to the segments with the local inside addresses using the command **ip nat inside** in the interface configuration mode.

5. Apply NAT on the interfaces connected to the segments with the global outside addresses using the command **ip nat outside** in the interface configuration mode.

To see how the configuration guidelines work, let's modify the task we performed to configure static NAT for a single host H1 (see the previous section) to configure dynamic NAT for hosts whose addresses are in the range 172.16.1.0/25. Let the global address space range from 10.100.0.50 to 10.100.0.100. In addition, let's require that only a TCP connection to a host on segment 2 can create a translation entry.

7. Special Cases Of Routing

Listing 7.24 shows the revised configuration of router R3. The other routers retain their configurations from the previous section.

Listing 7.24   Router R3's configuration.

```
ip nat pool pool172 10.100.0.50 10.100.0.100 prefix-length 24
ip nat inside source list TCP172 pool pool172

interface Loopback0
 ip address 10.100.0.1 255.255.255.0

interface Ethernet0
 ip address 172.16.1.1 255.255.255.0
 ip nat inside

interface Serial0
 no ip address
 encapsulation frame-relay
 frame-relay lmi-type ansi

interface Serial0.1 point-to-point
 ip address 10.255.0.10 255.255.255.252
 ip nat outside
 frame-relay interface-dlci 301

router eigrp 10
 network 10.0.0.0

ip access-list extended TCP172
 permit tcp 172.16.1.0 0.0.0.127 10.2.0.0 0.0.0.255
```

A useful command for monitoring NAT is **show ip nat translations**. This command displays the contents of the NAT table. If, however, the router is just configured for dynamic NAT, the NAT table may not contain any entries, and the command **show ip nat translations** produces no output.

To create entries in the NAT table, a router must first receive traffic that matches the access-list used in the NAT configuration. If the access-list is standard, any traffic whose source IP address matches the access-list will create an entry in the NAT table. If however, the access-list is extended, as in our case, the other characteristics of the traffic must also be matched by the access-list. In our case, the traffic eligible for NAT not only must be originated from a local inside address (that is, an IP address from the range 172.16.1.0/25), but also must be TCP and destined for a host on segment 2.

If we simply try to **ping** a host whose IP address belongs to the global outside address space, we won't succeed, because the command **ping** produces ICMP traffic. Listing 7.25 shows the results of attempts to **ping** host H2's and router R1's Ethernet interface.

Listing 7.25   *The results of pinging host H2 and router R1's Ethernet 0 interface from host H1 before the NAT table of router R3 contains an entry for host H1's IP address.*

```
C:\>ping 10.2.0.120

Pinging 10.2.0.120 with 32 bytes of data:

Request timed out.
Request timed out.
Request timed out.
Request timed out.

C:\>ping 10.1.0.1

Pinging 10.1.0.1 with 32 bytes of data:

Request timed out.
Request timed out.
Request timed out.
Request timed out.
```

The results of trying to Telnet to router R1 using the IP address configured on its Ethernet 0 interface will also be unsuccessful.

However, a Telnet session from host H1 to host H2 is successful (as shown in Listing 7.26).

Listing 7.26   *Telnet from host H1 to host H2 succeeds.*

```
C:\>telnet 10.2.0.120

Welcome to the Telnet Service on THUNDER

Username:
```

After that, the NAT table of router R3 contains an entry for host H1's IP address (172.16.1.111). Listing 7.27 shows the output of the command **show ip nat translations**.

Listing 7.27   The output of the command *show ip nat translations* on router R3.

```
R3#show ip nat translations
Pro Inside global  Inside local  Outside local Outside global
-- 10.100.0.50     172.16.1.111  --            --
```

After the entry is created, all connections from host H1 to the rest of the network are successful (see Listing 7.28, which shows how previously unsuccessful attempts to **ping** host H1 and router R1 now succeed). The connection is successful because the NAT table only contains pairs of local and global IP addresses, unlike the access-list that was used to verify if the outgoing traffic is eligible to create an entry in the NAT table.

Listing 7.28   After an entry for host H1's IP address is added to the NAT table, all connections from host H1 to the rest of the network succeed.

```
C:\>ping 10.2.0.120

Pinging 10.2.0.120 with 32 bytes of data:

Reply from 10.2.0.120: bytes=32 time=91ms TTL=125
Reply from 10.2.0.120: bytes=32 time=80ms TTL=125
Reply from 10.2.0.120: bytes=32 time=81ms TTL=125
Reply from 10.2.0.120: bytes=32 time=80ms TTL=125

C:\>ping 10.1.0.1

Pinging 10.1.0.1 with 32 bytes of data:

Reply from 10.1.0.1: bytes=32 time=60ms TTL=254
Reply from 10.1.0.1: bytes=32 time=50ms TTL=254
Reply from 10.1.0.1: bytes=32 time=50ms TTL=254
Reply from 10.1.0.1: bytes=32 time=50ms TTL=254
```

After a Telnet session to host H2 was established from host H1, the output of the command **netstat -n** entered on host H2 (shown in Listing 7.29) shows the inside global address that was used to replace the original IP address of host H1.

Listing 7.29   The output of the command *netstat -n* entered on host H2.

```
C:\WINDOWS\system32>netstat -n

Active Connections
```

Proto	Local Address	Foreign Address	State
TCP	10.2.0.120:23	10.100.0.50:1047	ESTABLISHED
TCP	127.0.0.1:1027	127.0.0.1:1028	ESTABLISHED
TCP	127.0.0.1:1028	127.0.0.1:1027	ESTABLISHED

TIP: *You can use the command **clear ip nat translation** * to remove all of the NAT table entries. In lieu of the asterisk, other parameters can be used to perform more specific removals.*

Using NAT In The Presence Of OSPF Routing

OSPF (as usual) adds a little "spice" to configuring NAT. In the previous section, we defined the range of global inside addresses using the interface Loopback 0 on router R3. We relied on EIGRP to establish dynamic routing in the network and to advertise the global inside address space to the rest of the network. However, if we replace EIGRP on routers R1 through R3 with OSPF, we'll find out that NAT does not work anymore.

Listings 7.30 through 7.32 show the configurations of all three routers in which EIGRP is replaced with OSPF. No other changes were made.

Listing 7.30   Router R1's configuration.
```
interface Loopback0
 ip address 10.0.0.1 255.255.255.255

interface Ethernet0
 ip address 10.1.0.1 255.255.255.0

interface Serial1
 no ip address
 encapsulation frame-relay
 frame-relay lmi-type ansi

interface Serial1.2 point-to-point
 ip address 10.255.0.5 255.255.255.252
 frame-relay interface-dlci 102

interface Serial1.3 point-to-point
 ip address 10.255.0.9 255.255.255.252
 frame-relay interface-dlci 103

router ospf 10
 network 10.0.0.0 0.255.255.255 area 0

ip classless
```

7. Special Cases Of Routing

Listing 7.31   Router R2's configuration.

```
interface Loopback0
 ip address 10.0.0.2 255.255.255.255

interface Ethernet0
 ip address 10.2.0.1 255.255.255.0

interface Serial0
 no ip address
 encapsulation frame-relay
 frame-relay lmi-type ansi

interface Serial0.1 point-to-point
 ip address 10.255.0.6 255.255.255.252
 frame-relay interface-dlci 201

router ospf 10
 network 10.0.0.0 0.255.255.255 area 0

ip classless
```

Listing 7.32   Router R3's configuration.

```
ip nat pool pool172 10.100.0.50 10.100.0.100 prefix-length 24
ip nat inside source list TCP172 pool pool172

interface Loopback0
 ip address 10.100.0.1 255.255.255.0

interface Ethernet0
 ip address 172.16.1.1 255.255.255.0
 ip nat inside

interface Serial0
 no ip address
 encapsulation frame-relay
 frame-relay lmi-type ansi

interface Serial0.1 point-to-point
 ip address 10.255.0.10 255.255.255.252
 ip nat outside
 frame-relay interface-dlci 301

router ospf 10
 network 10.0.0.0 0.255.255.255 area 0

ip classless
```

```
ip access-list extended TCP172
permit tcp 172.16.1.0 0.0.0.127 10.2.0.0 0.0.0.255
```

After the changes, the command **telnet 10.2.0.120** issued on host H1 no longer works. It does not work because NAT itself, on which we rely to issue this command, does not work anymore.

NAT does not work because of the way OSPF treats loopback interfaces. If we look at router R2's routing table (Listing 7.33), we'll notice that it contains a route for network prefix 10.100.0.1/32. This happens despite the fact that the Loopback 0 interface of router R3 is assigned the /24 subnet mask.

Listing 7.33   The routing table of router R2.

```
R2#show ip route
...
 10.0.0.0/8 is variably subnetted, 7 subnets, 3 masks
C  10.0.0.2/32 is directly connected, Loopback0
C  10.2.0.0/24 is directly connected, Ethernet0
O  10.1.0.0/24 [110/74] via 10.255.0.5, 00:12:40, Serial0.1
O  10.0.0.1/32 [110/65] via 10.255.0.5, 00:12:40, Serial0.1
O  10.100.0.1/32 [110/129] via 10.255.0.5, 00:12:40,Serial0.1
C  10.255.0.4/30 is directly connected, Serial0.1
O  10.255.0.8/30 [110/128] via 10.255.0.5, 00:12:40,Serial0.1
```

If we enter the command **show ip ospf interface Loopback 0** on router R3, we'll find that the last line of the command output indicates that the loopback interfaces are treated (and therefore advertised) as stub hosts.

*Listing 7.34   The output of the command **show ip ospf interface Loopback 0** on router R3.*

```
R3#show ip ospf interface Loopback 0
Loopback0 is up, line protocol is up
  Internet Address 10.100.0.1/24, Area 0
  Process ID 10, Router ID 10.100.0.1, Network Type LOOPBACK,
  Cost: 1
  Loopback interface is treated as a stub Host
```

In addition, because the Loopback 0 interface in our example has an IP address with a number higher than any global outside IP address, it is used as the OSPF router ID. It is inconsistent with the other router's OSPF IDs.

The straightforward solution is to define a static route for the global inside address space pointing to the Null 0 interface and to give the

Loopback 0 interface a consistent OSPF router ID. The static route then needs to be redistributed into the OSPF process.

Another solution is to give the Loopback 0 a consistent IP address (in our example, it is 10.0.0.3/32) and then to define a Tunnel interface whose source and destination addresses are equal to the Loopback 0's new IP address. As with loopback interfaces, the tunnel interfaces are logical. However, unlike loopback interfaces, tunnel interfaces are not treated by OSPF as stub hosts. Thus, if the global IP address is defined using a tunnel interface, it is advertised by OSPF correctly. This solution also eliminates the need to redistribute static routes into the OSPF process of router R3.

Listing 7.35 shows the updated configuration of router R3.

Listing 7.35   Router R3's configuration.

```
ip nat pool pool172 10.100.0.50 10.100.0.100 prefix-length 24
ip nat inside source list TCP172 pool pool172

interface Loopback0
 ip address 10.0.0.3 255.255.255.255

interface Tunnel0
 ip address 10.100.0.1 255.255.255.0
 tunnel source 10.0.0.3
 tunnel destination 10.0.0.3

interface Ethernet0
 ip address 172.16.1.1 255.255.255.0
 ip nat inside

interface Serial0
 no ip address
 encapsulation frame-relay
 frame-relay lmi-type ansi

interface Serial0.1 point-to-point
 ip address 10.255.0.10 255.255.255.252
 ip nat outside
 frame-relay interface-dlci 301

router ospf 10
 network 10.0.0.0 0.255.255.255 area 0

ip classless
```

```
ip access-list extended TCP172
 permit tcp 172.16.1.0 0.0.0.127 10.2.0.0 0.0.0.255
```

The routing table of router R2 (shown in Listing 7.36) now contains the route for the global inside address space.

Listing 7.36   The routing table of router R2 after the Tunnel 0 interface was added on router R3.

```
R2#show ip route
...
  10.0.0.0/8 is variably subnetted, 8 subnets, 3 masks
C   10.0.0.2/32 is directly connected, Loopback0
C   10.2.0.0/24 is directly connected, Ethernet0
O   10.0.0.3/32 [110/129] via 10.255.0.5, 00:00:11, Serial0.1
O   10.1.0.0/24 [110/74] via 10.255.0.5, 00:00:11, Serial0.1
O   10.0.0.1/32 [110/65] via 10.255.0.5, 00:00:11, Serial0.1
O   10.100.0.0/24 [110/11239]via 10.255.0.5,00:00:11,Serial0.1
C   10.255.0.4/30 is directly connected, Serial0.1
O   10.255.0.8/30 [110/128] via 10.255.0.5, 00:00:11,Serial0.1
```

NAT now functions properly.

Using The Parameter *type match-host* Of The Command *ip nat pool*

As mentioned in the previous section, the router allocates the inside global IP address from the pool in ascending order. Sometimes, however, you may want to preserve the host IDs when translating the network IDs. Specifically for this purpose, the optional parameter **type match-host** can be used at the end of the **ip nat pool** command.

If this parameter is used, the router calculates the inside global IP addresses using the following formula:

$$IGA = IGNA + (ILA - ILNA)$$

where IGA is the resulting inside global IP address, IGNA is the first IP address in the pool to which the pool's subnet mask was applied, ILA is the inside local IP address (that is, the address to be translated), and ILNA is the network ID of the inside local IP address. The pool's subnet mask is defined either by the parameter **prefix-length** *<length>* or by the parameter **netmask** *<subnet mask>*. All parameters must be treated as 32-bit numbers.

WARNING!   *The calculated inside global IP address must remain within the ranges of IP addresses defined by the pool. Otherwise, the translation is not performed.*

7. Special Cases Of Routing

Let's replace the pool of inside global IP addresses that we used in the previous section with a new one accompanied by the parameter **type match-host**. The revised configuration of router R3 is shown in Listing 7.37.

Listing 7.37   Router R3's configuration.

```
!
! IMPORTANT: The format of this book does not allow
! this command to print without a line break. In the
! actual configuration, this command is a single line.
!
ip nat pool pool172 10.100.0.96 10.100.0.127
                    prefix-length 24 type match-host

ip nat inside source list 1 pool pool172

interface Loopback0
 ip address 10.100.0.1 255.255.255.0

interface Ethernet0
 ip address 172.16.1.1 255.255.255.0
 ip nat inside

interface Serial0
 no ip address
 encapsulation frame-relay
 frame-relay lmi-type ansi

interface Serial0.1 point-to-point
 ip address 10.255.0.10 255.255.255.252
 ip nat outside
 frame-relay interface-dlci 301

router eigrp 10
 network 10.0.0.0

access-list 1 permit 172.16.1.0 0.0.0.127
```

The new NAT table is shown in Listing 7.38.

Listing 7.38   The NAT table of router R3.

```
R3#show ip nat translations
Pro Inside global  Inside local  Outside local Outside global
-- 10.100.0.111    172.16.1.111  --            --
```

NOTE: *The outside hosts cannot reach the inside hosts via the corresponding global inside addresses until the NAT table contains the corresponding entries. In the case of dynamic NAT, the entry in the NAT table is created only after traffic satisfying the access-list is routed to an outside network by the router performing NAT. In the case of static NAT, the entry is always present in the NAT table.*

Configuring NAT With Overloading Global Inside IP Addresses

Sometimes, it is not possible to define a large enough pool of global inside addresses. One such example is a network with private IP addresses that must be connected to the Internet. If the network is large and, therefore, uses a broad range of private IP addresses, such as 10.0.0.0/8, it may not be possible to get an equally sized pool of inside global IP addresses. (On the other hand, if it were possible to get such a big pool, then why bother using private IP addresses?)

A NAT solution is available specifically for such situations, referenced in RFCs as Network Address Port Translation (NAPT) and in the Cisco documentation as Port Address Translation (PAT). NAPT allows multiple hosts located on inside networks to access hosts located on outside networks using either a single inside global address or a limited number of those. This is made possible by translating Transport Layer identifiers—namely, TCP/UDP ports and ICMP query identifiers—created by the hosts on the inside networks into transport identifiers associated with a single or only few inside global addresses. The router performing NAPT has to keep track of Transport Layer identifiers and the corresponding inside local IP addresses.

To configure NAPT, you can use the procedure described in the section, "Configuring Dynamic Translation Of Inside IP Addresses," in this chapter, except in step 3, you must append the parameter **overload** to the command **ip nat inside source**.

Alternatively, you can use the following version of the command: **ip nat inside source list** {*<AL number>*|*<AL name>*} **interface** *<Interface>*. In this case, the router replaces the inside local IP addresses with the single IP address configured on the corresponding interface.

Listing 7.39 shows the configuration of router R3, which now performs translation of the inside local IP address into the IP address configured on subinterface Serial 0.1. The configurations of routers R1 and R2 are shown in Listings 7.16 and 7.17.

Listing 7.39   Router R3's configuration.

```
ip nat inside source list 1 interface Serial0.1 overload

interface Loopback0
 ip address 10.100.0.1 255.255.255.0

interface Ethernet0
 ip address 172.16.1.1 255.255.255.0
 ip nat inside

interface Serial0
 no ip address
 encapsulation frame-relay
 frame-relay lmi-type ansi

interface Serial0.1 point-to-point
 ip address 10.255.0.10 255.255.255.252
 ip nat outside
 frame-relay interface-dlci 301

router eigrp 10
 network 10.0.0.0

access-list 1 permit 172.16.1.0 0.0.0.127
```

The NAT table of router R3 is shown in Listing 7.40. Notice that the NAT table now has all fields filled out.

Listing 7.40   The NAT table of router R3.

```
R3#show ip nat translations
Pro Inside global      Inside local      ...
tcp 10.255.0.10:1054   172.16.1.111:1054  ...
                       ...       Outside local   Outside global
                       ...       10.2.0.120:23   10.2.0.120:23
```

NOTE: Because of the format limitations of this book, the lines of output shown in Listing 7.40 were broken in the middle using ellipses. Lines 1 and 2 are continued at lines 3 and 4, respectively.

Configuring NAT To Translate Between Overlapping Address Spaces

If two networks using the same IP addresses are merged and one of these networks is a stub network, it is possible to use NAT to perform IP address translation of the overlapped IP addresses.

This NAT solution is based on using DNS (Domain Name System) by the hosts on the stub network (an inside network) to resolve the IP addresses of the hosts located on the outside network. The router configured for NAT intercepts the DNS replies. If the returned IP address overlaps with an IP address in the stub network, the router translates it to a nonambiguous IP address routable in the stub network.

To configure NAT to translate between overlapping address spaces, follow these steps:

1. Using the command **ip nat pool**, define a pool of outside local addresses into which the IP addresses in the DNS replies will be translated. These addresses must be routable inside the stub network. The syntax of the command **ip nat pool** is the same as before.

2. Define an access-list specifying which traffic arriving on the interfaces labeled "outside" is eligible to create entries in the NAT table.

3. Establish an association between the eligible outside global addresses and the pool of outside local addresses using the command **ip nat outside source list** {*<AL number>*|*<AL name>*} **pool** *<name>*.

4. Apply NAT on the interfaces connected to the segments with the local inside addresses using the command **ip nat inside** in the interface configuration mode.

5. Apply NAT on the interfaces connected to the segments with the global outside addresses using the command **ip nat outside** in the interface configuration mode.

NOTE: *The IP addresses constituting the pool of outside local addresses to the router performing NAT must appear to be routable exactly as the outside global IP addresses that they will replace. Because the routers on the outside networks don't know anything about the outside local addresses, they can't advertise these addresses to the router performing NAT. Thus, it is possible that static routing is the only way to establish the necessary routing for the outside local address.*

TIP: *Translation of the outside addresses only makes sense if it is performed in conjunction with the inside address translation.*

Figure 7.3 shows the example of two merged networks, one of which (the gray area) uses the IP address from the other one. Luckily, the first network is not large, and it is a stub network from the second

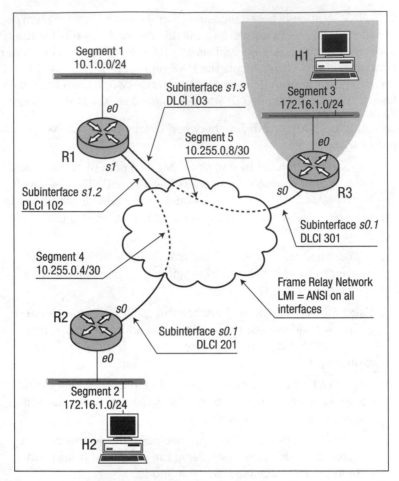

Figure 7.3   The IP address space used in the grayed area overlaps with an existing IP address space (segment 2).

network's perspective. Thus, NAT can be used to translate the overlapping IP addresses.

The configurations of all three routers are shown in Listings 7.41 through 7.43.

Listing 7.41   Router R1's configuration.

```
interface Ethernet0
 ip address 10.1.0.1 255.255.255.0

interface Serial1.2 point-to-point
 ip address 10.255.0.5 255.255.255.252
 frame-relay interface-dlci 102
```

```
interface Serial1.3 point-to-point
 ip address 10.255.0.9 255.255.255.252
 frame-relay interface-dlci 103

router eigrp 10
 network 10.0.0.0
```

Listing 7.42   Router R2's configuration.

```
interface Ethernet0
 ip address 172.16.1.1 255.255.255.0

interface Serial0
 no ip address
 encapsulation frame-relay
 frame-relay lmi-type ansi

interface Serial0.1 point-to-point
 ip address 10.255.0.6 255.255.255.252
 frame-relay interface-dlci 201

router eigrp 10
 network 10.0.0.0
 network 172.16.0.0
```

Listing 7.43   Router R3's configuration.

```
interface Loopback0
 ip address 10.100.0.1 255.255.255.0

interface Ethernet0
 ip address 172.16.1.1 255.255.255.0
 ip nat inside

interface Serial0
 no ip address
 encapsulation frame-relay
 frame-relay lmi-type ansi

interface Serial0.1 point-to-point
 ip address 10.255.0.10 255.255.255.252
 ip nat outside
 frame-relay interface-dlci 301

router eigrp 10
 network 10.0.0.0


ip nat pool ext172 10.200.0.30 10.200.0.80 prefix-length 24
ip nat pool int172 10.100.0.50 10.100.0.100 prefix-length 24
```

**7. Special Cases
Of Routing**

```
ip nat inside source list 1 pool int172
ip nat outside source list 1 pool ext172

ip route 10.200.0.0 255.255.255.0 10.255.0.9

access-list 1 permit 172.16.1.0 0.0.0.255
```

NOTE: Although two different NAT pools are used for translation of outside global addresses and inside local addresses, the access-list to match the IP datagrams establishing the NAT table entries remains the same for the inside and outside networks. This happens because the IP address spaces translated are overlapped and, therefore, can be matched using the same access-list. However, a single access-list in this NAT configuration is not a requirement.

The NAT table of router R3 is shown in Listing 7.44.

Listing 7.44   The NAT table of router R3.

```
R3#show ip nat translations
Pro Inside global   Inside local    Outside local  Outside global
-- 10.100.0.50      172.16.1.111    --             --
-- --               --              10.200.0.31    172.16.1.1
-- --               --              10.200.0.30    172.16.1.120
-- 10.100.0.50      172.16.1.111    10.200.0.30    172.16.1.120
```

Configuring NAT For TCP Load Balancing

As explained in the "In Brief" section in this chapter, it is possible to use NAT for load balancing. This version of NAT is called LSNAT (Load Sharing Using IP Network Address Translation). RFC 2391 documents this NAT technology.

If you have multiple servers that run the same service accessible via the network, such as a Web server or FTP server, you can use LSNAT to allow network access to the service via a single IP address called a *virtual server IP address*, still using all of the servers. A router performing LSNAT redistributes the connections incoming on that IP address to this service via all of the servers by translating the virtual server IP address into the real servers' IP addresses. Once such a connection is established, all subsequent packets of that connection are only forwarded to the same server that was originally chosen.

The first packet of those connections is used to establish a corresponding entry in the NAT table of the router. The segments on which the real servers reside are inside networks. The segments on which the hosts accessing the service via the virtual server IP address reside are outside networks.

To configure LSNAT, follow these steps:

1. Define the pool of IP addresses into which the virtual server IP address will be translated. All of the addresses that the pool defines must be the IP addresses of existing servers. If the IP addresses of the existing servers are not contiguous, you have to define a noncontiguous pool.

   Define the pool using the same command syntax as the one described in the "Configuring Dynamic Translation of Inside IP Addresses" section in this chapter with the keywords **type rotary** appended at the end.

2. Create an access-list that matches the virtual server IP address with the **permit** result.

3. Establish an association between the virtual server IP address and the pool using the command **ip nat inside destination list** {*<AL number>*|*<AL name>*} **pool** *<pool name>*.

4. Apply NAT on the interfaces connected to the segments on which the real servers reside using the command **ip nat inside** in the interface configuration mode.

5. Apply NAT on the interfaces connected to the segments with the global outside addresses using the command **ip nat outside** in the interface configuration mode.

NOTE: *The virtual server IP address must appear to be accessible via the router performing NAT.*

Figure 7.4 shows the network example suitable for deploying LSNAT. Servers S1 and S2 run the Telnet service, which is supposed to be accessible by hosts H1 and H2 via a single IP address.

Listings 7.45 and 7.46 show the configurations of routers R1 and R2. Notice that because the servers' IP addresses (10.0.1.111 and 10.0.1.222) collectively constitute a noncontiguous address space, we are forced to use a noncontiguous NAT pool.

Listing 7.45   Router R1's configuration.

```
interface Ethernet0
 ip address 10.0.1.1 255.255.255.0
 ip nat inside

interface Serial0
 ip address 10.255.0.5 255.255.255.252
 ip nat outside
```

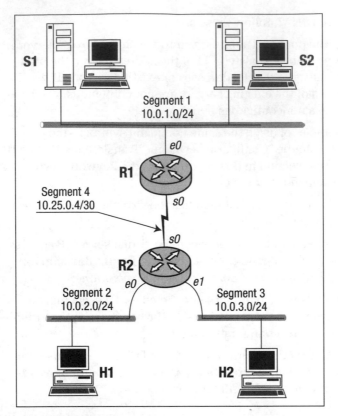

Figure 7.4   Router R1 performs load balancing of TCP sessions to servers S1 and S2.

```
router eigrp 10
 network 10.0.0.0

ip nat pool Servers prefix-length 24 type rotary
 address 10.0.1.111 10.0.1.111
 address 10.0.1.222 10.0.1.222

ip nat inside destination list 1 pool Servers

access-list 1 permit 10.0.1.100
```

Listing 7.46   Router R2's configuration.

```
interface Ethernet0
 ip address 10.0.2.1 255.255.255.0

interface Ethernet1
 ip address 10.0.3.1 255.255.255.0
```

```
interface Serial0
 ip address 10.255.0.6 255.255.255.252

router eigrp 10
 network 10.0.0.0
```

Listings 7.47 and 7.48 show the results of Telnetting from hosts H1 and H2, respectively, to the virtual server IP address. The outputs clearly indicate that, although the same destination IP address is used, the Telnet sessions are connected to two different servers (check the names—HUGEWAVE and LITTLEWAVE).

Listing 7.47   *Telnetting the virtual server IP address from host H1 succeeds.*
```
C:\>telnet 10.0.1.100

Welcome to the Telnet Service on HUGEWAVE

Username:
```

Listing 7.48   *Telnetting the virtual server IP address from host H2 succeeds.*
```
C:\>telnet 10.0.1.100

Welcome to the Telnet Service on LITTLEWAVE

Username:
```

Listings 7.49 and 7.50 show the outputs of the command **netstat -n** entered on hosts H1 and H2, respectively. The outputs show the IP addresses that replace the virtual server IP address.

Listing 7.49   *The output of the command **netstat -n** shows that this Telnet session is connected to server S1.*
```
C:\WINDOWS\system32>netstat -n

Active Connections

 Proto  Local Address       Foreign Address      State
 TCP    10.0.1.111:23       10.0.2.120:11004     ESTABLISHED
 TCP    127.0.0.1:1025      127.0.0.1:1026       ESTABLISHED
 TCP    127.0.0.1:1026      127.0.0.1:1025       ESTABLISHED
```

Listing 7.50   *The output of the command **netstat -n** shows that the Telnet session is now connected to server S2.*
```
C:\WINDOWS\system32>netstat -n

Active Connections
```

```
Proto   Local Address          Foreign Address        State
TCP     10.0.1.222:23          10.0.3.120:11005       ESTABLISHED
TCP     127.0.0.1:1025         127.0.0.1:1026         ESTABLISHED
TCP     127.0.0.1:1026         127.0.0.1:1025         ESTABLISHED
```

Finally, Listing 7.51 shows the NAT table of router R1.

Listing 7.51   The NAT table of router R1.

```
R1#show ip nat translations
Pro Inside global  Inside local        ...
tcp 10.0.1.100:23  10.0.1.222:23       ...
tcp 10.0.1.100:23  10.0.1.111:23       ...
                   ...   Outside local       Outside global
                   ...   10.0.3.120:11005    10.0.3.120:11005
                   ...   10.0.2.120:11004    10.0.2.120:11004
```

NOTE: *Because of the format limitations of this book, the lines of output shown in Listing 7.51 were broken in the middle using ellipses. Lines 1, 2, and 3 are continued at lines 4, 5, and 6, respectively.*

Configuring Hot Standby Router Protocol (HSRP)

In this section, we'll discuss two typical HSRP applications: *basic HSRP* and *HSRP with load balancing*.

Configuring Basic HSRP

Two or more Cisco routers can be configured for HSRP on their interfaces connected to the same LAN segment. To perform basic HSRP configuration, perform the following steps in the interface configuration mode:

1. Enter the command **standby** *<group #>* **ip** *<IP address>*. The *<group #>* parameter is the standby group number, which can range from 0 to 2 for TokenRing interfaces and from 0 to 255 for all other LAN interfaces. The *<IP address>* parameter is the IP address that the hosts on the segment will use as their default router (the router to which the default gateway route points as the next-hop router).

2. (This step is optional.) Enter the command **standby** *<group #>* **priority** *<priority>*. The *<priority>* parameter specifies the standby priority of the router. Assign the highest priority to the router that you want to be the active router under normal operation. If you do not enter this command, the router will use the default standby priority of 100.

3. (This step is optional.) Enter the command **standby** *<group #>* **preempt** if you want a standby router to become the active router, if the current active router decreases its priority lower than that of the standby router. Entering this command on the active router allows it to regain the active router status if it was lost either because the router was temporarily unavailable or because its priority decreased.

4. (This step is optional.) Enter the command **standby** *<group #>* **track** *<Interface>* [*<priority decrease>*] if you want the router to decrease its own standby priority if the interface specified using the parameter *<Interface>* goes down. The parameter *<priority decrease>*, if used, specifies the amount by which the router's priority must be decreased. If omitted, the amount defaults to 10.

Let's consider the network example shown in Figure 7.5. Routers R1 and R2 can be configured for HSRP to provide a redundant default router for the hosts connected on segment 1.

Listings 7.52 through 7.54 show the configurations of all three routers.

Listing 7.52   Router R1's configuration.
```
interface Ethernet0
 ip address 10.1.0.2 255.255.255.0
 no ip redirects
 standby 10 priority 100
 standby 10 preempt
 standby 10 ip 10.1.0.1
 standby 10 track Serial0 50

interface Serial0
 ip address 10.3.0.1 255.255.255.0

router eigrp 1
 network 10.0.0.0
```

7. Special Cases Of Routing

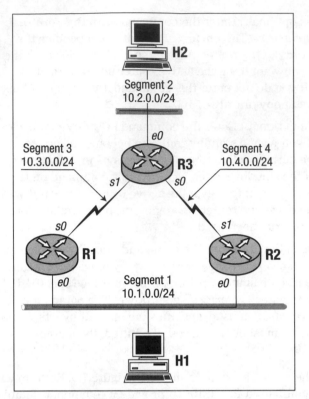

**Figure 7.5   Routers R1 and R2 are configured with HSRP to back up each
other in case either one of them or one of their interfaces fails.**

Listing 7.53   Router R2's configuration.

```
interface Ethernet0
 ip address 10.1.0.3 255.255.255.0
 no ip redirects
 standby 10 priority 80
 standby 10 preempt
 standby 10 ip 10.1.0.1

interface Serial1
 ip address 10.4.0.1 255.255.255.0

router eigrp 1
 network 10.0.0.0
```

Listing 7.54   Router R3's configuration.

```
interface Ethernet0
 ip address 10.2.0.1 255.255.255.0
```

```
interface Serial0
 ip address 10.4.0.2 255.255.255.0

interface Serial1
 ip address 10.3.0.2 255.255.255.0

router eigrp 1
 network 10.0.0.0
```

The command that you can use to verify the status of HSRP on routers is **show standby**. (The command has optional parameters. If you need more information on these parameters, refer to the Cisco documentation.)

Listings 7.55 and 7.56 show the output of the command **show standby** entered on routers R1 and R2. The output of the commands is fairly self-explanatory.

Listing 7.55 *The output of the command **show standby** entered on router R1.*

```
R1#show standby
Ethernet0 - Group 10
  Local state is Active, priority 100, may preempt
  Hellotime 3 holdtime 10
  Next hello sent in 00:00:01.056
  Hot standby IP address is 10.1.0.1 configured
  Active router is local
  Standby router is 10.1.0.3 expired
  Standby virtual mac address is 0000.0c07.ac0a
  Tracking interface states for 1 interface, 1 up:
    Up   Serial0 Priority decrement: 50
```

Listing 7.56 *The output of the command **show standby** entered on router R2.*

```
R2#show standby
Ethernet0 - Group 10
  Local state is Standby, priority 80, may preempt
  Hellotime 3 holdtime 10
  Next hello sent in 00:00:01.546
  Hot standby IP address is 10.1.0.1 configured
  Active router is 10.1.0.2 expires in 00:00:09
  Standby router is local
  Standby virtual mac address is 0000.0c07.ac0a
```

7. Special Cases Of Routing

NOTE: *The virtual MAC address, shown in the last line of Listing 7.56, corresponds to the virtual MAC address pattern for non-TokenRing media discussed in the "In Brief" section in this chapter.*

As mentioned in the "In Brief" section in this chapter, depending on the interface hardware type, the virtual MAC address may or may not be the same as the MAC address of the active router's interface on which HSRP is enabled. Router R1's Ethernet 0 interface is an example of hardware that forces the router to use the same MAC address as the interface MAC address and as the virtual MAC address. Because of this and because the router has to follow the pattern suggested for virtual MAC addresses for non-TokenRing media, the router changes the MAC address of the interface to the value of the virtual MAC address.

Listing 7.57 shows the first two lines of the output of the command **show interfaces Ethernet 0** entered on router R1. The first italicized text element in Listing 7.57 shows the current MAC address of the interface Ethernet 0. The second italicized text element shows the original "burned-in" MAC address of the interface.

*Listing 7.57   The output of the command **show interfaces Ethernet 0** entered on router R1.*

```
R1#show interfaces Ethernet 0
Ethernet0 is up, line protocol is up
  Hardware is Lance, address is 0000.0c07.ac0a (bia
00e0.b064.5063)
...
```

Nevertheless, router R2 still uses the original MAC address as the interface MAC address (see Listing 7.58).

*Listing 7.58   The output of the command **show interfaces Ethernet 0** entered on router R2.*

```
R2#show interfaces Ethernet 0
Ethernet0 is up, line protocol is up
  Hardware is Lance, address is 00e0.b064.30a9 (bia
00e0.b064.30a9)
...
```

However, if router R1 fails and R2 becomes the active router, it changes the interface MAC address to the value of the virtual MAC address, unless its interface hardware allows having different interface and virtual MAC addresses.

From the "In Brief" section in this chapter, remember that there can only be one active and one standby router. Thus, if we connect another HSRP router to segment 1 whose configuration is as shown in Listing 7.59, its state should be neither Active nor Standby.

Listing 7.59 *The configuration of the interface Ethernet 0 of router R4.*

```
interface Ethernet0
 ip address 10.1.0.4 255.255.255.0
 no ip redirects
 standby 1 priority 50
 standby 1 preempt
 standby 1 ip 10.1.0.1
```

As Listing 7.60 shows, its state is Listen.

Listing 7.60 *The output of the command **show standby** entered on router R4.*

```
R4#show standby
Ethernet0 - Group 10
  Local state is Listen, priority 50, may preempt
  Hellotime 3 holdtime 10
  Hot standby IP address is 10.1.0.1 configured
  Active router is 10.1.0.2 expires in 00:00:08
  Standby router is 10.1.0.3 expires in 00:00:07
```

Let's now see what happens if router R1 becomes temporarily un-available on segment 1. The first message (shown in 7.61) notifies you that router R1 is now the active router.

Listing 7.61 *The message that appears on router R1's console when it changes its state from Standby to Active.*

```
R2#
02:13:27: %STANDBY-6-STATECHANGE: Standby: 10: Ethernet0 state
Standby    -> Active
```

If we check the output of the command **show interfaces Ethernet 0**, it now indicates that the interface MAC address is equal to the virtual MAC address. In other words, to become the active router, router R2 had to make the interface MAC address equal to the virtual MAC address.

Listing 7.62 *The output of the command **show interfaces Ethernet 0** indicates that the router changed the MAC address of the interface to the value of the virtual MAC address.*

```
R2#show interfaces Ethernet 0
Ethernet0 is up, line protocol is up
  Hardware is Lance, address is 0000.0c07.ac0a (bia
00e0.b064.30a9)
  ...
```

Of course, this only happens if the interface hardware requires it.

7. Special Cases Of Routing

Let's now examine how long it takes the routers to switch over the virtual MAC and IP address to the new active router. To do this, I used a simple **perl** script that ran the command **ping** with the specified IP address—10.2.0.120, host H2's IP address—every second and displayed its output. (The **perl** script itself can be found in Appendix D.)

Listing 7.63 shows the output of the **perl** script and the command **ping 10.2.0.120** entered on host H1.

Listing 7.63   *The output of the command **ping 10.2.0.120** executed on host H1 from within the **perl** script, which also printed the time when the command was executed.*

```
C:\>perl tping.pl 10.2.0.120
[41:25] Reply from 10.2.0.120: bytes=32 time=10ms TTL=126
[41:26] Reply from 10.2.0.120: bytes=32 time=10ms TTL=126
[41:27] Reply from 10.2.0.120: bytes=32 time=10ms TTL=126
[41:28] Reply from 10.2.0.120: bytes=32 time=10ms TTL=126
[41:30] Request timed out.
[41:32] Request timed out.
[41:34] Request timed out.
[41:36] Request timed out.
[41:37] Reply from 10.2.0.120: bytes=32 time=10ms TTL=126
[41:38] Reply from 10.2.0.120: bytes=32 time=10ms TTL=126
[41:39] Reply from 10.2.0.120: bytes=32 time=10ms TTL=126
[41:40] Reply from 10.2.0.120: bytes=32 time=10ms TTL=126
[41:41] Reply from 10.2.0.120: bytes=32 time=10ms TTL=126
```

As the output shows, the default router was not available for only four seconds.

NOTE: *The timeout can also depend on the routing protocol convergence time. Even if the standby router has already taken over the virtual MAC and IP addresses, the routing protocol can still be converging.*

If we restore router R1, we may not see any timeout (see Listing 7.64). This happens because the previous active router supersedes the current active router; therefore, one of these routers is available all the time.

Listing 7.64   *The **perl** script executing the command **ping 10.2.0.120** was started, and router R1 was then made available. As the output shows, no timeout was detected when router R1 became the active router.*

```
C:\>perl tping.pl 10.2.0.120
[46:03] Reply from 10.2.0.120: bytes=32 time=20ms TTL=126
```

```
[46:04] Reply from 10.2.0.120: bytes=32 time=10ms TTL=126
[46:05] Reply from 10.2.0.120: bytes=32 time=10ms TTL=126
[46:06] Reply from 10.2.0.120: bytes=32 time=11ms TTL=126
[46:07] Reply from 10.2.0.120: bytes=32 time=10ms TTL=126
[46:08] Reply from 10.2.0.120: bytes=32 time=10ms TTL=126
[46:09] Reply from 10.2.0.120: bytes=32 time=10ms TTL=126
[46:10] Reply from 10.2.0.120: bytes=32 time=10ms TTL=126
[46:11] Reply from 10.2.0.120: bytes=32 time=10ms TTL=126
[46:12] Reply from 10.2.0.120: bytes=32 time=10ms TTL=126
[46:13] Reply from 10.2.0.120: bytes=32 time=10ms TTL=126
[46:14] Reply from 10.2.0.120: bytes=32 time=10ms TTL=126
[46:15] Reply from 10.2.0.120: bytes=32 time=10ms TTL=126
[46:16] Reply from 10.2.0.120: bytes=32 time=10ms TTL=126
```

Using MHSRP For Load Balancing

Using two routers just to back up each other is a waste of routing resources. However, using the same two routers to share the load of traffic requested by the local hosts is an efficient utilization of resources.

This sharing of resources can be addressed by modifying the basic HSRP configuration (to what is sometimes called *Multigroup HSRP* or *MHSRP*). The idea behind MHSRP is simple. If two routes are configured with two standby groups on the same interfaces, the first router can be active for the first group and the second router can be active for the second group. Obviously, the two groups can be only used to back up two IP addresses. Therefore, the local hosts should be divided into two groups: The first group must use the first IP address; the second group, the second IP address. Thus, the first group of hosts sends all outbound traffic to the first router, and the second group sends all outbound traffic to the second router.

The steps that must be taken to configure MHSRP on a router remain the same as in basic HSRP configuration. The only difference is that these steps must be taken for each standby group configured on the same interface.

Let's see how the routers from Figure 7.6 should be configured for MHSRP to provide two redundant default routers for hosts H1 and H2. Host H1 uses the first "redundant" IP address; host H2, the second IP address.

Listings 7.65 and 7.66 show the configurations of routers R1 and R2. Router R3's configuration remains exactly the same as in the previous section.

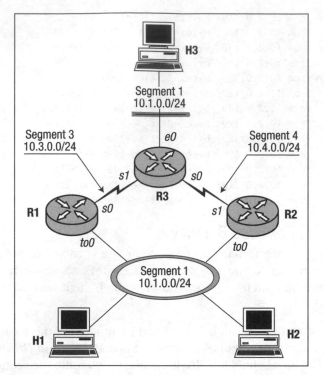

Figure 7.6   Routers R1 and R2 perform load balancing by being configured for two standby groups. Router R1 is the primary router in the first group, and router R2 is the primary router in the second group.

Listing 7.65   Router R1's configuration.

```
interface Serial0
 ip address 10.3.0.1 255.255.255.0

interface TokenRing0
 ip address 10.1.0.3 255.255.255.0
 no ip redirects
 ring-speed 16
 standby 1 priority 100
 standby 1 preempt
 standby 1 ip 10.1.0.1
 standby 1 track Serial0 50
 standby 2 priority 80
 standby 2 preempt
 standby 2 ip 10.1.0.2

router eigrp 1
 network 10.0.0.0
```

Listing 7.66   Router R2's configuration.

```
interface Serial1
 ip address 10.4.0.1 255.255.255.0

interface TokenRing0
 ip address 10.1.0.4 255.255.255.0
 no ip redirects
 ring-speed 16
 standby 1 priority 80
 standby 1 preempt
 standby 1 ip 10.1.0.1
 standby 2 priority 100
 standby 2 preempt
 standby 2 ip 10.1.0.2
 standby 2 track Serial1 50

router eigrp 1
 network 10.0.0.0
```

Listings 7.67 and 7.68 show the outputs of the command **show standby** entered on routers R1 and R2. Notice that the command **show standby** now displays two standby groups for each router. Router R1 is the active router for group 1 and the standby router for group 2, whereas router R2 is the active router for group 2 and the standby router for group 1.

Listing 7.67   The output of the command *show standby*.

```
R1#show standby
TokenRing0 - Group 1
  Local state is Active, priority 100, may preempt
  Hellotime 3 holdtime 10
  Next hello sent in 00:00:00.000
  Hot standby IP address is 10.1.0.1 configured
  Active router is local
  Standby router is 10.1.0.4 expired
  Standby virtual mac address is c000.0002.0000
  Tracking interface states for 1 interface, 1 up:
    Up   Serial0 Priority decrement: 50
TokenRing0 - Group 2
  Local state is Standby, priority 80, may preempt
  Hellotime 3 holdtime 10
  Next hello sent in 00:00:02.486
  Hot standby IP address is 10.1.0.2 configured
  Active router is 10.1.0.4 expires in 00:00:08
  Standby router is local
  Standby virtual mac address is c000.0004.0000
```

Listing 7.68   The output of the command show standby.

```
R2#show standby
TokenRing0 - Group 1
  Local state is Standby, priority 80, may preempt
  Hellotime 3 holdtime 10
  Next hello sent in 00:00:01.268
  Hot standby IP address is 10.1.0.1 configured
  Active router is 10.1.0.3 expires in 00:00:09
  Standby router is local
  Standby virtual mac address is c000.0002.0000
TokenRing0 - Group 2
  Local state is Active, priority 100, may preempt
  Hellotime 3 holdtime 10
  Next hello sent in 00:00:00.496
  Hot standby IP address is 10.1.0.2 configured
  Active router is local
  Standby router is 10.1.0.3 expired
  Standby virtual mac address is c000.0004.0000
  Tracking interface states for 1 interface, 1 up:
     Up    Serial1 Priority decrement: 50
```

Listings 7.69 and 7.70 show the output of the command **show interfaces TokenRing 0** entered on routers R1 and R2. Notice that now the interface hardware allows the routers to use different virtual and interface MAC addresses.

Listing 7.69   The output of the command show interfaces TokenRing 0 entered on router R1.

```
R1#show interfaces TokenRing 0
TokenRing0 is up, line protocol is up
  Hardware is TMS380, address is 0007.0d26.0a46
(bia 0007.0d26.0a46)
...
```

Listing 7.70   The output of the command show interfaces TokenRing 0 entered on router R2.

```
R2#show interfaces TokenRing 0
TokenRing0 is up, line protocol is up
  Hardware is TMS380, address is 0007.0d26.0c15
(bia 0007.0d26.0c15)
...
```

Configuring Dial-On-Demand Routing (DDR)

The following two sections describe the two most typical DDR solutions: *snapshot routing* and *dial backup*.

Configuring Snapshot Routing

Snapshot routing is an "economical" DDR solution. Snapshot routing allows you to use a distance vector routing protocol to establish dynamic routing over dialup connections while preventing the dialup lines from being brought up every time the routing protocol needs to send a routing update over them.

Snapshot routing defines two periods: *active* and *quiet*. The routing protocol is allowed to bring up the dialup line only during the active periods. During the quiet periods, the dynamic routing protocol must rely on the information it learned during the last active period. The data traffic, however, is allowed to bring up the dialup line regardless of which period the corresponding dialer interface is currently in. If the line was brought up by the used data traffic, the routing protocol may also perform exchange of routing updates.

Normally, the active period is rather short—about 5 to 10 minutes. The quiet period can be rather long—for example, 12 hours.

Snapshot routing configurations involve two types of routers: *snapshot servers* and *snapshot clients*. Snapshot clients perform dialing during the active periods; snapshot servers don't. Normally, snapshot clients are the routers connecting remote stub networks to the central site via dialup lines. Snapshot servers are usually located at the central "hub" site to which snapshot clients dial.

Snapshot routing only supports RIP Versions 1 and 2 and IGRP. Thus, if you need to deploy classless routing in conjunction with snapshot routing, your only choice is RIP Version 2.

Configuring snapshot routing consists of the following steps:

1. Configure the snapshot client using the command **snapshot client** *<active time> <quiet time>* in the dialer interface configuration mode (an example of the dialer interface is an ISDN BRI interface). The *<active time>* and *<quiet time>* parameters are numeric values specifying the active and quiet times, respectively, in minutes. The *<active time>* parameter can range from 5 to 100, and the *<quiet time>* parameter can range from 8 to 100,000.

2. Enable the snapshot client router to call the snapshot server router using the command **dialer map snapshot** *<seq #> <dial string>*. The *<seq #>* parameter is a numeric value uniquely identifying the dialer map. It can range from 1 to 254, inclusive. The *<dial string>* parameter is the dial string that the dialer interface should use to connect to the snapshot server router.

3. Configure the snapshot server router using the command **snapshot server** *<active time>*. The *<active time>* parameter is a numeric value specifying the active time in minutes. It can range from 5 to 100.

An example of a network that may benefit from snapshot routing is shown in Figure 7.7. The routers use RIP Version 2 throughout the network.

Listings 7.71 through 7.74 show the configurations of all four routers. Only routers R2 and R3 have snapshot routing-specific configuration commands, which are shown using italicized text.

Listing 7.71   Router R1's configuration.

```
interface Ethernet0
 ip address 10.0.1.1 255.255.255.0

interface Serial0
 ip address 10.255.0.5 255.255.255.252

router rip
 version 2
 network 10.0.0.0
```

Listing 7.72   Router R2's configuration.

```
username R3 password 0 cisco
isdn switch-type basic-ni

interface Ethernet0
 ip address 10.0.2.1 255.255.255.0
```

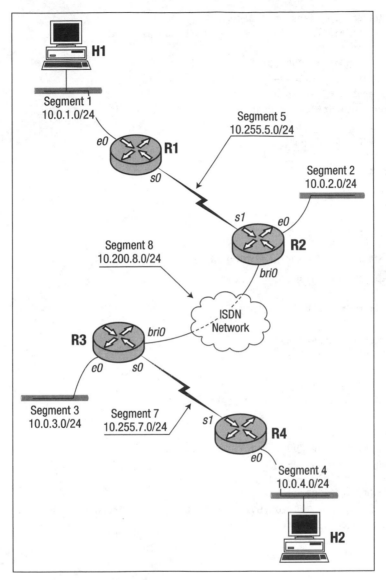

Figure 7.7   Routers R2 and R3 are configured for snapshot routing to provide overall network connectivity.

```
interface Serial1
 ip address 10.255.0.6 255.255.255.252

interface BRI0
 ip address 10.200.8.1 255.255.255.0
 encapsulation ppp
```

```
dialer map snapshot 1 384020
dialer map ip 10.200.8.2 name R3 broadcast 384020
dialer-group 1
isdn spid1 3840000001
isdn spid2 3840000002
snapshot client 5 20
ppp authentication chap

router rip
 version 2
 network 10.0.0.0

ip classless

dialer-list 1 protocol ip permit
```

Listing 7.73   Router R3's configuration.

```
username R2 password 0 cisco

isdn switch-type basic-ni1

interface Ethernet0
 ip address 10.0.3.1 255.255.255.0

interface Serial0
 ip address 10.255.0.14 255.255.255.252

interface BRI0
 ip address 10.200.8.2 255.255.255.0
 encapsulation ppp
 isdn spid1 3840200001
 isdn spid2 3840200002
 dialer map ip 10.200.8.1 name R2 broadcast 384000
 dialer-group 1
 snapshot server 5
 ppp authentication chap

router rip
 version 2
 network 10.0.0.0

dialer-list 1 protocol ip permit
```

Listing 7.74   Router R4's configuration.

```
interface Ethernet0
 ip address 10.0.4.1 255.255.255.0
```

```
interface Serial1
 ip address 10.255.0.13 255.255.255.252

router rip
 version 2
 network 10.0.0.0
```

After dynamic routing is stabilized, the routing tables of the routers should look the same, regardless of the current state of snapshot routing. Listing 7.75 shows the contents of router R4's routing table.

Listing 7.75   The routing table of router R4.

```
R4#show ip route
...
     10.0.0.0/8 is variably subnetted, 8 subnets, 3 masks
R     10.0.2.0/24 [120/2] via 10.255.0.14, 00:00:04, Serial1
R     10.0.3.0/24 [120/1] via 10.255.0.14, 00:00:04, Serial1
R     10.0.1.0/24 [120/3] via 10.255.0.14, 00:00:04, Serial1
C     10.0.4.0/24 is directly connected, Ethernet0
R     10.200.8.0/24 [120/1] via 10.255.0.14, 00:00:04, Serial1
R     10.200.8.1/32 [120/1] via 10.255.0.14, 00:00:04, Serial1
R     10.255.0.4/30 [120/2] via 10.255.0.14, 00:00:04, Serial1
C     10.255.0.12/30 is directly connected, Serial1
```

Notice that router R4 has routes for all segments of the network.

A useful command that allows you to check the state of snapshot routing is **show snapshot**, which produces slightly different results on snapshot clients and servers. (Regardless of the IOS version, the output of the command seems to carry the same misprint that probably happened quite a while ago—a line break is obviously missing in the first line between the words **up** and **Snapshot**.)

Listings 7.76 and 7.77 show the outputs of this command entered on routers R2 and R3, respectively. The output of the command is fairly self-explanatory.

*Listing 7.76   The output of the command **show snapshot** entered on router R2.*

```
R2#show snapshot
BRI0 is up, line protocol is upSnapshot client line state
down
 Length of active period:          5 minutes
 Length of quiet period:           20 minutes
 Length of retry period:           8 minutes
  Current state: active, remaining/exchange time: 3/2 minutes
  Updates received this cycle: ip
```

*Listing 7.77   The output of the command **show snapshot** entered on router R3.*

```
R3#show snapshot
BRIO is up, line protocol is upSnapshot server line state up
  Length of active period:          5 minutes
   For ip address: 10.200.8.1
    Current state: active, remaining time: 1 minute
```

Configuring Dial Backup

Dial backup is a powerful and very useful solution. Two routers connected via a dedicated link, such as a T1 connection, use a dialup link if the dedicated link fails.

To configure dial backup, follow these steps:

1. In the interface configuration mode of the interface to be backed up, enter the command **backup interface** <*Dialer Interface*>. The <*Dialer Interface*> parameter specifies the dialer interface that must be used if the backed-up interface fails.

2. Using the command **backup delay** <*enable delay*> <*disable delay*> in the backed-up interface configuration mode, define how quickly the backup interface must kick in when the backed-up interface fails and how quickly it should go down after the backed-up interface is restored. Both parameters are numeric values measured in seconds, which can range from 0 to 4294967294 or take the value **never**. If the latter value is used as the <*enable delay*> parameter, the backup interface is never brought up. If it used as the <*disable delay*>, the backup interface once being brought up remains up forever or until it is manually disconnected.

The dial backup configuration relies on correct dialer configuration. However, the dialer configurations used for regular DDR and for dialer backup are different. Using regular dialer interface configuration guidelines to configure dial backup interfaces can result in nonworking configurations or superfluous expenses associated with unnecessary dialing. Following is the list of "tips and tricks" that can help you perform "cleaner" dial backup configurations:

- Dial backup configuration must be performed only on one of two routers. The counterpart router must have a regular DDR configuration.

- The counterpart router should not have any interesting traffic defined. Otherwise, it tries to bring the dialer interface up each time interesting traffic needs to cross the dialup connection. You still must have the **dialer-group** *<gr #>* command under the dialer interface configuration. It is also a good idea to define explicitly that all traffic is *uninteresting* by using the command **dialer-list** *<gr #>* **protocol ip deny**.

- Define a very long idle timeout on the dialer interface of the counterpart router. Because no traffic is interesting and idle timeout is 120 seconds by default, the counterpart router will be disconnecting its dialer interface every 3 minutes during the period the backup connection is up if the default idle timeout value is used.

- Check the workability of the dialup connection before adding the dial backup specific commands. It may be more difficult to troubleshoot misconfigurations associated with authentication, dialer strings, and so on after the backup commands are put in place. Pay special attention to authentication commands, such as **username** *<router name>* **password** *<passwd>*. Depending on the authentication method used (CHAP or PAP), this command may require identical passwords on the routers involved.

Let's see how dial backup can be used in the network example shown in Figure 7.8. The different between this network and the one that we considered in the previous section is that routers R2 and R3 are now also connected with segment 6. Segment 6 is the main link, and the dialup segment 8 is supposed to back it up.

Listings 7.78 through 7.81 show the configurations of all four routers. The portions of the configurations for routers R2 and R3 that are specific to dial backup are shown using italicized text.

Listing 7.78   Router R1's configuration.

```
interface Ethernet0
 ip address 10.0.1.1 255.255.255.0

interface Serial0
 ip address 10.255.0.5 255.255.255.252

router eigrp 10
 network 10.0.0.0
```

Listing 7.79   Router R2's configuration.

```
username R3 password 0 cisco

isdn switch-type basic-ni
```

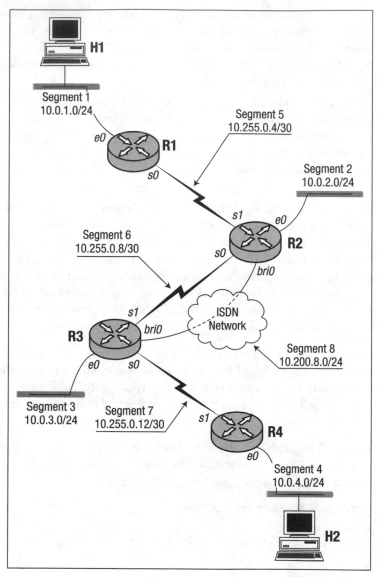

Figure 7.8   Routers R2 and R3 can use segment 8, an ISDN BRI connection, to back up segment 6.

```
interface Ethernet0
 ip address 10.0.2.1 255.255.255.0

interface Serial0
 ip address 10.255.0.9 255.255.255.252
 backup delay 3 20
 backup interface BRIO
```

```
interface Serial1
 ip address 10.255.0.6 255.255.255.252

interface BRI0
 ip address 10.200.8.1 255.255.255.0
 encapsulation ppp
 dialer map ip 10.200.8.2 name R3 broadcast 384020
 dialer-group 1
 isdn spid1 3840000001
 isdn spid2 3840000002
 ppp authentication chap

router eigrp 10
 network 10.0.0.0

dialer-list 1 protocol ip permit
```

Listing 7.80   Router R3's configuration.

```
username R2 password 0 cisco

isdn switch-type basic-ni1

interface Ethernet0
 ip address 10.0.3.1 255.255.255.0

interface Serial0
 ip address 10.255.0.14 255.255.255.252

interface Serial1
 ip address 10.255.0.10 255.255.255.252

interface BRI0
 ip address 10.200.8.2 255.255.255.0
 encapsulation ppp
 isdn spid1 3840200001
 isdn spid2 3840200002
 dialer idle-timeout 2147483
 dialer map ip 10.200.8.1 name R2 broadcast 384000
 dialer-group 1
 ppp authentication chap

router eigrp 10
 network 10.0.0.0

dialer-list 1 protocol ip deny
```

Listing 7.81   Router R4's configuration.

```
interface Ethernet0
 ip address 10.0.4.1 255.255.255.0

interface Serial1
 ip address 10.255.0.13 255.255.255.252

router eigrp 10
 network 10.0.0.0
```

To see how dial backup works when segment 6 fails, let's use the command **debug backup**. The output of this command entered on router R2 is shown in Listing 7.82. Remember, it only makes sense to use this command on router R2 as it is the only router that has dial backup specific commands. The router is also configured with the command **service timestamps debug uptime**. This command makes the router print the time elapsed since it was powered on and then the debug message. This enables us to see how fast the backup interface kicks in when the main interface fails.

*Listing 7.82   The output of the command **debug backup** on router R2 during which the serial link between routers R2 and R3 went down.*

```
02:23:18: %LINK-3-UPDOWN: Interface Serial0, changed state to
          down
02:23:18: BACKUP(Serial0): event = primary went down
02:23:18: BACKUP(Serial0): changed state to "waiting to
          backup"
02:23:19: %LINEPROTO-5-UPDOWN: Line protocol on Interface
          Serial0, changed state to down
02:23:21: BACKUP(Serial0): event = timer expired
02:23:21: %LINK-3-UPDOWN: Interface BRI0:1, changed state to
          down
02:23:21: %LINK-3-UPDOWN: Interface BRI0:2, changed state to
          down
02:23:21: BACKUP(Serial0): secondary interface (BRI0) made
          active
02:23:21: BACKUP(Serial0): changed state to "backup mode"
02:23:21: %LINK-3-UPDOWN: Interface BRI0, changed state to up
02:23:21: %ISDN-6-LAYER2UP: Layer 2 for Interface BR0, TEI 65
          changed to up
02:23:23: %ISDN-6-LAYER2UP: Layer 2 for Interface BR0, TEI 64
          changed to up
02:23:24: %LINK-3-UPDOWN: Interface BRI0:1, changed state to
          up
```

```
02:23:25: %LINEPROTO-5-UPDOWN: Line protocol on Interface
          BRIO:1, changed state to up
02:23:30: %ISDN-6-CONNECT: Interface BRIO:1 is now connected
          to 384020 R3
```

The router noticed that the main interface went down at 02:23:18. The router started to initiate the backup interface at 02:23:21. The difference between these two times is 3 seconds, which corresponds exactly to the time interval configured via the *<enable delay>* parameter.

If we try to **ping** host H1 from H2 continually during the dial backup operation, we will be unpleasantly surprised to find that the recovery actually takes longer than 3 seconds. Listing 7.83 shows the results of timed pinging of host H1 from host H2.

Listing 7.83   The results of timed pinging of host H1 from host H2.

```
C:\>perl tping.pl 10.0.1.120
[35:01] Reply from 10.0.1.120: bytes=32 time=30ms TTL=124
[35:02] Reply from 10.0.1.120: bytes=32 time=30ms TTL=124
[35:04] Request timed out.
[35:06] Request timed out.
[35:07] Reply from 10.0.4.1: Destination host unreachable.
[35:08] Reply from 10.0.4.1: Destination host unreachable.
[35:09] Reply from 10.0.4.1: Destination host unreachable.
[35:10] Reply from 10.0.4.1: Destination host unreachable.
[35:11] Reply from 10.0.4.1: Destination host unreachable.
[35:12] Reply from 10.0.4.1: Destination host unreachable.
[35:13] Reply from 10.0.4.1: Destination host unreachable.
[35:14] Reply from 10.0.4.1: Destination host unreachable.
[35:15] Reply from 10.0.4.1: Destination host unreachable.
[35:16] Reply from 10.0.4.1: Destination host unreachable.
[35:18] Request timed out.
[35:19] Reply from 10.0.1.120: bytes=32 time=40ms TTL=124
[35:20] Reply from 10.0.1.120: bytes=32 time=30ms TTL=124
```

The actual time interval during which the affected network segments are not accessible from segment 4 is around 16 seconds. The actual inaccessibility interval is longer than the time interval specified using the **backup delay** command because the routing protocol used to perform dynamic routing in the network has to reconverge over the backup connection, which previously was unavailable.

We used EIGRP, whose convergence time is short. It may take other protocols, especially RIP and IGRP, longer to reconverge over the backup connection. Thus, it is important to use either quickly converging routing protocols or static routing to achieve fast network availability if backup connection must be used.

Luckily, the reversed process—that is, disconnecting the backup link after the main link is recovered—may not introduce any connectivity delay because the two links can be set to run in parallel for some time. Again, this length of time depends on the convergence time of the dynamic routing protocol used. In our case, the dynamic routing protocol is EIGRP; therefore, the configured 20 seconds should be enough for EIGRP to reconverge, and the backup link can be brought down safely without introducing any interruption.

Chapter 8

IP Multicast Routing

If you need an immediate solution to:	See page:
Configuring PIM-DM	427
Configuring PIM-SM	433
Configuring PIM-SM And PIM-DM On The Same Interface Simultaneously	437
Configuring PIM-SM Over NBMA Networks	437

In Brief

In Chapter 1, I mentioned that a group of IP addresses, called *multicast* addresses, are used to address groups of hosts. It was also mentioned that the number of multicast addresses constitutes class D IP addresses. The high-order four bits of the first byte of the IP address equal to 1110 (in binary) denote multicast IP addresses. This produces a range of IP addresses, which in dotted decimal notation is 224.0.0.0 through 239.255.255.255.

As we know, some of these addresses are used for purposes other than those commonly perceived to be intended for multicast communications. For example, some routing protocols, such as EIGRP, OSPF, and RIP Version 2, use predefined multicast IP addresses to communicate with neighboring routers. This use of multicast addressing is perfectly justified. The hosts that are not interested in receiving routing updates receive none, while the involved routers are kept updated using the minimal possible number of packets per update—one.

The document that describes the preassigned multicast IP addresses is RFC 1700, *Assigned Numbers*. Some of the officially assigned multicast IP addresses are shown in Table 8.1.

NOTE: *Some of the documents referenced in Table 8.1 may have updated versions. Please check the RFC index.*

Table 8.1   Some of the officially assigned multicast IP addresses.

IP Address	Description	Associated RFC Document
224.0.0.0	Base Address (Reserved)	RFC 1112
224.0.0.1	All Systems on This Subnet	RFC 1112
224.0.0.2	All Routers on This Subnet	N/A
224.0.0.4	DVMRP Routers	RFC 1075
224.0.0.5	OSPF All Routers	RFC 2328
224.0.0.6	OSPF Designated Routers	RFC 2328
224.0.0.9	RIP2 Routers	N/A
224.0.0.10	IGRP Routers	N/A
224.0.1.1	NTP Network Time Protocol	RFC 1119

Basics Of Multicast Routing

Obviously, multicast IP routing must differ tremendously from regular unicast IP routing. As we remember, the IP unicast routing paradigm is routing based on the network part of the address. In the case of multicast IP addresses, this paradigm no longer works. The group of hosts addressed by a single multicast address can be spread among multiple IP networks. This means that the multicast IP address itself cannot be used to identify individual network segments and hosts. Therefore, some other logic must be applied when making routing decisions on how to route datagrams destined for multicast IP addresses.

Before considering available techniques of routing multicast IP traffic, let's familiarize ourselves with some other specific aspects of multicast routing.

Because of the nature of multicast IP addresses, they are often called *multicast groups* rather than *multicast addresses*, which is how they are referred to in this book.

In unicast IP routing, a host sending traffic to a certain destination in most cases also receives some traffic back from this destination. In multicast routing, this rule is broken quite often. Some hosts only send traffic to the group and do not expect any traffic back. Some hosts also only receive the traffic sent by somebody else to the group, but these hosts do not send anything to the group. The first type of hosts is, therefore, called a *sender* or *source*, whereas the latter is called a *receiver* or *member* of the group. Not surprisingly, the multicast routing often uses the knowledge of who is a sender and who is a member to optimize the delivery of multicast traffic across networks comprising multiple segments.

Mapping Multicast IP Addresses To MAC Addresses

Another important aspect of multicast routing is mapping multicast IP addresses to the Network Access Layer addresses. In multicast IP—even in LAN environments—ARP is no longer used to perform such mapping. Methods similar to ARP in multicast environments are undesirable for two reasons. First, a single ARP request, if it were used to perform mapping of a multicast IP address to MAC addresses, in most cases would cause multiple ARP replies, which would congest the segment. (In addition, there would also be issues with storing and using multiple MAC addresses corresponding to a single multicast IP address.) Second, and even more important, ARP does not provide for utilizing LAN media's built-in multicast addressing functionality.

As discussed in Chapter 2, the structure of the MAC addresses used in most LAN media includes a so-called *group bit*. This bit, being set in the destination MAC address, indicates that the address is a group address as opposed to an individual address. Hence, the multicast IP addresses are mapped to the MAC addresses whose group bit is set using the following rule: The low-order 23 bits of the multicast IP addresses are placed into the low-order 23 bits of MAC address 01-00-5E-00-00-00. (Obviously, the number of possible multicast IP addresses is larger than the number of MAC addresses producted by this rule. Thus, it is possible that two or more different multicast IP addresses can be mapped to a single MAC address. This should not create a problem.) Both Ethernet and FDDI support this mapping, although the order of the bits in the bytes constituting the MAC address must be reversed in the case of FDDI.

TokenRing MAC addressing could support this mapping, because TokenRing MAC addressing also defines the group bit in the same fashion as do Ethernet and FDDI MAC addressing. However, this mapping may not be possible because of the limitations of many existing TokenRing controller chips. There are two more possibilities. The first is to map all multicast IP addresses to the broadcast address, which must use all-rings broadcast in the presence of source-route bridging. The second possibility is to map all IP multicast addresses to a single TokenRing functional address, which for multicast IP is C0-00-00-04-00-00 in the TokenRing format. The latter is preferable; however, not all hosts support it. Hence, the hosts that support mapping of multicast IP addresses to the TokenRing functional address must also support mapping to the broadcast address.

NOTE: Functional TokenRing MAC address C0-00-00-04-00-00 is not dedicated to multicast IP. It may also be used by some other protocols.

Source-Based Trees

As mentioned before, unicast IP routing cannot be used to route IP datagrams destined for multicast IP addresses. One possibility is simply to flood such an IP datagram via all router interfaces except the one on which the datagram was received. However, such an approach is not acceptable. Flooding datagrams through all router interfaces may lead to enormous network congestion in the topologies with redundant paths. However, what if we first disable the redundant links and then flood the multicast traffic through the remaining links? This is very similar to spanning tree algorithms used in transparent bridging. Although this approach is feasible, it still suffers from one significant shortcoming—it does not utilize the redundant paths. This solution may be acceptable in bridged LAN environments where the bandwidth is normally plentiful, but it is often unsatisfactory in mixed media routing environments.

What if we create a separate spanning tree rooted at the source of multicast traffic instead of building a single multicast delivery spanning tree for the whole network? This approach is feasible from a multicast routing perspective for the same reason that a single spanning tree is. At the same time, it allows building an optimal multicast delivery tree for every source of multicast traffic. Such spanning trees are called *source-based trees*.

The way in which the source-based trees are built depends on a particular multicast routing protocol implementation. Normally, the procedure responsible for building source-based trees is referenced as a *topology discovery mechanism* or simply *topology discovery*. Interestingly enough, the topology discovery mechanism may or may not be a part of the multicast routing protocol itself. The topology discovery mechanism also provides sufficient information for a router to tell if the neighboring system, whether another router or a receiver, is upstream or downstream with respect to the source.

Multicast environments are more dynamic than unicast environments. As was already mentioned, the routing in unicast environments is performed based on the network portion of the IP address. The network portion or network prefix normally addresses a physical network—or a number of physical networks—if the network prefix is a summary address. Physical networks are not supposed to be created and then disappear often. Normally, such events are caused by either new network deployments or network components failures. In a multicast world, however, new hosts can join or leave multicast groups frequently. Therefore, topology discovery should address frequent group membership changes.

Group membership changes are handled using so-called *prune* and *join* messages. A router sends a prune message to the routers enroute to the source if it has no group members left and there are no downstream routers forwarding traffic for this group. The intermediate routers can also send prune messages toward the source if all of their downstream neighbors pruned themselves from the multicast group.

If, however, a certain member joins or rejoins the group for which the router has previously sent a prune message, the router sends a join message to restore the multicast traffic delivery.

The described multicast routing methodology lies in the basis of multicast routing protocols called *dense-mode* protocols. Many dense-mode protocols only use join messages when a receiver joins a group that has been previously pruned. If, however, a sender starts sending traffic to a multicast group, the routes simply flood the traffic to all downstream neighbors. If a certain neighbor does not have any active members, it prunes itself from the group using prune messages.

Shared Trees

Dense-mode protocols operate well in the multicast environments where the groups are widely represented or where the network bandwidth is not an issue. However, in environments where the multicast groups may be scattered sparsely, such as the Internet, dense-mode protocols may be quite inefficient. For such cases, a modification of source-based trees exists, called *shared trees*.

A source-based tree must be built for every source sending to a particular group. Contrary to that, a single shared tree is built for a group, and this shared tree is used to forward traffic from every source sending to this group.

Source-based trees are rooted at the sources of multicast traffic. Shared trees are rooted at routers, which are called *rendezvous points*. Therefore, the multicast traffic from every source must first be sent to the rendezvous point, from which it is distributed among the members of the group using the shared tree. At any given time, only a single rendezvous point can exist for a particular multicast group.

Shared trees create a basis for the multicast routing protocols called *sparse-mode* protocols. Unlike dense-mode protocols, sparse-mode protocols allow the groups to be distributed in the network in a more sparse way. (The "official" definition of "more sparse way" is rather vague. For more information on which groups have to be considered "sparse groups," see the documentation referenced at the end of the "In Brief" section of this chapter.) In addition to shared trees, sparse-mode protocols require explicit join messages from members of a group, which are propagated between the routers toward the rendezvous point. If a join message is not received from a certain router for a certain multicast group, the traffic destined for this group is not sent to the router.

Multicast Routing Table

Routers, when making multicast routing decisions, use a data structure called a *multicast routing table*. The multicast routing table consists of entries containing the multicast group, the incoming interface, the list of outgoing interfaces, and some other fields.

If an entry represents a multicast group routing that is performed using a source-based tree, the entry also contains the IP address of the source. Such entries are often denoted as *(S,G)*, where *S* is for source and *G* is for group and are called *source-specific*. If an entry represents a group routing that is performed using a shared tree, the source is not contained in the entry. Such entries are often denoted as *(*,G)*, where the asterisk, like a wildcard, reflects the fact that the tree is shared. Hence, (*,G) entries are called *wildcard entries*.

Reverse Path Forwarding Algorithm

Regardless of which type of tree is used to forward multicast traffic, routers always use a procedure called a *reverse path forwarding (RPF) algorithm* when making routing decisions.

The reverse path forwarding algorithm can be defined as follows:

- The algorithm defines an interface that is used to forward unicast traffic to the source in the case of source-based trees, or the rendezvous point in the case of shared trees, as the *RPF interface*.

- If a datagram arrives on an RPF interface, it is forwarded via the interfaces listed as outgoing interfaces in the multicast routing table entry for that group.

- If a datagram arrives on a non-RPF interface, it is silently dropped.

Existing IP Multicast-Related Protocols

Although IP multicast routing is still under development, some protocols already exist, and many of them are implemented in the Cisco IOS. The following sections provide a brief description of most well-known multicast-related protocols currently available.

Internet Group Management Protocol (IGMP)

One of the most important is *Internet Group Management Protocol (IGMP)*. Currently, IGMP exists in two versions—Versions 1 and 2—IGMP Version 3 is under development.

The main purpose of IGMP is to provide routers with the ability to monitor members of multicast groups on the segments to which the routers have direct connections. Routers use IGMP to query the status of the groups' members periodically. IGMP helps the routers determine that there are no members left belonging to a particular group and that it is time to start sending prune messages. Likewise, the members announce that they join or leave a certain group by sending appropriate IGMP messages.

IGMP Version 1 is documented in RFC 1112, whose status is an Internet standard. IGMP Version 2 is documented in RFC 2236, whose status is a proposed Internet standard.

Protocol Independent Multicast-Dense Mode (PIM-DM)

Protocol Independent Multicast Dense Mode (PIM-DM) is a dense-mode multicast routing protocol. It is called *protocol independent* because it does not have its own topology discovery mechanism. Instead, PIM-DM relies on the unicast routing protocols running in parallel with PIM-DM and on a reverse path forwarding algorithm when making multicast routing decisions.

PIM-DM routers with no local members of a certain group and no downstream neighbor routers prune themselves from that group by means of prune messages. The neighbors that receive the prune messages stop sending multicast traffic destined for this group to the routers that sent the prune messages. The pruned messages are not sent regularly. The routers receiving the prune messages start a timer. When the timer expires, the routers resume sending the multicast traffic destined for the pruned group to the routers that sent the prune messages. This is called the *broadcast and prune cycle*, which is typical for dense mode protocols.

PIM-DM utilizes "hello" messages to discover and monitor neighbors.

The details of PIM-DM are documented in the *Protocol Independent Multicast Version 2 Dense Mode Specification*. This draft document is available on the Internet at www.ietf.org/ids.by.wg/pim.html.

Protocol Independent Multicast-Sparse Mode (PIM-SM)

Protocol Independent Multicast Sparse Mode (PIM-SM) is more like a separate multicast routing protocol than a modification of PIM-DM. Still, PIM-SM shares many features with PIM-DM. Like PIM-DM, PIM-SM also does not have a built-in topology discovery mechanism and relies on existing unicast routing protocols and the reverse path forwarding algorithm (namely, its modification for shared trees) when making forwarding decisions.

Following are the key features of PIM-SM:

- Creates a single shared tree for each multicast group. The tree is rooted at the rendezvous point.

- Creates source-based trees for sources whose data traffic rate justifies it.

- Requires explicit join messages in order to pass the traffic toward the member. PIM-SM routers propagate the join messages that they receive from a member toward the rendezvous point of the corresponding group.

The details of PIM-SM are documented in RFC 2362, *Protocol Independent Multicast-Sparse Mode (PIM-SM): Protocol Specification*. The status of this RFC is an experimental Internet protocol.

Other Multicast Routing Protocols

The protocols discussed so far are fully implemented in the Cisco IOS. There are two more popular multicast routing protocols, one of which is partially implemented in Cisco IOS, and the other one is not implemented at all. These protocols are Distance Vector Multicast Routing Protocol (DVMPR) and Multicast Extensions to OSPF (MOSPF).

DVMPR is an experimental protocol that was designed for and implemented in the experimental Internet multicast backbone called *MBONE*. Cisco routers provide enough DVMPR functionality to interoperate with DVMPR routers. DVMPR is documented in RFC 1075, *Distance Vector Multicast Routing Protocol*.

MOSPF is documented in RFC 1584, *Multicast Extensions to OSPF*.

There are some additional multicast routing related protocols that are beyond the scope of our discussion in this book.

Immediate Solutions

This section gives only basic configuration guidelines for configuring multicast routing on Cisco routers. A comprehensive discussion of multicast routing configuration would require several chapters and go beyond pure IP routing, which is the subject of the book. Still, the introduction presented here provides a good start toward understanding how multicast routing works and how to configure it on the Cisco routers.

NOTE: As you have already noticed, **ping** is one of the most important tools used throughout this book to verify if routing works. Unfortunately, pure **ping** is not very helpful for verifying whether multicast routing works.

Because I wasn't able to find anything similar to **ping** in terms of simplicity and clarity of the results, I created my own application, called MCASTER. I will use MCASTER as a testing tool in this chapter.

MCASTER runs on Windows NT based computers (however, it does not work under Windows 95). MCASTER can join a specified multicast group and receive multicast UDP-encapsulated packets similar to those of **ping** and send packets to the same group from the same UDP number. It allows you to assign the multicast group address, UDP port, and some other parameters.

Figure 8.1 shows the main window of MCASTER and explains the most important elements of it. I tried to design MCASTER to be as user friendly and easy to use as possible. MCASTER is absolutely free and is available from www.hugewave.com/blacktools. I will gladly accept any bug reports and improvement recommendations.

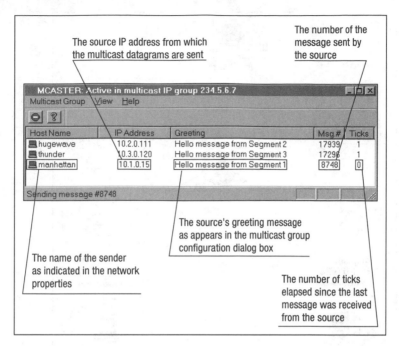

The source IP address from which
the multicast datagrams are sent

The number of the
message sent by
the source

```
MCASTER: Active in multicast IP group 234.5.6.7          _ □ ×
Multicast Group   View   Help
 ⊝  ?
 Host Name        IP Address    Greeting                        Msg.#   Ticks
 🖳 hugewave       10.2.0.111    Hello message from Segment 2    17939   1
 🖳 thunder        10.3.0.120    Hello message from Segment 3    17296   1
 🖳 manhattan      10.1.0.15     Hello message from Segment 1    8748    0
 Sending message #8748
```

The source's greeting message
as appears in the multicast group
configuration dialog box

The name of the sender
as indicated in the network
properties

The number of ticks
elapsed since the last
message was received
from the source

Figure 8.1   A snapshot of the MCASTER application window.

Configuring PIM-DM

Configuring PIM-DM is easy. You only have to enable PIM-DM on the interfaces you wish to participate in multicast routing using the command **ip pim dense-mode**. This command automatically enables IGMP on the same interface.

WARNING!   The nature of PIM (both DM and SM) requires correct unicast routing in the area serviced by PIM.

To understand how to configure PIM-DM and how it works, let's consider the network example shown in Figure 8.2.

Listings 8.1 through 8.3 show the configurations of all four routers. Notice that EIGRP is the unicast routing protocol used along with PIM-DM.

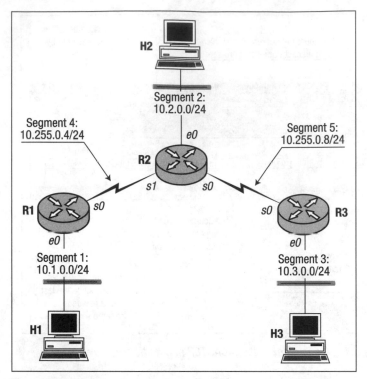

Figure 8.2   The routers are configured for PIM-DM to allow the hosts to communicate via multicast IP.

Listing 8.1   Router R1's configuration.

```
ip multicast-routing

interface Ethernet0
 ip address 10.1.0.1 255.255.255.0
 ip pim dense-mode

interface Serial0
 ip address 10.255.0.6 255.255.255.252
 ip pim dense-mode

router eigrp 10
 network 10.0.0.0
```

Listing 8.2   Router R2's configuration.

```
ip multicast-routing

interface Ethernet0
 ip address 10.2.0.1 255.255.255.0
 ip pim dense-mode
```

```
interface Serial0
 ip address 10.255.0.9 255.255.255.252
 ip pim dense-mode

interface Serial1
 ip address 10.255.0.5 255.255.255.252
 ip pim dense-mode

router eigrp 10
 network 10.0.0.0
```

Listing 8.3   Router R3's configuration.

```
ip multicast-routing

interface Ethernet0
 ip address 10.3.0.1 255.255.255.0
 ip pim dense-mode

interface Serial1
 ip address 10.255.0.10 255.255.255.252
 ip pim dense-mode

router eigrp 10
 network 10.0.0.0
```

All three hosts are Windows NT machines, whose names are MAN-HATTAN (H1), HUGEWAVE (H2), and THUNDER (H3). All of them run MCASTER, configured to join multicast group 234.5.6.7 and to use UDP port 3456 to receive and send multicast traffic. The main window of MCASTER run on host H1 is shown in Figure 8.3.

As you can see, host H1 can see the other two hosts. You would see the same setup if you had a look at MCASTER run on the other hosts.

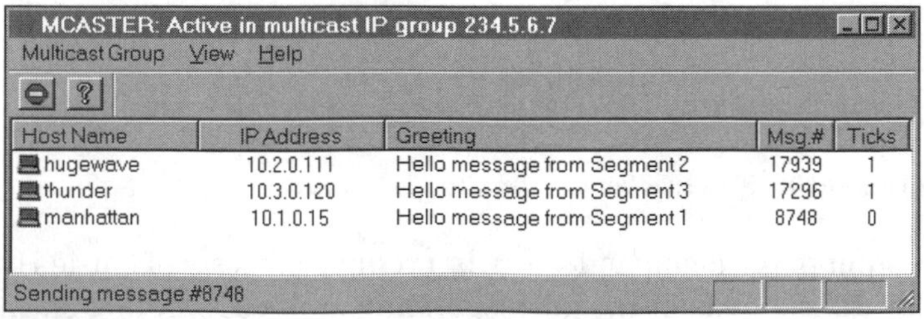

Figure 8.3   The snapshot of the MCASTER application window of host H1.

The command used to display the multicast routing table is **show ip mroute**, which is similar to **show ip route**. The output of this command entered on router R1 is shown in Listing 8.4.

Listing 8.4   The output of the command show ip mroute entered on router R1.

```
R1#show ip mroute
IP Multicast Routing Table
Flags: D-Dense, S-Sparse, C-Connected, L-Local, P-Pruned
       R-RP-bit set, F-Register flag, T-SPT-bit set, J-Join SPT
Timers: Uptime/Expires
Interface state: Interface, Next-Hop or VCD, State/Mode

(*, 224.0.1.40), 05:30:47/00:00:00, RP 0.0.0.0, flags: DJCL
  Incoming interface: Null, RPF nbr 0.0.0.0
  Outgoing interface list:
    Ethernet0, Forward/Dense, 05:30:47/00:00:00
    Serial0, Forward/Dense, 05:30:47/00:00:00

(*, 234.5.6.7), 05:30:47/00:02:59, RP 0.0.0.0, flags: DJC
  Incoming interface: Null, RPF nbr 0.0.0.0
  Outgoing interface list:
    Ethernet0, Forward/Dense, 02:29:40/00:00:00
    Serial0, Forward/Dense, 05:30:47/00:00:00

(10.1.0.15, 234.5.6.7), 02:29:39/00:02:59, flags: CT
  Incoming interface: Ethernet0, RPF nbr 0.0.0.0
  Outgoing interface list:
    Serial0, Forward/Dense, 02:29:39/00:00:00

(10.2.0.111, 234.5.6.7), 02:32:47/00:02:59, flags: CT
  Incoming interface: Serial0, RPF nbr 10.255.0.5
  Outgoing interface list:
    Ethernet0, Forward/Dense, 02:29:47/00:00:00

(10.3.0.120, 234.5.6.7), 02:32:46/00:02:59, flags: CT
  Incoming interface: Serial0, RPF nbr 10.255.0.5
  Outgoing interface list:
    Ethernet0, Forward/Dense, 02:29:47/00:00:00
```

The output of the command **show ip mroute** consists of entries that display the contents of the corresponding multicast routing entries. This includes the combination of the source and multicast group, which can be in either (S,G) or (*,G) formats, where *S* is the source's IP address and *G* is the multicast group address (multicast IP address). Further, this includes the incoming interface, the outgoing interfaces list, flags indicating whether the entry was created using dense- or sparse-mode protocol, plus some additional characteristics of entry and some other information.

Notice that although a wildcard routing entry (*,234.5.6.7) was created, its incoming interface is Null (which indicates that there is no incoming interface—it has nothing to do with the Null interface available on the Cisco routers). This is because a wildcard entry in a multicast routing table indicates that a shared tree is used for the group. As we know, PIM-DM does not use shared trees.

You can use the commands **debug ip igmp** to see the IGMP transactions and the command **debug ip pim** to see the PIM transactions.

TIP: *The command **debug ip pim** can be used for both PIM-DM and PIM-SM.*

Listing 8.5 shows the output of these two commands during which MCASTER running on host H1 (MANHATTAN, IP address 10.1.0.15) was stopped. When MCASTER is stopped, it sends out an IGMP message indicating that the host has left the multicast group.

Listing 8.5   *The output of the commands **debug ip igmp** and **debug ip pim** on router R1.*

```
R1#debug ip igmp
IGMP debugging is on
R1#debug ip pim
PIM debugging is on
R1#
PIM: Send v2 Hello on Serial0
IGMP: Received Leave from 10.1.0.15 (Ethernet0) for 234.5.6.7
IGMP: Send v2 Query on Ethernet0 to 234.5.6.7
IGMP: Send v2 Query on Ethernet0 to 234.5.6.7
PIM: Send v2 Hello on Ethernet0
IGMP: Deleting 234.5.6.7 on Ethernet0
PIM: Send v2 Prune on Serial0 to 10.255.0.5 for
  (10.2.0.111/32, 234.5.6.7)
PIM: Send v2 Prune on Serial0 to 10.255.0.5 for
  (10.3.0.120/32, 234.5.6.7)
PIM: Send v2 Prune on Serial0 to 10.255.0.5 for
  (10.2.0.111/32, 234.5.6.7)
PIM: Send v2 Prune on Serial0 to 10.255.0.5 for
  (10.3.0.120/32, 234.5.6.7)
```

Notice that after host H1 left the group, router R1 sent out several prune messages over the interface Serial 0, because host H1 was the only member of group 234.5.6.7.

8. Multicast Routing

Listing 8.6 shows the output of the command **show ip mroute** entered on router H1 after host H1 left the group and after router R1 pruned itself from the group. Notice that the entries pointing for the sources located on remote segments (that is, 10.2.0.111 and 10.3.0.120) now have flag *P* (prune) set.

Listing 8.6 *The output of the command **show ip mroute** after host H1 (MANHATTAN) left the multicast group.*

```
R1#show ip mroute
...
(*, 234.5.6.7), 05:35:08/00:02:58, RP 0.0.0.0, flags: DJ
  Incoming interface: Null, RPF nbr 0.0.0.0
  Outgoing interface list:
    Serial0, Forward/Dense, 05:35:08/00:00:00

(10.1.0.15, 234.5.6.7), 02:33:59/00:02:35, flags: T
  Incoming interface: Ethernet0, RPF nbr 0.0.0.0
  Outgoing interface list:
    Serial0, Forward/Dense, 02:33:59/00:00:00

(10.2.0.111, 234.5.6.7), 02:37:00/00:02:38, flags: PT
  Incoming interface: Serial0, RPF nbr 10.255.0.5
  Outgoing interface list: Null

(10.3.0.120, 234.5.6.7), 02:37:01/00:02:37, flags: PT
  Incoming interface: Serial0, RPF nbr 10.255.0.5
  Outgoing interface list: Null
```

To see what happens when host H1 rejoins the group, let's examine Listing 8.7, showing the output of the commands **debug ip igmp** and **debug ip pim** on router R1. Notice that now router R1 uses so-called *graft* messages, which are analogs of join messages, to speed up the process of reverting the pruned state of group 234.5.6.7 on router R1.

Listing 8.7 *The output of the commands **debug ip igmp** and **debug ip pim** on router R1 after host H1 (MANHATTAN) rejoined the multicast group.*

```
R1#debug ip igmp
IGMP debugging is on
R1#debug ip pim
PIM debugging is on
R1#
PIM: Received v2 Hello on Serial0 from 10.255.0.5
IGMP: Send v2 Query on Ethernet0 to 224.0.0.1
IGMP: Set report delay time to 3.0 seconds for 224.0.1.40
 on Ethernet0
```

```
IGMP: Received v2 Report from 10.1.0.15 (Ethernet0) for
  234.5.6.7
PIM: Building Graft message for 234.5.6.7, Ethernet0:
  no entries
PIM: Building Graft message for 234.5.6.7, Serial0:
      10.2.0.111/32 10.3.0.120/32
PIM: Send v2 Graft to 10.255.0.5 (Serial0)
PIM: Received v2 Graft-Ack on Serial0 from 10.255.0.5
      Group 234.5.6.7:
      10.2.0.111/32 10.3.0.120/32
```

Configuring PIM-SM

Configuring PIM-SM is not much more difficult than configuring PIM-DM. It consists of entering the command **ip pim sparse-mode** on the interfaces that are supposed to forward multicast IP traffic. It also involves configuring the rendezvous point IP address on the routers connecting leaf networks (the segments with members of multicast groups).

TIP: *You do not have to configure a router to be a rendezvous point. It will find it out automatically when you specify one of the router's IP addresses in the configurations of the (other) routers connected to leaf networks.*

To configure the rendezvous point address, use the command **ip pim rp-address** *<IP address>* [{*<AL number>*|*<AL name>*}]. The *<IP address>* parameter is the IP address of the rendezvous point. The optional parameter is the access-list, which can be used to limit this particular rendezvous point only to certain multicast groups. Only the multicast groups that pass the access-list with the **permit** result are serviced by this rendezvous point.

Let's consider the network topology shown in Figure 8.4. Suppose the routers must be configured for PIM-SM to provide overall multicast connectivity in the network infrastructure. The routers are configured with EIGRP as their unicast routing protocol and use loopback interfaces with IP addresses of 10.0.0.X/32, where X is the router number.

Let's make the Loopback 0 interface IP address of router R2 the rendezvous point for all possible multicast groups. Listings 8.8 through 8.11 show the configurations of all four routers.

8. Multicast Routing

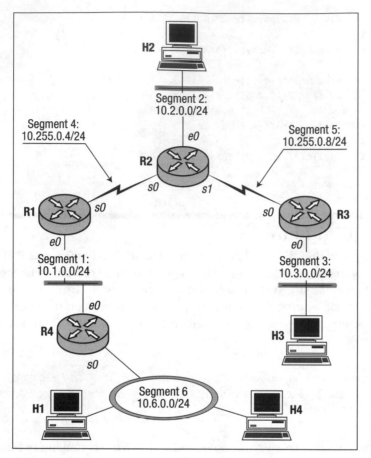

Figure 8.4   *The routers are configuring for PIM-SM to allow the hosts to communicate via IP multicast.*

Listing 8.8   Router R1's configuration.

```
ip multicast-routing

interface Loopback0
 ip address 10.0.0.1 255.255.255.255

interface Ethernet0
 ip address 10.1.0.1 255.255.255.0
 ip pim sparse-mode

interface Serial0
 ip address 10.255.0.6 255.255.255.252
 ip pim sparse-mode
```

```
router eigrp 10
 network 10.0.0.0
```

Listing 8.9   Router R2's configuration.

```
ip multicast-routing

interface Loopback0
 ip address 10.0.0.2 255.255.255.255

interface Ethernet0
 ip address 10.2.0.1 255.255.255.0
 ip pim sparse-mode

interface Serial0
 ip address 10.255.0.5 255.255.255.252
 ip pim sparse-mode

interface Serial1
 ip address 10.255.0.9 255.255.255.252
 ip pim sparse-mode

router eigrp 10
 network 10.0.0.0
```

Listing 8.10   Router R3's configuration.

```
ip multicast-routing

interface Loopback0
 ip address 10.0.0.3 255.255.255.255

interface Ethernet0
 ip address 10.3.0.1 255.255.255.0
 ip pim sparse-mode

interface Serial0
 ip address 10.255.0.10 255.255.255.252
 ip pim sparse-mode

router eigrp 10
 network 10.0.0.0

ip pim rp-address 10.0.0.2
```

Listing 8.11   Router R4's configuration.

```
ip multicast-routing

interface Loopback0
 ip address 10.0.0.4 255.255.255.255
```

```
interface Ethernet0
 ip address 10.1.0.2 255.255.255.0
 ip pim sparse-mode

interface TokenRing0
 ip address 10.6.0.1 255.255.255.0
 ip pim sparse-mode
 ring-speed 16

router eigrp 10
 network 10.0.0.0

ip pim rp-address 10.0.0.2
```

Listing 8.12 shows the output of the command **show ip mroute** entered on router R4. Notice that now the (*, 234.5.6.7) entry in the routing table has an incoming interface defined (Incoming interface: Ethernet0), is labeled as sparse (flags: S...) and has a defined rendezvous point (RP 10.0.0.2). This became possible because PIM-SM is used, and because of its sparse nature, uses shared trees.

Listing 8.12   The output of the command show ip mroute entered on router R4.

```
R4#show ip mroute
IP Multicast Routing Table
Flags: D-Dense, S-Sparse, C-Connected, L-Local, P-Pruned
    R-RP-bit set, F-Register flag, T - SPT-bit set, J-Join SPT
Timers: Uptime/Expires
Interface state: Interface, Next-Hop or VCD, State/Mode

(*, 224.0.1.40), 00:11:08/00:00:00, RP 10.0.0.2, flags: SJPCL
  Incoming interface: Ethernet0, RPF nbr 10.1.0.1
  Outgoing interface list: Null

(*, 234.5.6.7), 00:11:08/00:02:59, RP 10.0.0.2, flags: SJC
  Incoming interface: Ethernet0, RPF nbr 10.1.0.1
  Outgoing interface list:
    TokenRing0, Forward/Sparse, 00:11:08/00:02:23

(10.2.0.111, 234.5.6.7), 00:11:08/00:02:59, flags: CT
  Incoming interface: Ethernet0, RPF nbr 10.1.0.1
  Outgoing interface list:
    TokenRing0, Forward/Sparse, 00:11:08/00:02:23

(10.3.0.120, 234.5.6.7), 00:11:08/00:02:59, flags: CT
  Incoming interface: Ethernet0, RPF nbr 10.1.0.1
```

```
Outgoing interface list:
   TokenRing0, Forward/Sparse, 00:11:08/00:02:23

(10.6.0.10, 234.5.6.7), 00:11:09/00:02:59, flags: CT
  Incoming interface: TokenRing0, RPF nbr 0.0.0.0
  Outgoing interface list:
     Ethernet0, Forward/Sparse, 00:10:27/00:02:26

(10.6.0.15, 234.5.6.7), 00:11:09/00:02:59, flags: CT
  Incoming interface: TokenRing0, RPF nbr 0.0.0.0
  Outgoing interface list:
     Ethernet0, Forward/Sparse, 00:10:27/00:02:26
```

Configuring PIM-SM And PIM-DM On The Same Interface Simultaneously

By entering the commands **ip pim dense-mode** and **ip pim sparse-mode**, you assign the corresponding version of PIM on the interface as a whole. Sometimes, you may need to run PIM-DM for certain groups and PIM-SM for other groups. You can do this by using the command **ip pim sparse-dense-mode** instead of the two previous commands. If you use the command **ip pim sparse-dense-mode**, the routers use PIM-SM for all groups for which rendezvous points are available and PIM-DM for all other groups.

Thus, you can use this command in conjunction with the command **ip pim rp-address** *<IP address>* [{*<AL number>*|*<AL name>*}] on the routes connecting leaf networks. Using the access-list, you will define the groups whose traffic must be routed using PIM-SM or PIM-DM.

Configuring PIM-SM Over NBMA Networks

As usual, NBMA networks represent a special case even for multicast routing. If a router is connected to a non-fully meshed NBMA network using a single interface, it may need to use the same interface for forwarding transit traffic to the rest of the network. Normally, this is not possible because an outgoing interface cannot coincide with the incoming interface.

8. Multicast Routing

To make multicast routing possible in those situations, PIM-SM provides a so-called *NBMA mode*. In NBMA mode, PIM-SM can maintain separate outgoing interface lists for each neighbor accessible over the NBMA network.

To enable NBMA mode, use the command **ip pim nbma-mode** in the interface configuration mode of the interface connecting the router to the NBMA network.

Figure 8.5 shows a modified version of the network that we used to examine PIM-SM configuration. In this new version, router R2 is connected to two frame relay PVCs assigned to a single interface Serial 0. Thus, we have to use NBMA mode to restore the multicast communication in the network.

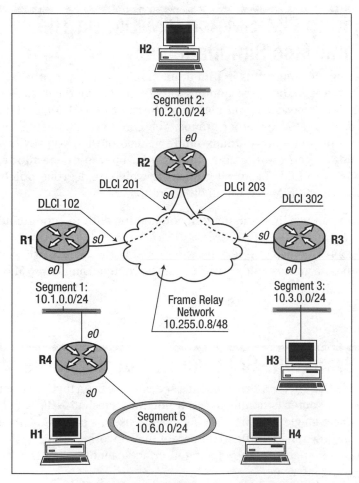

Figure 8.5   *Router R2 must take into account that it is connected to a non-fully meshed frame relay network.*

Let's configure all of the routers using the command **ip pim sparse-dense-mode** and run two instances of MCASTER—one for multicast group 234.5.6.7 and one for multicast group 234.9.9.9—on hosts H1, H2, and H3.

TIP: *If you decide to try this experiment, be sure to use a different UDP port for each of the two different groups.*

For group 234.5.6.7, we will define a rendezvous point using the command **ip pim rp-address 10.0.0.2 1**, where 10.0.0.2 is the IP address of router R2's Loopback 0 interface, and 1 is the number of the standard access-list that permits only group 234.5.6.7.

Thus, we conclude that PIM-SM is used for group 234.5.6.7 and PIM-DM is used for group 234.9.9.9.

Listings 8.13 through 8.16 show the configuration of all four routers.

Listing 8.13   Router R1's configuration.

```
ip multicast-routing

interface Loopback0
 ip address 10.0.0.1 255.255.255.255

interface Ethernet0
 ip address 10.1.0.1 255.255.255.0
 ip pim sparse-dense-mode

interface Serial0
 encapsulation frame-relay
 frame-relay lmi-type ansi

interface Serial0.1 point-to-point
 ip address 10.255.0.10 255.255.255.248
 ip pim sparse-dense-mode
 frame-relay interface-dlci 102

router eigrp 10
 network 10.0.0.0
```

Listing 8.14   Router R2's configuration.

```
ip dvmrp route-limit 20000

interface Loopback0
 ip address 10.0.0.2 255.255.255.255
```

```
interface Ethernet0
 ip address 10.2.0.1 255.255.255.0
 ip pim sparse-dense-mode

interface Serial0
 ip address 10.255.0.9 255.255.255.248
 ip pim nbma-mode
 ip pim sparse-dense-mode
 encapsulation frame-relay
 no ip split-horizon eigrp 10
 bandwidth 64
 frame-relay map ip 10.255.0.10 201 broadcast
 frame-relay map ip 10.255.0.11 203 broadcast
 frame-relay lmi-type ansi

router eigrp 10
 network 10.0.0.0
```

Listing 8.15   Router R3's configuration.

```
ip multicast-routing

interface Loopback0
 ip address 10.0.0.3 255.255.255.255

interface Ethernet0
 ip address 10.3.0.1 255.255.255.0
 ip pim sparse-dense-mode

interface Serial0
 encapsulation frame-relay
 frame-relay lmi-type ansi

interface Serial0.1 multipoint
 ip address 10.255.0.11 255.255.255.248
 ip pim sparse-dense-mode
 frame-relay map ip 10.255.0.9 302 broadcast

router eigrp 10
 network 10.0.0.0

ip pim rp-address 10.0.0.2 1

access-list 1 permit 234.5.6.7
```

Listing 8.16   Router R4's configuration.

```
ip multicast-routing

interface Loopback0
```

```
  ip address 10.0.0.4 255.255.255.255

interface Ethernet0
  ip address 10.1.0.2 255.255.255.0
  ip pim sparse-dense-mode

interface TokenRing0
  ip address 10.6.0.1 255.255.255.0
  ip pim sparse-dense-mode
  ring-speed 16

router eigrp 10
  network 10.0.0.0

ip pim rp-address 10.0.0.2 1

access-list 1 permit 234.5.6.7
```

Listing 8.17 shows the output of the command **show ip mroute** entered on router R4. Notice that now the multicast routing table contains a separate set of routing entries for group 234.5.6.7 and a separate set for group 234.9.9.9. Notice also that the wildcard entry (*,234.5.6.7) is labeled as established by PIM-SM (flags: S...), whereas the wildcard entry (*,234.9.9.9) is labeled as established by PIM-DM (flags: D...).

*Listing 8.17   The output of the command **show ip mroute** on router R4.*

```
R4#show ip mroute
IP Multicast Routing Table
Flags: D-Dense, S-Sparse, C-Connected, L-Local, P-Pruned
       R-RP-bit set, F-Register flag, T-SPT-bit set, J-Join SPT
Timers: Uptime/Expires
Interface state: Interface, Next-Hop or VCD, State/Mode

(*, 224.0.1.40), 00:33:02/00:00:00, RP 0.0.0.0, flags: DJCL
  Incoming interface: Null, RPF nbr 0.0.0.0
  Outgoing interface list:
    Ethernet0, Forward/Sparse-Dense, 00:33:02/00:00:00

(*, 234.9.9.9), 00:25:30/00:02:58, RP 0.0.0.0, flags: DJC
  Incoming interface: Null, RPF nbr 0.0.0.0
  Outgoing interface list:
    TokenRing0, Forward/Sparse-Dense, 00:22:49/00:00:00
    Ethernet0, Forward/Sparse-Dense, 00:25:30/00:00:00

(10.2.0.111, 234.9.9.9), 00:15:11/00:02:59, flags: CT
  Incoming interface: Ethernet0, RPF nbr 10.1.0.1
```

```
    Outgoing interface list:
      TokenRing0, Forward/Sparse-Dense, 00:15:11/00:00:00

(10.6.0.15, 234.9.9.9), 00:22:22/00:03:29, flags: CT
  Incoming interface: TokenRing0, RPF nbr 0.0.0.0
  Outgoing interface list:
    Ethernet0, Forward/Sparse-Dense, 00:22:23/00:00:00

(*, 234.5.6.7), 00:34:10/00:02:59, RP 10.0.0.2, flags: SJC
  Incoming interface: Ethernet0, RPF nbr 10.1.0.1
  Outgoing interface list:
    TokenRing0, Forward/Sparse-Dense, 00:34:10/00:02:07

(10.2.0.111, 234.5.6.7), 00:12:19/00:02:59, flags: CJT
  Incoming interface: Ethernet0, RPF nbr 10.1.0.1
  Outgoing interface list:
    TokenRing0, Forward/Sparse-Dense, 00:12:19/00:02:07

(10.3.0.120, 234.5.6.7), 00:34:10/00:02:59, flags: CT
  Incoming interface: Ethernet0, RPF nbr 10.1.0.1
  Outgoing interface list:
    TokenRing0, Forward/Sparse-Dense, 00:34:10/00:02:06

(10.6.0.10, 234.5.6.7), 00:01:32/00:01:57, flags: CT
  Incoming interface: TokenRing0, RPF nbr 0.0.0.0
  Outgoing interface list:
    Ethernet0, Forward/Sparse-Dense, 00:01:32/00:03:23

(10.6.0.15, 234.5.6.7), 00:21:40/00:03:29, flags: CT
  Incoming interface: TokenRing0, RPF nbr 0.0.0.0
  Outgoing interface list:
    Ethernet0, Forward/Sparse-Dense, 00:21:40/00:03:22
```

If we display the multicast routing table of router R2 (shown in List-ing 8.18), we'll notice that it now contains an entry with separate sets of outgoing interfaces for each neighbor.

Listing 8.18   The output of the command *show ip mroute* on router R2.

```
R2#show ip mroute
...
(*, 234.5.6.7), 00:01:11/00:02:59, RP 10.0.0.2, flags: S
 Incoming interface: Null, RPF nbr 0.0.0.0
 Outgoing interface list:
  Serial0, 10.255.0.11,Forward/Sparse-Dense,00:00:35/00:02:54
  Serial0, 10.255.0.10,Forward/Sparse-Dense,00:00:21/00:03:08
```

It becomes obvious that PIM-DM does not work over the non–fully meshed frame relay network, despite the presence of the command

ip pim nbma-mode in router R2's configuration, if we check the contents of the MCASTER applications running on the three hosts.

Figures 8.6 through 8.11 show the contents of the main window of MCASTER on the three hosts. The figures are grouped in pairs. The first pair (Figures 8.6 and 8.7) show the MCASTER windows for groups 234.5.6.7 and 234.9.9.9 on host H1 (MANHATTAN). Notice that although both groups have the same number of members (three), MCASTER for group 234.5.6.7 shows all three members, whereas MCASTER for group 234.9.9.9 shows only two. The latter does not display host H3 (THUNDER), which is behind the frame relay could. As we know, group 234.9.9.9 is served by PIM-DM; hence this is evidence that PIM-DM does not work over non-fully meshed NBMA networks.

The situation differs in the case of host H2 (HUGEWAVE). Host H2 can see all three members of both groups. The reason why it's possible is that host H2 is behind router R2, which is the only router that can accept traffic from both parts of the network, even though it is using PIM-DM.

The situation on host H3 (THUNDER) is very similar to that on host H1 (MANHATTAN). Host H3 cannot see host H1 in group 234.9.9.9.

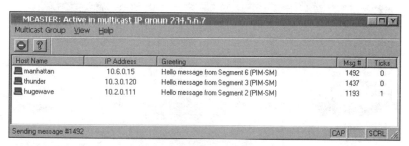

Figure 8.6   The MCASTER main window on host H1 (MANHATTAN) for group 234.5.6.7.

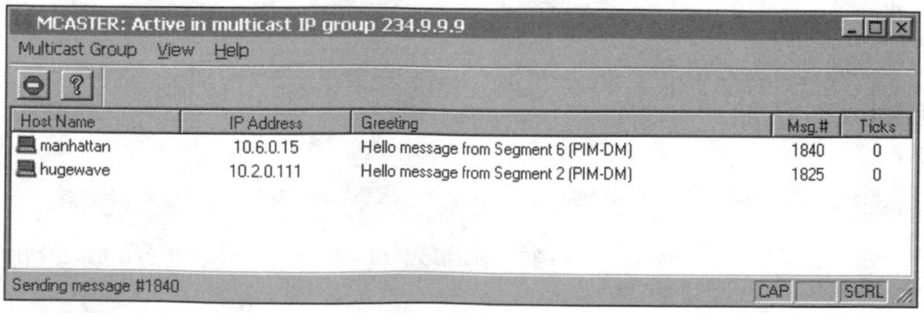

Figure 8.7   The MCASTER main window on host H1 (MANHATTAN) for group 234.9.9.9.

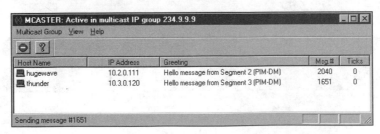

MCASTER: Active in multicast IP group 234.5.6.7

Multicast Group   View   Help

Host Name	IP Address	Greeting	Msg.#	Ticks
thunder	10.3.0.120	Hello message from Segment 3 (PIM-SM)	1669	0
manhattan	10.6.0.15	Hello message from Segment 6 (PIM-SM)	1723	1
hugewave	10.2.0.111	Hello message from Segment 2 (PIM-SM)	1424	1

Sending message #1425

Figure 8.8   The MCASTER main window on host H2 (HUGEWAVE) for group 234.5.6.7.

MCASTER: Active in multicast IP group 234.9.9.9

Multicast Group   View   Help

Host Name	IP Address	Greeting	Msg.#	Ticks
hugewave	10.2.0.111	Hello message from Segment 2 (PIM-DM)	1952	0
manhattan	10.6.0.15	Hello message from Segment 6 (PIM-DM)	1967	1
thunder	10.3.0.120	Hello message from Segment 3 (PIM-DM)	1563	1

Sending message #1952

Figure 8.9   The MCASTER main window on host H2 (HUGEWAVE) for group 234.9.9.9.

MCASTER: Active in multicast IP group 234.5.6.7

Multicast Group   View   Help

Host Name	IP Address	Greeting	Msg.#	Ticks
thunder	10.3.0.120	Hello message from Segment 3 (PIM-SM)	1746	0
manhattan	10.6.0.15	Hello message from Segment 6 (PIM-SM)	1800	1
hugewave	10.2.0.111	Hello message from Segment 2 (PIM-SM)	1501	1

Sending message #1746

Figure 8.10   The MCASTER main window on host H3 (THUNDER) for group 234.5.6.7.

MCASTER: Active in multicast IP group 234.9.9.9

Multicast Group   View   Help

Host Name	IP Address	Greeting	Msg.#	Ticks
hugewave	10.2.0.111	Hello message from Segment 2 (PIM-DM)	2040	0
thunder	10.3.0.120	Hello message from Segment 3 (PIM-DM)	1651	0

Sending message #1651

Figure 8.11   The MCASTER main window on host H3 (THUNDER) for group 234.9.9.9.

Connecting Two Cisco Routers Back-To-Back Using Two Serial Cables

For testing purposes, it is sometimes necessary to connect two Cisco routers back-to-back. To do this, you need two cables: a Cisco serial cable with a male DTE connector, such as a CAB-V35MT, and a Cisco serial cable with a female DCE connector, such as a CAB-V35FC. As soon as you connect the cables to the routers, the router hardware and Cisco IOS automatically determine the type of the cable's connector.

After the routers are interconnected using these two cables and before the connection can be used, a source of clocking is required since the serial interfaces are synchronous. Normally, the clocking is provided by a CSU/DSU unit, to which the router is connected. A CSU/DSU does not exist in our configuration, so one of the routers should provide clocking. The router allows clocking to be defined only on a DCE interface. The command used to define clocking is **clock rate** *<value>*, where *<value>* is the desired speed of the connection measured in bits per second (bps). Depending on the version of IOS, the router may or may not be able to display the available values using the syntax **clock rate ?**. In general, the values shown in Table A.1 should work with most versions of IOS.

Table A.1 Values available for use with the command clock rate.

Value	Value
1200	125000
2400	148000
4800	250000
9600	500000
19200	800000
38400	1000000
56000	1300000
64000	2000000
72000	4000000

An alternative version of the command **clock rate** can also be used in the form of **clockrate** *<value>*, but the router will not display help for this version of the command.

Configuring Frame Relay Switching On A Cisco Router

Cisco routers can be used as frame relay switches. To configure a Cisco router as a frame relay switch, perform the following steps:

1. Enable frame relay switching using the command **frame-relay switching** in the global configuration mode.

2. Configure frame relay encapsulation using the command **encapsulation frame-relay** on the serial interfaces that you wish to perform frame relay switching.

3. Configure the serial interfaces configured with frame relay encapsulation as frame relay DCE interfaces using the command **frame-relay intf-type dce**.

NOTE: *The interfaces you configure for frame relay DCE do not have to be physical DCE interfaces.*

---

4. Establish desired frame relay PVC switching using the command **frame-relay route** *<Input DLCI>* **interface Serial** *<interface #>* *<Output DLCI>* in the interface configuration mode of the interfaces involved in frame relay switching. The parameter *<Input DLCI>* is the DLCI of the PVC that this interface must service. The **interface Serial** *<interface #>* specifies the interface to which the PVC must be routed. Finally, the *<Output DLCI>* is the DLCI of the PVC on the output interface.

TIP: *Alternatively, you can switch the PVC to a Tunnel interface, instead of a Serial interface. This way, you can encapsulate frame relay traffic into IP and route it through a TCP/IP network to a desired location.*

---

5. (This step is optional.) Configure a desired LMI type using the command **frame-relay lmi-type {ansi|cisco|q933a}** on the interfaces involved in frame relay switching. By default, the LMI type is **cisco**.

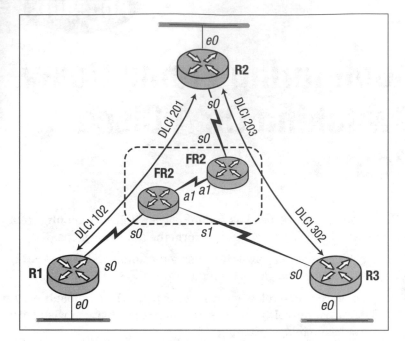

Figure B.1   Routers FR1 and FR2 are configured for frame relay switching.

Let's examine the network example shown in Figure B.1.

Figure B.1 demonstrates a very economical way to implement frame relay switching in a lab if you don't have routers with more than two serial interfaces. This solution also employs normally forgotten AUX lines of the routers as Async (asynchronous) interfaces, allowing you to use the remaining interfaces possibly at some other locations of the network.

Listings B.1 through B.5 show the configuration of all five routers. Only routers FR1 and FR2 implement frame relay switching.

Listing B.1   Router FR1's configuration.

```
username FR2 password 0 cisco
frame-relay switching

interface Tunnel0
 tunnel source 1.0.0.1
 tunnel destination 1.0.0.2

interface Ethernet0
 ip address 169.124.84.34 255.255.255.0
```

```
interface Serial0
 encapsulation frame-relay
 clockrate 64000
 frame-relay lmi-type ansi
 frame-relay intf-type dce
 frame-relay route 102 interface Tunnel0 421

interface Serial1
 encapsulation frame-relay
 frame-relay lmi-type ansi
 frame-relay intf-type dce
 frame-relay route 302 interface Tunnel0 423

interface Async1
 ip address 1.0.0.1 255.255.255.0
 encapsulation ppp
 async default routing
 async mode dedicated
 ppp authentication chap

line aux 0
 rxspeed 38400
 txspeed 38400
```

Listing B.2   Router FR2's configuration.

```
username FR1 password 0 cisco
frame-relay switching

interface Tunnel0
 tunnel source 1.0.0.2
 tunnel destination 1.0.0.1

interface Ethernet0
 ip address 169.124.84.36 255.255.255.0

interface Serial0
 encapsulation frame-relay
 frame-relay lmi-type ansi
 frame-relay intf-type dce
 frame-relay route 201 interface Tunnel0 421
 frame-relay route 203 interface Tunnel0 423

interface Async1
 ip address 1.0.0.2 255.255.255.0
 encapsulation ppp
 async default routing
 async mode dedicated
```

```
 ppp authentication chap

line aux 0
 rxspeed 38400
 txspeed 38400
```

Listing B.3   Router R1's configuration.

```
interface Ethernet0
 ip address 10.1.0.1 255.255.255.0

interface Serial0
 encapsulation frame-relay
 frame-relay lmi-type ansi

interface Serial0.1 point-to-point
 ip address 10.255.0.10 255.255.255.248
 frame-relay interface-dlci 102
```

Listing B.4   Router R2's configuration.

```
interface Ethernet0
 ip address 10.2.0.1 255.255.255.0

interface Serial0
 ip address 10.255.0.9 255.255.255.248
 encapsulation frame-relay
 clockrate 64000
 frame-relay map ip 10.255.0.10 201 broadcast
 frame-relay map ip 10.255.0.11 203 broadcast
 frame-relay lmi-type ansi
```

Listing B.5   Router R3's configuration.

```
interface Ethernet0
 ip address 10.3.0.1 255.255.255.0

interface Serial0
 encapsulation frame-relay
 clockrate 64000
 frame-relay lmi-type ansi

interface Serial0.1 multipoint
 ip address 10.255.0.11 255.255.255.248
 frame-relay map ip 10.255.0.9 302 broadcast
```

If you decide to use AUX lines as Async interfaces, prepare to be patient. You may need to try several different versions of Cisco IOS before you'll be able to make the connection between two Async interfaces become stable. If PPP used in the above example does not work, try SLIP, the other encapsulation available for Asynchronous interfaces.

A command that you can use to verify how frame relay switching is performing is **show frame-relay route**. The output of this command entered on routers FR1 and FR2 is shown in Listing B.6 and B.7.

*Listing B.6   The output of the command **show frame-relay route** on router FR1.*

```
FR1#show frame-relay route
Input Intf    Input Dlci    Output Intf    Output Dlci    Status
Serial0       102           Tunnel0        421            active
Serial1       302           Tunnel0        423            active
Tunnel0       421           Serial0        102            active
Tunnel0       423           Serial1        302            active
```

*Listing B.7   The output of the command **show frame-relay route** on router FR2.*

```
FR2#show frame-relay route
Input Intf    Input Dlci    Output Intf    Output Dlci    Status
Serial0       201           Tunnel0        421            active
Serial0       203           Tunnel0        423            active
Tunnel0       421           Serial0        201            active
Tunnel0       423           Serial0        203            active
```

Using RSH And RCP With Cisco Routers

In this appendix we'll discuss two extremely useful commands that are nonetheless somewhat obscure features of the Cisco IOS. These commands are RSH and RCP. Because they use the same protocol used by RSH and RCP Berkley-style commands, the commands are interoperable with the RSH and RCP daemons running on the Unix systems. Moreover, a Cisco router itself can run both RSH and RCP daemon processes, and thus become available through RSH and RCP client applications on Unix, Windows NT, and other systems.

Use the following guidelines to configure RSH and RCP features on the Cisco routers:

- To enable RSH daemon process on a router, use the command **ip rcmd rsh-enable** in the enable configuration mode.

- To enable RCP daemon process on a router, use the command **ip rcmd rcp-enable**.

- Both RCP and RSH daemons on most systems, including Cisco routers, require a certain level of authentication. Normally r-style authentication is achieved via specifying which user on which system can communicate with RSH and RCP daemons under which local user name. To configure r-style authentication on a Cisco router, use the command **ip rcmd remote-host** <local username> {<remote IP address>|<remote system name>} <remote username> [enable]. The <local username> parameter specifies the name configured on the router using the command **username** <local username>. The parameter {<remote IP address>|<remote system name>} specifies either the IP address or DNS name of the remote system allowed accessing the router via RSH and RCP.

NOTE: If a DNS name is used, the router must have a valid DNS configuration. If you do not use DNS on your routers, however, turn off DNS lookup completely using the command **no ip domain-lookup**. This command can also save you a lot of time if you experiment with the routers in a lab, where you normally do not use DNS.

The parameter *<remote username>* specifies the name under which the remote user must log in onto the remote system to be eligible to execute commands on the router. This name the RCP and RSH protocols pass in their PDUs along with the other parameters of the connection.

The optional parameter enable specifies that authenticated remote users can issue privileged (enable mode) commands using RSH.

• Use the command **ip rcmd remote-username** *<username>* to specify the name this router must use when the users issue the command RCP from this router to a remote location.

Listing C.1 shows a sample router configuration that enables RSH and RCP daemon processes.

Listing C.1   Router R1's configuration.

```
username Admin1


ip rcmd rcp-enable
ip rcmd rsh-enable
ip rcmd remote-host Admin1 10.6.0.15 Administrator enable


interface TokenRing0
 ip address 10.6.0.1 255.255.255.0
 ring-speed 16
```

Listing C.2 shows how the command RSH can be used on a Windows NT machine to execute commands on the router.

Listing C.2   The command **rsh** is used from a Windows NT computer to execute commands remotely on router R1.

```
C:\>rsh 10.6.0.1 -l Admin1 -n show ip route

Codes: C-connected, S-static, I-IGRP, R-RIP, M-mobile, B-BGP
  D-EIGRP, EX-EIGRP external, O-OSPF, IA-OSPF inter area
  N1-OSPF NSSA external type 1, N2-OSPF NSSA external type 2
  E1-OSPF external type 1, E2-OSPF external type 2, E-EGP
  i-IS-IS, L1-IS-IS level-1, L2-IS-IS level-2, *-candidate
 default
  U-per-user static route, o-ODR
  T-traffic engineered route

Gateway of last resort is not set

     10.0.0.0/24 is subnetted, 1 subnets
C        10.6.0.0 is directly connected, TokenRing0
```

Notice that you have to specify the name under which you want to execute the commands on the router. In the Windows NT implementation of RSH, this is done using the parameter **-l** *<username>*, which in our case was Admin1. This is the name specified on the router in the commands **ip rcmd remote-host** and **username**.

If you omit this parameter, usually the host uses the name under which you've logged in to the system in lieu of the explicitly specified name. For example, if you logged in to a Windows NT system as "Administrator", the RSH tries to login to the remote system as "Administrator".

Listing C.3 shows that the command RSH fails if it is entered without the **-l** parameter.

Listing C.3   The command RSH entered on the Windows NT host fails if entered without the valid user name under which the command must be executed on the router.

```
C:\>rsh 10.6.0.1 -n show ip route
10.6.0.1: Permission denied.
rsh: can't establish connection
```

In some situations, it may be difficult to understand why the RSH and RCP commands fail when used to access a router. An easy way to understand why it happens is to use the command **debug ip tcp rcmd**. Because this command is not processing-intensive, it should not lead to a router lockup.

For example, if the command **debug ip tcp rcmd** had been entered before the RSII command from Listing C.3 was issued, we would see the output shown in Listing C.4.

Listing C.4   The output of the command debug ip tcp rcmd on router R1.

```
R1#debug ip tcp rcmd
RCMD transactions debugging is on
R1#
RCMD: [514 <- 10.6.0.15:1018] recv 1017\0
RCMD: [514 <- 10.6.0.15:1018] recv
 Administrator\0Administrator\0show ip route\0
RCMD: [514 <- 10.6.0.15:1018] recv --
 Administrator 10.6.0.15 Administrator not in trusted hosts
 database
RCMD: [514 -> 10.6.0.15:1018] send <BAD,Permission denied.>\n
```

Even if we didn't know why the RSH command failed, we would be able to easily figure it out by consulting the output of the command

debug ip tcp rcmd. The command shows the output **Administrator 10.6.0.15 Administrator not in trusted hosts database**. This must be interpreted as the local user Administrator from host 10.6.0.15 on which he or she is logged on as Administrator does not have the corresponding authentication entry on the router, which must be created using the command **ip rcmd remote-host**. The "local user Administrator" means the name under which the remove user tries to execute the command on the router. This name must be specified as the first parameter of the command **ip rcmd remote-host**; in addition it must also be explicitly defined in the router's configuration using the command **username**.

A client version of RSH is also available on Cisco routers. If you need to execute some command remotely using RSH then you have to type in the command **rsh {**<*remote IP address*>l<*remote system name*>**}** [/user <*username*>] <*router command*>. The parameter **rsh {**<*remote IP address*>l<*remote system name*>**}** specifies the IP address or DNS name of remote system (such as another router). The optional parameter [/user <*username*>] is used to specify which name you want to execute the command under on the remote system. Finally, the last parameter is the command that you want to execute.

NOTE: *If you do not log in to a router under a defined user name (which can be defined using the command **username** or via some authentication mechanism such as RADIUS, TACACS+, and the like) the router will use its own name (specified in the command **hostname**) in the RSH and RCP communication.*

To demonstrate how the note above applies, let's examine what happens if we try to use the command RSH on a router to which we connected without specifying a user name. Suppose there is another router called R2 on the same TokenRing segment to which router R1 configured as shown in Listing C.1 is connected. Listing C.5 shows the result of the command RSH entered on router R2.

Listing C.5   *The command RSH entered on router R2 fails if it is used to execute a command on router R1.*

```
R2#rsh 10.6.0.1 /user Admin1 show ip route
%Permission denied.
```

If we use the command **debug ip tcp rcmd** we'll see the reason of the failure. The output of the command **debug ip tcp rcmd** on router R1 is shown in Listing C.6.

Listing C.6   *The output of the command* **debug ip tcp rcmd** *on router R1*
                   shows that the RSH connection is made using the router name
                   (R2) as the remote login name.

```
R1#debug ip tcp rcmd
RCMD transactions debugging is on
R1#
01:48:07: %SYS-5-CONFIG_I: Configured from console by console
01:48:37: RCMD: [514 <- 10.6.0.2:1016] recv \0
01:48:37: RCMD: [514 <- 10.6.0.2:1016] recv R2\0Admin1\0show
 ip route\0
01:48:37: RCMD: [514 <- 10.6.0.2:1016] recv --
 Admin1 10.6.0.2 R2 not in trusted hosts database
01:48:37: RCMD: [514 -> 10.6.0.2:1016] send
 <BAD,Permission denied.>\n
```

RCP is very useful if you need to download a new Cisco IOS image to
a router when an RCP server is available. It is much faster and more
reliable than regular TFTP, and therefore is preferable to TFTP.

You can specify the keyword **rcp** instead of **tftp** in the **copy** commands. For example, if you would like to copy a Cisco IOS image
from an RCP server, you can use the command **copy rcp flash**. The
output of the command **copy rcp flash** is shown in Listing C.7.

Listing C.7   *The output of the command* **copy rcp flash** *entered on router R2.*

```
R2#
R2#copy rcp flash
                    ****  NOTICE  ****
Flash load helper v1.0
This process will accept the copy options and then terminate
the current system image to use the ROM based image for the
copy. Routing functionality will not be available during
that time. If you are logged in via telnet, this connection
will terminate. Users with console access can see the results
of the copy operation.
                ---- ******** ----

Proceed? [confirm]
Address or name of remote host []?10.6.0.1
Source username [R2]? Admin1
Source filename []? c2500-d-l.120-2a.bin
Destination filename [c2500-d-l.120-2a.bin]?
The returned username is R2(8CF68)
```

TIP: It's a good idea to switch to the ROM version of Cisco IOS before downloading a new Cisco IOS image to a router. The command that you use to switch to the ROM version of Cisco IOS depends on the router platform and the version of Cisco IOS currently running on the router. Nevertheless, all versions of the command begin with the keywords **boot system**, which is followed by version-dependent parameters. For example, in the Cisco IOS version 11.1 on the 2500 series routers, this command is **boot system rom**. The command must be entered in the global configuration mode, after which the configuration needs to be saved in the router's NVRAM (**copy running-config startup-config** or old fashioned **write memory**), and the routers itself must be rebooted.

If you use the ROM version of Cisco IOS, you can download a new image without reloading the router. Remember, however, that the ROM version of Cisco IOS does not support routing. You have to use the command **ip default-gateway** <IP address>, where the <IP address> parameter is the IP address of another router that can serve as the default gateway.

The combination of the ROM version of Cisco IOS and RCP can be very helpful if you need to upgrade the Cisco IOS image on a router at a remote location connected to your site via some type of WAN, such as frame relay.

Ping With Time Stamps

The **ping** command available on most systems does not, unfortunately, produce output with time stamps. A time stamp feature would be quite useful in the situation when you need to know the time that it takes some resource to become available, or how long a resource is unavailable during network recovery caused by network components failures.

We considered a couple of similar situations in Chapter 7 when testing HSRP and dial backup solutions. Especially for those situations, I wrote a short perl script that actually runs the command **ping** once every second and then time stamps **ping's** output. The text of the script is shown in Listing D.1.

*Listing D.1   Perlscript that runs command **ping** and time stamps its output.*

```
# This procedure creates a stamp on the moment it's invoked.
sub tstamp
{
    local($sec,$min,$hour) = localtime;
    return sprintf( "%02i:%02i", $min, $sec );
}


# This variable will be used to invoke the NT ping command
# to ping the remote destination only once. In other
# operating systems the option "-n 1" must be replaced
# with the option that makes ping send only a single
# ICMP packet.
$OS_SPING = 'ping -n 1 ';

# The destination IP address is passed as the first and the
# only command line argument. I do not perform any command
# line syntax checking, so it's important to pass the
# correct IP address.
$IP_ADDR = $ARGV[0];
$T_PREV = '';

while (1)
```

```
{
    # Wait until one second expires
    while( $T_PREV eq &tstamp ) {}

    # Parse ping output
    ( $tmp1,$tmp2, $tmp3, $P_RES ) =
        split( "\n", `$OS_SPING $IP_ADDR` );

    # Print time stamp
    print "[". &tstamp ."] ";

    # Print the fourth line of ping output
    print $P_RES . "\n";

    # Refresh the time stamp
    $T_PREV = &tstamp;
}
```

As you may notice, the script runs indefinitely. To stop it, use the
Ctrl+Break keystroke.

Appendix E

Using Windows NT Computers As Hosts

Using computers running the Windows NT 4.0 operating system may be very handy when testing various routing configurations. The OS allows having multiple NICs, running routing protocols such as RIP and OSPF, and so on. However, you should be aware that if you have multiple NICs, Windows NT will install multiple default gateway routes. You can see that using the Windows NT command **netstat -rn**. These multiple default gateway routes confuse Windows NT a lot—it just can't figure out which one to use. Thus, it makes sense to add more specific routes in accordance with your testing procedures. For example, if you have two NICs, and the first one is configured with IP address 10.1.1.10/24, and the other one with IP address 172.16.1.10/24, it makes sense to add two specific routes as follows:

```
route add 10.0.0.0 mask 255.0.0.0 10.1.1.1 metric 1
route add 172.16.0.0 mask 255.255.0.0 172.16.1.1 metric 1
```

Index

A

ABRs (area border routers), 227, 238, 245
access-list <*AL number*> [**permit|deny**] <*source IP address*> < *wildcard mask*> command, 287
Access-lists, 42-43, 287
   extended access-lists, 291-293
   filtering routing updates, 312-315
   named access-lists, 293-294
   standard access-lists, 287-290, 291
Active periods, 405
Active router, 355, 398
Address resolution, 41-42
Address Resolution protocol. *See* ARP.
Administrative distance, 144-146, 169
Algorithms
   classless routing algorithm, 108, 109
   distance vector algorithm, 139-144
   reverse path forwarding algorithm, 423
   shortest path algorithm, 222-225
   spanning tree algorithm, 64-68, 89
All routes broadcast, 69
All routes explorer, 70
All stations broadcast, 71
ANSI Annex D, 54
Application Layer
   Internet model, 7, 40
   OSI/RM, 5, 6
Application Layer protocol, 11
area <*area*> **range** command, 236, 238, 239
area <*area*> **range** <*IP address*> <*subnet mask*> command, 235
area <*area*> **stub** command, 242

area <*area*> **virtual-link** <*OSPF ID*> command, 245
Area border routers. *See* ABRs.
ARP (Address Resolution protocol), 42, 54
   InARP (Inverse ARP), 54
   multicast IP, 419
   PDU, 101
   ProxyARP, 48-52, 119
   source-route bridging, 81
ARP reply, 42
ARP requests, 42
ARP table, 42
ASBRs (autonomous system boundary routers), 228, 333-342
Authentication, ISDN, 59
Autonomous system, 227
Autonomous system boundary routers. *See* ASBRs.
Auto-summarization, 157
   disabling EIGRP, 213-214
   disabling RIP version 2, 208-209

B

Backbone, 227, 235, 245-255
backup delay <*enable delay*> <*disable delay*> command, 410
backup interface <*Dialer Interface*> command, 410
bandwidth <*B*> command, 234
bandwidth command, 185, 189
Basic congestion control, 12
Basic match step, classless routing algorithm, 108, 109
Basic Rate Interface service. *See* BRI service.

B-channel, 48
Best-effort service, 14
Bit-count notation, 30-31
BPDUs, 89
bridge crb command, 86
Bridged LAN, 62
bridge-group <*group number*>
command, 73, 75, 80, 83
bridge-group <*group number*>
path-cost <*cost*> command, 96
bridge <*group number*> **priority**
<*priority*> command, 94
bridge <*group number*> **protocol**
<*protocol*> command, 73, 75, 80, 83
bridge <*group number*> **route ip**
command, 89
bridge irb command, 87
Bridge priority, 89, 94-96
Bridge virtual interface, 87
Bridging, 13, 62
over ISDN, 83-86
MAC Addressing, 62-63
mixed-media transparent
bridging, 77-96
multiple bridge groups, 75-77
source-route bridging, 68-71, 97-103
spanning tree algorithm, 64-68
transparent bridging, 64-68, 72-77
BRI (Basic Rate Interface) service, 58
Broadcast bits, 69-70
Broadcast network, 39

C

Channel, 59
Cisco LMI, 54
Cisco routers, 13
access lists, 42 43, 287-294
bridging with, 61-103
data traffic filters, 282-294
Dial-On-Demand routing (DPR),
357, 405-416
HSRP, 354-357, 394-405
IP multicast routing, 417-444
network address translation
(NAT), 352-354, 369-394
policy-based routing, 352-358
redistribution, 282-286, 297-350

routing updates filters, 294-297
serial interface, 52-57
static routing, 105-135
Class A addresses, 26
Class B addresses, 26
Class C addresses, 26
Classful dynamic routing protocols, 49
Classful routing protocols, 28, 146
configuring IGRP, 182-192
configuring RIP, 148-181
classless command, 264
Classless routing, configuring, 123-125
Classless routing algorithm, 107-109
Classless routing protocols, 28
configuring EIGRP, 210-218
configuring RIP version 2, 202-208
VLSM and, 192-202
clear ip route command, 331-332
Concurrent routing and bridging.
See CRB.
Congestion control, 12
Connected route redistribute, 306-308
Connectionless service, 14
Contiguous subnet masks, 29, 30, 31
Convergence time, 141
Counting-to-infinity problem, 141-142
CRB (concurrent routing and
bridging), 72, 86-87

D

Data Communication Equipment
node. *See* DCE node.
Datagrams, 8, 15
fragmentation, 16
policy-based routing, 358
Data Link Circuit Identifiers.
See DCLCs.
Data Link Layer, OSI/RM, 5, 6, 7, 10, 62
Data Link Layer technologies, 39
Data Terminal Equipment node. *See*
DTE node.
Data traffic, filtering. *See* Filtering.
DCE node, 53
D-channel, 58
DCLCs (Data Link Circuit
Identifiers), 54

DDR (Dial-On-Demand Routing)
  dial backup, 357, 410-414
  snapshot routing, 357, 405-410
debug arp command, 121, 122
debug backup command, 414
debug command, 43
debug ip igmp command, 431, 432
debug ip igrp transactions
  command, 183, 187, 297, 327-329
debug ip packet command, 129, 134
debug ip pim command, 431, 432
debug ip policy command, 367-368
debug ip rip command, 152, 153,
  156, 162-163, 166, 169, 177
debug ip route command, 181
dec bridging protocol, 73
Default gateway, 125
Default gateway route, 45
default-information originate
  always command, 240
default-information originate
  command, 160
default-metric command, 299, 331
default-metric <*routing protocol*
  specific metric> command, 308
Default redistribution metric, 308-309
Delay field, IP datagram, 18-19
Demultiplexing, 4, 6
Dense-mode protocols, 422
Designated bridge, 65
Designated port, 65
Designated router, 275
Destination Unreachable message,
  37, 290
Dial backup, 357, 410-414
dialer-group <*dialer group*>
  command, 83
dialer-list <*gr #*> **protocol ip deny**
  command, 411
dialer-list <*list number*> **protocol**
  bridge [permit list <*Ethernet-*
  typecode access-list number>]
  command, 83
dialer map bridge ... command, 84
Dial-On-Demand Routing. *See* DDR.
Digital telephony, 58
Directed broadcast, 26, 28
distance commands, 169-173
distance 255 command, 309

Distance vector algorithm, 139-144
Distance Vector Multicast Routing
  Protocol. *See* DVMPR.
Distance vector protocols, 137-218
  configuring classful protocols,
    146, 148-192
  configuring classless protocols,
    146, 192-218
  distance vector algorithm, 139-144
distribute-list 10 out eigrp 10
  command, 338-339
distribute-list <*AL number*> **out**
  <*source of routing information*>
  command, 313, 319
Djikstra, Edsger, 222
Dotted decimal notation, 24, 27
DTE node, 53
DVMPR (Distance Vector Multicast
  Routing Protocol), 425
Dynamic NAT, 354
Dynamic routing, 107, 161-165
Dynamic routing protocols, 107, 138
  classful, 146, 148-192
  classless, 146, 192-218
  distance vector protocols, 137-218
  link state protocols, 219-279

E

Echo message, 36
Echo Reply message, 36
EGPs (exterior routing protocols), 138
EIGRP, 13, 282
  auto-summarization, disabling,
    213-214
  configuring over non-fully meshed
    frame relay networks, 216-218
  configuring route summarization
    with, 214-216
  metrics, 213
  redistributing between EIGRP and
    IGRP, 324-332
  redistribution with, 323-332
EIGRP external routes, 323
Encapsulation, 5, 6, 15, 52-53
encapsulation frame-relay
  command, 55, 56, 80
End-to-end communication, 9
Entity, 3, 5

Equal cost load balancing, 109
   configuring with IGRP, 187-190
   configuring with RIP, 173-175
Ethernet, MAC addresses, 62
Extended access-lists, 291-293
Extended offset-lists, 176
Exterior routing protocols. *See* EGPs.

F

Fast switching, 129
Filtering, 284
   access-lists, 42-43, 287-294
   data traffic filters, 287-294
   routing updates filters, 294-297
Filter packets, 42-43
Flags field, IP datagram, 20
Floating static routes, 115-118
Fragmentation, 15-16, 21-22
Fragment Offset field, IP datagram, 20-22
Frame relay, 53, 79-82
frame-relay interface-dlci *<DLCI>* command, 56
frame-relay lmi-type *<lmi-type>* command, 55, 56, 80
frame-relay map bridge *<DLCI>* **broadcast** command, 80
frame-relay map ip *<IP address> <DLCI>* command, 265, 266
frame-relay map ip *<remote IP address> <DLCI>* command, 56
Frame relay networks
   fully meshed, OSPF with, 261-268
   non-fully meshed, EIGRP with, 216-218
   non-fully meshed, OSPF with, 268-279
   non-fully meshed, RIP with, 177-181
Frames, 39
Fully meshed NBMA networks, configuring OSPF over, 261-268

G

Garbage collection timer, 144
Gateways, 8

Global/Local bit, 63
Group/Individual bit, 63, 420

H

HDLC, bridging over HDLC, 78-79
HDLC encapsulation, 52-53
Header, 6, 17, 40
Header Checksum field, IP datagram, 23
HELLO protocol, 261
Hierarchical routing, 227-228
High-Level Data Link Control. *See* HDLC.
Holddowns, 144
Hop-to-hop communication, 9
Host, 8, 114
Host ID, 24, 27
Host-to-host communication, 9
Hot Standby Router Protocol. *See* HSRP.
HSRP (Hot Standby Router Protocol), 354-357, 394-401
Hub-spoke topology, 359

I

ibm bridging protocol, 73
ICMP (Internet Control Message protocol), 13, 33-34
ICMP control messages, 34-38
   Destination Unreachable message, 37, 290
   Echo message, 36
   Echo Reply message, 36
   Redirect message, 38
   Source Quench message, 37-38
   Time Exceeded message, 38
   types, 35-36
Identification field, IP datagram, 20
ieee bridging protocol, 73
IGMP (Internet Group Management Protocol), 424
IGPs (interior routing protocols), 138
IGRP, 13, 49, 148, 282
   configuring, 182-184
   load balancing and, 187-191
   metrics, 148, 184-187

redistributing between EIGRP and IGRP, 324-332

InARP (Inverse ARP), 54

Incoming routing updates, administrative distance for, 169

Individual host addresses, with RIP, 158-159

Individual host routes, configuring, 125-126

Inside IP addresses
- configuring dynamic translation of, 374-384
- configuring static translation of, 369-374
- inside global addresses, 354
- inside local addresses, 353-354

Integrated routing and bridging. *See* IRB.

interface BVI *<bridge group number>* command, 87

interface loopback *<number>* command, 158

Interior routing protocols. *See* IGPs.

Intermediate System to Intermediate System. *See* IS-IS.

"Internet Assigned Numbers" (RFC 1700), 25, 28

Internet Control Message protocol. *See* ICMP.

Internet Group Management Protocol. *See* IGMP.

Internet Layer, Internet model, 7, 9

Internet model, 2, 7-11

IP (Internet protocol), 12-13
- configuring over ISDN, 58-60
- IP routing, 14-17
- source-route bridging, 71
- TCP/IP protocol suite, 13-14

ip access-group *<AL number>* command, 288

IP addresses, 23-24
- design, 24-28
- DLCIs, 54
- HSRP router, 355
- inside global addresses, 354, 385-386
- inside local addresses, 353-354
- NAT, 352-354, 369-394
- outside global addresses, 354

outside local addresses, 354
- overlapped, 386-390
- subnetting, 27, 29-33
- virtual IP address, 355
- virtual server IP address, 390
- with VLSM, 192-202

ip address *<IP address>* **255.255.255.255** command, 158

ip address *<IP address> <subnet-mask>* command, 55, 56

IP address mask, 169

ip classless command, 123, 125, 161

IP datagrams, 16, 17-23

IP header, 40

IP Header Length (IHL) field, IP datagram, 18

IP multicast routing. *See* Multicast routing.

ip nat inside destination list [*<AL number>|<AL name>*] **pool** *<pool name>* command, 391

ip nat inside source command, 385

ip nat inside source list [*<AL number>|<AL name>*] **interface** *<Interface>* command, 385

ip nat inside source list [*<AL number>|<AL name>*] **pool** *<name>* command, 375

ip nat outside source list [*<AL number>|<AL name>*] **pool** *<name>* command, 387

ip nat pool command, 383, 387

ip nat pool *<name> <start IP address> <end IP address>* [**netmask** *<subnet mask>*|**prefix-length** *<prefix length>*] command, 374

ip ospf network broadcast command, 265-268

ip ospf network point-to-multipoint command, 272-275

ip ospf network point-to-point command, 272

ip ospf priority *<priority>* command, 276

ip pim dense-mode command, 427, 437

ip pim nbma-mode command, 438, 443

ip pim rp-address 10.0.0.2.1
command, 439
ip pim rp-address *<IP address>*
command, 433
ip pim sparse-mode command, 437
ip policy route-map *<RM name>*
command, 359
ip rip receive version [1|2]
command, 209
ip rip send version [1|2]
command, 209
ip route-cache command, 129
ip route *<IP address>* **0.0.0.0
0.0.0.0** *<next-hop router>*
command, 125
ip route *<IP address>*
255.255.255.255 *<next-hop
router>* command, 125
ip route *<remote network address>*
<subnet mask> <next-hop router>
command, 111, 115
ip route *<remote network address>*
*<subnet mask> <output
interfacer>* command, 119
IP routing, 14-17, 40-41, 106
static routing, 105-135
unicast, 419-420
ip subnet-zero command, 264
ip summary-address eigrp *<AS
number> <IP address> <subnet
mask>* command, 214, 227
IRB (integrated routing and bridging),
72, 87-89
ISDN
bridging, 83-86
configuring IP over, 58-60
isdn switch-type *<switch type>*
command, 83
ISIS (Intermediate System to
Intermediate System), 220
ITU-T Q-933 Annex A, 54

J

Join message, 421-422

L

LAN interface, configuring on
router, 45-52
LAN segments, 62
LAPB (Link Access Procedure
Balanced protocol), 52
LAPD (Link Access Procedure for the
ISDN D Channel), 52
Layered communication model, 2-5
components, 9-12
Internet model, 7-9
OSI/RM, 2, 5-7
Layer stacks, Internet model, 8
Link Access Procedure Balanced
protocol. *See* LAPB.
Link Access Procedure for the ISDN
D Channel. *See* LAPD.
Link state advertisements. *See* LSAs.
Link state database, OSPF, 221,
241-242
Link state protocols, 200, 219-279
OSPF, 220-229
outbound routing updates
filters, 295
LLC (Logical Link Control)
protocol, 52, 62
LMI (Local Management Interface), 54
Load balancing, 109
equal cost load balancing, 109,
126, 130, 131, 173-175, 187-190
with IGRP, 187-191
MHSRP for, 401-404
NAT, 353, 390-394
unequal cost load balancing, 109,
132-135, 190-191
Load Sharing Using IP Network
Address Translation. *See* LSNAT.
Load splitting, 109
Local broadcast, 25-26
Local Management Interface.
See LMI.
Logical Link Control protocol.
See LLC.
Longest match lookup, classless
routing algorithm, 108
Longest match step, classless routing
algorithm, 108
Loopback address, 26

Loopback interface, 158
LSAs (link state advertisements), 228-229
LSNAT (Load Sharing Using IP Network Address Translation), 390, 391

M

mac-address command, 96
MAC addresses, 39, 62-63, 96
    HSRP router, 355
    mapping multicast IP addresses to, 419-420
    virtual MAC address, 355, 398
Manual mapping, 42
Mapping, multicast IP addresses to NAL addresses, 419-420
Maximum Transfer Unit. *See* MTU.
MCASTER application, 426, 443-444
Metric domain, 283-284
Metrics, 139
    default redistribution metric, 308-309
    EIGRP, 213
    IGRP, 148, 184-187
    redistribution, 283
    RIP, 148, 175-177
    with static routing, 115
MHSRP (Multigroup HSRP), load balancing, 401-404
Microsoft Network Monitor, 43, 290
Mixed-media transparent bridging, 77-78
    CRB, 86-87
    IRB, 87-89
    over frame relay, 79-82
    over HDLC, 79-79
    over ISDN, 83-86
    spanning tree parameters, 89-96
Module 5
MOSPF (Multicast Extensions to OSPF), 425
MTU (Maximum Transfer Unit), 9, 15
Multicast addresses, 24, 418, 419
Multicast Extensions to OSPF. *See* MOSPF.
Multicast groups, 419

Multicast IP addresses, mapping to MAC addresses, 419-420
Multicast MAC addresses, 63, 419-420
Multicast-related protocols, 423-425
Multicast routing, 419
    RPF (reverse path forwarding algorithm, 423
    shared trees, 422
    source-based trees, 420-422
Multicast routing table, 423
Multigroup HSRP. *See* MHSRP.
Multiplexing, 4, 6
Multipoint subinterface, 54, 272
Multiprotocol routers, 13
multiring ip command, 97
Muscle RIP, 184

N

Named access-lists, 293-294
NAPT (Network Address Port ·Translation), 385
NAT (Network Address Translation), 352-354
    dynamic NAT, 354
    IP addresses, dynamic translation of, 374-384
    IP addresses, static translation of, 369-374
    load balancing, 353, 390-394
    with OSPF routing, 379-383
    overlapped IP addresses, 386-390
    with overloading global inside IP addresses, 385-386
    static NAT, 354
NAT table, 354
NBMA (Non-Broadcast Multiple Access) networks, 39, 177
    EIGRP, 216-218
    OSPF, fully meshed, 261-268
    OSPF, non-fully meshed, 268-279
    PIM-SM, 437
    RIP, 177-181
neighbor command, 261-265
neighbor <*IP address*> command, 168, 261
Neighbors, 139
netstat -n command, 373-374, 378-379, 393

Network Access Layer, Internet
  model, 7, 10, 12
Network address, 26, 106
Network Address Port Translation.
  See NAPT.
Network Address Translation.
  See NAT.
Network Associates Sniffer
  (software), 43
Network classes, 25
network command, 147, 211, 233
Network ID, 24, 27
network *<IP Address> <wildcard*
  mask> **area 0** command, 230, 236
Network Layer, OSI/RM, 5
network *<network IP address>*
  command, 147
Network prefix, 106, 139
Next-hop router, 39-40, 115
no auto-summary command, 208, 213
no ip route-cache command, 129
no ip routing command, 73, 75, 80,
  83, 86, 97
no ip split-horizon eigrp *<AS*
  Number> command, 216
Non-Broadcast Multiple Access
  networks. *See* NBMA networks.
Non-contiguous subnet masks,
  29-30, 31
Non-fully meshed frame relay
  networks
    configuring EIGRP over, 216-218
    configuring OSPF over, 268-279
    configuring RIP over, 177-181
no shutdown command, 55
NSSA (not-so-stubby area), configuring, 342-350
Null interface, route summarization,
  318-323

O

offset-list command, 175, 189
offset-list 0 command, 189
One-way redistribution, 309-312
Open Shortest Path First. *See* OSPF.
Open System Interconnection
  Reference Model. *See* OSI/RM.

Options field, IP datagram, 23
OSI/RM (Open System Interconnection Reference Model), 2, 5-7
OSPF (Open Shortest Path First),
  177, 220-229
    configuring 235-245, 261-279
    costs, 234
    default route, 240
    hierarchical routing, 227-228
    link state advertisements (LSAs),
      228-229
    link state database, 221, 241-242
    link state routing protocols, 295
    NAT with, 379-383
    network types, 225-226
    outbound routing updates
      filters, 295
    redistribution with, 332-350
    secondary IP addresses, 234
    shortest path algorithm, 222-225
    types 1 and 2 external metrics,
      333-340
    virtual links, 245-260
OSPF external routes, 333
Outbound routing updates filters, 295
Output interface, static
  routing, 119-122
Outsidc global addresses, 354
Outside local addresses, 354

P

Packet encapsulation, 5
Packet filtering, 42-43
Padding field, IP datagram, 23
Partitioned backbone, restoring with
  virtual links, 245-255
passive-interface *<interface>*
  command, 165
passive-interface TokenRing 0
  command, 168, 171
PAT (Port Address Translation), 385
Payload, 17
PCM (pulse code modulation), 58
PDUs (protocol data units), 3, 6, 101
Per-destination load balancing,
  109, 129
Permanent virtual circuits. *See* PVCs.

Per-packet load balancing, 109, 129
Physical Layer, OSI/RM, 5, 7, 10, 62
PIM-DM (Protocol Independent
  Multicast-Dense Mode), 424, 427-433
PIM-DM routers, 424
PIM-SM (Protocol Independent
  Multicast-Sparse Mode), 425, 433-437
ping 10.2.0.120 command, 400
Ping, 36, 114, 122, 181, 252, 254, 289,
  290, 377, 426
Point-to-point network, 39
Point-to-point subinterface, 54, 272
Policy-based routing, 352
  application-sensitive, 365-369
  configuring, 358-369
  dedicated link, 359-365
Port Address Translation. *See* PAT.
ppp authentication command, 83
ppp chap authentication, 59
Presentation Layer, OSI/RM, 5
Primary IP address, 50
Primary Rate Interface service. *See*
  PRI service.
PRI (Primary Rate Interface)
  service, 58
Protocol data units. *See* PDUs.
Protocol field, IP datagram, 22-23
Protocol Independent Multicast-
  Dense Mode. *See* PIM-DM.
Protocol Independent Multicast-
  Sparse Mode. *See* PIM-SM.
Protocols, 3
ProxyARP, 48-52, 119
Prune message, 421
Pseudo-connected static route,
  119, 122
Pulse code modulation. *See* PCM.
PVCs (permanent virtual circuits),
  53-54

Q

Quiet periods, 405

R

Random ports, 11
Redirect message, 38

redistribute command, 308, 324, 333
redistribute connected
  command, 307
redistribute <*routing information
  source*> **metric** <*routing protocol
  specific metric*> command, 298
redistribute static command, 307
Redistribution, 282-284, 297
  access-lists used during, 312-315
  configuring, 298-308
  connected route redistribute,
    306-308
  default redistribution metric,
    308-309
  with EIGRP, 323-332
  one-way redistribution, 309-312
  with OSPF, 332-350
  problems with, 284-287
  route-maps used during, 315-318
  routing loops, 302-305
  static route redistribution, 306-308
Reliability field, IP datagram, 18-19
Remote source-route bridging.
  See RSRB.
Reverse path forwarding algorithm.
  See RPF.
RFC 950, 192-193
RFC 1042, 71
RFC 1075, 425
RFC 1112, 424
RFC 1583, 220
RFC 1584, 425
RFC 1631, 353
RFC 1700, 25, 28, 418
RFC 2236, 424
RFC 2281, 355
RFC 2328, 220
RFC 2362, 425
RFC 2391, 353, 390
RFCs (Requests for Comments), 2
RIF (routing information field), 69
RIP, 49, 148, 282
  auto-summarization, 157
  configuring, 148-158, 160, 173-181
  IGRP compared to, 184, 190
  individual host addresses with,
    158-159
  metrics, 148, 175-177
  routing updates, preventing, 165-167

secondary IP addresses, 161-165
unicast routing updates with, 167-169
using simultaneously with RIP version 2, 209-210
RIP version 2, 202, 318
  auto-summarization, disabling, 208-209
  configuring, 207-208
  using simultaneously with RIP version 1, 209-210
Root bridge, 65
Root port, 65
Routed protocols, 138
route-map *<RM name>* [permit|deny] *<sequence #>* command, 316
Route-maps, 315
  policy-based routing, 358
  to filter routing updates, 315-318
router *<routing protocol>* command, 147
router eigrp command, 231
router igrp *<AS number>* command, 182, 184, 190
router igrp command, 231
router ospf command, 231
router ospf *<Process ID>* command, 230, 235
router rip command, 148
Routers, 13, 106
  ABRs, 227, 238, 245
  active router, 355, 398
  ASBRs, 228, 333-342
  Cisco routers. *See* Cisco routers.
  designated router, 275
  join message, 421-422
  load balancing, 126, 130-131, 132
  multiprotocol routers, 13
  neighbors, 139
  next-hop router, 39-40, 115
  PIM-DM, 424, 427-433
  prune message, 421
  secondary IP addresses, 161-165
  standby router, 355, 398
Routes, 106
Route summarization
  configuring with EIGRP, 214-216
  null interface for, 318-323

Routing
  connected interfaces for, 110-111
  DDR, 357, 405-416
  dial backup, 357, 410-414
  dynamic routing, 107, 161-165
  hierarchical routing, 227-228
  IP routing. *See* IP routing.
  IRB, 72, 87-89
  multicast routing, 419-423
  over dedicated link, 359-365
  policy-based routing, 352, 358-369
  snapshot routing, 357, 405-410
  static routing, 105-135
Routing algorithms, 28, 107-109
Routing information field. *See* RIF.
Routing information redistribution. *See* Redistribution.
Routing loops, redistribution, 302-305
Routing protocols, 138, 282-284
Routing table, 19, 106, 423
Routing update filters, 294-297
Routing updates, 107, 138
  incoming, discriminating, 169-173
  preventing RIP from sending, 165-167
  unicast, 167-169
RPF (reverse path forwarding algorithm), 423
RPF interface, 423
RSRB (remote source-route bridging), 98

S

Samples, 58
SAP (service access point), 3
Secondary IP address, 50
  OSPF and, 234
  RIP and, 161-165
Segments, 8, 39
Serial interface, configuring, 52-57
Service access point. *See* SAP.
service timestamps debug uptime command, 414
Session Layer, OSI/RM, 5
Shared trees, 422
Shortest path algorithm, 222-225
show bridge command, 74

show interfaces command, 180, 185, 186

show interfaces Ethernet 0 command, 110, 111, 398, 399

show interfaces *<Interface> <number>* command, 234

show interfaces Serial 1 command, 185

show interfaces TokenRing 0 command, 404

show ip interface command, 180

show ip interfaces *<interface> <interface number>* command, 110

show ip mroute command, 430, 432, 441, 442

show ip nat translations command, 376, 378

show ip ospf database command, 241

show ip ospf interface Loopback 0 command, 381

show ip ospf neighbor command, 265, 272, 275

show ip ospf virtual-links command, 250-251

show ip route command, 110, 150, 151, 152, 155, 166, 191, 238

show route-map command, 369

show snapshot command, 409

show spanning-tree *<bridge group number>* command, 91

show spanning-tree command, 91

show standby command, 397, 399, 403

Single route broadcast, 69

Single route explorer, 70, 71

Snapshot clients, 405

Snapshot routing, 357, 405-410

snapshot server *<active time>* command, 406

Snapshot servers, 405

Sniffer (software), 43

Source-based trees, 420-422

source-bridge *<physical ring-number> <bridge number> <virtual ring number>* command, 97

source-bridge remote-peer... command, 98

source-bridge ring-group *<ring-number>* command, 97

Source Quench message, 37-38

Source-route bridging, 68-71
  configuring, 98-103
  using, 97-98

Source-route translational bridging, 100

Spanning explorers, 71

Spanning tree algorithm, 64-68, 89

Spanning tree recalculation, 65

Spanning tree topology, 64, 91, 94

Sparse-mode protocols, 422

Split-horizon with poisoned reverse rule, 143

Split-horizon rule, 143

Standard access-lists, 287-290, 291

Standby group, 356

standby *<group #>* **ip** *<IP address>* command, 394

standby *<group #>* **preempt** command, 395

standby *<group #>* **priority** *<priority>* command, 395

standby *<group #>* **track** *<Interface>* [*<priority decrease>*] command, 395

Standby priority, HSRP, 356

Standby router, 355, 398

Static NAT, 354

Static route redistribution, 306-308

Static routing, 107
  classless routing, 123-125
  configuring, 111-114
  default gateway, 125
  equal cost load balancing, 126-131
  floating static routes, 115-118
  individual host routes, 125-126
  load splitting, 109
  metrics with, 115
  with output interface, 119-122
  pseudo-connected static route, 119, 122
  routing algorithm, 107-109

Stub areas, configuring, 242-245

Subinterface, 54, 269-272

subinterface multipoint command, 56

subinterface point-to-point
  command, 56
Subnet address, 28
Subnet directed broadcast, 28
Subnet ID, 27
Subnet mask, 27-28, 29-33, 46
Subnetting, 27, 29-33
summary-address command,
  340-342, 348
Supernets, 28, 318
SVCs (switched virtual circuits), 54

T

TCP/IP model. *See* Internet model.
TCP/IP protocol suite, 13-14, 27
TCP port, 11, 365
telnet 10.2.0.120 command, 381
Telnet, 10-11, 365
Throughput field, IP datagram, 18-19
Time Exceeded message, 38
Time to Live (TTL) field, IP
  datagram, 22
TokenRing networks
  MAC addresses, 62, 420
  source-route bridging, 68-71
Topology discovery, 421
Total Length field, IP datagram, 19-20
traceroute command, 254-255,
  363, 367
tracert -d command, 363-364
Transparent bridging, 64
  configuring, 72-77, 78-89
  spanning tree algorithm, 64-68
  spanning tree parameters, 89-96
Transport Layer
  Internet model, 7, 9
  OSI/RM, 5
Transport Layer protocol, 11, 13
Triggered updates, 144
Tsunami Computing, URL, 43
Type of Service (ToS) field, IP
  datagram, 18-19

U

UDP (User Datagram protocol), 11,
  13, 40
Unequal cost load balancing, 109
  configuring, 132-135
  configuring, with IGRP, 190-191
Unicast addresses, 24-25
Unicast routing, 419-420
Unicast routing updates, with
  RIP, 167-169
Unrealiable service, 14
User Datagram protocol. *See* UDP.
username *<router name>* **password**
  <passwd> command, 411
username *<user name>*
  command, 83

V

Variable Length Subnet Masks.
  See VLSM.
variance *<multiplier>* command, 190
Version field, IP datagram, 18
Virtual circuits, 53
Virtual IP address, 355
Virtual links, 246
  restoring a partitioned
    backbone, 245-255
  to connect remote areas, 255-260
Virtual MAC address, 355, 398
Virtual server IP address, 390
VLSM (Variable Length Subnet
  Masks), 192-202
Voice-grade channel, 58

W

Well-known ports, 11